# The Transformative
# Humanities

Invention is of two kinds much differing – the one of arts and sciences, and the other of speech and arguments. The former of these I do report deficient; which seemeth to me to be such a deficience as if, in the making of an inventory touching the state of a defunct, it should be set down that there is no ready money. For as money will fetch all other commodities, so this knowledge is that which should purchase all the rest …. So it cannot be found strange if sciences be no further discovered, if the art itself of invention and discovery hath been passed over. That this part of knowledge is wanting, to my judgment standeth plainly confessed …

—FRANCIS BACON

Mental interests, hypotheses, postulates, so far as they are bases for human action – action which to a great extent transforms the world – help to make the truth which they declare.

—WILLIAM JAMES

I am enough of an artist to draw freely upon my imagination. Imagination is more important than knowledge. Knowledge is limited. Imagination encircles the world.

—ALBERT EINSTEIN

# The Transformative Humanities

## A Manifesto

*Mikhail Epstein*

*Translated and edited by*
*Igor Klyukanov*

BLOOMSBURY

NEW YORK · LONDON · NEW DELHI · SYDNEY

**Bloomsbury Academic**

An imprint of Bloomsbury Publishing Plc

175 Fifth Avenue           50 Bedford Square
New York                   London
NY 10010                   WC1B 3DP
USA                        UK

**www.bloomsbury.com**

First published 2012

© Mikhail Epstein, 2012

**Library of Congress Cataloging-in-Publication Data**
Epstein, Mikhail.
The transformative humanities : a manifesto / Mikhail Epstein ; translated and edited by Igor Klyukanov.
p. cm.
Includes bibliographical references and index.
ISBN 978-1-4411-5507-8 (pbk. : alk. paper)– ISBN 978-1-4411-0046-7 (hardcover : alk. paper)  1. Humanities–Philosophy. 2. Learning and scholarship.  I. Klyukanov, Igor. II. Title.
AZ103.E67 2012
001.3–dc23
2012020542

ISBN: HB: 978-1-4411-0046-7
      PB: 978-1-4411-5507-8

Typeset by Fakenham Prepress Solutions, Fakenham, Norfolk NR21 8NN
Printed and bound in the United States of America

# CONTENTS

# ACKNOWLEDGMENTS

I have worked on this book for approximately ten years, and it would not have been finished without the generous support of a number of individuals and institutions.

First of all, I am immensely grateful to Michael Holquist of Yale University, whose support and endorsement were crucial for the transformation of my project into a book. As a reviewer, Michael was most generous in his evaluations, and most helpful in his insightful comments and recommendations that led to a significant improvement of the manuscript.

I want to express my deepest gratitude to Caryl Emerson of Princeton University for her long-standing interest in my work, and her encouragement of this project from its early stages on. Her preface is, in my view, a masterpiece of dialogical thinking penetrating to the very core of the issues raised in this book, while at the same time offering their most original and inspiring interpretation. Her personal voice and the force of her argumentation set the tone for the book and considerably broaden its scope. Caryl Emerson's text is a powerful vision of the transformative role of the humanities in its own right.

I owe a unique debt to Igor Klyukanov, the translator and editor of this book, with whom I have collaborated since 2007. Professor of Eastern Washington University and Editor-in-Chief of *Russian Journal of Communication*, Igor Klyukanov has brought to our joint project his vast knowledge and experience in the theory of communication and methodology of the humanities. Invariably, I have found in Igor Klyukanov an exceptionally perceptive and kindred spirit, and our discussions have prompted me to formulate new ideas and approaches. He has my heartfelt thanks for his careful and sensitive translations, which capture the language as well as the tonality of my Russian text. Igor Klyukanov helped me enormously to organize the material of the book into a coherent conceptual framework. In all issues of form and content, I was a beneficiary of his intellectual generosity, wise advice, and prompt collaborative action, which is reflected in only a small degree in his editorial footnotes. His innumerable suggestions concerning style and composition, and his valuable comments on many of the ideas as well as their expression, have given this book its present shape.

My special thanks go to my friend and colleague Walter Reed of Emory University, whose intellectual and practical encouragement was invaluable in many areas, as was his generous support of my applications for grants and fellowships to various programs and institutions. Teaching together with Walter Reed a course on Mikhail Bakhtin, and our numerous discussions in and out of class, gave a significant impulse to my thinking on the nature of the humanities. My colleagues and friends at Emory Juliette Stapanian Apkarian and Elena Glazov-Corrigan were instrumental in providing the necessary creative atmosphere in my department and in helping me to obtain the funds and release time necessary for my work on the project.

I owe gratitude to my former graduate student Svetlana Corwin, who typed and edited the initial fragments of the book in 2002–3; to Sheldon Kohn, who helped me to edit earlier versions of Chapters 3 and 4; to Edward Demenchonok, who helped me to edit an earlier version of Chapter 19; and to Vallan Kantner of Emory University, who helped me persistently and diligently in editing a significant part of the initial manuscript.

I am deeply grateful to my new colleagues at Durham University, UK, Alex Harrington, Alastair Renfrew, Marianna Taymanova, and Andy Byford, who helped me to integrate my thinking on the future of the humanities in a new intellectual community and enriched it with interesting insights and perspectives. Alex Harrington read several chapters and generously provided most useful comments and suggestions both on content and language, which were very helpful for my work on the book and its subsequent editing. Durham graduate Samuel Thompson read attentively a considerable part of the manuscript, and his remarks and proposals were also most insightful and helpful.

I thank Edward Skidelsky and Vern W. MacGee, whose excellent translations of my Russian texts are used in two chapters (respectively 2 and 19). I am deeply grateful to Jeffrey M. Perl, Editor-in-Chief of *Common Knowledge*, who accepted for publication and brilliantly edited my articles that later became integrated into this book (Chapters 2, 3, 5 and 10).

I also wish to thank several institutions. I am very thankful for the continuing support that I have received from Emory University, its administrators and staff, as well as my colleagues, in pursuing my research goals. As an inaugural Senior Fellow at The Bill and Carol Fox Center for Humanistic Inquiry at Emory University in 2002–3, I was fortunate to devote the entire academic year to my project that, at that time, was titled *The Future of the Human Sciences: Paradigmatic Shifts and Emerging Concepts*. I am grateful to the Center's Director Martine Brownley and Associate Director Keith Anthony for organizing discussions on various issues related to the humanities and creating a productive atmosphere for my work. I want to thank Emory University Research Committee for the grant I received in the spring of 2009, which allowed me to concentrate on the project for one semester.

Finally, in 2011 as a Fellow at the Institute of Advanced Study at Durham

University, I had the privilege to participate for three months in the project on the subject of "Futures", which allowed me to work on the completion of my book. I am deeply grateful to the administrators of the Institute, to its Acting Executive Director Michael O'Neill and Director Colin Bain, and to its members of staff for their hospitality and for creating the best possible conditions for intellectual exchange. I am indebted to the fellows of the Institute, particularly to Andrew Crumey with whom we discussed in depth, and corresponded on, many ideas related to the future of the humanities. As a Prowse Fellow at Van Mildert College where I resided, I am thankful to its then Master Patrick O'Meara for his hospitality.

Haaris Naqvi, Senior Commissioning Editor at Bloomsbury, was instrumental in making this book possible. I am deeply grateful to him for his interest in the proposed manuscript, and for his patient guidance and excellent advice throughout my work on the book. I wish to thank Ally Jane Grossan, Assistant Editor at Bloomsbury, Kim Storry, Project Manager, and James Tupper, Production Editor at Bloomsbury, who carefully and patiently oversaw the production of the book.

There are many more people who have influenced this work in various ways, either personally or through their research. I apologize if I have missed any of them.

# FOREWORD

*Caryl Emerson (Princeton university)*

The manifesto is a curious genre. Like a shout, it signals urgency, impatience with the present, a break and a boundary beyond which other principles should apply. But the most effective manifestos are always sunk deep in history. Alert to historical tensions and turning points, a manifesto is able, from the perspective of the future, to look back at itself as a threshold utterance even if its judgments are not heeded—as most often they are not. It accomplishes its cultural work if it anticipates the tools and goals of the future without bleaching them out into utopia or apocalypse. Manifestos are filled with the energetic faith that we will *go on*. Little wonder, then, that Mikhail Epstein's transformative humanities has a long and rich back-story.

Two dozen books by him in Russian and English precede it, as well as a multitude of essays that test its ideas under various names and rubrics. Among these trial concepts are the "improvisational community", transculturalism, the "dehumanities" (our discipline stripped of its living subjects), futuristics, minimal or "poor" religion, "possibilistics". All of these topics will be found in the present volume but with their agenda sharpened, the neologisms multiplied, the intellectual contexts deepened and made more polemical. Epstein opens and closes on the intonation of a true manifesto: first what is wrong, and at the end a "task-sheet" of practical suggestions. These latter include "the restoration of realities left out by hard science", the birth of new humanistic disciplines (rather than our current habit of timidly yoking together existing disciplines), and a "University Center for Humanities Innovation" where our "informational universe" could explore strategies for becoming a "transformational multiverse". To found a center or a site is one of Epstein's signature motifs. In the 1980s in Moscow, he organized "experiments in dialogical thinking". By the late 1990s, already in the USA, these workshops had evolved into "collective improvisations" on university campuses, designed to explore creativity, technology, and the role of spirituality in everyday mental processes. The present volume is both a manifesto and a user's manual to this growing, ever more virtual infrastructure. In between its balance sheet and its task sheet comes the cautionary message: that the humanities, endowed with such huge potential and staffed by such well-educated people, flounders without articulate definition or defense— and at times even doubts that its workers are professionals with skills sufficient to produce a competitive product or to train others. How might we humanists rid ourselves of the bondage, the embarrassment, the defensiveness and unproductiveness that we now feel in relation to other branches of knowledge and technology?

One enabling place to start is with Epstein's special brand of personalism— what he calls, in Chapter 15, "Differential Ethics". The chapter is deeply beholden to the moral philosophy of Mikhail Bakhtin. Here Epstein supplements the homogenizing Golden Rule (based on a reciprocity of human wills) with the differentiated, multifaceted "Diamond Rule": *"Do that which others need and no one else can do in your place"*. Although this "dutiful [obligation-generating] uniqueness"—the phrase is Bakhtin's— has little power to address issues of justice or even of justification, it remains our best weapon against any absorption by a coercive ideology or any caving-in to a passive rhetoric of victimhood. Act according to the Diamond Rule, and you cannot be superfluous; your actions will be strapped to your back and to the back of your neighbor. But to be humanly answerable, rules are not enough. We also need new scholarly forms to legitimate partial, tentative utterances. The current roster of academically respectable genres must be broadened to re-embrace those more "creative, succinct, energetic" forms of profound thinking that were a mainstay of intellectual wisdom in earlier eras—the working notebook, manifesto, theses, aphorism, fragment, preamble—and are amateurish today (or relegated to quasi-literate blogs or chat rooms). As Epstein put it in 1982 in his "Essay on the Essay": what we need now is modesty, brevity, tentativeness combined with depth of thought, a *"boldness of propositions and meekness of conclusions."*[1]

Epstein is of course aware that bold prepositions are extremely difficult to keep appropriately meek, that is, small and individualized. If given free rein, a bold claim will naturally swell up in size and authority. It will strive toward a systematic Whole and from there to the status of Truth. Epstein, chronicler of a country whose truth narrative collapsed two decades ago in disastrous and comedic fashion, is expert at extracting potentials for human freedom from the surviving parts of a crumbled or exploded system. That freedom is one theme of the present book.

[1]Mikhail Epstein, "An Essay on the Essay" [Moscow, 1982], in Ellen E. Berry and Mikhail N. Epstein, *Transcultural Experiments: Russian and American Models of Creative Communication* (New York: St. Martin's Press, 1999): 189–93, esp. 193.

A second, equally potent theme of this book is that humanistic organisms, like any other organism, must cope with environmental change. Yet mostly what we do, Epstein notes, is complain. His fear is that academic humanists will die out as a profession before we redefine ourselves and seize the heights. In his Introduction he resolutely parts company with the crisis-mongers. He hints gently—and gentleness is everywhere Epstein's great asset—that humanists have succumbed to nostalgia, anger, self-pity, the comfort zone of fixed texts and slow-moving traditions ("the canon"), attitudes that paralyze our field. Without the petulance of past Futurists who discredited cultural legacies as a matter of principle, we must investigate new means for activating our accumulated wealth. One bad habit has been thinking "post-": postmodern, postwar, post-communist, post-human. The logistics of post- can only be reactive and "reactionary" in a brutal sense. The operative prefix, Epstein has long insisted, is *proto-* : where we might be headed rather than whence we dispiritedly came. Of course the maps here are speculative, but positing ourselves as the beginning of a new thing rather than the tail-end of an old thing can only improve our potency and flexibility. Since the way to get at the new is to name it, we must continually be thinking up new words to explain unfamiliar glimpsed spaces. "To tell you the truth," Epstein told an interviewer in November 2002 for his faculty profile in *The Chronicle of Higher Education*, "my favorite intellectual occupation is inventing new disciplines, new methods. . . . This is what actually the humanities enterprise may be: finding mutenesses and lacunae in the languages of existing disciplines and trying to fill them."[2]

To this powerfully Russian conviction that "finding the word means creating the thing" we shall return, but it is important to note that the silences and gaps in language are not "filled in" for the sake of mere talk. In fact, one of the big problems Epstein sees with our existing crisis-ridden models for renovating the humanities is that they remain just talk. "Imagine botany without agriculture, forestry or gardening, i.e. without any cultivation and experimentation with plants", he counsels in his "In Place of a Conclusion". "Or imagine cosmology without cosmonautics and space technology . . . And yet, this is exactly the situation with the humanities today, where scholarship, without developing its own practical and experimental branches, degenerates into scholasticism". Fired by this faith that words can be more than mere talk—that they not only fill conceptual voids but generate real and valuable matter—Epstein displays the sleuthing appetites of an astrophysicist out to map the universe, filling

[2]*The Chronicle of Higher Education*, November 22, 2002: "A Cultural Hero of the Soviet Era Looks to the Future. Now at Emory, Mikhail Epstein envisions new modes of thought in the humanities." Interview conducted by Peter Monaghan.

it in with new planets by ingenious strategies to measure the micro-wobble of orbits or minuscule light-reduction across the face of a star.

Instead of applying ourselves in rigorous practice, however, humanists cower and complain. Look around and listen: digital technology is blamed for depersonalizing, dis-integrating, hyper-accelerating and reifying the modern world. Epstein protests loudly. Never before, he insists, have humanists had such access to tools for face-saving (literally) and personality-sharing. Never has temporal or spatial distance mattered so little in pulling together people, ideas, and cognitive pleasures. Never has the problem of storage and retrieval been so close to elegant resolution. True, an on-line text is not a graspable book in the library. Also true, cozying up to a computer screen is not the same as snuggling up to a living body. But our new environment requires that we redefine our bodies, or at least our inborn drive for body warmth, for emotional and mental security. Human organisms have always had this creative edge on other creatures: we can co-think our way out of a trap, and even refashion the trap into a new sort of home. It is insufficient to argue that without a fixed canon we will lose precious permanent values amid the torrent of the transitory in cyberspace. Such anxieties have been with us for millennia.[3] Our response must be not self-pity or panic but a fresh surge of "inventorship", the courage to devise new forms of responsible retention and interaction alongside new definitions of permanent and transient worth. Tectonics, electronics, mnemonics we have long known; let there also be culturonics. Similar to more abstract sciences, humanists are now well positioned to think boldly, across boundaries, and to arrive at an *aha!* synthesis without any of the dependency on statistics or norms that so fetters the social sciences to the present and the past (a fetter that legitimizes them, rightly or wrongly, *as* a science). The more visionary natural sciences have always needed our products and love them. Instead of experimenting in our own way, however, humanists too often fall back indignantly on the truism that human experience, so unrepeatable and private, cannot be turned into an experiment that laboratory science would respect.

Epstein would say that we have long held too impoverished a view of "laboratories". It is simply not true that human beings must become mechanized, predictable, or objectified in them. Theater, music, and dance ensembles are classic examples of highly disciplined, rule-bound working groups that set a common goal and experiment their way through

---

[3]For a reminder (which Epstein would appreciate) that our fear of being "mentally overwhelmed" is very old, see Ann M. Blair, *Too Much to Know: Managing Scholarly Information before the Modern Age* (New Haven: Yale University Press, 2010).

to a collectively acknowledged, expressive solution. But Epstein takes
on more than the routine teamwork of performance art. By the 1980s,
he had turned even writing and thinking, those most private bastions
of creativity in the humanities, into a laboratory. On the assumption
that communication, to be responsibly creative, must transcend mere
conversation by incorporating "moments of privacy, isolation, and
meditation", he devised "improvisational communities" made up of writers
engaged alternately in multi-dimensional thinking and uni-dimensional
speaking, the virtues of silence and the satisfactions of speech—thereby
uniting "the experiences of public eloquence characteristic of the West and
silent meditation characteristic of the East".[4] What was an experiment in
the 1980s has become, of course, the norm of our nonstop text-messaging
today. Why, then, do humanists fret rather than rejoice? Too often we go
bitter, nostalgic, defensive—and worst of all, technophobic. Little wonder
that we cannot gain the trust or attention of corporations (including our
own universities) that produce the more marketable goods of our time:
bombs, consumer contrivances and conveniences, colorfully packaged
info-bytes, media entertainment.

Epstein opens his Chapter 3 on a tribute to Russia's first transculturalist
thinker, Mikhail Bakhtin. One of the exquisite paradoxes of Epstein's book
is that Bakhtin, unlike Epstein, was a technophobe. Even the telephone, it
appears, was too much for him. What might explain Bakhtin's disinterest
in, and even aversion to, the mechanical equipment of long-distance,
instantaneous communication? Was it connected to his passion for the
unmediated face? The undiluted voice? His instinctive sense that machinery
always speeds us up, and yet to grasp both a work of art and one another
we must learn to slow down? Or perhaps for Bakhtin, the important
dialogues were with past consciousnesses that had been caught in words—
that is, with the fictive and the dead rather than with people we can dial up
now. Bakhtin, survivor of Stalin, lived in an era where personal dialogue
was precious and often dangerous. We live in an era where dialogue costs
nothing and is carried around (and carried on) endlessly over everyone's
tiny portable machines. Epstein does not address Bakhtin's archaic side. But

---

[4]In these laboratories, Epstein makes a strong case for the written character of creative
improvisation (and a speculative case for Russia and the Near East as the meeting ground of
public rhetoric and silent meditation, which explains in part to its "love of books, literacy,
and writing"). "In front of a sheet of paper or a computer screen," he writes, a person experiences the full measure of her individuality as a creator. Without writing, improvisation tends
to dissolve into conversation, exchange of opinions, that is, pure communication. . . . It is
writing that resolves the dilemma of speech and silence." See Chapter 17, "Improvisational
Community", in Berry and Epstein, *Transcultural Experiments*, 201–13, esp. 207.

he is deeply invested in Bakhtinian hybridity, centrifugal energy, and the inevitable inadequacy of any mind standing alone.

In Bakhtin's dialogic spirit, Epstein asks two questions of the humanities in the current proto-global age. "Is the multicultural model—the pluralistic world of self-enclosed cultures, each valuable in itself—sufficient for understanding new intercultural flows? Or do global studies have to work out a new model that will challenge the mosaic multiculturalism, just as multiculturalism had earlier challenged the melting-pot model and the 'universal' cultural canon?" The transition from multicultural to transcultural had been the focus of Epstein's 1999 book (with Ellen Berry), *Transcultural Experiments: Russian and American Models of Creative Communication*. But institutional inertia on these matters is immense. In continuing to prod the regnant infrastructure of most humanities programs, Epstein is in good company. One useful book to read in tandem with *The Transformative Humanities: A Manifesto* is an anthology from 2009 in the same genre, edited and framed by Stephen Greenblatt under the title *Cultural Mobility: A Manifesto*.[5] Greenblatt too considers our disciplinary segmentation into departments of literature and language a formidable handicap to our return to health as a profession, for it suggests (and rewards) a far greater degree of fixity and purity than has ever anywhere been real. It is a fantasy, he insists, to believe that "settled, coherent, and perfectly integrated national or ethnic communities" ever existed anywhere (2); the norm for the world has always been fantastic hybridity and flux. "Only the increasingly settled and bureaucratized nature of academic institutions in the nineteenth and early twentieth centuries, combined with an ugly intensification of ethnocentrism, racism, and nationalism, produced the temporary illusion of sedentary, indigenous literary cultures making sporadic and half-heated ventures toward the margins," Greenblatt writes. "The reality, for most of the past as once again for the present, is more about nomads than natives" (6). But the fact that our "established analytical tools have taken for granted the stability of cultures" burdens us with the myth that "robust cultural identity" must entail searching for, and finding, roots and a singular "at-homeness" (3).

Greenblatt's manifesto on behalf of mobility and heterogeneous exchange is nudged by Epstein beyond its initial geographical and political implications into the digital age. The canon as a fixed set of texts has long ago frayed away. The next step is to embrace the fluid, intervenable "textoid" as a transitorily authoritative utterance, and translation as "interlation" (a juxtaposition of many approximate versions for the multilingual subject).

---

[5] Stephen Greenblatt et al., *Cultural Mobility: A Manifesto* (Cambridge: Cambridge University Press, 2009). Further page references in text.

And further: the subject itself must be reconfigured and co-created as a "transsubject" available through a more trustful, needy type of writing that Epstein calls "scriptorics" (see his Chapter 7). If we do not turn this new digitized environment to our benefit, we have ourselves to blame. Epstein is not naïve about crises in academic funding, shrinking enrollments, disappearing jobs, or the collapse of morale in the creative arts brought about by a commodification of the humanities. But he is losing patience with our uncreative response to these conditions. Keep the cultural heritage alive, of course, but also reconceive ourselves as organisms capable of acquiring radically new skills and tools. Epstein devotes several chapters to innovative disciplines that might address the most fearful realities head-on: research into cultures paralyzed by information trauma, for example, or the new field of *horrology* ("the study of the self-destructive mechanisms of civilization, which make it susceptible to all forms of terrorism"). His Chapter 11 ends on the *horrification* of our entire way of life after 9/11. In sum: it is certainly bad out there, and nothing promises us that in thinking up one more word to describe this badness we will alleviate it. But—Epstein would immediately add—until you send a useful articulate idea out into the world detached from the old static structures, no amount of funding will save you.

How are ideas best sent out? The November 2002 "featured faculty" column on Epstein in *The Chronicle of Higher Education* devoted considerable space to what was at that time his most recent "mode of thought in the humanities", a product of the glasnost 1990s published in English by Paul Dry Books only that year: *Cries in the New Wilderness: From the Files of the Moscow Institute of Atheism*. Both the wilderness and the atheism deserve a careful look. An intentionally partial and transitory text, *Cries* is also a mystifying triple spoof: a novel wrapped in several quasi-fictional frames posing as a classified document compiled in 1985 by one Raisa Omarovna Gibaydulina, PhD, an academic on the Party's research staff assigned the task of cataloguing the vital new spiritual sects then emerging on the exhausted soil of Marxist-Leninist ideology.

The core of the book is Gibaydulina's classified report, *The New Sectarianism*, which reveals a rich nascent spiritual world. Doomsday sects of Arkists and Steppies (or void-worshippers) proselytize alongside the literary sect of Pushkinians; the nationalist groups Red Horde and Khazarists co-exist with atheists (Good-Believers and Sinnerists) and the neo-fetishistic "everyday sects" of Foodniks and Thingwrights. Gibaydulina, a professional non-believer and a veteran of many years front-line service in the USSR's struggle for atheism, is at first baffled by the results of her research. But she is a devoted materialist, trained to take empirical evidence seriously, and continues to collect the most astonishing data. In the book's back matter, we learn that Gibaydulina survived the collapse of Communism, developing in her final decade an interest in cyber-technology and virtual space as the ultimate liberated phase of the communist (collective-communicative) ideal. Drawing on this global "syntellect", she devises a new "creative atheism" that is capable, thanks to Hegelian sublation, of loving all faiths equally. The end of censorship dismays her, as it does many of her generation. Postmodern texts flooding the Russian market are devoid of that disciplined skepticism she had always brought to her cultural work: they strike her as frightfully anti-humanist, pagan, animist, idolatrous "sign systems at play". The new theorists, she notes sadly, are as vulgarly superstitious as the old theists, with their "distracting little godlets" (linguistic structures, epistemic codes, the id) that "aren't even capable of entering into serious moral relations". When, in 1996, Gibaydulina (now in retirement) comes across an essay by Mikhail Epstein on "Poor Religion" in the Soviet journal *October,* she writes an excited, agitated Letter to the Editor. Before Epstein can respond, however, she dies in a Moscow hospital. Posthumously published notes toward her next project, *Spiritual Movements of the Future*, seem to echo several themes dear to Epstein himself.

Is this book—that is, Epstein's edition of her book—a work of fiction? Hard to say, Epstein tells his interviewer. If these persons and cults did not exist they would have to be invented, in order to understand the twilight years of Soviet Communism as well as the steep learning curve of Professor R. O. Gibaydulina, PhD. As so often is the case with Epstein, the more bizarre the name or passion invoked, the more seriously he frames it. He ends his *Cries* with an Afterword, "The Comedy of Ideas". There he calls for a release of the creative concept from all the linear ideologies and institutionalized bureaucracies that have boxed it in and for its return to "speculative phantasmagorias", where it can migrate or mutate into transient forms, at peace with the "partiality of its content". We can now appreciate *Cries in the New Wilderness* as an early, meek prototype for the applied or experimental humanities.

Much in this book will inspire and enchant the reader. Epstein's wide and informed reading across a global curriculum; his optimism about science as a handmaiden to human development; his fascination with the future rather than his dread of it; and the sheer inventiveness and pliability of his mind, which finds almost nothing threatening and almost everything interesting. It comes as no surprise that Epstein devotes an entire section (Chapter 16) to the concept of "interesting"—not as Deleuze and Guattari defined the word in the 1980s, in defiant opposition to the static truth-claims of knowledge, but as a more gently induced (and thus a more productive) quality of mind. The "interesting", Epstein writes, is a category "constituted not merely in opposition to truth, but in the juxtaposition of the truthful and trustworthy on the one hand, and on the other, the improbable and wondrous. . . . An interesting theory presents the *most consistent and plausible proof* for what appears to be the *least probable*. In other words, the interest of a theory is *inversely proportional to the probability of its thesis and directly proportional to the provability of its argument*. . . . The interesting is what comes in between two *mutually exclusive* and *equally indispensable aspects* of a phenomenon." Glinting below the surface here—as beneath the surface of the later Bakhtin[6]—is a metaphysics that shares less with Plato, Marx, and Kant than it does with the Christianization of Aristotle in the work of St. Thomas Aquinas. For Thomist ontology presumes that every question posed by science or philosophy has two aspects: it is both a *problem* and a *mystery*. The problem side is empirical, a puzzle that is in principle solvable; it can be pried up by the analyst. Mystery, however, is a matter of reverence and intuition, so only the seeker's prior faith in its existence will bring its essence into being.[7] Epstein has no problem seeing mystery in the most mechanical scientific breakthroughs, for he is interested in mysteries as routes to practical knowledge.

A warm glow illuminates Epstein's faith in the future of the humanities, and by extension his faith in humanity itself. But three positions in this book might startle the reader and are sure to stimulate further questions. In the spirit of *proto*-ism, I preview them here. The first has been hinted at throughout: Epstein's passionate belief in the power of the word to pin down a problem, point the way toward its solution, satisfy its sender and its receiver, and accomplish a quantitative change in the world. No one would dispute that the word is a wonderfully flexible, efficient all-purpose instrument. But does it cover every creative concept and communicative impulse? Leaving to one side the reductive "linguistic turn" that took Continental theory by storm in the middle of the past century, one can detect in this belief Bakhtin's near-maniacal commitment to the utterance, as expressed in his comment in a late essay that "language and the word are almost everything in human life."[8] Epstein's conception of the humanities

---

[6]See Mikhail Bakhtin's "Toward a Methodology for the Human Sciences [Humanities]," where he remarks on the inadequacy of the current "trivially human attitude toward the future (desire, hope, fear); there is no understanding of evaluative non-predetermination, unexpectedness, as it were "surprisingness,' absolute innovation, miracle, and so forth." M. M. Bakhtin, *Speech Genres & Other Late Essays*, transl. Vern W. McGee (Austin: University of Texas Press, 1986a): 159–72, esp. 167.
[7]The most celebrated twentieth century spokesman for this metaphysical position is the Catholic Thomist philosopher Jacques Maritain; see especially his *Preface to Metaphysics: Seven Lectures on Being* (1934). But the interaction between speculative and practical knowledge, and within the practical realm between making and doing, is constant throughout Maritain's work (as it is in Epstein's).
[8]See Bakhtin, "The Problem of the Text" [1959], in *Speech Genres & Other Late Essays*, 118.

(and arguably of the human) is litero- and *logos*-centric. Although his relevant Chapter 6 ("Semiurgy: From Language Analysis to Language Synthesis") does make a point of invoking signs in general rather than only phonemes or syllables, his categories are clearly deduced from the word, his examples are poets and folkloric bards. Readers of Epstein's book who are also dancers, theatrical mimes, musicians, sculptors, portrait painters, set designers—the "fine arts" side of the humanities, where people express and communicate their individuality with absolute precision, but non-verbally— might feel excluded from this vision of the creative humanities.

The issue, then, is whether faith in the transformative power of the word, and specifically the word, is indispensible to Epstein's manifesto. Could his marvelous neologisms (infinition, informatization, noocracy, interlation, ichnosphere) find their functional equivalents in a newly-coined dance step, an original elbow gesture, an unusual chord sequence, voice timbre, stone carving, stunningly sketched face? Does the energy of Epstein's transformational model extend to "speakers" in those non-linguistic expressive systems? After all, there is no reason why a dancer, violinist, water-colorist, or architect should have to think or speak in words at all, rather than in movements, tones, pitches, rhythms, shades, volumes, spatial or temporal relationships. Within those imaginary communities (imaginary, because willy-nilly it seems we all have to pass through words) you see a building and build your own in response; hear a melody and sing one back; join a round dance and make your intent clear with your feet; tie down your tongue and still communicate fully with people similarly inclined, trained, and inspired. If literary humanists are seeking only to save one another, then of course no problem exists. The word is their instrument. They can use it to talk—or type—their way out; all it takes to join Epstein's InteLnet is to "press a key". The destination will still be constrained by the medium, however, which is at best "applied words". This in itself will be transformative for many, especially for those who believe that our most powerful ideas and creative visions are born in the word and expressible in words (or, on occasion, through the withdrawal of words). But many forms of creative expression have nothing to do with verbal language, present or absent. And one senses in Epstein, as one does in the semiotics of Yury Lotman, a more cosmic, interdisciplinary ambition that would tap these other rich modes of creativity, but is not sure how.

The other two startling, potentially most controversial theses in this book concern the ancient turf war between body and spirit. Let us begin with the body. Among Epstein's most provocative sections is Part Three, "Humans and Machines", especially its Chapter 8, "The Fate of the Human in the Posthuman Age". The title is a tease, of course, because Epstein rejects any reasoning from "post-"; his real topic is *proto-technohumanism*, a concept he considers wholly compatible with humanism "because the most human feature of humans is to transcend and technologize themselves". What does this entail? The new discipline of humanology will eventually map out the task, but in brief: being a cyborg, a hybrid cybernetic organism, must cease to seem monstrous or comic and begin to be seen as enhanced. And further: an enhanced body—a body plugged in and covered with tiny machines that personalize its environment in all dimensions at every second—is not just a glorious cyborg, it is a work of art. "Techno-humanism", Epstein writes, "provides a way of upholding humans as a species through technology as an artistic creation of the highest order." Endorsing this way and appreciating its results as artistic, I am afraid, will take major work. We must part from old models of community and make our peace with people around us living in their own individualized time and space, looking up only to cross the street (and not always even then). We must outgrow those old habits of perception that sentimentalize the body according to the heroic or intimate models provided by Greek sculpture or Rembrandt. And we must redefine our sense of the beautiful, emphasizing cognitive and design delights over the merely proportional or physiological.

At this point Epstein does venture beyond words to other types of tissue—even though one might still be obliged first to "type them in". The available infosphere will eventually become "an active part of my mind", he predicts; "I will communicate with the network by using my voice, touch and gestures, which will also become part of the infinitely growing and, in its own way, creative memory of *syntellect* …" (Epstein's name for the combined intellectual resources of people and machines). In Chapter 14, "From Body to Self, or What Is It Like To Be What You Are?", he muses that the noosphere (the "sphere of human thought" after the geosphere and the biosphere) might some day operate directly with consciousness, "giving up the need for the body as an intermediary". This is a startling sentiment from a humanist, and it comes as a relief that Epstein is so wholly unapologetic about it. Intimacy can now be distanced, mediated, micro-managed by all parties. We are overwhelmed by all the new channels we can boot up for fighting loneliness. But in every crucial individualizing dimension, Epstein insists, We Are Still What We Are. The body that matters to him, and that he recommends to us, is the body of knowledge: mobilized, accelerated, and split asunder by the energy of thinking. In a gorgeous metaphor in Chapter 20, Epstein boldly applies Einstein's formulas to the humanities: "The energy of thought is extracted from the body of knowledge by producing multiple, fast, light-like, fleshless, fictive, virtual combinations of its former particles." Few people would deny that on occasion, a great thought can indeed feel that mobile and exciting. The controversy comes in the body-mind balance, in the contrast between the vulnerable organism, absurdly attempting to defend itself against age and infirmity, and the magnificent indestructible noosphere, where all can partake and none can lose. To be potentially a proto-superman is a riveting thought. But does this relieve the traditional mortal body of its anxieties?

This question leads us to a third startling moment in Epstein's manifesto, also in Part Three but now on the spirit-oriented side of the human: *technotheism*. Epstein holds that the recent discoveries in cosmology, together with the digital revolution, global networks, informational matrices, and the proto-syntellectual condition of human beings (what he calls collectively "cognitive faith") has made it easier than ever to believe in Supreme Mind. He will not allow the mystery of the multiverse to default to anti-intellectual fundamentalists. Nor does he take kindly to the likes of Richard Dawkins, whose preemptory atheism on behalf of scientific method strikes him as defensively short-sighted. If it is true that *In the Beginning was the Word*, then "informational patterns precede corporeal existence"—and the humanities as well as the sciences should draw strength from this hypothesis. "The time has come", Epstein writes, "to speak of the religiosity of knowledge, not only of the religiosity of faith. . . . Why should not science, relying on these physically verifiable facts, find a common language with theology?" One suspects that Bakhtin had something like this integrated picture in mind when he added "miracle" after "absolute innovation" in his essay on methodology in the humanities.

*  *  *

As a cultural theorist, Mikhail Epstein belongs to the "healthy-minded" (to evoke an epithet made famous by William James in *The Varieties of Religious Experience*). In his Lecture Six, James remarks whimsically that "the healthy-minded live habitually on the sunny side of their misery-line"[9]—and Epstein commits wholly to this admirable mental behavior. The unknown buoys him up. Mystery is on a continuum with data-banks. Part contemplator and part pragmatist, Epstein strives to bring together "the reality of the unseen" (the topic of James's Lecture Three) with "the instrumentality of pure ideas", a prerequisite, James says, for any positive belief.[10] Whatever evil or apprehension there is in our life and thought processes can be isolated, named, investigated, targeted piecemeal and perhaps even driven out. To the healthy-minded, the bad and the inadequate are not first principles but, with some input of effort, curable conditions, "only a maladjustment with *things*, a wrong correspondence of one's life with the

---

[9] William James, *The Varieties of Religious Experience* [1902], in *Writings 1902–1910* (New York: The Library of America, 1987): 1–477, esp. 128.
[10] Ibid., 55.

environment."[11] For Epstein, the existing *things* of the world (organisms, texts, bodies, machines) are by definition "interesting". They always reward study, through a Center or better yet, a website. Addressed by technologies under our control, these modified hybrid things can become supports for the spirit. Reading this book, even for the multitude of "sick souls" lamenting the fate of the humanities, can be a revelation. Or if revelation runs too great a risk of short-circuiting the wires, plugs, and screens that hold our body and soul together, this book promises its reader (at the very least) a robust, wholly new variety of cognitive-religious experience.

---

[11] Ibid., 127.

# Introduction

## The crisis of the humanities

A reaction I often encountered in response to my work in progress, *The Future of the Humanities*, was surprise: "Do you really believe that the humanities have a future?" Unfortunately, such a reaction is not surprising: one day, in the not too distant future, we may find the humanities an extinct species among academic disciplines. A recent article in the *Boston Globe* puts it clearly:

> At college campuses around the world, the humanities are hurting. Students are flocking to majors more closely linked to their career ambitions. Grant money and philanthropy are flowing to the sciences. And university presidents are worried about the future of subjects once at the heart of a liberal arts education. (November 8, 2010)

The statistics are eloquent: in the last 40 years, the number of students majoring in the humanities in the US has declined by more than half, according to the American Academy of Arts and Sciences. As the figures below indicate, the popularity of the following subjects among undergraduates has significantly decreased from 1970/71–2003/04 :

> English: from 7.6 per cent of the majors to 3.9 per cent
> Foreign languages and literatures: from 2.5 per cent to 1.3 per cent
> History: from 18.5 per cent to 10.7 per cent (Chace, 2009).

All these dry figures cannot convey the whole measure of the bitterness which those of us working in the humanities feel when witnessing the lack of demand for our expertise, our vocation, and when we observe an arrogant contempt towards that which we consider the focus of our life. Therefore many pronouncements on the plight of the humanities seem to combine two distinct genres: the diagnosis of a doctor and the complaint of the patient, as, for example, in the recent book of Martha Nussbaum, *Not for Profit: Why Democracy needs the Humanities*:

> The humanities and the arts are being cut away, in both primary/ secondary and college/university education, in virtually every nation of the world. Seen by policy-makers as useless frills, at a time when nations must cut away all useless things in order to stay competitive in the global market, they are rapidly losing their place in curricula, and also in the minds and hearts of parents and children. (Nussbaum, 2010, p. 2)

But, before asking society to embrace once again the value of the humanities, we should ask ourselves a simple question: what is it in contemporary humanities that holds special value and promise for society? How many ideas coming from literary, philosophical, and historical departments have recently achieved any prominence at an international level, or at least at the level of interdisciplinary academic debates? Can we imagine the next era being heralded by a particular treatise on aesthetics, a philological study, philosophical aphorisms, or poetic meditations? Not by politicians, scientists, or technologists, but by a new Novalis or Schlegel brothers, Byron or Hugo? Physics and genetics, medicine and informatics, cosmology and sociology invest heavily in the climate of intellectual innovation. Ideas from these fields easily cross the thresholds of their mother disciplines. This has all but ceased to be the case with the humanities.

Frank Donoghue (2010), professor of English at Ohio State, offers a melancholic comment: "What *has* happened is that the center of gravity at almost all universities has shifted so far away from the humanities that the most pertinent answer to the question 'Will the humanities survive in the twenty-first century?' is not 'yes' or 'no,' but 'Who cares?' … Curricula change over time, and the humanities simply don't have a place in the emergent curriculum of the 21st century."

Why? Perhaps twenty-first-century society, and conceivably even the academe itself, are turning away from the humanities because in the twentieth century, and especially in its second half, the humanities turned away from humans? Instead they focused on texts. To a certain extent, humanities stopped being human studies and became textual studies. No one now seems to expect anything from the humanities except readings and re-readings, and, first and foremost, criticism rather than creativity and suspicion rather than imagination. As a result, the humanities are no longer focusing on human self-reflection and self-transformation. Philosophy, for instance, is no longer thinking about the foundations, purpose, and meaning of the Universe; instead, it is focusing on analysis of the philosophical texts. As a result, there is now a vacuum of human meaning and purpose that technology cannot, and the humanities will not, fill. As they retreat from the forefront of history and society, the humanities lose the best and brightest to other fields, becoming a shelter for those less creative and those with more "archival" inclinations.

I believe that those of us in the humanities should be responsible enough to accept at least part of the blame for the decline of our professions, rather than pointing an accusing finger at the job market, the economic crisis, the greed of corporations, the indifference of the government, shallow consumerism, or superficial obsession with new technologies. The humanities should look more critically at their own methods in order to see what is wrong with their self-proclaimed intentions to keep the moral and liberal spirit of humanity alive.

Unfortunately, the prevailing tone of contemporary works on the state of the humanities is one of resentment. Many lamentations come from the academics condemning the dry pragmatic spirit of our century, and looking at their professions as a safe haven of mental and moral purity in a world driven by profit. It is this type of intellectual that Richard Hofstadter—an American historian and public intellectual himself—singled out as "paradoxical" in his famous book *Anti-intellectualism in American Life*:

> Many of them [intellectuals] have come to feel that alienation is the only appropriate and honorable stance for them to take. What they have come to fear is not so much rejection or overt hostility, with which they have learned to cope and which they have almost come to regard as their proper fate, but the loss of alienation... This is the fundamental paradox in their position—that while they do resent evidences of anti-intellectualism, and take it as a token of a serious weakness in our society, they are troubled and divided in a more profound way by their acceptance. (Hofstadter, 1963, p. 393)

Hofstadter wrote his book in what later came to be known as the last decade of the industrial age (1960s), when intellectuals could still justify their alienation from the establishment by the spirit of nonconformism and resistance to the power of capital. Today, however, ideas rather than material riches make up the wealth of a society; the world is open to conceptual innovations more than ever before. That is why the position of a voluntary alienation of intellectuals is today even more striking and self-defeating[1].

In the nineteenth century John Ruskin, an English art critic and social thinker, complained that machines had robbed workers of their nobility, freedom, and individuality. Challenging that view, James Martin, a contemporary English social thinker remarks on the intellectual machines of the future: "The machines of the twenty-first century will be the opposite.

---

[1]Even Humanities and Technology Association, hosted by the Department of History and Government, Bowie State University, is not sufficient to fix the broken connection between the two worlds. The association publishes the annual *Humanities and Technology Review* (http://htronline.weebly.com/index.html), which offers three articles a year by humanists interested in issues of technology. This exception only proves the rule.

Inability to use them will rob workers of their nobility, freedom and individuality" (2007, p. 387). The alienation of intellectuals from the increasingly intellectualized world becomes less explicable and justifiable as the post-industrial world moves from a manufacturing-based economy to a society based on the growth of information and value of innovation. More and more often people today earn their living by producing ideas and images, not things, and by operating with words, symbols, and numbers, not with material objects.

Meanwhile, the word "technology" still has a negative ring in the humanities, and an escape from technological society is seen as a way of salvation of intellectual values. John Paul Russo ends one of the chapters of his book, entitled *The Future without a Past: the Humanities in a Technological Society,* with an appeal to the monastic tradition:

> [I]t is worthwhile to recall that monastic refuge happened once in Western culture and the humanities survived. The light of learning at Lindisfarne and Citeaux, at St. Gall and Monte Cassino, could be rekindled by an apprenticeship to the word in the midst of our necessary participation in technological society. As Burckhardt said, the culture of the West may once again be saved by ascetics. (Russo, 2005, p. 42)

However appealing the image of the humanities taking "a monastic refuge" may be, I believe that the humanities are worthy of a better future, and one very different from their past. The crisis in the humanities is first and foremost a crisis of imagination. There is no future for those disciplines and methods that turn away from the future.

# The world as a project

Today the word "project" has become ubiquitous. Even that which was, at one time, presumed to be immutable or, at the least, slowly changeable now becomes an open project—be it a culture, a country, or a language, cf. "USA as a project", "English as a project", "the Antarctica as a project", "the planet Earth as a project", or "the Universe as a project".

In this way, theory is increasingly turning into practice as a project of systemic transformation of its subject area. In pure theory, which literally means "contemplation", a certain period of stability is required for its object. In the twentieth and twenty-first centuries this temporal gap between a real object and its transformation becomes smaller and smaller. History has increased its speed to such an extent that theory, rather than explaining its object, now anticipates and produces it. The very existence of an object in the informational universe is now derivative from the system of concepts. Moreover, the informational universe itself is now morphing into the transformational one.

More and more often, cognition approaches the limits of what can be cognized, only to discover limitless possibilities of creation beyond such limits. Sciences turn into technologies, with knowledge emerging within the very process of such a transformation. We learn about the characteristics of nanoparticles through the process of their engineering while creating new materials from them. We learn about the characteristics of the genome through the process of constructing its working model while developing genetic medicine and engineering. The very process of learning about a certain object, therefore, turns into an act of its creation. No longer does such an act simply involve the knowledge of a static and unchanged object; instead, cognition and creation of an object are brought together in a single *projective* act of thinking.

Theorizing, thus, should be treated both in terms of "theories of", focusing on representation of objects, and "theories for", highlighting their re-entry into the social fabric and thus enabling further practices. In other words, all theories must be viewed as "social inventions that intervene with, transform, create, or maintain the realities we experience" (Krippendorff, 1994, p. 102). Theory that is aiming to transform its object can be called "projective" theory, and it is related to the genre of a project as described by Friedrich Schlegel—a founder of German Romanticism, which was itself one of the greatest projects in cultural history:

> A project is the subjective embryo of a developing object. A perfect project should be at once completely subjective and completely objective, should be an indivisible and living individual ... . The feeling for projects—which one might call fragments of the future—is distinguishable from the feeling for fragments of the past only by its direction: progressive in the former, regressive in the latter ... the feeling for fragments and projects is the transcendental element of the historical spirit. (Schlegel, 1991, pp. 21–2)

Natural sciences have been quick to appreciate the power of projects overflowing with all kinds of intellectual energies, and brimming with concepts and ideas to define the future of humanity. Scientists have been following in the footsteps of Giordano Bruno

> who swept away the last sphere of the fixed stars and opened the universe in all directions.... It is said he was not a scientist; he did not make any systematic observations or experiments; he was only a metaphysician and his view of the universe was a poetic vision, not a scientific discovery. (Čapek, 1976, p. xxii)

Bruno's "poetic vision" of multiple worlds, however, became an important contribution to the birth of modern science and its projective methods. In physics and biology, for example, the search for patterns is conducted more and more often through a comparison of real processes with their imaginary or experimentally designed alternatives. Until recently, there has been only one reality at scientists' disposal: one Universe, one terrestrial form of life, and one—human—form of intellect. No generalizations about its nature could be made because only one reality could be observed, while any generalization calls for a comparison of various forms of a phenomenon. Computer simulations of natural processes have made it possible to compare the "real" reality with its alternative forms; as a result, more generalizations have become possible. To quote Christopher Langton, who pioneered the theory of artificial life:

> You end up with a much larger set. You can then probe this set not just of existing chemical compounds but of possible chemical compounds. And it's only really within that ground of the possible chemical compounds that you're going to see any regularity. The regularity is there but you can't see it in the very small set of things that nature initially provided you with … . So part of what artificial life is all about, and part of the broader scheme that I just call synthetic biology in general, is probing beyond, pushing beyond the envelope of what occurred naturally. (see: Horgan, 1997, p. 199)

New electronic technologies radically change the structure of knowledge by allowing instantaneous transformations of knowledge accumulated over centuries. Every new discovery and every new invention is immediately reflected in a relevant database, while in the past, in the Gutenberg galaxy, such a process used to take a very long time as information slowly travelled from one paper publication to another. New electronic technologies act as a means for new methodologies, which can be called 'synthetic': consider, for example, disciplines such as "synthetic biology", developed by Langton, or "synthetic physics", "synthetic chemistry", "synthetic linguistics", or "synthetic aesthetics". Each such discipline is looking not so much for the units of analysis at their boundaries—"atoms" in its field, so to speak—as for such methods of synthesizing them that would broaden the very field of the phenomena under study. Horgan takes Langton's thought further by stating that

> Science had obviously made enormous progress by breaking things up into pieces and studying those pieces. But that methodology provided only limited understanding of higher-level phenomena, which were created to a large extent through historical accidents. One could transcend those limitations, however, through a synthetic methodology, in which the basic components of existence were put together in new ways in computers to explore what might have happened or could have happened. (1997, p. 200)

In the 2000s, the quantum transportation experiments conducted in the US, Europe, and China, opened up amazing prospects for the computer industry. They confirmed the phenomenon of quantum superposition whereby a particle can simultaneously exist in two states, allowing a quantum bit (qubit) to keep two numerical values at the same time. Thus, a quantum computer with 300 qubits can run more calculations in a moment than there are atoms in the universe (Choi, 2005). What are we to do with such quantum computers if each of them can potentially contain information about all the particles in the Universe? We will start creating new universes, figuratively speaking; in other words, we will go beyond our knowledge of the existing Universe and therefore beyond the Universe itself. And this is where the humanities become indispensable with their capacity to create new signs, ideas, and modes of subjectivity. The vector in the development of science turns from the cognized to the cognizer, i.e. the human being, which opens the perspective for the new, humanistic, or anthropocentric turn in sciences.

# The humanities and sciences

The crucial distinction between the humanities and sciences is that in the humanities the subject and the object of the study coincide; in the humanities, humans are studied by humans and for humans. Therefore, to study the human being also means to create humanness itself: every act of the description of a human is, by the same token, an event of one's self-construction. In a wholly practical sense, the humanities create the human, as human beings are transformed by the study of literature, art, languages, history and philosophy: the humanities humanize. When those of us in the humanities are asked by university administrators or our colleagues in the sciences to show them the results of our work, the most natural thing to do would be to point at the interlocutor as if to say, 'It is you, and I, and all of us.' Whether dealing with the aesthetics of the Italian Renaissance or epic stories of ancient India, the interrelationships between the Romanic and Germanic languages, or Kant's philosophy of time and space, every humanistic study brings up in front of us an image of another human being, another mind. As we compare us to them, drawing distinctions and finding commonalities, we keep becoming ourselves and thus more human. This way, we are becoming more universal and more distinctly ourselves.

Let us make one qualification. The humanities are so called not because they study humans in all of their diverse manifestations; many other disciplines study the human being as well. The human body, for example, is examined by physiology, anatomy, medicine; labor activity and the exchange of its products are explored by economics; and modes of human social organization are discussed by sociology and political science. Yet all of these listed examples are natural or social—that is to say, not human—sciences. In the humanities, one is least capable of conceptualizing oneself as an empirical entity, a physical individual or a social body. The humanities focus on those processes of creativity, thinking, speaking, writing, or inter-personal relations in which a human being is least definable or finalizable. The field that is the humanities is made up of the dissipating fragments of language and the growing symbolic lacunas as gaps in which reflexivity is slipping away from itself. The *critical* side of the humanities consists in the denaturalization of a human being, i.e. in the unmasking of every-thing viewed by the natural and social sciences as the solid and positive foundation of objectivity. The humanities are engaged in the demystifi-cation of their own scientific claims as much as those forms of knowledge about humans that are claimed by physics, physiology, or economics. The *constructive* dimension of the humanities suggests that humans create new images, signs and concepts of themselves. In this process, humans do not so much discover something in the world of objects as build their very subjec-tivity by way of self-description and self-projection.

It is this constructive dimension of the humanities that is today in such high demand in the exact and natural sciences. Throughout the twentieth century, the humanities suffered from an inferiority complex. However, the entire system of the scientific knowledge in the twentieth century was shaken by this paradoxical nature of the humanities, affecting even those disciplines that seemed to be the most methodologically stable, such as mathematics, logics, or cybernetics. All of them have to accept and integrate those "strange loops" of self–reflexivity that, in the humanities, make humans simultaneously objects and subjects of study. Cf. the testimony by Douglas R. Hofstadter:

> All the limitative Theorems of metamathematics and the theory of computation suggest that once the ability to represent your own structure has reached a certain critical point, that is the kiss of death: it guarantees that you can never represent yourself totally. Gödel's Incompleteness Theorem, Church's Undecidability Theorem, Turing's Halting Theorem, Tarksi's Truth Theorem —all have the flavor of some ancient fairy tale which warns you that 'To seeks self-knowledge is to embark on a journey which … will always be incomplete, cannot be charted on any map, will never halt, cannot be described. (1980, p. 697)

And so, in the twenty-first century, as mathematics, physics, and biology develop newer and newer technologies, coming closer to the creation of artificial intelligence and life, they inevitably find themselves straying into territory that previously belonged uniquely to the humanities. It turns out that the natural sciences are most interested in what makes the humanities 'less scientific', their subject–object reversibility, for example, their semantic fuzziness, and even the metaphoric nature of their language. The natural sciences cannot strive for the pinnacle of self-organized and self-reflective knowledge without the humanities' critical contribution.

More and more scientists have been turning to the humanities when taking up problems of consciousness, creativity, intuition, free will, language, as well as ethical and even theological problems. In this respect, one can mention such scientists as David Bohm, John D. Barrow, Freeman Dyson, Paul Davies, Roger Penrose, Frank J. Tipler, and John Wheeler. Significantly, they turn to the humanities when trying to find answers to questions within their own disciplines (mostly physics, cosmology, and biology). Even the hard-core natural scientists are forced to introduce the human factor into their grand theories. The so-called 'theory of everything'—supposedly the grandest theory of all theories and the ultimate dream of contemporary physics—cannot be completed without the humanistic mind providing the missing piece in the overall puzzle of how all known physical forces and interactions can be integrated into one. According to Eugene Wigner, a Nobel laureate in physics, "it was not possible to formulate the laws of quantum mechanics in a fully consistent way, without reference to the consciousness ... the very study of the external world led to the conclusion that the content of the consciousness is the ultimate reality" (Kaku, 2006, p. 165). Another physicist who believes in the defining role of consciousness is Andrei Linde, a founder of the inflationary theory of universe: "For me as a human being, I do not know any sense in which I could claim that the universe is here in the absence of observers. We are together, universe and us. ... I cannot imagine a consistent theory of everything that ignores consciousness" (Kaku, 2006, p. 166).

Science seems to have exhausted its resources of experimental study, reaching the limit of the human ability to describe the Universe. It is precisely at this point, where traditional sciences end, that the projective sciences take over. Consider, for instance, John Horgan's book *The End of Science: Facing the Limits of Knowledge in the Twilight of the Scientific Age* (1997). The work features interviews with leading scientists from ten distinct disciplines—from physics to chaos theory to evolutionary biology—who question the potential of positive science. Horgan calls modern science "ironic" and states that it "resembles literary criticism in that it offers points of view, opinions, which are, at best, interesting, which provoke further comment. But it does not converge on the truth" (Horgan, 1997, p. 7). It does, however, converge on the human being, searching for new ways of self-reflexivity.

The future of our civilization depends upon many scientific disciplines, including mathematics, cybernetics, informatics, cognitive science, semiotics, neuropsychology, and the theory and practice of artificial intelligence. All of these disciplines, however, depend upon the humanities' focus on the self-reflexivity of any consciousness—be it that of God, human, or machine. No technologies, powerful as they may be in their capacities of calculation, can exist without self-reflexivity. The supreme technology can exist only insofar as it can learn what it means "to be itself" or "to know itself" or "to speak about itself". As Douglas Hofstadter puts it, "In the end, we are self-perceiving, self-inventing, locked-in mirages that are little miracles of self-reference" (2007, p. 363). In this sense, the humanities should always be ahead of any and all breakthroughs in cyber-, neuro- or bio-technologies and thus closer to the future.

However, the humanities of today are enveloped in the paradigms of the past. Even the most recent attempts to deal with the state and prospects of the humanities in the twenty-first century largely explore the socio—political and educational aspects of humanistic teaching and research in the academy, the place of the humanities in the curriculum, and their interaction with the natural and social sciences in the infrastructure of a university. Many of such attempts are devoted to historical ideas in the humanities and do not have much to say about their path to the future (Hoyrup, 2000; Tindemans et al., 2003). Other works focus in a nostalgic manner on the decline of traditional literary culture in a society driven by technology (Paulson, 2001; Russo, 2005). These works do not propose any strong alternative to current trends, holding out arguments for the intrinsic worth of humanistic studies pretty much as they have been constituted since at least the radical university reforms of the nineteenth and early twentieth centuries (Nussbaum, 2010; Menand, 2010). But, while it may have been natural in the past to pay homage to a slow pace of historic time, today focusing exclusively on the past means ignoring looking past everything that is taking place in the transformational universe.

Without a doubt, the humanities need a healthy dose of conservatism, and those studying ancient literature or Shakespeare's plays should not completely give up the objects of their study in order to catch up with the newest trends in science and technology. At the same time, some kind of methodological fermentation must take place in the humanities, reflecting a faster pace of the technological, social, and cultural dynamics of humankind and thus a new approach to language, literature, and philosophy. In their current configurations, sciences and technology take the responsibility for shaping the future, while the humanities commit themselves to the elucidation of the past. But, is such a temporal polarity necessarily linked to the specifics of these branches of knowledge? The world of culture and history is much more dynamic than the world of nature; why, then, should the sciences of nature be more dynamic and future oriented than the study of culture? Why cannot the humanities share their constructive potentials for the future with technologies, in the same way that technologies can make (and are already making) a huge contribution into the preservation of the past, for example, by collecting information about the early stages of civilization and building digital archives? It would be preposterous to stage a confrontation between the traditional scholarship and projective thinking, between the domains of cultural memory and intellectual imagination: both expand the potential of human consciousness and creatively complement each other.

What is at stake today is not technological innovations in rockets or computers, it is the radical enhancement of human potential and new capacities for the self–creation of human beings. According to Joel Garreau, the author of *Radical Evolution*,

> this cultural revolution in which we are immersed is no more a tale of bits and bytes than the story of Galileo is about paired lenses. In the Renaissance, the big deal was not telescopes. It was about realizing that the Earth is a minor planet revolving around an unexceptional star in an unfashionable part of the universe. Today, the story is no less attitude-adjusting. It is about the defining cultural, social and political issue of our age. It is about human transformation ... . The goal is to seamlessly merge mind and machine, engineering human evolution so as to directly project and amplify the power of our thoughts throughout the universe. (2006, pp. 11, 20).

For the first time in history, humans now have the ability to create something (or even somebody) similar to humans themselves. Not just tools or symbols, but artificial intelligence, artificial organisms, new forms of life, and holistic human–like creatures. This can infinitely expand the sphere of humanness. Our time may be remembered by the distant future as the first epoch of creation of humans by humans through combined efforts of culture and technology. The evolution that for millions of years has been in nature's hands is now passing, through the use of info- and biotechnologies, into human hands: "This change from nature-based evolution to human-based evolution is, by far, the largest change to occur since the first single-cell life appeared" (Martin, 2007, p. 275). Will the humanities let this evolutionary dynamic go by without their own attempt to enhance the role of humans in the transformation of the universe and their own nature? Will the humanities depart from their mission of serving human self-fulfillment? Will the humanities miss the astonishing opportunities of exploring the very phenomenon of the human in the time of its greatest and most dramatic transformation?

## The transformative humanities

In no way does such an active and transformative approach to one's object of study contradict the traditions of the humanistic thought that for centuries determined the vector for humankind's development and provided it with its historical meaning. In the eighteenth and nineteenth centuries, the humanities were the disciplines about human beings and humankind, e.g. metaphysics, logics, political and social philosophy, philosophy of religion, ethics, aesthetics, history, psychology, philology, the study of art and literature, and linguistics. The humanities used to determine, and give meaning to, historic eras. The era of Enlightenment was inaugurated by philosophy and literature: by the works of Voltaire, Rousseau, and Diderot. The era of Romanticism came into being thanks to the creative efforts of literary critics, linguists, poets, and writers, such as Novalis, the brothers Schlegel, Byron, Hugo, and Madame de Staël. It has traditionally been the role of the humanities to lead humankind.

Thus, the future-oriented humanities must not limit themselves to scholarship, but rather should seek to create their own ways of changing what they study and transforming the human world. And yet, the creative aspect of the humanities has not yet found its recognition in the established classification and methodology of scientific disciplines. The crucial question is whether the humanities are a purely scholarly field, or whether there should be some active, constructive supplement to them. We know that technology serves as the practical extension ("application") of the natural sciences, and politics as the extension of the social sciences.[2] Both technology and politics are designed to transform what their respective disciplines study objectively: nature and society. Is there any activity in the humanities that would correspond to this transformative status of technology and politics? In the following schema, the third line contains a blank space, indicating an open status of the practical applications of the humanities:

| Nature | – | natural sciences | – | *technology* | – | transformation of nature |
| Society | – | social sciences | – | *politics* | – | transformation of society |
| Culture | – | the humanities | – | ? | – | transformation of culture |

The blank space and question mark in the third line suggest that we need a *practical branch of the humanities*, which will function similarly to technology and politics, but which is specific to the cultural domain. [3]

What are we to call such a new, practical branch of the humanities? Naming is sometimes the best way to deal with a problem; a name contains

---

[2]This does not mean that technology and politics are secondary to, and derivative from, natural and social sciences. In many respects, practical disciplines precede theory and actively shape it, the way medicine precedes physiology or biology, and political life precede social studies. There is a mutually transformative correlation between theories and practices in these areas.

[3]Arts and literature cannot serve in this capacity because they constitute one of the objects of the humanities (including aesthetics, literary, and art theory) just as nature constitutes the object of natural sciences.

the embryo of a concept and the beginning of a future theory. While the current embryonic stage of theorizing leaves the future open to multiple possibilities, several terms can be suggested that could operate in that blank space:

*Culturonics* might denote a discipline that deals with culture practically, in the mould of "electronics", "bionics", "avionics", "tectonics" (the art of building), "mnemonics" and other applied, constructive disciplines;

*Pragmo-humanities* would suggest that the humanities have a pragmatic aspect that regulates the relationship between their practitioners and users, their authors and addressees;

*Techno-humanities* would refer to the *art of the humanities*. This includes the art of building new intellectual communities, new paradigms of thinking and modes of communication, rather than simply studying or criticizing the products of culture. We should bear in mind that the humanities constitute the level of *meta-art*, different from the primary arts of literature, painting, or music, all of which comprise the objects of humanistic inquiry. The fact that the humanities belong to this meta-discursive level does not preclude their practical, productive orientation. The humanities do not produce works of art, but rather generate new cultural positions, movements, perspectives, and modes of reflexivity. The concept of *techno-humanities* does not imply that the humanities should "steal" the idea of "techno" from scientific technology; on the contrary, it was technology that took "techno" (Greek 'techné', meaning "art, skill, craft") from the humanities. By utilizing the term "techno", we do not intend to "scientize" the humanities, but, on the contrary, we intend to draw them closer to art and creativity in the sphere of ideas and communications.

However, the broadest term for this transformative branch of the humanities would be *trans-humanities*; that is, the humanities that aim to transform the area of their studies. The transformative humanities encompass all humanistic technologies and all practical applications of cultural theories. When offering a certain theory, we need to ask ourselves if it can inaugurate a new cultural practice, a new artistic movement, a new disciplinary field, a new institution, a new life-style, or a new intellectual community.

I will give an example of what I understand by the transhumanities. The main insights of literary theory, as we study its innovative ideas and peak achievements, are found not in scholarly monographs or articles, but in literary manifestos, which are products of theoretical imagination, rather than of empirical study and scholarly scrutiny. The manifestos of Neoclassicism, Romanticism, Naturalism, Symbolism,

Futurism, or Surrealism are not based on the discipline of research; that is, the "careful, systematic, patient study and investigation in some field of knowledge", as defined in Webster's Dictionary. Instead, manifestos proclaim new literary movements and cultural epochs, and they trigger these movements by the very act of their proclamation. Manifestos are performative rather than descriptive speech acts; they implement what they pronounce.

The majority of the key concepts that laid the ground for literary studies in the past initially came from such imaginative proclamations, which were not supported by any systematic research. It is primarily from manifestos that we learn about the irony and the grotesque, the image and the symbol, the "naïve" and the "sentimental", and the poetic landscape and the realistic character. Those who found new literary movements typically are not scholars, but a separate breed of creators of ideas and theories. They are transformative thinkers and humanistic inventors.

Under which existing academic categories can such constructive theoretical activity be placed? Manifestos are neither factual nor fictional—they are *formative*. They aim to produce new literary facts, rather than to register and analyze facts of the past and present. The proper place of manifestos is precisely in the as yet unmarked domain of *theoretical inventions*, or *the transhumanities*. The transhumanities embrace both modes of cognitive advancement recognized by the sciences: the *discovery* of some existing principles and facts, and the *invention* of those tools and ideas that can transform a given area of study. *Inventorship*, as a mode of creativity, is as indispensable a companion to scholarship in the humanities as technology is to science. The transhumanities can be defined in Bakhtin's words as "the co-creativity of those who understand [culture]", (1986a, p. 142.) as the constructive and transformative potential of cultural theories.

Our academic institutions, however, currently have no place for such avenues of conceptual creativity. There are departments of literary theory and scholarship ("comparative literature"); departments or programs of fiction and creative writing; but there are no departments of constructive writing in "practical theory", no transhumanities departments.

Is there any institution in contemporary academia in which such *literary inventors and builders* as Friedrich Schlegel, Vissarion Belinsky, Friedrich Nietzsche, André Breton, or Walter Benjamin, could flourish as professionals? Imagine Friedrich Nietzsche applying for the position of assistant professor in a department of philosophy somewhere in the United States. He brings his book *Thus Spake Zarathustra* as confirmation of his credentials—a book without a single reference, with no list of sources, devoid of scholarly apparatus, and full of pompous and vague metaphysical declarations voiced by an arrogant author in the guise of an ancient Persian prophet. Most likely Nietzsche would be denied even the position of an instructor, while, following his death, dozens of distinguished professors of philosophy have made their careers studying Nietzsche's oeuvre and commenting on his philosophy of the superman. Nietzsche himself was not a researcher in the academic sense of the word. He was a seeker and a visionary, who invented ideas that inspired a number of highly influential social, artistic, and philosophical movements in the twentieth century.

The contemporary academy dismisses humanistic inventorship, while retrospectively holding it in such high esteem. This paradox can be compared to the improbable scenario in which a university would exclude a computer technology department or an engineering school on the grounds that, unlike departments of physics or chemistry, they deal with inventions and not discoveries. Invention in the humanities is no less important.

The academy's failure to recognize the cognitive status of the transhumanities raises the question of whether various intellectual capacities are adequately represented at our universities. According to Alfred North Whitehead, one of the greatest philosophers of the twentieth century, "the task of a University is the creation of the future, so far as rational thought, and civilized modes of appreciation, can affect the issue" (Whitehead, 1938, p. 233). Humanistic *inventorship*, even more directly than humanistic scholarship, shapes our future. For the humanities to survive and to enhance their intellectual impact on society, their transformative branches need to be recognized and institutionalized in contemporary universities by establishing programs in creative thinking and humanistic inventions. The academy needs creative minds in these fields no less than they need the academy.

This book focuses on the transformative potential of the humanities and on those practices that can evolve on the basis of cultural, literary, and philosophical theories. My central concern is the need for deep methodological changes in the humanities that would enrich them with a new, creative dimension. The concept of "transhumanities" emphasizes the constructive aspect of humanistic inquiry and calls for a reexamination of far-reaching questions such as: "How can the humanities affect the areas of their study?", "Which practices can be built on the basis of our studies of language, literature, and philosophy?", "Can the analysis of language lead to the synthesis of new lexical units, terms and concepts?", or "Can philosophy be involved in strategic thinking about 'virtual worlds' and their technological implementation?"

# The invention of new disciplines.
# Futurologisms

The invention of new disciplines, such as the transhumanities, needs imagination. Today the distinction between reality and imagination is increasingly being blurred, and we enter a world in which fiction becomes a form of knowledge of near or distant future. In fact, science and fiction switch roles; and we are moving from science fiction to fictional science. Rather than inspire fiction, science is inspired by it. Science translates our imagination into the knowledge of future things, the cognition of such things being tantamount to their creation. Thus, a sphere of imagination enters the very structure of contemporary scientific knowledge. In the late nineteenth century Engels wrote the book entitled *The Development of Socialism from Utopia to Science*. In our time, to oppose science to utopia means to ignore the imaginative and utopian impulses behind scientific progress.

The first conscious synthesis of science and imagination was Francis Bacon's "desirable sciences" found in his treatise *De Dignitate et Augmentis Scientiarum* (1623). Bacon not only described those branches of knowledge that had already existed in his time, but anticipated new disciplines that he believed would emerge in the future:

> Thus have I made as it were a small globe of the intellectual world, as truly and faithfully as I could discover; with a note and description of those parts which seem to me not constantly occupate, or not well converted by the labour of man. (Bacon, 1803, v.1, p. 234)

Bacon claims that certain disciplines are missing in the system of knowledge and thus need to be created. For instance, Bacon placed in the category of "desiderata" "the history of sciences and arts", "the theory of machines", "the doctrine on the state's expansion", and several other disciplines developed only centuries later (Bacon, 1878, p. 120). Bacon also provided examples of discipline-building creativity such as experimental treatises in non-existent area, e.g. *Consulem Paludatum. Exemplum Tractatus Summarii de Proferendis Finibus Imperii* (Bacon, 1878, p. 120). Today, this discipline about the "expansion of the frontiers of the empire" would be identified as geopolitics. Thus, almost 500 years ago, Bacon created a kind of periodic table designed to both classify and predict scientific disciplines. Some of the blank spaces in this table have been filled as a result of the subsequent advances of the sciences, just as the empty squares of undiscovered elements have been gradually filled in Mendeleev's periodic table of elements.

Sometimes, the role of fantasy in science is deemed to be subservient to the task of popularization and accessible presentation of its achievements (cf. popular physics or popular linguistics). However, along with *popular* science, *fictional*, or *fantastic* science has to be acknowledged as a separate branch of intellectual activity. It embraces the variety of possible and desirable disciplines, such as humanology, culturonics, realogy, micronics, semiurgy, and technosophy, all presented in this book as "desiderata". At present, none of these can claim the status of an academic discipline or institutional recognition. Along with the *classification of sciences*, we need to delineate the *construction of sciences* or, in Bacon's words, the "logic for the invention of arts and sciences" as a separate, experimental realm of contemporary theory of knowledge. According to Bacon, such invention of disciplines is the primary intellectual pursuit, the *art of arts* and the *science of sciences*:

> Invention is of two kinds much differing – the one of arts and sciences, and the other of speech and arguments. The former of these I do report deficient; which seemeth to me to be such a deficience as if, in the making of an inventory touching the state of a defunct, it should be set down that there is no ready money. For as money will fetch all other commodities, so this knowledge is that which should purchase all the rest. And like as the West Indies had never been discovered if the use of the mariner's needle had not been first discovered, though the one be vast regions, and the other a small motion; so it cannot be found strange if sciences be no further discovered, if the art itself of invention and discovery hath been passed over. That this part of knowledge is wanting, to my judgment standeth plainly confessed. (1803, p. 132)

For centuries, Bacon has been hailed as the founder of empirical methods in science. However, Bacon's loyalty to the experience and experiment did not prevent him from unleashing the powers of intellectual imagination that now can be viewed as his even more vital contribution to the methodology of science. Bacon's enthusiasm for constructive activity even surpasses his admiration for empiricism. In fact, such enthusiasm resonates deeper with the contemporary scientific mind and its proclivity for paradigmatic shifts as described by Thomas Kuhn in *The Structure of Scientific Revolutions*. While he is commonly seen as the father of the "normal science" of the Modern Age, Bacon's "desirable sciences" put him on the level of a visionary exemplifying the spirit of scientific revolution.

It is noteworthy to mention that Bacon's famous aphorism "Knowledge is power" inspired Albert Einstein to coin a new slogan for twentieth century science: "Imagination is more important than knowledge. Knowledge is limited. Imagination encircles the world". Einstein argues with Bacon, yet at the same time enhances Bacon's vision of the "logic of invention" ("What Life Means to Einstein: An Interview", by George Sylvester Viereck, 1929).

\* \* \*

This faculty of invention is especially lacking in the humanities. And yet, through studying the products of human imagination, such as art, literature, and philosophy, the humanities are potentially even more open to the constructive work of theoretical imagination than natural sciences. One, perhaps most ostensible, aspect of this constructive work is neology.

The reader of the present book may find the use of many new terms to denote *desirable* disciplines, including their methods and concepts, rather excessive and even annoying. However, the use of neologisms is determined by the projective approach to the future of the humanities adopted in this book. Usually neologisms follow the progress of the society rather than anticipate and initiate it. They tend to be reactive, i.e. reflect what has already happened or designate emerging trends, fashions, and commodities. In contrast, the majority of neologisms used in this book are *futurologisms*, i.e. language signs that denote nonexistent, yet thinkable and imaginable entities. Futurologisms as new coinages articulate in advance those concepts that can engender the corresponding realities in the future. Thus, the signifier of such signs serves as a prototype or generative model of their signified, rather than the other way around, as is usually the case with neologisms, where the signified comes before the signifier. For instance, 'corputer' is a futurologism signifying a *corporeal computer*, an electronic prosthetic device that, through interconnected microchips and artificial neurons, becomes a part of the human body. In the future, computers may be transformed into *corputers* and integrated with human bodies.

Jonathon Keats, the editor of *Wired*'s "Jargon Watch", has investigated the origins and development of many new words, such as "cubit", "singularity", "tweet", and "copyleft", that accompanied or even instigated certain technological and social trends. Keats observes

> a remarkable symbiosis between scientific and lexical innovation, a potent coevolution. Ideas inspire words, which inform ideas ad infinitum. ... [L]anguage is a technology, arguably our first, possibly, our most resilient, developing with us as a species and facilitating all other technological advances from agriculture to the internet. The language of technology and science illuminates the science and technology of language. (2011, p. VIII).

Thus, futurologisms are "virtual words" that anticipate and predetermine the conceptual structure of those phenomena that they projectively describe. For example, Paul Grutzen, a Nobel prize-winning atmospheric chemist, coined the word "Anthropocene" to designate the current geological epoch succeeding the Holocene. And, while he made up it on the spur of the moment, the word has stuck and has had a profound impact on our environmental thinking, since the effect of humans on the environment is now terminologically recognized as a geological factor. And, to quote Keats again, "given that language can impact thought, there's even a chance to observe the reciprocal influence of words on science and technology" (2011, pp. YII–YIII).

The category of futurologisms has a special significance for the humanities and social sciences, where concepts, initially speculative and hypothetical, can gradually take on real historical flesh, for instance, the way it happened with such presumably fantastic and purely prognostic terms as "utopia" and "communism" (see more on verbal creativity and its role in the humanities in Chapter 6 "Semiurgy: From Language Analysis to Language Synthesis").

The multitude of futurologisms in this book is in accordance with its genre of manifesto. In fact, each futurologism is a micro-manifesto compressed into one word, while a manifesto in general can be seen as a futurologism extended to the size of an entire book. Both manifesto and futurologism are not constative, but performative types of discourse: they do not describe what already exists, but attempt to implement the future through the very act of its manifestation. Such performative discourse is more appropriate for the humanities than for any other branch of knowledge, precisely because, unlike nature and society, individual human beings are themselves a projection. Their realities coincide with the spheres of their intentions, desires, expectations, and possibilities. The entire field of the transhumanities is a self-projection of the human species and thus encourages a projective type of discourse, be it a single word or an entire book.

# The structure of the book

In the first part of the book, entitled *An Open Future*, I focus on the marks of the historical changes in our perception of time, temporality, and contemporaneity. I discuss the present moment in the history of the humanities and delineate a transition from finality to initiation as a mode of critical thinking. I show how Mikhail Bakhtin's concept of "embryonic genres" can be applied to many cultural formations whose birth we are witnessing today. Thinking in terms of beginnings and initiations presupposes an open future, rather than a consummated past.

The second part of the book, entitled *Humans and Texts*, addresses language and text, the most canonical fields of the humanities, which in the twentieth century experienced a "linguistic turn" and increasingly morphed into textual studies. I attempt to answer the question of whether the traditional notion of text, central to the humanities, remains intact in the digital era. Or, if the immutable, self-identical texts now give way to more flexible, dynamic, nomadic *text-like* formations that wander from site to site and are modified by their users, much like the epic song was modified in a preliterate community. Further I argue that, while preserving their loyalty to textuality, the humanities can offer a synthetic, rather than analytic, approach to language and initiate language games of their own designed to expand the field of the speakable and thinkable. Language is approached here as a form of life that needs permanent expansion and revitalization. This indicates the direction of a new synthesis where Wittgensteinian theory of language games merges with Nietzschean philosophy of life.

The third part, entitled *Humans and Machines*, takes the opposite side of the disciplinary frontier. If textuality is considered to be the territory native to the humanities, then "techno" is usually viewed as an adversarial dehumanizing force, which humanists have to resist. My approach is different. Technology is an extension of the creative potential of humans in the same, or even more radical, way than arts, crafts, or any other cultural practices. Machines not only serve as powerful tools for humans, but also provide the traditional humanities with a new opportunity to transition from the methods of speculative metaphysics into the area of technologically based practices. Instead of being a threat or a limitation, I view technology as the prospect for innovation that will bring the humanities into the very center of intellectual activities in the twenty-first century.

The fourth part, entitled *Humans and Humans*, explores the self-reflexive and self-transformative tasks of the humanities. It raises the perspective of our return to those concepts of *universality*, *wisdom* and *self* that have been sharply criticized and almost obliterated by poststructuralist (anti)humanists, but now deserve a radical rethinking and re-evaluation. This part discusses the ways from cultural relativism that dominated recent theory toward a new kind of critical, or apophatic, universalism, which assumes the humility and insufficiency of each culture in relation to others. There are further questions in this part for humanistic self-reflection, such as: "How can we reformulate the millenia-old golden rule of ethics in such a way that it preserves its universality and, at the same time, emphasizes the uniqueness of each subject, the value of an individual gift and vocation?"

In the fifth part of the book, entitled *The Future of Wisdom and Creative Theory*, I present some criteria of productive thinking, which may lead to the renovation of the humanities and increase their transformative potential. Thus, I return to the central issue of creativity in the humanities but, distinct from the first part of the book, discuss it more in methodological rather than historical terms. To that end, I raise a number of questions: "What makes a theory interesting?", "How can these criteria be equally applied to a work of fiction and to a work of scholarship?", "What is the modality of humanistic discourse?", "Why does the category of possibility acquire a new meaning in contemporary philosophy?", and "What is understood by research in academia and why should the acquisition of knowledge as its goal be complemented, in our professional orientation, with the value of conceptually creative and hypothetical thinking?"

# PART ONE

# An open future

# 1

# From post- to proto-: Toward a new prefix in cultural vocabulary

This chapter raises the following strategic question: "What in contemporary culture comes *after the post-*, e.g. postmodernism, poststructuralism, post-communism, and post-utopianism?" I propose and examine a number of paradigmatic shifts or modes of possible transition, such as the transition from finalizing to initiating approaches in the humanities. I do so always in the subjunctive rather than in the indicative mood; any response to the above question can deal only with what *may be*, not what *will be*.

Thomas Kuhn introduced the concept of a "paradigm shift" to describe the mechanism of methodological innovations in the natural sciences. In considering the application of this concept to the humanities, we should bear in mind that "paradigm shift" is an inherently humanistic concept that Kuhn borrowed from Gestalt psychology. It is also implicitly related to the legacy of Russian Formalism, represented by Viktor Shklovsky, Boris Eikhenbaum, Yury Tynianov, and Roman Jakobson. The following passage from *The Structure of Scientific Revolutions* (Kuhn, 1996) reminds us immediately of Shklovsky's notion of *defamiliarization* [*ostranenie*]:

> It is rather as if the professional community had been suddenly transported to another planet where familiar objects are seen in a different light and are joined by unfamiliar ones as well ….
>
> Rather than being an interpreter, the scientist who embraces a new paradigm is like the man wearing inverting lenses. Confronting the same

constellation of objects as before and knowing that he does so, he nevertheless finds them transformed through and through in many of their
details. (pp. 11, 122)

In fact, Kuhn demonstrates the applicability of Shklovsky's model of artistic
estrangement to the great revolutionary shifts in science. Literary devices and
scientific postulates both involve a change of vision and defamiliarization
of the established canons. As Shklovsky writes, "The technique of art is to
make objects 'unfamiliar' …. Art removes objects from the automatism of
perception" (Davis et al., 1985, pp. 55–6).

This parallel between the thought of Shklovsky and Kuhn is one
example of the gradual convergence of the theory of science and the theory
of art in the twentieth century. Another literary thinker from the same
cohort of Russian formalists of the 1920s, Yury Tynianov, studied the
change of literary paradigms in the dynamics of assimilation and defamiliarization. According to Smith, "Tynyanov's overview of artistic paradigm
shift overshadows Kuhn's concept of revolutionary and normal science"
(1995, p. 8).

Science itself is now increasingly seen as a mental and linguistic
construction, rather than an objective presentation of reality. Thus, the
technique of defamiliarization reveals the *artfulness* of science and explains
the mechanism of its cognitive and *stylistic* transformations.

Kuhn further illustrates the change of scientific paradigms by pointing
to the Gestalt experiments in which drawings can be read in two different
ways: "What were ducks in the scientist's world before the revolution are
rabbits afterwards" (Kuhn, 1996, p. 111). In what follows, I examine
similar instant transformations of conceptual patterns that presently
prevail in the humanities; in a manner of speaking, where we habitually
see a duck, a rabbit's shape may be emerging. These animals' roles in
our conceptual field are played, respectively, by two antonymic prefixes:
"post-" and "proto-".

# From "post-" to "proto-"

If we try to single out one specific concept that dominated the late
twentieth century humanities, it would be denoted neither by a noun nor
an adjective, but by a prefix: "post-". *Post-modernism, post-structuralism,
post-communism, post-colonialism*, and many other "posts-" were regularly
attached to both nouns and adjectives, and sometimes even verbs, e.g. "to
postmodernize". The magic of this prefix allowed theoreticians to put any
concept under the sign of its transcendence, relegating the term to the past.

This conceptual mode, however, was ambivalent and, in a certain sense, self-defeating, because it presumed the new concept's dependence on the existing one. For example, *post-structuralism* describes a theoretical position that claims to supersede structuralism; ironically, in so doing, it binds itself to the very concept that it attempts to overcome. Similarly, "post-historicism" binds itself to historicism, and "post-utopianism" to utopianism. There was nothing positively new in the concept of "post-modernism" except being "after modernism", with modernism as a positive term. The prefix "post-" was a sort of arrogant and, at the same time, parasitic addition to the existing cultural vocabulary. This irony becomes even more evident with the proliferation of "posts-" themselves, signifying supposedly new stages of their self-transgression. A typical example of this "post-post" discourse can be found on a website devoted to academic philosophy:

> Recent debates within the humanities have explored the alleged time of post-history, post-postmodernity, post-art, post-capitalism, post-philosophy, post-poststructuralism, post-gender, post-race, post-metanarratives: the list is as unending as the debates themselves. (http://www.um.edu.mt/news/philosophysoc.html)

Now, in the early twenty-first century, we are witnessing a major shift in cultural attitudes: from retrospectivism to prospectivism. We live not so much *after* (modernity, structuralism, or Communism) as in the very beginning of a new epoch whose features must now be more positively defined in terms of "proto-" rather than "post-": *proto-global, proto-informational, proto-virtual,* and *proto-cyborgian,* to name but a few.

To take one example, our civilization can be called *proto-global,* because the term "global" in fact implies a civilization that has mastered all the sources of energy on the Earth and is able to regulate its climate completely, a condition which, according to the famous Russian astrophysicist Nikolai Kardashov, might take about three to four hundred years to achieve.

There are a number of prominent scientists who clearly define the character of our time as *proto-,* rather than *post-.* Stephen Hawking, for instance, writes in his book *The Universe in a Nutshell*: "Now we are at the beginning of a new era, in which we will be able to increase the complexity of our internal record, the DNA, without having to wait for the slow process of biological evolution" (2001, p. 165). This implies that our present condition is *proto-biotechnic.* Edward O. Wilson, a leading figure in contemporary biosciences, remarks in his book *Consilience: The Unity of Knowledge* that "predictive syntheses [between various branches of knowledge – M.E.], the ultimate goal of science, are still in an early stage, and especially so in biology" (1999, p. 136). Thus, the current stage of interdisciplinary collaboration can be called *proto-synthetic.*

Britain's leading futurologist, James Martin, writes:

The true computer revolution is yet to come – with ubiquitous sensors, nanotechnology, global data warehouses and totally pervasive access to networks of extreme bandwidth. The main reason the true computer revolution is ahead of us is that machines will become intelligent. Computers can be immensely more powerful than the human brain because their circuits are millions of times faster than the neurons and axons of the brain.... We are now seeing the first baby steps of this new intelligence. (2006, pp. 207, 219)

Thus, the current stage of computing can be called "proto-intelligent" or "proto-nano".

The growing power of computers presents evidence of artificial *proto-intelligence*; genetic and cloning experiments are examples of artificial *proto-life* and electronic networks are examples of *proto-global* community and collective *proto-mind*.

A question that springs to mind while considering "proto-" as a term for a new cultural paradigm concerns its possible deterministic and teleological implications.. By naming a certain trend "proto-X", do we assume that the future imposes on us "X-ization"? By calling our civilization "proto-global", do we mean that it is in some sense doomed to globalization? The use of "proto-" by no means implies such fatalistic outcomes. When applied to contemporary phenomena, "proto-" indicates a possibility rather than a necessity. "Proto-" simply means "having the potential to become" or "starting to move in a certain direction". Unlike the prefix "pre-", which presupposes succession in time (cf. "pre-global"—"prior to becoming global"), "proto-" suggests a beginning, an embryo rather than a precursor, an open possibility rather than a sequence. If "pre-" is a sign of temporality, "proto-" is a sign of modality, a prefix of the subjunctive mood. "Proto-X" means "having the propensity to become X".

The term "post-" is sometimes applied to phenomena that might be more properly characterized "proto-". In her influential book *How We Became Posthuman: Virtual Bodies in Cybernetics, Literature, and Informatics*, N. Katherine Hayles defines our present cultural condition in terms of "post-": "First, the posthuman view privileges informational pattern over material instantiation, so that embodiment in a biological substrate is seen as an accident of history rather than an inevitability of life" (1999, p. 2). According to this explanation, however, the current stage of humanness should be called "proto-informational". The human body is now progressively explained as a semiotic network and transformed into an informational resource.

This perspective resonates with Norbert Wiener's suggestion that in the future it would be possible to telegraph a human being:

...there is no absolute distinction between the types of transmission which we can use for sending a telegram from country to country and the types of transmission which at least are theoretically possible for transmitting a living organism such as a human being. Let us then admit that the idea that one might conceivably travel by telegraph, in addition to traveling by train or airplane, is not intrinsically absurd, far as it may be from realization. (1989, p. 103)

Hans Moravec, a pioneer in the theory of thinking machines, has subsequently updated Wiener's argument by suggesting that it will be possible to download human consciousness into a computer (1988, pp. 108–9). These predictions now appear more realistic than in Wiener's and Moravec's times; they point not to the end of the human, but to the beginning of an informational conversion of the human being. Although Hayles persists in employing the "post-" terminology throughout her book, in her conclusion (*What does it mean to be posthuman?*), she begins to question the relevance of the term: "But the posthuman does not really mean the end of humanity. It signals instead the end of a certain conception of the human …, as autonomous beings exercising their will through individual agency and choice" (1999, p. 286). The phenomenon that Hayles describes is, by her own admission, not "posthuman", but rather "*protohuman*"; it is the beginning of humans' expansion beyond the limits of their bodies:

> In the model that … the posthuman helps to authorize, human function-
> ality expands because the parameters of the cognitive system it inhabits
> expand. In this model, it is not a question of leaving the body behind
> but rather of extending embodied awareness in highly specific, local, and
> material ways that would be impossible without electronic prosthesis.
> (1999, pp. 290–1)

Thus, the so-called "posthuman" does not involve any elimination of the human, but rather the expansion, even the extension of embodied awareness through a system of electronic implants and digital enhancements.

The humanistic potential of new technologies was evident to its early prophets, such as M. McLuhan, for whom media as any technologies are "the extensions of man", giving humans new powers of perception and thought. In his view, "after more than a century of electric technology, we have extended our central nervous system itself in a global embrace …. Rapidly, we approach the final phase of the extensions of man – the technological simulation of consciousness, when the creative process of knowing will be collectively and corporately extended to the whole of human society…" (McLuhan and Zingrone, 1995, p. 149).

As an example of theoretical approaches favoring "proto-" over "post-", I would refer to Mikhail Bakhtin's concept of "embryonic genres". It can be applied to many cultural formations whose birth we are witnessing today. Bakhtin notes with regret the state of literary studies:

What we foreground is the *ready-made* and *finalized*. Even in antiquity we single out what is ready-made and finalized, and not what has originated and is developing. We do not study literature's pre-literary embryos. (1986a, p. 139)

Elsewhere, Bakhtin opposes two fundamental theoretical tenets—"finalizing" and "initiating"—or, in our terminology, "post-" and "proto-". Each offers a different approach to the question of "genre as a definite (essentially, petrified) whole, and [of] embryonic genres (thematic and linguistic), with a still undeveloped compositional skeleton, so to speak, the 'first signs' of a genre" (Bakhtin, 1986a, p. 513).

The prefix "proto-", with which I propose to designate the "first signs" of a genre, would reflect a radical Bakhtinian transition from finality to initiation as a mode of thinking. A "post-post-postmodern" culture suddenly views itself as a proto-global, proto-virtual, proto-biotechnic, proto-synthetic one. Everything that the previous generation perceived under the sign of "post-", this generation views as "proto-"; not as a completion, but rather as a first draft of new cultural formations.

## *Début de siècle*

The obsession with the past, even under the guise of its transgression in various "posts", is typical of the worldview that the late nineteenth century had dubbed *fin de siècle*. That sensibility was characterized by a sense of fatigue and exhaustion of creative impulses in a culture that appeared to be doomed to repetition and self-repetition. Here is, for example, Thomas Mann's elucidation of the nineteenth century *fin de siècle*:

Irrespective of which contents were given to the expression 'fin de *siècle*' that was fashionable then in all of Europe, whether it was thought to be neo-Catholicism or demonism, intellectual crime or decadent super-refinement of nervous intoxication – in any case, one thing was clear: it was the formula of the near end, a 'superfashionable' and somewhat pretentious formula that expressed the feeling of death of a certain epoch, that is the bourgeois epoch. (1990, p. 311)

In the last decades of the twentieth century, the *fin de siècle* atmosphere resurfaced in the form of postmodernism, not decadence. Instead of the refined nervousness and obsession with illness and death, postmodernism was characterized by a skeptical and hedonistic feeling of consummation and weariness of all cultural forms, a spiritual and formal *kenosis*. Towards the end of the twentieth century, the theme of the "end" becomes predominant, manifested in the proclamations of the end of modernity and Enlightenment, the end of history and progress, the end of ideology and rationalism, and the end of subjectivity and objectivity. John Barth (1967), a leading novelist of American postmodernism, called the literature of this new *fin de siècle* "the literature of exhaustion" because it is so clearly aware of "used-up-edness" of all its forms and the impossibility of telling lively, truthful stories. What is left is solely the possibility of the repetition, citation, and recombination.

At the turn of the nineteenth and twentieth centuries, the *fin de siècle* moods gradually made way for a more positive and optimistic mindset that can be called the *début de siècle*. Historically, this was a transition from decadence to what was later named "avant-garde". If we understand "avant-garde" broadly, i.e. as a radical break with the past, whether in arts, sciences, or politics, it can be said that the beginning of the twentieth century was marked by avant-garde movements and phenomena in a number of fields:

In literature and art—futurism, cubism, dada, and suprematism;
In philosophy and the humanities—pragmatism, intuitivism, and Nietzscheanism; birth of psychoanalysis, scientific sociology and psychology;
In politics—Bolshevism and Zionism;
In science—the discovery of X-rays, radioactivity, quantum, electron, special theory of relativity, and crisis of "matter" in physics;
In technology—automobiles, aviation, and cinema;
In religion—Pentacostals, Anthroposophy, God-seeking, God-building, and numerous apocalyptic sects.

In the early twentieth century, manifesto became the most productive genre in literature and philosophy, proclaiming new approaches to the future. The range of those proclamations was very broad: from The *Futurist Manifesto* by F. T. Marinetti in Italy (1909) to the radically conservative Russian philosophical collection *Landmarks* (1909). Thus, decadence was succeeded by avant-garde, which was determined to break resolutely with the past while striving towards the future.

I believe that the beginning of the twenty-first century has its own avant-garde, although its moods and intentions are yet to be clarified. In general, our cultural vocabulary should include the expression *début de siècle* to refer to the recurrent pattern of innovative, futuristic orientation that can be observed at least throughout the beginnings of the last three centuries. The early nineteenth century was dominated by Romanticism, which came into sharp contrast not only with neo-Classicism, but also with Sentimentalism, which had colored the *fin de siècle* of the eighteenth century. Romanticism is the purest expression of *début de siècle*' sensibility, setting the pattern both for the avant-garde of the early twentieth century and this enigmatic beginning of the twenty-first century, for which we still need to find a proper definition.

What signs of a new beginning can we identify in today's cultural moods? In the middle of the 1990s, despite the continuing discussions of postmodernism and poststructuralism in the humanities, the intellectual initiative was taken up by a new generation formed by the revolution in informational technologies. The Generation of the Internet (GIN) was not interested in deconstruction and splitting verbal hairs in order to demonstrate that there is nothing real signified in signifiers. The Generation of the Internet left the dead to bury their dead, so to speak, moving forward to those new fantastic post-real, or, more precisely, proto-virtual, objects that it could construct creatively. The cultural world, which seemed doomed to self-mirroring and self-deconstruction, witnessed with a sense of surprise the impulses to expand into the new territories of psycho-reality, info-reality, and bio-reality.

Thus, what seemed to be the *fin de siècle* turns out, in fact, to be a prologue to *the début de siècle*. Take, for example, *the end of reality* about which the "post-ists" or "post-niks" talked so much. It turns out to be only the beginning of the era of virtuality. Our shallow dives into the computer screen are only the first approaches to the ocean behind it. Virtonautics, i.e. our further departure into the virtual world, entails the disappearance of the shoreline, that is, the computer screen itself, and the creation of a three-dimensional milieu that would involve and impact all five senses. It is plausible that later in the twenty-first century various parts of our planet will be covered with fragments of a hyperspace, first the size of boxes, then a room, a house, a stadium, a city, and then maybe the entire 'virtoland.' In terms of perception, such hyperspaces would be indistinguishable from the physical world; at the same time, they will have different laws, or, more precisely, will allow us to choose laws more or less freely[1]. The virtual reality of the twenty-first or twenty-second centuries will be authentic in terms of psycho-physical perception, while still controllable and susceptible to intellectual and volitional regulation.

Alternatively, let us consider *the end of history* that was so eloquently discussed by numerous neo-Hegelians. It is now strange to assume that the course of history can be exhausted by the full self-realization of its underlying idea as this would contradict all known paradoxes of self-reflection and self-reference. Self as an object of self–reflection always eludes itself,

---

[1]An interesting example of such creative use of hyperspaces is found in William Gibson's novel *Spook Country* (2007). The main character is researching a story on locative art, i.e. 3D pieces, which are invisible to everyone unless you know specific GPS coordinates for each work of virtual art and have a special web-enabled visor for viewing it.

and, therefore, even if history is produced by a super-mind, it can never come to full self-cognition, which makes history permanently incomplete and open to continuation. Here, Hegel comes into contradiction with Gödel (1931), and absolute idealism with the theorems of incompleteness. The French neo-Hegelian thinker Alexandre Kojève saw the end of history in the creation of an absolute total state, with Stalin's USSR as its prototype, while the American neo-Kojèvian Francis Fukuyama saw the end of history in the victory of the liberal model and Western democracy all over the world, with Reagan's US as its prototype. Decades after their prophecies, it is clear that the course of history did not slow down, but rather accelerated. In Russia, for example, history resumed its flow only in the last 25 years after many decades of a totalitarian freeze. Similarly, for China or the Islamic world, the 1990s and 2000s turned out to be a signal for a new awakening to history. In all probability, it is only now that we come out from the millennia of pre-history, which moved unevenly in spurts, freezing for decades and centuries and then exploding in revolutions, wars, falls of empires, or big migrations. We became accustomed to view history as a series of bloody events, shocks and upheavals, whereas in a dynamic society history is more like ceaselessly flowing water.

Or, take *the death of the author* with its erasure of the signature, which was the agenda of Roland Barthes, Michel Foucault, and their numerous followers. Incidentally, they never crossed out their own signatures or put them "under erasure". They never practiced what they preached[2].

As it happens, *the death of the author* is not the end, but rather the beginning of a new epoch of *hyperauthorship*, multiplication of avatars and conceptual persona that wander through virtual worlds in increasingly oblique and obscure relationships to their biological parents.

Or, take the *death of utopia and universality* (or metanarrative), one of the idioms of postmodern theory, as expressed by Jean-François Lyotard and Jean Baudrillard. The "metanoia", the turn of the creative mind to the future, defines the way in which young Moscow artists and art scholars have been attempting to revive that which their postmodern fathers denounced. As Viktor Miziano, an art critic, a curator of the Centre for Contemporary Art in Moscow, and the editor-in-chief of the *Khudozhestvennyi zhurnal*, writes, "It is crucial that the problem of the universal be raised as a contemporary issue. I understand that it is a utopia. It is done completely consciously; yes, utopia is dead, so long live utopia. Utopia endows the

---

[2]Rare as they may be, one still finds the actual instances of writing under erasure. For example, in the silk-screen print "Untitled (Skull)" from the portfolio *Reality and Paradoxes*, 1973 (figure 6), Jasper Johns crosses out his signature (see: Galpin, 1998). This way, while the authorship is not denied, its authenticity is open to doubt. It is reasonable to expect postmodern writers to follow through with the deconstructive approach in their own works and cross out their signatures.

individual with a more significant and wider horizon" (*Kto est' kto v sovre-mennom iskusstve Moskvy*, 1993, no pagination). Anatolii Osmolovskii, a leader of the anti-postmodernist movements of E.T.I. and the Revolutionary Rival Program *NETSEZUDIK*, argues: "The future of contemporary art is in the will to utopia, in sincerity and pathos, and in the breakthrough into reality through a membrane of quotations" (Ibid.). This "revolutionary program" suggests the resurrection of utopia after its death, no longer as a social project claiming to transform the world, but as a new intensity of experience and a broader horizon for the individual.

Finally, take *the death of the human*, proclaimed by the posthumanists inspired by Michel Foucault. Just as humans once departed from the animal kingdom, today we depart from our own biological species, enhancing our bodies technologically. Everything that humans have created as a part of their external technical and cultural environment now integrates back into human beings themselves and transforms their organic nature. We should, then, talk about the triumph rather than the death of the human. We should view this "death" as a new stage of the humanization and intellectualization of machines and tools, which progressively acquire the capabilities of movement, calculation, perception, and perhaps even thinking.

# The proteism of contemporary civilization

Thus, it is "proto-" (from the Greek "πρῶτος", *protos*, meaning "the first") that best describes the mindset of the early twenty-first century. *Proto-* signals a humble awareness of the fact that we live in the earliest stage of an unknown civilization; that we have tapped into some secret source of power and knowledge that can eventually destroy us; that all of our glorious achievements to this point are only pale prototypes of what the coming bio- and info- technologies promise to bring. Nietzsche expressed this *proteic* sensitivity in his *Gay Science*: "We, the new, the name-less, the hard-to-understand, we firstlings of a yet untried future – we require for a new end also a new means" (Nietzsche, 1910, p. 351).

We live in the earliest stage of an unknown civilization. We are all embryos of a future society and, looking at ourselves from that distant future, perceive ourselves as relics of the past. I define the mindset of the early twenty-first century as *proteism*, which combines experimental and nostalgic moods, the propelling force of imagination and the archival sense of our time as the remote past in relation to the distant future.

Proteism is an alternative to the "post-", e.g. postmodernism, poststruc-turalism, post-utopianism, and post-industrialism. The "post-" negated the past and simultaneously was unable to break away from it. By contrast, *proto-* defines itself *vis-à-vis* the coming future. Proteism studies emerging, not yet-formed phenomena in the earliest fluid stages of their development, when they only promise, or tend to become. Proteism deals with beginnings, not with middles or ends. It is an embryology of culture that approaches each phenomenon as if it were an early sketch or a rough draft.

Proteism is a field of self-consciousness and a dramatic sensitivity to the new as immediately becoming "the old" in the face of the future. Proteic humans perceive themselves as remote prototypes of some unknown future, and their self-attitude is imprinted with a sense of both embryology and archeology. Proteism is an elegiac optimism that in the birth of new things foresees their demise. Our era is *paleonoic* (from Greek "nous", meaning "reason"), i.e. the era of ancient forms of reason (cf. *paleozoic*, meaning "the ancient forms of life"). In terms of our proto–informational technological development, we live in the "paleonoic" epoch of primitive computers, or the steam engines of the digital age. In terms of literature, we live in the epoch of Beowulf and medieval epic songs. An abysmal gap separates us from the future Tolstoys and Joyces, whom we are unable even to predict.

As a proto-something, I am crawling like an antediluvian monster out from the second half of the twentieth century. I see myself as a thinking protoplasm of the late Communism and the early information age with its primitive psychic life and naively over-complicated computer tools. It is a tragi-comic situation to feel like a prototype of something so unknown that it is uncertain if it will ever become actualized or will vanish in the past, having failed to correspond to anything in the future.

Proteism refers to the figure of Proteus in ancient Greek mythology whose name comes from the same root "πρῶτος" ("the first"). The deity of the seas and waves, he was famous for his power to assume any shape at will, transforming into fire, water, trees, and animals. Proteus can foretell the future, but is always ready to change his shape to evade such foretelling; he will answer only to someone who can capture him, which is virtually impossible to do. Proteus presents precisely this figure of the elusive future that I try to capture in this book. In fact, Proteus could be seen as the allegorical patron of the transformative humanities.

Civilization of the future is itself *proteistic* because it consists of flows of energy and information that easily change their material form. In Francis Bacon's allegory *Proteus or Matter* (1597), Proteus is viewed as a symbol of all changing matter. Were Bacon to have witnessed the discovery of nuclear power, radiation, light waves, or gravitation fields, he would most likely see the world differently. Matter is rather the principle of stasis, or arrested motion, as compared with the proteism of energy and even greater proteism of information, which can be transmitted in the package of words, numbers, formulas, genes, organisms, light rays, and quantum interactions.

Thus, we can characterize the contemporary condition in terms of "proto-", as a remote past in the face of a remote future. The early twenty-first century civilization shows various tendencies, some of which are promising, while others are potentially threatening. Let us look at some of these "proto-"s.

## Proto-global

The majority of the world population is still divided by language, national, political, cultural, and religious barriers. At the early stage of our species' history, people lived within small nomadic tribes with no more than 50 members each because only that size could guarantee their survival. Gradually, they formed more populous communities reaching the size of contemporary nations and states. Eventually, the globe will transform into a global village (McLuhan & Powers, 1992). But even now, no more than 2 or 3 per cent of the population lives "across barriers" in the so-called global noosphere, which includes intellectual and business elites, politicians, artists, and journalists. One can call such people *globers*, i.e. residents of the entire globe who travel more than they dwell in a single place.

## Proto-quantum and proto-nano

The quantum level of matter that was discovered by science in the twentieth century will become the starting point for future creative and transformational practices. Although still in its infancy, both the power and speed of quantum computing promise to exceed the current silicon models by several degrees. More importantly, the manipulation of particles on nano- and quantum levels will allow us to create any forms of matter, including organic tissues. A molecular assembler will process raw materials and deliver a final product according to desired parameters, from a juicy apple to a fashionable coat. This way, all food and energy problems of humanity could be solved once every industry is converted on a pollution-free micro-particle level.

## Proto-polymorphic, proto-transformative

Up until now, our civilization has been ontologically "poor": the overwhelming majority of objects and subjects have had only one form of existence. For example, reason exists only in the form of one species—*Homo Sapiens*—that only now begins to develop an alternative, artificial form of intelligence. Further development of civilization will lead from the universe to a multiverse, the multiplication of alternative modes of existence for every individual. The same information can be transmitted as hand-written or printed text, oral speech, binary code, numerical formula, or visual image. Similarly, any kind of existence can change its form, or clone its multiple versions. All modes of existence will become more flexible and convertible, including the polymorphous transformations of the human body.

As early as the 1970s, psychologists described the emergence of a proteic type of personality, denoting the propensity of individuals for self-experimentation and multiplication of selves (see Lifton, 1970). This is not a schizophrenically split personality, but one rich in roles, a *multividual* that cannot be confined to a single self. This multiplicity of selves often reveals itself in acts of inspiration and artistic creativity when an individual assumes a new personality on stage or in a novel. If a human being is inherently inclined to chafe at the limits imposed by a single body, we can assume that eventually these multiple selves will acquire not only symbolic and imaginative embodiments, but also independent bodies connected by invisible ties of integral personality, as both unmergable and indivisible physically as they are now psychologically. For example, Michio Kaku's description of the quantum multiverse involves the following understanding of the concept of a multividual: "although our parallel selves living in different quantum universes may have precisely the same genetic code, at crucial junctures of life, our opportunities, our mentors, and our dreams may lead us down different paths, leading to different life histories and different destinies" (2006, p. 353). A personality could spread and manifest itself across continents and planets, assuming various material guises and performing various social and professional roles, while simultaneously remaining conscious of its own unique vocation and moral responsibility. A strong creative personality can populate whole worlds with its infinitely multiplying selves. Then the ancient art of play and drama will be reconceptualized as the epoch of proto-polymorphism, or symbolic anticipation of *proteic* personalities.

## Proto-nootic

In the course of evolution, the brain transforms from an organism's tiny appendage, such as ganglia in invertebrates, into a central organ. The same evolution occurs in the history of civilization: the thinking matter increases its mass in nature, and geo-sphere and bio-sphere grow into noosphere. The future of humankind can be envisioned as *noocracy*—that is, the power of the collective brain rather than separate individuals and social groups. The Internet is only a prototype of such *InteLnet* (intellectual network) that will connect all thinking beings, both natural and artificial, into one communicational network and will develop into a new form of consciousness—*Syntellect*. This integral intellect will accumulate the potential of all thinking beings and operate on both biological and technical levels. We find ourselves now in the very first stage of electronic Syntellect (co-reason). To consider an analogy of paleozoic era, we could identify ourselves as people of the Palaeonoic era, when the first artificial forms of thinking come into existence and when reason gets released from the prison of the cranium, creating computers and other increasingly complex self-organizing forms of intellect.

## Proto-metaphysical

Up until now, metaphysics has been the most speculative division of philosophy as a discipline dealing with the most general principles and attributes of the world: life and death, identity and difference, reality and illusion, being and knowledge. Only recently did metaphysics prove itself applicable to the whole range of problems of multiple worlds and their construction. Metaphysics has the potential to become inseparable from physics, since physical knowledge itself has reached the observable limits of matter and now extends into the realm traditionally defined as "meta-physical". Contemporary science begins to explore "the hidden reality", "parallel worlds" and "physics of immortality", to use the phrases found in the titles of the famous books by physicists Brian Greene, Michio Kaku, and Franc Tipler. Thus quantum physics turns into *quantum metaphysics*, redefining causality, freedom, and possibility. Genetics acquires a metaphysical dimension as it delves into such problems as the nature of identity (cf. cloning) and life and death (cf. the genes of aging). The transition from the physical to the metaphysical at the advanced frontiers of knowledge makes all metaphysics of the past only an introduction to the "post-scientific" metaphysics of the future, the realm beyond physics as it was originally meant to be.

So far, since we had at our disposal only one universe, metaphysics was a speculative and unpractical science. But, as soon as the boundaries of the world become something palpable and we gain the power to create new forms of life and reason, metaphysics becomes a practical and effective discipline of setting the foundational parameters and properties for various new worlds. A time may come when a specialist in metaphysics will be assigned to draft a blueprint for a new universe, or a new planet, or at least a fragment of world-like virtual reality. This way, a new world will be brought into existence as a logical possibility that later may be put in place by astronauts, engineers, constructors, technicians, and computer programmers.

## Proto-angelic

Medieval people, were they to listen to our telephone conversations or soar up in a plane over the clouds, would believe that they had encountered angels or were transformed into them. Technology alleviates and accelerates all physical processes, dissolves matter into flows of energy and information, makes our existence volatile and ubiquitous, and allows our consciousness to spread momentarily without obstacles at the speed of light or electricity. Because these technical miracles have become routine, we often fail to appreciate just how transparent our material environment has become: it embraces a multiplicity of virtual and ethereal bodies and acquires more and more of the characteristics that our ancestors ascribed to a heavenly kingdom. Human beings are still not free from the biological limitations of their species, but they learn to change—by force of medicine, by prostheses, by sensory extensions, and by communicational devices— the chemical and physical composition and functions of their bodies and therefore are morphing into angeloids, angel-like creatures.

As mentioned earlier, Norbert Wiener predicted that one day a human being may be turned into a beam of light or an electronic matrix that can be transmitted in any material form. This supra-material informational core of humanness, initially developed in the biological form of a primate and then transcending this evolutionary limit, could be called a *humangel*. Some thinkers of our time use the concepts of medieval angelology to characterize computer-generated, virtual worlds. For example, according to the French thinker Pierre Levy (1997, p. 97), angelic or heavenly worlds evolve into virtual worlds, where human minds constitute forms of collective intellect (or what I call *Syntellect*). It is worth noting, however, that virtual reality is only the initial stage of techno-angelism. We first enter virtual worlds through our vision and hearing, and then by using smell, taste, and touch. This way, different levels of our existence are radically transformed, and we enter possible worlds with transfigured flesh, as supernatural beings, or anthropo-angels. The border between the artificial and supernatural is as contingent and penetrable as the border between the natural and artificial. Humans are natural beings who create artificial worlds and can, therefore, potentially become supernatural. We cannot predict at which point in the development of civilization the artificial will turn into the supernatural. But it is already clear that the ancient conception of humans as a transitional link between animals and angels is being revived thanks to new technologies.

## Utopia and apocalypse

However, the twenty-first century shows tendencies that are potentially threatening the future of humanity. One of them is the danger of *pan-psychism*, the historically growing internalization of the world and the collapse of the category of reality as such. History becomes an omnivorous vortex of triumphant reason—or madness, since, in the absence of reality, reason and madness become indistinguishable. In the simulated reality of the future, everything is artificially constructed, and there are no objective correlatives to the psychic, which becomes the black hole hidden within us, sucking in external reality. There are at least two varieties of such pan-psychic internalizations: the black magic of brain chemistry and the white magic of virtuality. The latter may even be more dangerous because it projects an appearance of objectivity and psychic health, the additional ecstasy provided by the consciousness of the exteriority of pleasurable virtual objects and our mastery of them as something independent.

Another danger of civilization is illustrated by the spread of viruses in computer networks. It is only with the development of the Internet as a perfect communicational organ that we come to understand how these artificial organisms are vulnerable to their own self-generated diseases (see Chapter 11, "Horrology: The Study of Civilization in Fear of Itself"). Having surveyed these remote ends of several current trends, we can console ourselves by the fact that we belong to their earliest stages, appropriately named *proto–psychic* and *proto-viral,* when fatal illnesses of future humanity can still be properly diagnosed and promptly treated.

Thus, our attitude to the future is as utopian as it is apocalyptic. We dread the same things that we impatiently await: the arrival of the technotronic and psychotronic civilization and the age of the intelligent machines that could transform us into their tools and servants. We anticipate the fulfillment of all our desires, and, at the same time, fear that this ultimate techno-revolution will erase the thin line between the psychic and the real, between the internal and the external, and between thought and being. Unlike the decadents of the late nineteenth century, we do not long for the destructive, but we are aware of the possible destructiveness of our longings.

For previous generations, utopia and anti-utopia, the aspiration for the ideal future and the fear of such compulsive ideals, were clearly opposed. The generation of the early twentieth century was utopian, whereas by the second half of the century anti-utopian moods became predominant. The generation of the early twenty-first century is utopian and anti-utopian at the same time, we are both attracted to, and repelled by, the future. Utopianism and anti-utopianism have much in common, e.g. hypersensitivity to the future, intense anticipations and expectations, the projection of images and models of the possible, and extremely enthusiastic or suspicious attitudes to novelties and innovations. This mindset could be called *ambi-utopianism* (the prefix "ambi-" means "from both sides", cf. "ambivalent"). Those with the mind of ambiutopianism, as a combination of utopianism and anti-utopianism, are particularly aware of their dramatic interchangeability. Having experienced both the periods of fiery utopianism and ardent anti-utopianism in the twentieth century, we can now appreciate the thinness of their divide. The most frightening aspect of utopias, according to Nicholai Berdiaev's *bon mot*, is that they have the propensity to come true. This is why every utopian impulse contains anti-utopian premonitions, which keep us from reckless leaps of progress. Such fear is a noble feeling and part of what the Ancient Greeks called *prudentia*, and what Aristotle and Thomas Aquinas considered the greatest virtue.

Never before in human history was reality so shapeable in the hands of *Homo Faber*. Yet, according to Kierkegaard, angst is born from the experience of nothingness: "dread is the dizziness of freedom" (1957, p. 55). A human being that knows how to create something out of nothing and to annihilate the real is full of angst. We are capable of too much and therefore fear ourselves. As a result of our pursuits of the unbounded freedom, we fear becoming slaves of our own desires and creations in the absence of the obstacles that were traditionally imposed by reality, laws of nature, or providence.

Armed with our knowledge of the dangers of utopia, we are left with some hope of avoiding them since we share neither the enthusiasm of our grandfathers, nor the skepticism of our fathers. With the acceleration of progress, the role of the brakes becomes more important. Visions of impending apocalypse slow the race of technological progress as we maneuver through the sharp turns of history. People are afraid of the advent of clones, genetic engineering, and a new race of robots, because all these advances may lead us to a dystopian ending. If people continue to press the gas pedal of technological advances with one foot, they also must keep the other foot on the eschatological brakes. Only by using both pedals can we proceed safely through the rough terrain of the future.

# Proteism and avant-garde

Proteism as the mindset of the *début de siècle* of the twenty-first century has much in common with the avant-garde of the early twentieth century: an orientation towards the future, experimental audacity, openness to everything new, prognostics and futurology/futuroscopy, and the genre of manifesto. However, these similarities make their differences even more striking. The new *début de siècle* accepts and integrates the critique that postmodernism turned against the avant-garde and its companions, such as utopianism and totalitarianism, denial of tradition, political and aesthetical radicalism, and faith in the purity of a new idea or a new style that will soon conquer the world. *Avant-garde* literally means an advanced military detachment that leads the masses lagging behind, or recklessly abandons them in a daring raid into the unknown. Proteism, on the contrary, already possesses sufficient historical experience in order to claim its place not in the distant future, but in the distant past of the future that it anticipates. It positions itself not as an avant-garde, but as a arrière-garde of those trends that will soon turn it into an archeological layer of our rapidly changing society.

We can contrast and judge our beginnings against our ends, an experience not available to the avant-garde generations of the first half of the twentieth century. Having euphorically attained the peak of certain technological and political innovations, they did not witness their demise and so identified themselves with the future in its ultimate and irrefutable truth. In the twenty-first century, the pace of innovations has accelerated to such an extent that our generation can already foresee its own decline in a future that views us as its distant past. This double, forward-and-back vision is our distinctive feature. Proteism sees itself as if it were looking through the other end of binoculars; as a result, the contemporary world appears small and recedes into the historical past.

Avant-garde is conceptually linked to Albert Einstein's relativistic cosmology and Edwin Hubble's discovery of the expanding universe. Avant-garde pumps up the muscles of its style and magnifies its imagery to gigantic proportions, leaning towards hyperboles. Consider the following excerpt from *The Futurist Manifesto* by F. T. Marinetti's (1909):

> We are on the extreme promontory of the centuries! What is the use of looking behind at the moment when we must open the mysterious shutters of the impossible? Time and Space died yesterday. We are already living in the absolute, since we have already created eternal, omnipresent speed. ... We will sing of the great crowds agitated by work, pleasure and revolt; the multi-colored and polyphonic surf of revolutions in modern capitals: the nocturnal vibration of the arsenals and the workshops beneath their violent electric moons: the gluttonous railway stations devouring smoking serpents; factories suspended from the clouds by the thread of their smoke; bridges with the leap of gymnasts flung across the diabolic cutlery of sunny rivers: adventurous steamers sniffing the horizon; great-breasted locomotives, puffing on the rails like enormous steel horses with long tubes for bridle, and the gliding flight of aeroplanes whose propeller sounds like the flapping of a flag and the applause of enthusiastic crowds. (http://cscs.umich.edu/~crshalizi/T4PM/futurist-manifesto.html)

This is the style of gigantomania typical of avant-guarde. Proteism, on the contrary, has a propensity towards litotes, or understatements. It is a trend of decreasing and minimalizing all phenomena, congenial to those nano-technologies that reduce the scales of industry and cybernetics to the size of an atom or a quantum.

# The paradoxes of the "proto-"

As a rule, it is possible to judge anything as "proto-" only once its mature stage and completion have already been reached. How do we know that Dante and Giotto belong to proto-Renaissance? Evidently, such a conclusion can be drawn only after the Renaissance itself has already taken place. Indeed, the term "proto-Renaissance" emerged only in the nineteenth century, while the term "Renaissance" itself only emerged in late eighteenth century in France.

The uniqueness of our contemporary situation is that we can define something as "proto-" in advance, not with hindsight, but rather with foresight. When we refer to the current electronic technologies as "proto-virtual", we set the parameters for the development of these flat screens into mature, multidimensional, and comprehensive virtual worlds. Simultaneously, we designate our own place in the preliminary, two-dimensional stage of this process. By forecasting the future, we position ourselves in its distant past. Thus, futurology becomes inseparable from the projective archeology of our own time.

In the late seventeenth to early eighteenth centuries, the debate between the parties of the "Ancients" and the "Moderns" began in France and England as the two most developed countries of that period. The "Ancients" proclaimed the unconditional superiority of the classical authors of antiquity, while the "Moderns" argued that contemporary authors could surpass them. Charles Perrault, the author of *Red Riding Hood,* and Bernard de Fontenelle, the author of *Conversations on the Plurality of Worlds,* can be seen as the first avant-gardists of European culture. While they did not call for throwing Homer and Sophocles off the ship of modernity, as did many futurists later on, they did believe that the "Moderns" can surpass the "Ancients". This was the beginning of the secular conflict of the new and the old that has continued for three centuries, taking more and more sophisticated and sometimes radical forms, such as Romantics vs Neoclassisists, Realists vs Romantics, Symbolists vs Realists, Futurists vs Symbolists, Socialist Realists vs Modernists, Sots-artists vs Socialist Realists, and Postmodernists vs Neo-Avant-Gardists.

Today, we may be witnessing the end of this conflict and the merging of the opposing sides because, culturally, we rejuvenate at the same rate as we grow old. We are super-modern and super-ancient; we are neo-archaics. The rapid renewal that we project for the future determines the speed of our own recession into the past.

# 2

# Chronocide: A prologue to the resurrection of time

## Chronocide and the spectre of revolution

Regicide, matricide, parricide, ecocide … The suffix *cide* has had an especially remarkable career since 1944, when the word *genocide* was introduced by Raphael Lemkin (1946), an American lawyer of Polish extraction. At the commencement of our new century, I would like to propose, generalizing from the rich criminal experience of the last century, another neologism: *chronocide*—the murder of time.

Chronocide, genocide, and ecocide are linked, as a rule, in a straight line of revolutionary development. The first victim of any revolution, right or left wing, is time. Revolution begins with chronocide, the murder of time past in the name of an abstract future. Only when time, a given time, has been killed does a revolution begin to devour human lives. Genocide is a matter of condemning whole nations, estates, or classes deemed unworthy of the future to remain in the past. In the end, the exhausted revolution, despairing of giving what it promised and having destroyed society's industrial forces, ends in ecocide, i.e. the rapacious consumption and destruction of defenceless nature. Chronocide is an invisible cataclysm in consciousness, but it comes first; and later cataclysms depend upon it.

There are three fundamental forms of chronocide: the utopian obsession with the future ("the happiness of coming generations"), the nostalgic obsession with the past ("the Great Tradition"), and the postmodern infatuation with the present ("the disappearance of time in a synchronic play of significations"). The three fundamental modes of time—future, past, and present—are thus transformed into three techniques of chronocide.

# Anomalies of time in Russia

To liberate the future from the past ... To liberate the past from the future ... For these two apparently contradictory concepts there is one word: *revolution*. It might be made in the name of the Great Utopia or the Great Tradition, but it cannot but be bloody.

In the early years of the twentieth century, revolution was considered to be a victory over the autocratic past and a leap into the kingdom of freedom. By the close of the twentieth century, with the legacy of this totalitarian era serving as a haunting reminder of its false promises, a widespread nostalgia for pre-revolutionary times had emerged. The ideas of the right, or the counter-revolution, began to hold sway over people's minds: the Great Tradition, forgotten over the course of the millennium, must now be freed from the rotten deposits of chimerical progress. Let us heed the voice of the new revolution, proclaiming the freedom of the past from the future:

> Our basic task ... is the restoration of the Integral Tradition in all its dimensions. Tradition, according to René Guénon, is the sum of divinely revealed, super-temporal knowledge. It constituted the order of all sacred civilisations – from the heavenly empires of the golden age, which disappeared many millennia ago, to the civilisation of the middle ages.˙ (Dugin, *Milyi Angel*, 1991, p. 1)

In other words, everything that happened after the Middle Ages, including Michelangelo and Leonardo, Shakespeare and Goethe, Mozart and Kant, must be seen as a retreat from the Great Tradition, a betrayal or a mistake. All the novelties of the modern era, including the idea of novelty itself, must be burnt in the penitential fire of the last revolution: "The fire of the global national revolution, the socialistic revolution, the last revolution, which will terminate human history's cycle of decline, is on the march" (Dugin, 1993, p. 17).

Again we see an assault on time, only now the murder of a cursed future in the name of a holy past. As always, chronocide summons the spectre of revolution, this time not a left-progressive revolution, but a Fascist or a National-Socialist one. The crime of revolutions is not only in that they negate time and the lives of entire nations, but also in that they create their own monstrous negations. The right wing revolution, proclaimed by the new Russian fundamentalists who call themselves 'Eurasianists', is the negation of the left wing revolution, which repudiated the inheritance of the "exploitatory" society, opening the door to the classless future.

Chronocide has happened nowhere with such insane consequences as in Russia. For here, the victim was the present. The present—perceived as an echo of the past or a stepping stone to the future—has never had an independent value in Russia. Diderot, who corresponded with Catherine II and despaired of bringing the fruits of Enlightenment here, said that Russia had "gone rotten before ripening." (see Skalkovsky, 1904, p. 6). In other words, the present never ripened and the future turned out to be this country's past. Thoughts similar to Diderot's were subsequently expressed by Russian thinkers: "Russia is fated to useless escapades, hastily embarked on and hastily abandoned" (Prince M. Sherbatov), "We are growing, but not ripening" (Petr Chaadaev), and "We were born well, but have grown very little" (V. V. Rozanov) (see Skalkovsky, 1904, pp. 10, 21, 39).

If the past corresponds to youth, the present to maturity, and the future to old age, then Russia is at once youthful and senile, having quietly skipped maturity altogether. Its relationship to time distinguishes Russia both from the great Eastern civilizations, in which the present is linked to the past by a continuous ethnic and religious tradition, and from the modern civilizations of the West, in which the present is screwed to the future by uninterrupted technological progress. Russian civilization is at the same time archaic and futuristic; and that is its special value for cultural study. The mechanisms of renewal are naked where the future and past are so directly joined, without the bridge provided by the present.

Yury Lotman and Boris Uspensky have analyzed Russian culture as dualistic in character. In Russia, the gods of pagan antiquity were thought an impure force or else merged with images of Christian saints—but never evaluated impartially. The attitude of Russia to the West has passed through many stages: a "new" Russia gains ascendancy over an "ancient" West, a "new" West humiliates an "ancient" Russia, back and forth, forth and back. In the same way, Russian religious consciousness has always recognized hell and heaven, but not purgatory. The present is too middling for Russian culture, which moves, not through smoothly negotiated oppositions, but by means of dramatic reversals (see Lotman and Uspensky, 1985, pp. 31, 33, 63).

Let us look at several recent examples. Yesterday, Communism, or "the classless society", was the future; suddenly, unable to become the present, it became the past. Overnight, Communism became a burdensome, disposable relic. And, vice versa, the more distant past—free market, the constituent assembly, even perhaps monarchy and class division—has been speedily transferred into the desirable future. But Russia, having lived for seven decades in the avant-garde of the world history, has suddenly found herself in the *arrière*-garde—on the fringe of capitalism or even feudalism and serfdom.

It seemed that the most radical of possible interpretations was Francis Fukuyama's: no more global conflict and thus the end of world history. But for Russia, teleology is never radical enough. The end is, after all, the end: a normal point in the temporal process, eventually inevitable. In the consciousness of Russia, the collapse of Communism rearranged beginning and end. The communist future traded places with the bourgeois and feudal past. The shock of this temporal anomaly affected not only Russia, but humanity as a whole. The world had, after all, been dragged into the communist project, if only in opposition to it.

At any moment in history there may exist different epochs as much as different nations. The destruction of stationary and conservative elements of society is "of the future"; the destruction of novelty is "of the past". Middling elements, in which the future and the past find their living connection, are termed the present. In Russian, the word meaning "present" has a dual significance: not just "now", but also "genuine", "veritable", and "real". The drama of Russian history can be summarized as a linguistic paradox, as an antonymy of synonymic meanings: in its desperate quest for the "real", Russia has always ignored the present.

Which brings us to Germany. As genocide was condemned at Nuremberg, so chronocide should be arraigned in Weimar. "Do not look into the distance, or into the past", Weimar's favorite son writes in *Faust*: "Only in the present is happiness and delight".

# The utopia of the present. Time as deferral

Goethe's thought is ironic. To live only in the present is just another—the most refined—form of chronocide. To halt the moment, however wonderful, transforms it into an eternal corpse. Faust himself, who wanted time to stop, drops dead: "I take my joy, my highest moment this" (*Faust sinks back into the arms of the Lemurs, who lay him upon the ground.*)

Faust's dream was realized only with the aid of Mephistopheles (negation himself). The frozen moment, the full and final "beauty of life", is death for the decrepit Faust. In his last moments, he seems to hear the sound of free labor on the free earth. What he actually hears is the noise of the spades with which, to the accompaniment of Mephistopheles' laughter, the demons are digging his grave.

Postmodernism is a frozen moment, an inflated soap bubble of time. On its fine film, all ages—past and future—are reflected. Its prototype is the exhausted Faust. At the end of all his global travels (in the words of Mephistopheles), Faust

would no joys content, no fortune please,
And thus he wooed his changing fantasies.
This wretched, empty moment at the last
He sought, poor wretch, to grasp and hold it fast.

*(Faust,* part 2, act 5, scene 6, lines 11587–90)

Goethe's ironic parable is a history. The West could not, initially, quench its thirst for all that exceeds the limits of time. But surrendering, finally, to the charm of the passing moment, lack of substance, and the play of mercurial shadows, all the ideals once pursued are now reduced to shadow theater—stylish signs in a game of signs: "Then to the passing moment might I say/ Thou art so beautiful, wilt thou not stay." The arrested present is but a parody of eternity.

But Faust is, notoriously, the hero of the modern age. His companion Mephistopheles is the genius of what comes after. "I'd rather", Mephistopheles admits (indeed boasts), "have Eternal Emptiness". He not only terminates—at least, in theory—all former strivings ("all is finished"), but also persistently asks: "Was there a beginning at all?" He abolishes the category of origin and thus originality. Only emptiness (das *Ewig-Leere*) is not cast in doubt or postponed. Time itself is postponement, free from past and future, an endless interval.

Postmodernism is the most sophisticated form of burying time in the present under the pretext of saving and immortalizing it in countless repetitions and postponements. While devotees of tradition are bewitched by the distant past, by some mythical golden age, postmodern thinkers, disclaiming any kind of beginning, celebrate the end and completion of everything in the here-and-now of the eternal present. This is how Frederic Jameson describes the condition of the newest posthistoricism, which transforms time into the condition of space: "If history has become spacial, then even her repression has become spacial, and all those ideological mechanisms by means of which we avoid thinking historically" (1993, p. 374).

The radical distinction between time and space is thus attenuated. Jacques Derrida explains: "In constituting itself, in dividing itself dynamically, this interval is what might be called *spacing*, the becoming-space of time or the becoming-time of space (*temporization*). And it is this ... that I propose to call archi-writing, archi-trace, or *différance*. Which (is) (simultaneously) spacing (and) temporization" (1982, p. 13). *Différer* in French means both "to differentiate" and "to postpone, defer, slow down". Time resembles space insofar as there is no difference in quality between its moments, only distance—or a delay when nothing happens: "*Différer* in this sense is to temporize, to take recourse, consciously or unconsciously, in the temporal and temporizing mediation of a detour that suspends the accomplishment or fulfillment of 'desire' or 'will'" (Derrida, 1982, p. 8).

Each next moment is only the postponement of a previous. Such time is familiar to us from Beckett's play *Waiting for Godot*. Postponement is a difference that functions as identity. *Différance* is transformed into *indifférance*. The same postponement that, according to Derrida, establishes time, allows time to flow, also abolishes time, transforming distinct moments into identical moments, the last being the postponement of the first. "What is intermediate is not transitory", Mark Taylor, a theologian–deconstructionist, writes, "what is interstitial is 'permanent.' Though always betwixt 'n' between, the 'eternal' time of the middle neither begins nor ends" (1986, pp. 526–7).

In the language of *différance*, "later" sounds like "never". The Girl says to her Father: "Let's go for a walk!" He, seated comfortably on the sofa with a book, replies: "Later!" The Citizen asks the State: "When will we end violence and guarantee a right to life?" The State—its muscles swelling—replies: "Later!" "Later!" is the flesh and blood of our time. Postmodernism, our vivacious sepulcher, derives from, or simply is, the philosophy of deferred expectation. What remains for us is to await the coming of time with the same fear and hope with which we once awaited the coming of eternity.

Yet the moment postponed is reproduced again and again. The Girl repeats her suggestion to her Father, the Citizen his question to the State, all human beings their hope for Godot, and—nothing occurs.

"Eternal recurrence" was Nietzsche's term for this, and Derrida expounds his *différance* in connection with Nietzsche's myth: "And on the basis of this unfolding of the same as *différance*, we see announced the sameness of *différance* and repetition in the eternal return" (Derrida, 1982, p. 17). Eternal recurrence is the most metaphysical of Nietzsche's notions, the price he paid for the quest to defeat metaphysics. The difference in *différance* only creates intervals between the elements in repetition. If postponement is not temporal, if there is nothing behind the frontier of postponement, then the moment postponed will be repeated, can never complete itself and give way to the next moment, like a gramophone needle on an LP that has been scratched.

Corresponding to the three fundamental modes of time—future, past, and present—are three fundamental forms of chronocide: utopian obsession with the future, nostalgic obsession with the past, and postmodern obsession with the present. All three have happened and recurred. Can we initiate a resurrection of time?

# Love for the future

Our priority must be to establish confidence in the future. Obsession with the future was the great seduction and curse of the twentieth century, a legacy of nineteenth century optimism and progressivism. For decades, Communism appeared to many to be the inevitable future; countless sacrifices were made on its altar. Is it still indecent to talk about the future? The future itself is innocent. Priests of the revolution took it for a bloodthirsty god, but the future overthrows every idol, even those fashioned in its honor. The communist future remains in the past; the future itself is purged of yet another specter. The purification of time is the future's special function. So let the future approach us again, though punctuated differently now: without the exclamation point. Perhaps a question mark?

As for the epoch in which we live, "the interval between the death and resurrection of the future" would be less stylish a description than "postmodern", but more accurate. Now, after the epoch of the grand utopias and antiutopias has passed, we need—conceivably for the first time in history—to plumb the full depth and deceptiveness of the future's purity, the irony of its innocence. That purity is not the purity of the *tabula rasa*, on which we can write grandiose projects; rather, the future has the purifying capacity of an eraser, reducing all projects to a dim blur—the remnants of evaporated utopias.

The new vision—a future that cannot be objectivized, a future unamenable to prognosis—was the revelation of Mikhail Bakhtin. The future, he wrote, is a comedian: "Nothing definitive in the world has yet taken place; the last word of the world, about the world, has not yet been spoken; the world is open and free; everything is still to come and will always be still to come. This, you see, is the purifying meaning of ambivalent laughter" (Bakhtin, 1979, p. 193). The word for "future" in Russian [budushchee] has the same root as "being" [byt], whereas "past" and "present" are formed from entirely different concepts and words: "to pass" and "to stand", respectively The mysterious thing about being is its ceaselessness, its tirelessness, its "futuricity".

Does my paean to the future sound like a new utopian heresy? Anti-utopianism is necessary but insufficient. We must reawaken love for the future—though not the love of *What Is to Be Done?* Nikolai Chernyshevsky wrote: "Love the future! Bring from it into the present as much as you can carry!" But the lovable future, a future that deserves love, is one from which it is impossible to carry anything into the present, because it retreats into nowhere with the same speed that the present retreats into the past. As one moves forward, what is distant becomes closer; but distance itself moves on ahead. This reminds us of Proteus, who was able to foretell the future, but avoided this task by permanently changing his shape and escaping anybody who would try to capture him to get a definite prediction.

In fact, the future has two interplaying planes: the approaching object and the retreating distance. The future is always double-faced, like an ironic utterance in which "yes" means "no". One future approaches swiftly and physically surrounds us, becoming the present. It is summoned by utopians of all ages, impatiently demanding its arrival. The other future retreats from us with the same speed that the first future approaches. The future is like a cannon: it fires the event toward us, but itself rolls backward.

The future is allegedly algebraic rather than arithmetical, so we approach the future as an unknown. We know that winter always comes after autumn, and summer after spring. But do winter and summer belong to the future? No, they are elements of a repeating cycle. They appear as future only in relation to prior phases of the cycle, and thus as past in relation to the phases following. Still, the future as such cannot be construed as a rhythm of repetitions. Any event appears first as future, then as present, and, finally, as past: it is played in all three registers, and hence the event is always multicolored and three-dimensional; we perceive it from the front, the side, and the back. But it does not follow from this metaphorical fact that we can mix and muddle up the colors. The communist, the traditionalist, and the postmodernist all suffer from color blindness with respect to time.

# Models of development. Multiple futures

The period we are entering is no longer a period after something: postcommunist, postmodernist, "postthis", or "postthat". The present era is "proto-", but a preface to *what*, we do not know. *Proto-* is noncoercive, nonpredictive, and unaccountable: a mode of maybe. The future is a language without grammar, an unconscious without dreams, pure nothing. Inescapably the future becomes everything so as again and again to remain nothing.

To restore trust in the future means to develop a model of development in harmony with the passage of time. That fatal mechanism, which triggered revolutionary-utopian thinking and then caused the chain reaction of traditionalism and postmodernism, was a metaphysical substitute. In it, the present appears as a realm of ideas and ideals, the future as a realm of their fulfillment. The present is a realm of possibilities, while the future is the process of their realization.

European metaphysics created the kingdom of general ideas, whose backside is European history. The aspiration of European history was to bring abstract ideas down to earth and incarnate them as political, moral, and legal institutions. Nothing attracted Europeans like abstraction. The very abstraction of freedom, equality, national greatness, racial supremacy, and religious exclusivity made them attractive ideas and required their involvement in history.

Even the most radical oppositional movements that threatened to explode European civilization did little to change its mentality. The more abstract the ideas, the more separated they were from life, the more persistently they demanded embodiment. The slogans shouted in May 1968 from the student barricades in Paris—"All power to the imagination!" and "Paradise now!"—were an act of profound self-expression on the part of European civilization, demanding for every dream to come true.

This model, which faithfully served the development of Western civilization over many centuries, refuses to work any longer. There is no enthusiasm for either metaphysics or history. Now, another model operates: the incessant production of new possibilities that do not demand realization. The future is not something that will be, but something that may be. A possibility never comes alone, but only in the form of doubling and multiplying possibilities. Possibilities clash yet do not exclude one another. A possibility that excludes all others is a fact, a mere necessity. A possibility must remain a possibility, valuable and efficacious in itself.

I will remind you that, until the twentieth century, the word *culture* was used only in the singular, in the sense of a norm or model. The concept of cultural pluralism emerged slowly, and the plural has begun to prevail. I wonder if a similar metamorphosis will take place with the word *future*, and the binding singular *be* will become the plural *maybes*. Discredited by utopian ideologies and totalitarian regimes, the concept *future* can be justified for the future only as the coexistence and interaction of different *futures*.

The process of opening the present to a multiplicity of futures might be termed "potentiation", because it increases the potential of reality, or of what we regard as real. Facts are transformed into probabilities, theories into hypotheses, assertions into suggestions, necessities into possibilities. Our reality is made up more and more of potentialities; it is becoming more and more conditional. If we are fortunate, one day, *is* may be transformed into *if*, and *to be* into *might be*.

Societies of the First World are often called "Lands of Opportunity". What is meant is not opportunity in the abstract, but a system of insurance and credit that translates everyday life into the subjunctive mood. I live on resources (credit) that I could potentially earn; I pay for services (insurance) that I could potentially need. The modern West is a civilization of opportunities or possibilities in the sense that, here, I do not "possess what I possess", but rather "what I might possess if …." Credit and insurance companies busy themselves with estimating my life-chances; they deal not only with my actual existence, but with my probable future states. Thus both the positive and negative sides of life appear conditional.

For people accustomed to a non-Western way of life, with its hard realities and binding norms, it is very difficult to switch into this game of possibilities, where nothing exists "just-so", in the indicative mood, but more in terms of "as if". One possibility opens on to another, and the whole of reality consists of alternating possibilities that are realized but rarely.

The expressions "Land of Opportunity" and "Free Society" characterize different aspects of Western democracies. Freedom is opposed to, or
inhabits the same plane of meaning as, political repression. The definition
of Western society as free, therefore, began to look outdated after the
communist regimes in Europe had collapsed. For, at the structural level,
Western society is not free at all: it is much more harshly constrained by
internal economic and technological relations than totalitarian societies
(hence its amazing historical stability). Defined in terms not of freedom, but
of potentiality, Western society bears a more consequential meaning.

Consider the role of the polls and primaries carried out in anticipation
of elections. Polls and primaries are hypothetical models of the election,
but nevertheless seriously affect the final result. American observers have
pointed out how the introduction of polls has significantly influenced
elections and the election system in the United States, where now each
conditional assumption about the political future depends on previous
conditional assumptions. Politics is not merely, as for Bismarck, "the art of
the possible," but the art of "possibilizing" reality, i.e. giving reality a more
conditional character.

# From the real to the possible: Culture and ethics

I am by no means inclined to consider this model to be ideal. The category
of the "ideal" has been compromised by the old progressive-revolutionary
model. In any case, the dictatorship of the possible (potentiocracy?)
has its positive traits. It is a truism to state that capital has given way
to information as the basic social resource; however, a far from trivial
conclusion follows from this statement. The value of any communication is
in proportion to the unexpectedness of what is communicated. Surprise is
a fluid quantity; it increases to the extent that the probability of what has
been communicated diminishes. Naturally, the information society is keen
to increase the volume of information it possesses, because that is its main
source of wealth. The growth of information presupposes an increase in the
probabilistic character of social life, while information itself grows only to
the extent that the world becomes less predictable and consists of less and
less probable events.

Thus, the novel takes primacy over the epic, or, rather, our conception
of the novel takes primacy over our conception of the epic. Bakhtin, distin-
guishing between the two, concludes that, if in the epic necessity prevails, in
the novel possibility prevails: "The epic world … is completed, conclusive
and immutable, as a fact, an idea and a value" (Bakhtin, 1981, p. 17). Not
only does the hero of the epic act in the sphere of necessity, but also the
author pictures the epic reality as the only true one, unarguable in its value

and factuality. The hero of the novel, on the other hand, is presented as pure potentiality that can never be realized externally: "An individual cannot be completely incarnated into the flesh of existing sociohistorical categories .... Reality as we have it in the novel is only one of many possible realities; it is not inevitable, it is arbitrary, it bears within itself other possibilities" (Bakhtin, 1981, p. 36).

On the same grounds as we prefer the novel to the epic, we prefer (or should prefer) the essay to the novel. Montaigne wrote: "I like these words which soften and moderate the rashness of our propositions: 'perhaps,' 'to some extent,' 'some,' 'they say,' 'I think,' and the like" (1973, p. 788). 'May be' as the formula of the essay refers, in distinction to the novel, not only to represented reality, but also to the methods of representation. According to Robert Musil, the author of *The Man without Qualities*, the "essayism" as the creative credo of the twentieth century is the art of "living hypothetically". Essayism has transformed every culturally fixed role into one of possibilities for authentic existence. Humanity has no qualities by nature; what exists is a quintessence of human possibilities, a porous subtext of many other meanings.

Culture as a whole is coming to be understood as only one set of possibilities. No longer locked in a single cultural reality of birth and upbringing, each of us stands at a crossroads of different ethnic, historical, and professional cultures. Thus each has a possibility for surmounting the obsessional complexes, manias, and phobias of our "given" (native) culture.

What becomes of moral life at the crossroads of possibilities? Ethics has traditionally been considered a sphere of normative judgments. Its statutes have been formulated as duties and very often addressed to the entire human race. The most convenient and generally accepted form of ethical judgment is in the imperative: "Do not kill", "Do not fornicate", or "Do not do to others what you would not have them do to you". The practical philosophy of Kant, the most influential doctrine in Western ethical thought, is summed up in the categorical imperative: "I should never act in such a way that I could not also will that my maxim should be universal law" (Kant, 1969, p. 21).

It is obvious that the imperative form of ethical injunctions is connected to their generality. But the general should not be confused with the universal. The universal is not abstracted from, but contained within, the individual (Leonardo da Vinci was a universal, not a general, mind and genius); therefore a universal ethical principle appears not as obligation, but as possibility. Can we imagine a universal ethics constructed in the subjunctive, not the imperative, mood—an ethics of possibility, not of duty?

Nietzsche wrote: "How naive it is in general to say, 'Human beings *should* be such and such!' Reality shows us a captivating treasury of types, the exuberance of an evanescent play and alteration of forms. And some pathetic bystander of a moralist says to all this, 'No! Human beings should be *different*!'" (1997, p. 28). Nietzsche's rebellion against duty in the name of "life as it is" easily slides into a rebellion against morality as such. Ethics cannot be a mere justification of existence, a description of humanity as it is. But is ethics possible beyond the imperative and indicative moods? Nikolai Berdyaev saw the moral crisis of the past century in positive terms, as "the transition from a consciousness for which morality is obedience to general laws, to a consciousness for which morality is the individual's creative task" (1985, p. 299). If morality does not call humanity to duties, it can still call on us to create possibilities.

Ethics enters the world of possibility at its most basic level—the ABC of etiquette, so to speak. Etiquette in speech consists of avoiding the imperative mood and replacing it with the subjunctive. Instead of *Hand me the salt!*, we ask *Could you please pass the salt?* Polite people do not burden each other with their needs, but delicately grant each other the opportunity of satisfying them. Etiquette expresses the emancipatory priority of possibility over necessity in human relations.

It is doubtful, however, that the higher ethics were established in contradiction to basic etiquette. More likely, the former is an outgrowth and elaboration of the latter. If the initial moral intuition is to conceal my own necessity under the cover of another's opportunity, then the essence of ethics may be to widen the sphere of opportunity for others. Eventually, the opportunities we open for others cease to be sophisticated means for the satisfaction of our own desires and become ends in themselves, i.e. they come to represent an opening of possibilities, on the whole. Ethics may now consist of our creating possibilities for one another.

## History in the subjunctive mood

History is a process of accumulating possibilities. Each era absorbs the unrealized possibilities of the previous era. In our social and spiritual life, we observe a continual process diametrically opposed to the process known as "realization". The past, which undoubtedly was what it was, involuntarily allows the possible into its own completed world. Every fact, to the extent that it is distanced from us, becomes a hypothesis. In the words of Max Weber:

> Hence, the historian is able to consider the question: which consequences were to be anticipated had another decision been taken, with better chances of success than, for example, Bismarck himself [had]. It is clear that this way of looking at the matter is very far from being 'idle' .... . The judgment that, if a single historical fact is conceived of as

absent from or modified in a complex of historical conditions, it *would* condition a course of historical events in a way which would be different in certain *historically important* respects, seems to be of considerable value for the determination of 'historical significance' of those facts. (1949, pp. 165–6)

History, from the point of view of the historian, is not only that which was, but also that which could have been; otherwise the individual fact, outside of this fictional or conditional context, loses its meaning. In this light, historical reality is becoming transparent, permeated by bubbles of air. Arnold Toynbee happily named this process "etherealization"—the transmutation of the material substrata of history into a more spiritual condition. If the creative Word, by which the world was made, is a verb, i.e. a word-act, then history represents its conjugation or perhaps its translation from the indicative into the subjunctive mood.

The subjunctive mood offers new experience, tolerance, and intellectual generosity. It opens up a peaceful meandering trail between the present and the future, and permits us to see the past behind us as a multitude of alternative paths. It allows us to grasp the meaning of historical events to the extent that they might not have been (or could very well have been otherwise).

At the commencement of this new historical era, we are blessed with a superabundance of being that is ready for translation into the "if" mode. The only way towards the resurrection of time is following the future, or rather, the futuricity as a garden of forking paths into various futures.

# 3

# Mikhail Bakhtin and the future of the humanities

## From "finalizing" to "initiating"

Since the 1970s, the humanities have been passing death sentences on culture as if they were presiding at a military tribunal: the death of metaphysics, the death of the author, the death of history, the death of utopia, the death of originality, the death of humanity, and, finally, as a consequence, the *death of the humanities themselves*. Today, however, it becomes clear that the Socratic art of philosophical midwifery, assisting at the birth of the new, is a more appropriate vocation for the humanities. The Bakhtinian "embryonic approach" to nascent genres and cultural formations is an important contribution to this ancient Socratic tradition.

I first became interested in Bakhtin as a student of the philological department at Moscow State University in 1967. While I was studying literary theory and analysis, I wondered if it was possible to use his ideas in a practical way different from the predominant ideology of Soviet Marxism. Without a doubt, I was heavily influenced by Marx's ideas of transforming theory into practice. In the second thesis on Feuerbach, Marx presented what he considered to be the most reliable criterion of truth: "The question whether objective truth can be attributed to human thinking is not a question of theory but is a practical question. Man must prove the truth – i.e. the reality and power, the this-sidedness of his thinking in practice. The dispute over the reality or non-reality of thinking that is isolated from practice is a purely *scholastic* question" (*Theses on Feuerbach*, Thesis 2).

Practice, however, is not simply a way to verify theory. Practice creates something new altogether that was not contained in the object previously explored or explained by theory. When we apply theory to the existing world, the world becomes something different as it embraces new facts created by the practical application of theory itself. Thus practice, even when it is based on a particular theory, cannot simply be reduced to that theory. It creates a possibility for new theories that in turn create possibilities for new practices.

I was also questioning the obsession of Soviet Marxism with politics. It was assumed that even art and literature were active participants in the ideological struggle against capitalism, and therefore all cultural issues were to conform to the party line and turn into political practices. Of course, politics is an important part of culture, but why should it be privileged over literature, science, technology, religion, or ethics? Skeptical of this political reductionism in Marxist theory, I was pondering the following questions: "How can literary theory turn into literary practice?", "How can theory of art turn into the practice of art?", "How can theory of an essay turn into the practice of an essay?", and "How can the theory of 'X' turn into the 'X-ization' of the world?" Marxism, with its political preoccupations, gave no answer to these questions because it neglected the specifics of each of these cultural spheres.

The most consistent alternative to Marxism in the 1960s–70s was offered by the rise of structuralism and semiotics, which adhered to the ideal of a purely scientific approach to literature by using precise mathematical and quantitative procedures. Yury Lotman, as the leader of Soviet structuralism, was critical of Marxist ideological approaches to literature. Aiming to transform literary theory into a rigorous science, he wrote in an article tellingly titled *Literary Study Must Become Science* (1967):

> A literary scholar of a new type is the researcher who needs to integrate broad mastery of the independently obtained empirical material with the habits of deductive thinking as elaborated by exact sciences. ... He has to train himself to cooperate with mathematicians, and he ideally combines a literary scholar, a linguist and a mathematician. (1997, p. 765)

Even though I sympathized with Lotman's bold challenge to official Marxism, I could not support his claim that the humanities should turn to mathematics and natural sciences for criteria of scientific rigor. I was not satisfied with reducing literature either to politics and class struggle, or to mathematics and information theory (although I found the latter more honest and attractive). In my view, literary theory needed to establish itself as a branch of the humanities rather than that of social or exact sciences. I was thus looking for a third way that would fall somewhere between

Marxism and structuralism, as well as between ideological engagement and statistical calculations.

My strongest attraction was to Mikhail Bakhtin who, in his younger years in the 1920s, positioned himself as a Marxist and later, in 1960s and 1970s, was greeted as one of the forerunners of structuralist poetics, although he himself never was a member of any party, political or methodological. As a cultural thinker, he focused on the problem of dialogue in a literary work, but his approach could be expanded to include the dialogical relationship between literary study and literature itself. Following the tradition of German hermeneutics and "the sciences of spirit" (Dilthey's *Geisteswissenschaften*), Bakhtin sought to align methods of cognition with their objects. He distinguished between the "objective" cognition of the natural world and the dialogical cognition of human beings and their creative endeavors:

> The exact sciences constitute a monologic form of knowledge: the intellect contemplates a *thing* and expounds upon it. ... But a subject as such cannot be perceived and cognized as a thing, for as a subject it cannot, while remaining a subject, become voiceless, and, consequently, cognition of it can only be *dialogic*. (Bakhtin, 2002, p. 161)

Scholars enter into a dialogue with their "subjects", literary texts, authors and characters, and theory thus acquires a dialogical dimension. Simply put, Bakhtin's approach represented for me the most attractive "third path": not ideological or logical, but dialogical. It applies to the broadest varieties of dialogue as discussed in this chapter: the dialogue among cultures and the dialogue between the humanities and humanity.

# From multicultural to transcultural

According to Bakhtin, "the most intense and productive life of culture takes place on the boundaries of its individual areas and not in places where these areas have become enclosed in their own specificity" (1986a, p. 2). This famous statement carries a special relevance for our *proto-global* age. Is the multicultural model—the pluralistic world of self-enclosed cultures, each valuable in itself—sufficient for understanding new intercultural flows? Or do global studies have to work out a new model that will challenge the mosaic of multiculturalism, just as multiculturalism had earlier challenged the melting pot model and the "universal" cultural canon? Assuming that the most beautiful patterns in culture (as in nature) are created by overlapping waves from various traditions, epochs, and disciplines, can we move from the model of "difference" (or *différance*) that dominated the humanities in the 1970s–90s to a model of *interference*?

"Interference" is not taken here to mean an intrusion or intervention, but, in line with its definition in physics, denotes the mutual action of two or more waves of sound or light. Such an effect is found, for instance, in the butterfly's colorful markings. The *interferential* model in the study of cultures may succeed models based either on one-directional influences of mono-cultural canons or on impenetrable "differences" of multicultural diversity. This *interferential* model no longer isolates cultures from each other; rather, it opens up perspectives of their self-differentiation and mutual involvement. While recognizing all cultures as valuable in themselves, the Bakhtinian approach invites us to take the next step. By emphasizing the life of cultures on the boundaries, we can conclude that they are inherently insufficient when isolated from one another. People from different cultures need to develop the quality of *humility* and openness to each other, rather than revel in the pride of self-identity and self-aggrandizement: "only in the eyes of an alien culture, does another culture open itself in a fuller and deeper way" (Bakhtin, 1986a, p. 7). We cannot fully visualize our own faces; only others can see our true appearance. For instance, the distinctiveness of Russian culture can, paradoxically, be perceived more deeply by non-Russians, or the distinctiveness of the "white" culture by "non-whites", and vice versa. This Baktinian approach leads us from multiculturalism to *transculturalism*. Transculturalism is not simply a method based on the value of "outsidedness", but also a mode of being located at the crossroads of cultures. Culture, by releasing us from physical limitations, imposes new limitations on a symbolic level with its own idiosyncrasies, manias, phobias, ideological assumptions and restrictions, modes of indoctrination, and informational filters. As physical beings, we are governed to an extent by our bodily instincts, such as hunger and sexuality; culture transforms these instincts into rituals and generic routines through which we may come to possess what possesses us. We develop patterns of cultural behavior that curb these instincts and delay our gratification through the mediation of symbols, etiquette, and customs. Each culture has its own sets of rules and prescriptions that become second nature for its members; for instance, each culture has its particular rituals for eating, dating, and speaking. *Transculture* is the next step in the ongoing human quest for freedom, in this case the liberation from the prison-house of language and a variety of artificial, self-imposed, and self-deifying cultural identities.

An eloquent case for transculturalism can be found in the life and philosophy of Merab Mamardashvili (1930–90). Although Mamardashvili lived for many years in Moscow and Prague, he spent his last years in his native Tbilisi, where he suffered from the excesses of Georgian cultural and political nationalism exacerbated by the downfall of the Soviet empire. Mamardashvili sympathizes with multiculturalism as a mode of liberation from a monolithic cultural canon, but objects to the glorification of ethnic diversity for its own sake. In response to the arguments that favor cultural specificity along the lines of "each culture is valuable by itself", or "people should be allowed to live within their own cultures", Mamardashvili objects that:

> The defense of autonomous customs sometimes proves to be a denial of the right to freedom and to another world. It seems as if a decision were made for me: 'you live in such an original way, that it is quite cultural to live as you do, so go on and live this way.' But did anyone ask me personally? ... Perhaps I am suffocating within the fully autonomous customs of my complex and developed culture? (1992, p. 335)

Thus, what needs to be preserved is one's right to live beyond one's own culture:

> [It is necessary] to take a step transcending one's own surrounding, native culture and milieu not for the sake of anything else, not for the sake of any other culture, but for the sake of nothing. Transcendence into nothing. Generally speaking, such an act is truly the living, pulsating centre of the entire human universe. This is a primordial metaphysical act. (Ibid., 1992, p. 337)

From this standpoint, *transculture* does not mean adding yet another culture to the existing array. It is rather transcendence into "no culture" or "meta-cultural beyond", in the same sense that culture is "meta-physical beyond" in relation to nature. If culture positions itself outside nature, then transculture is the new emerging sphere in which humans position themselves *outside their primary, "inborn" naturalized cultures.* Cultures develop their own sets of values, identities, and predispositions that tend to become an oppressive cultural environment for their members, leading to a new process of "denaturalization", or, more precisely, "deculturalization". Transculture is the outcome of such a process of interaction between cultures. More and more individuals find themselves outside of their native ethnic, racial, sexual, ideological, and other cultural limitations. However, I need to stress the distinction between transculturalism and the cosmopolitan ideal of the Enlightenment: it is precisely this relevance of the primary (e.g. ethnic, national) cultures emphasized by the former that the latter attempts to ignore or bypass. The cosmopolitan person, as a citizen of the world, claims to belong directly and immediately to humankind as a whole, disregarding ethnic, racial, and other differences. Transcultural persons fully identify with their roots in a certain cultural ground, while not clinging to them.

Transculture, of course, does not completely release us from our "primary" cultural bodies, just as culture does not release us from our physical bodies. Each successive sphere of existence—nature, culture, transculture—is irreducible to the previous one, while at the same time changing its meaning. Freedom achieved through transculture may be characterized in Bakhtin's words: "[it] cannot change existence, so to speak, materially (nor can it want to) – it can change only the *sense* of existence" (1986a, p. 137). The *sense* of the existence of natural objects, such as a stone or water, is changed as they are interwoven in the context of various cultures. Similarly, the *sense* of the existence of a certain cultural tradition with its rituals and symbols, such as ethnic food or a literary convention, is changed when interwoven in the expanding transcultural context. As a simple gastronomic example, I would suggest that, for the contemporary New Yorker, rice has a more subtle and differentiated taste than for a medieval Chinese peasant, who never tasted anything like French Roquefort, Russian caviar, or Italian pizza.

We can freely choose the elements of transculture since they are not dictated by rules and prescriptions within any given culture. In the same way, artists choose colors in order to combine them creatively in their paintings. Transculture offers a universal symbolic palette on which any individual can blend colors to produce an expressive self-portrait. As a transcultural being, I can adhere to any ethnic or confessional tradition and decide the degree to which I make it my own. This transcultural condition, which gives a new meaning to all elements of existing cultures, can be described by using Bakhtin's concept of *vnenakhodimost'*, "outsidedness" or "being located beyond". This realm *beyond* all cultures is located *within* transculture (for more on transculture see: Berry and Epstein, 1999, pp. 1–6, 15–27, 79–90).

# The rehumanization of the humanities

Bakhtin's late writings assume that the fundamental human characteristic is one's capacity to be other to oneself. To put it simply, self-consciousness splits us into a subject and an object. If otherness grows from the very foundation of what it means to be human, we can reinterpret the postmodern paradox of the *dehumanization of the humanities* from Bakhtin's perspective as a necessary stage in the development of human self-awareness.

One of the general tenets of poststructuralism has been to assign the source of our activity to some non-human, impersonal, unconscious structures speaking through us and challenging our capacity to understand and command them. From the Bakhtinian viewpoint, however, such unknowables belong to the hidden potential of human self-knowledge. If we understand these alienated sources of our activity as an indispensable otherness inherent in the nature of human self-awareness, then an entirely new perspective of rehumanization becomes possible. The earlier emphasis on dehumanized knowledge, including psychoanalysis, Marxism, semiotics, structuralism, and poststructuralism, can be reinterpreted in new terms as the signs of human self-objectifying or self-othering capacity.

Bakhtin's ultimate project (never implemented) was the construction of a philosophical anthropology that would focus on the phenomenon of humanity in a much broader sense than the contemporary humanities usually consider. According to Bakhtin, the existence of human consciousness transforms the entire meaning of the world even if this world is never reflected and interiorized by consciousness. This assumption challenges the traditional concept of humanization as the appropriation and transformation of the world for, and by, human subjectivity. The world is radically changed in the presence of humans precisely because it cannot be contained within human consciousness. It remains *unknown and untouched*, which gives it an entirely different meaning in the presence of a "witness" capable of knowing and touching.

> Let the [human] witness see and know only an insignificant corner of existence, and all existence that is not cognized and not seen by him changes its quality (sense), becoming uncognized, unseen existence, and not simply existence as it was before, that is, without any relationship to the witness. (Bakhtin, 1986a, p. 138)

In other words, the unknown existence is as related to humans and as meaningful in human terms as is the known existence. The non-knowledge and the non-knowable, including economic, psychological, and semiotic determinants of human behavior, are humanistic categories related to, and derived from, specific human conditions. The Socratic thesis *I know that I know nothing* makes it clear that *ignorance is the product and object of knowledge*. It is impossible to state one's non-knowledge meaningfully without the knowledge of what remains beyond the known. If Kant developed a critique of knowledge, Bakhtin's remark suggests a *critique of ignorance* as a humanly produced form of knowledge. The statement *I know that I know nothing* is an axiom of what I call *optimistic epistemology*. Because *we know that we do not know*, our knowledge always surpasses our non-knowledge.

Humanness, as Bakhtin defines it, presupposes its otherness to itself: "*Not-I* in me, that is, existence in me; something larger than me in me" (1986a, p. 146). There are two different versions of *me*: one is "me" in the narrow sense, as I know myself; the other is "Me" embracing both me and my other, the part of myself hidden from me. To make this distinction clearer, I use capital and lower-case letters for the different versions of *me*, one Me embracing the other "me". The "not-I in me"—the other—includes language and the unconscious speaking through me.

This 'not-I' is a major theme and stronghold of the humanities in the twentieth century, and the basis of their anti-humanistic and anti-personal stance. This dehumanized version of the humanities, propagated by Michel Foucault, views humans as determined by non-human factors, such as economics, language, or the unconscious, beyond human comprehension and control. Bakhtin reminds us, however, that this "not-I" is "in me", although it is "larger than me in me". Although all of these non-human entities are larger than "me", they still belong to the structure of Me in its self-division, self-consciousness, and therefore non-knowledge of itself. This opens the dehumanized humanities to the prospect of rehumanization.

It is remarkable that, for Bakhtin, the other, the not-I, is more susceptible and open to consciousness than Me: "My temporal and spatial boundaries are not given for me, but the other is entirely given" (1986a, p. 147). Therefore, Me is a more complex object for the humanities than "me" or "the other". The radical fallacy of the dehumanized humanities was the reduction of Me to "me" and the belief that "the other" is beyond cognition, as distinguished from the "me" that allegedly is "immediately given to itself" through introspection. Bakhtin paradoxically shifts the perspective: it is Me that cannot be fully cognized and objectified, in distinction from "the other" that "is entirely given". Thus, the sphere of the non-known in the humanities is a part of the human subject as Me. Humanness, in its capacity for permanent self-othering, dividing into me and "the other", comprises the ultimate concern and enigma of all humanistic disciplines.

Thus, *three stages* in the development of the humanities can now be outlined. In the first stage, when the very concept of *humanitas* emerged in Renaissance Italy, the humanities were mostly preoccupied with "me" in Me. Humanness was defined in radical contradistinction from God, nature, and everything else in the world. In the second stage, the phenomenon of humanity was objectified and analyzed as "the other" in Me. For example, this otherness was interpreted by Marx as the totality of social relationships and, in a capitalist society, as the product of alienated economic conditions. Freud interpreted this otherness as the "id", i.e. as the unconscious spontaneously determining and mastering the human ego. The Saussurian and post-Saussurian developments in semiotics interpreted this otherness as those language mechanisms that predetermine the form and meaning of our speech acts. This rise of the *dehumanities* (to suggest a term for this second stage) was not a mistake or deviation, but a necessary stage of exploration of "otherness" constitutive of humanness in its capacity of self-transcendence and self-awareness.

The entire thrust of Marxist, Freudian, Saussurian, structuralist, and poststructuralist thought can be described in Bakhtin's words: "The *I* hides in the other and in others, it wants to be only the other for others, to enter completely into the world of others as an other, and to cast from itself the burden of being the only *I* (*I-for-myself*) in the world" (Bakhtin, 1986a, p. 147).

Now that "the other" in its opposition to "me" has been theoretically recognized and examined, we enter the third stage, in which the phenomenon of Me in its entirety is the focus of humanistic exploration. This new stage of the humanities can be called *trans-humanistic*, since it embraces both the human in its narrow, Renaissance sense ("me") and the non-human as postulated by the dehumanities of the twentieth century ("the other"). Trans-humanistic knowledge is addressed both to intra-human capacities and extra-human forces, as the latter are inherent in the former. According to Bakhtin's original coinage, Me is "*nadchelovek*", literally translated as "transhuman" (Bakhtin, 1979, p. 342). Bakhtin connects this discovery of "otherness" in the human being with Me's "trans-human" capacity for self-transcendence and self-awareness:

> This is analogous to the problem of man's self-awareness. Does the cognizer coincide with the cognized? ... Something absolutely new appears here: the supraperson [*nadchelovek*], the *supra-I*, that is, the witness and the judge *of the whole* human being, of the whole *I*, and consequently someone who is no longer the person, no longer the *I*, but the *other*. (1986a, p. 137)

Thus, the rupture at the foundation of the humanities is created as a result of the impossibility by the human being to understand oneself completely; it is in this space of self-differentiation that the humanities are prone to turn into the dehumanities which at the next stage can be reappropriated by the transhumanities.

For Michel Foucault, too, the object of the humanities contains an original gap between their subject and object as something radically unthinkable. By its very nature, the humanities' self-reflexivity posits a dark, incomprehensible double next to every person:

> Man and the unthought are, at the archaeological level, contemporaries. Man has not been able to describe himself as a configuration in the episteme without thought at the same time discovering, both in itself and outside itself, at its borders yet also in its very warp and woof, an element of darkness, an apparently inert density in which it is embedded, an unthought which it contains entirely, yet in which it is also caught. The unthought (whatever name we give it) is not lodged in man like a shriveled-up nature or a stratified history; it is, in relation to man, the Other: the Other that is not only a brother but a twin, born, not of man, nor in man, but beside him and at the same time, in an identical newness, in an unavoidable duality. (Foucault, 2004, pp. 355–6)

Supra-I, or Me, is posited here precisely as the open space of non-coincidence between "the cognizer" and "the cognized", or "me" and "the other", or "Man" and the "unthought". This non-coincidence is the sphere of humanly creative and responsible self-awareness that includes the possibility of self-deception and "non-knowledge".

Thus semiotic, genetic, economic, and other unconscious and non-human structural forces are constitutive of the phenomenon of humanness and comprise the potential field of the *transhumanities*. In this third stage, the otherness that was previously apprehended as a dehumanizing factor is reinterpreted and reappropriated as self-transcendence of humanity.

*  *  *

René Magritte's famous painting *Decalcomania* (1966) depicts two male figures. The solid silhouette on the left covers up a panorama comprising three elements: the earth, the sea and the sky. The silhouette on the right is cut out of the folds of a red curtain: through this blue aperture the same panorama is revealed. Naturally, Magritte had no intention of representing in these two silhouettes an emblem of human knowledge, but there is nothing to stop us interpreting them in this way. Man is a blank space in his knowledge about himself. We see him only from behind, as an object of humanistic inquiry, as a "he"—a historical figure, a cultural figure, a writer, a thinker, a warrior, a lover, a ruler or a child of nature, an interlocutor or a rival of God. But we cannot glimpse the face of the gazing man, that is, as a thing in itself: instead, we see an empty silhouette. In our time, we can no longer discern a coastal landscape through this aperture which is cut out in the shape of a man, but rather a "technoscape"—little figures of clever machines, which have ousted their biologically imperfect human forefathers. Formerly, man, seeking himself in himself, found God; then, nature; now—he finds the machine. Man sees everything except himself; he sees himself only from behind, as an Other. The task of the humanities is to turn man's face back towards himself—a completely unattainable goal: but precisely in this resides its greatness and nobility.

# PART TWO

# Humans and texts

# 4

# Reconfigurations of textuality

## From interpretation to a new performativity

Does the traditional notion of text being central to the humanities remain intact in the digital era? Or, is the immutable, self-identical text now being converted into flexible, dynamic, nomadic *text-like* formations that wander from site to site, modified by users, much like an epic song in a traditional community? Perhaps electronic discourse is closer to folklore than to the culture of fixed literary texts. Can we pertinently apply the term "text" to *oral* and *digital* genres in *preliterate* and *postliterate* societies? Or could the term *textoid* (the suffix "-oid" of Greek origin meaning "like", "like that of") be more precisely used to denote those unstable entities easily changed in the process of their perception?

Bakhtin's concept of utterance as a speech unit modelled on oral communication, as distinct from text, can illuminate this transition from literary to digital textuality:

> The utterance (speech product) as a whole enters into an entirely new sphere of speech communication. ... The term 'text' is not at all adequate to the essence of the entire utterance. There can be no such thing as an isolated utterance. It always presupposes utterances that precede and follow it. No one utterance can be either the first or the last. Each is only a link in the chain, and none can be studied outside this chain. (Bakhtin, 1986a, pp. 135–6)

On the one hand, the digital textual formations that can be called *textoids* are similar to *utterances* in Bakhtin's sense. Unlike stable, finished texts, they are fluid configurations of signs obedient to such commands as "cut", "copy", "paste", "find", or "replace". On the other hand, the Web allows its users even greater freedom than oral communication: we can insert our voice into utterances of other people, and interrupt, or spontaneously transform, others' texts. In fact, electronic textoids are even more fluid than utterances as defined by Bakhtin:

> [T]he change of speaking subjects, by framing the utterance and creating for it a stable mass that is sharply delimited from other related utterances, is the first constitutive feature of the utterance as a unit of speech communication …. In each utterance —from the single-word, everyday rejoinder to large, complex works of science or literature—we embrace, understand, and sense the speaker's *speech plan* or *speech will*, which determines the entire utterance, its length and boundaries. (1986a, pp. 76–7)

For Bakhtin, the utterance is a separate unit of communication produced by a single speaker, which preserves its integrity within a certain interval of speech. This notion of utterance, however, appears too rigid for electronic dispersal of voices and authorships. The Web is a different aggregate state of verbal communication: like watches in Salvador Dali's paintings, textoids are fluid texts that can acquire any form and blend freely with any other texts and voices.

Another aspect of Bakhtin's theory of utterance is the role of dialogical context:

> The text lives only by coming into contact with another text (with context). Only at the point of this contact between texts does a light flash, illuminating both the posterior and anterior, joining a given text to a dialogue. (1986a, p. 162)

According to Bakhtin, contextualization implies that the meaning of each text can be understood only through its dialogical relationship with other texts, while the text itself supposedly remains unchanged by this textual environment.

Bakhtin's concepts of utterance and context clearly help to theorize the patterns of electronic communication; however, his conceptual system still falls short of super-fluid forms of textuality now found on the Web. The Web develops a more radical form of contextualization, which can be viewed as *retextualization*. Texts do not simply "live" by contacting other texts; they are also reshaped by such contacts. In digital networks, contextuality transforms the structure and substance of texts, not only their meanings. For example, we answer emails by altering the received text, inserting our responses and reactions into it. In oral communication, what has been said can never be "unsaid"; the oral message is locked into an immutable past, just as the written text is connected to an immutable presence of its printed medium. In the electronic universe, however, there is only an ever-open future, and everything written can be unwritten and rewritten in multiple ways. Even intellectual discussions on the Web tend not so much to interpret electronic publications as *retextualize* them, performing new semi-critical and semi-transformative writing on the basis of what has been read.

Web texts lose their fixed character not only because they are subject to spontaneous rewriting, but also because their own structure depends on the activity of reading. In the past, it was the order of writing that determined the linear order of reading; now, on the contrary, what we find published on the Web is determined by what we read and how we read it. Instead of following a ready-made text, we compile a new text in the process of its creative perception. Searching the Web is an increasingly productive method of *compositional reading* that constructs new *supra-textual* unities, such as virtual anthologies, collections, compilations, and encyclopedias.

Today, to read means not only to follow a text with one's eyes, but also to compile it with one's own hands. The position of the reader becomes that of a curator, who arranges and displays artwork at an exhibition. In the world of literature, this corresponds to the role of the compiler of anthologies and collections. Readers compose new texts from the materials provided by the original authors. The position of a hyper-reader contains various possibilities as it combines functions of both the traditional reader and the traditional compiler. In fact, any hyperlink is a multiplier of virtual books emerging in the process of our creative hyper-reading. The hyperlink fastens numerous texts by various authors, organizing them in a different way: repaginating, reshuffling, and thus retextualizing them. Any hyper-linked word, phrase, or idiom can serve as an entry into an entirely different textual universe. We are now reading rhizomatically, in all possible direc-tions along and across the screen. The floating and soaring quality of our gaze, incessantly changing its focus, brings forth the ephemeral quality of those texts that we are creating in the process of reading. It is possible to speak of floating signifieds in the process of reconfiguration of textuality. In this sense, the *textoid* is a virtual text that exists only in the process of its reading: it has no author other than its reader.

The art of *interpretation*—the constitutive procedure of the human-ities—has developed in response to literary texts as fixed and immutable utterances. Interpretation modifies the meaning of a text based on the assumption that its verbal identity is preserved. Interpretation and literary criticism as we know them are the ingredients of paper culture, reactions to the solid stature of verbal production. In preliterate societies, utterances are not fixed and can be adjusted to the changing conditions of perception through direct performative acts of textual variations. For instance, if one hears a popular song from a neighboring village and wants to perform it to one's own community, one simply changes it, incorporating local names to adjust it to the needs of the audience. Why do we need to interpret something that can be easily transformed?

Similar performativity applies to the *post-literate* conditions of digital culture. Instead of interpreting the online text, one simply recites it differently. With the transition to textoids, *performativity* may supplement or even succeed interpretation in the textual economy of digital networks. A new reading is enacted through *rewriting*. In literary culture, text has a sacred status, whereas digital culture desacralizes it. If there is no finished aesthetic product, there is nothing to interpret. Understanding a text now involves not simply processing its meaning, but enacting its transformation. Or, in the words of Bakhtin: "understanding supplements the text: it is active and also creative by nature. Creative understanding continues creativity, and multiplies the artistic wealth of humanity" (1986a, p. 142). The Web challenges readers, scholars, and critics to participate creatively in what they previously observed, studied, and interpreted.

# Megatext, supratext, unitext, and other configurations

One of Bakhtin's foremost theoretical concerns was the expansion of our understanding of the text beyond its actual borders, the placing of it in the multiplicity of contexts that surround it both at a given point of time, and in the overall time of history as an open and unending whole. Bakhtin was against the "enclosure of analysis (cognition and understanding) in one given text" (1981, p. 161). He wrote:

> Each word (each sign) of the text exceeds its boundaries. Any understanding is a correlation of a given text with other texts.... Understanding as correlation with other texts and reinterpretation, in a new context (in my own context, in a contemporary context, and in a future one).... Stages in the dialogic movement of *understanding*: the point of departure, the given text; movement backward, past contexts; movement forward, anticipation (and the beginning) of a future context. (1986a, p. 161)

This new level of critical understanding can be achieved by the development of electronic communications that brings forth new textual configurations that were invisible or even non-existent in the age of printed texts.

*Megatext, supratext, unitext, pertext*—all these concepts reflect the upper levels of textuality, which manifest themselves on the Web and must be studied on their own terms.

*Megatext* is the totality of texts perceived or studied as one discursive whole, characterized by common topics, symbols, archetypes, keywords, leitmotifs, or stylistic devices. For example, we can talk about the megatext of German Romanticism, or of Chinese Landscape lyrics, or of the superfluous man in Russian literature[1].

*Supratext* designates the same textual configuration but, unlike megatext, it is a relational term that links any text or its fragment of it with megatexts on other levels. *Supratext* is a text of a higher, more general plane in relation to the given text. For example, 'English romanticism' or the genre of 'lyrical ballads are supratexts for S. T. Coleridge's poem The Rime of the Ancient Mariner (1797–8). Many motifs in Andrey Belyi's poetry can be understood only within the supratexts of Russian Symbolism and the Antroposophic movement. If *context* is the environment of a text on the same systematic level, then *supratext* is a unit of the next, higher level. If Russian Symbolism is a supratext in its relation to the poetry of Belyi, then Russian Modernism or European Symbolism are supratexts in relation to Russian Symbolism. Any literary work, as well as any image, motif, or textual unit has a variety of supratexts and can be understood only in relation to them.

Here is, for instance, a list of some supratexts of Alexander Pushkin's most famous poem "K***" ("I remember a wonderful moment..."):

1 All texts, which include certain lines or expressions of the poem, such as "in a remote corner of the Earth", "like a fleeting vision", and "life, tears, and love";

2 All texts that incorporate the names of Anna Kern (the addressee of the poem) and Alexander Pushkin;

3 All texts that were written in Russian in 1825 because the date of the text's creation is also a supratextual unit, a common marker of a certain megatext;

---

[1]The phrase "superfluous man" (*lishnii chelovek* in Russian) is used to describe a type of character in nineteenth century Russian literature, who is typically well-educated, intelligent, and idealistic, yet unable to engage in effective social action. Such archetypal characters are drifting individuals who experience inner turmoil, as they feel alienated from society and cannot set up a foundation for their life. The phrase became popular following the publication of Ivan Turgenev's story "The Diary of a Superfluous Man" (*Dnevnik lishnego cheloveka*) (1850). One often-quoted example of the "superfluous man" is Pechorin in Mikhail Lermontov's story "A Hero of Our Time". It is interesting to note that all examples of such characters in nineteenth century Russian literature are men although the phrase "*lishnii chelovek*" literally means "superfluous person". (Editor's Note).

4  All texts that were written by Pushkin in the village of
   Mikhailovskoe because the place of the text's creation is also a
   supratextual unit;

5  All texts about love;

6  All texts about memory.

The list of such supratexts can be continued *ad infinitum*.

Thus, the same text can have many supratexts, depending on which of
its components is regarded as the constitutive feature of a given supratext.
Supratext is a totality of all the texts united by a common element that can
be a phrase, a metaphor, the name of the author, the name of the hero, etc.

The supratext of all existing texts can be called *Unitext*—the universal
text of humanity. *Unitext* embraces to all texts as the universe embraces
to all components of the material world. In 1827, Goethe introduced the
concept of "world literature" (*Weltliteratur*), pointing to the growing unity
of national literatures: "National literature is now a rather unmeaning
term; the epoch of world literature is now at hand, and everyone must strive
to hasten its approach" (quoted in: Damrosch, 2003, p. 12).

With the development of digital technologies, the unitext becomes a
tangible manifestation of the world literature, in which every word is
potentially connected to all others. The unitext is both a universal text and
a unique text. Just as our universe is unique, there is only one unitext that
encompasses everything that has ever been written. This "unitextuality"
becomes increasingly achievable through the growing capacity of electronic
libraries and automatic translation on the Internet.

Contemporary authors, therefore, must take into account all supratexts
in which their texts will be inscribed, including the unitext as the supratext
of all supratexts. Before using certain words or expressions, one may want
to check the presence, frequency, and combinational capacities of these
units on the Web. This can help the author to avoid repetitions, inscribing
the text into multiple thematic, disciplinary, ideological supratexts, and
even making the text's key words entries in the dictionary-like, hypertextual
structure of the entire Internet.

Today, any text must be submitted not only to syntagmatic, but also
paradigmatic, reading and writing. The syntagmatic dimension connects
each text unit with the surrounding context and is manifested on the
printed surface of paper. The paradigmatic dimension connects the text
and all its units with their supratexts, which are presented in digital form
through actual and potential hyperlinks. This new art of *paradigmatic*
writing and reading weaves each textual thread into the multi-dimensional
whole of unitext. In this respect, authors interact with the entire Web,
which requires them to be responsible and responsive when selecting words
and images. Each word has to be properly placed not only in its immediate

context within a certain text, but also in the supratext of its usage by all other authors throughout the history of writing. For example, while writing about "time as a dynamic image of eternity", one must place this expression within the *vertical* context of supratext, in which it would be compared to the same expressions used by Plato, Bergson, Semyon Frank, and many other less famous authors.

The Web makes visible and comprehensible those orders of supratextuality that Bakhtin envisioned as the "festival" of rebirth for every single meaning lost over the past centuries.

> There is neither a first nor a last word and there are no limits to the dialogic context (it extends into the boundless past and the boundless future). Even *past* meanings, that is, those born in the dialogue of past centuries, can never be stable (finalized, ended once and for all)—they will always change (be renewed) in the process of subsequent, future development of the dialogue.... Nothing is absolutely dead: every meaning will have its homecoming festival. (1986a, p. 170)

The information retrieved by a search engine—the list of the Web pages that contain a certain word or phrase—is also a new type of textual formation. It can be called *pertext* (from Larin "per", meaning "through"), and it functions as a table of contents for megatexts or supratexts[2].

For example, the first four lines of the pertext for the word 'poem,' according to Google, are as follows:

1 PoemHunter.Com—Thousands of poems and poets... Poetry Search
...

www.poemhunter.com/

2 Poems

www.poemhunter.com/poems/

Best *poems* from famous *poets*. Read romantic love *poems*, ...

3 Poetry—Wikipedia, the free encyclopedia

en.wikipedia.org/wiki/Poetry

The oldest surviving epic *poem* is the Epic of Gilgamesh, from the 3rd millennium BC in Sumer ...

4 Love Poems And Quotes—Romantic Love Poetry & More

---

[2] We must distinguish between the "pertext", as a web phenomenon, and the more conventional literary term "paratext", which Gérard Genette (1997) defines as those elements that accompany a published work, such as its title, preface or introduction, its illustrations, the name/s of the work's author/s, etc.

The pertext is a textual thoroughfare of many different texts connected by a certain unit, such as a word (in this case, "poem"). The pertext is complementary to the concept of the hypertext. The hypertext is a coherent text containing links to many other texts, while the pertext is a collection of links (or references) to many texts connected by a single word or phrase. We encounter *pertexts* more and more often along with traditional "syntexts", i.e. coherent texts that are read syntagmatically. Pertexts contain the titles of the sites, the names of the authors, initial sentences of their works, Web addresses, and links to those pages where certain words or expressions are used. If all texts that contain the word "poetry" in them make up a megatext, then the pertext "poetry" serves as a table of content or a collection of references for this gigantic text that, according to Google, contains about 330 million pages.

Multiple *virtual books* are inscribed in any single pertext and may be open for vertical, rather than horizontal, reading. By a "virtual book", I mean not simply a digitized paper book, but rather a potential book unique to the compositional capacities of the Web. Using various search engines, it is easy to compile a virtual book of any imaginable content, e.g. an anthology of texts or utterances on any topic. For example, a collection entitled *The Dynamic Image of Eternity* would be composed of all the texts in which this expression is used.

Thus, we read what we ourselves "write", our own compositions being compiled from Web searches. This new reconfiguration of textuality imposes new obligations on writers and simultaneously expands the potential scope of their works. Each writer becomes a transformer of unitext, a voluntary or involuntary contributor to the hundreds of virtual anthologies, collections, and online dictionaries. Any textual unit (e.g. a sentence, a paragraph, or a page) becomes a wanderer in the digital world, inserted into the multitude of virtual books that emerge only when Web readers need them. It is interesting to note that the Russian word for page is *stranitsa*, which is derived from the same root as *strannitsa* ("a wanderer"). Thus, released from its binding, the emancipated page migrates through disciplines and languages.

From the multitude of such "pages-wanderers", "stapled" together by the keyword from a Web search, a new virtual book can be compiled in an instant, with the pertext acting as its spine. Writers need to foresee the possibility that each of their pages not only belongs to the original text, but may also fit in the variety of virtual books produced by Web searchers.

# Interlation and stereotextuality

Transculturalism presupposes *translingualism*, or what Bakhtin called *polyglossia*: "Only polyglossia fully frees consciousness from the tyranny of its own language" (1981, p. 161). The globalization of cultures radically changes the role of languages and translation. With the spread of multi-lingual competence, translation is becoming a dialogical counterpart to the original text rather than its substitution.

The text and its foreign counterpart together comprise a multidimensional, multilingual, culturally curved discourse. While bilingual or multilingual persons have no need for translation, they may still enjoy *interlation*—a simultaneous contrastive juxtaposition of allegedly "equivalent" texts in two or more different languages. *Interlation* is a multilingual variation on the same theme, with the roles of source and target languages becoming interchangeable. In his essay *The Homeric Versions*, J. L. Borges famously argued that we could only evaluate a translation and original fairly if we had no prior knowledge of which is which. What is more important here, however, is not the comparative value of the original and its translation(s), but their complementarity and mutual enrichment. One language allows the reader to perceive what another language misses or leaves unclear.

I will cite one example of interlation from a poem by Joseph Brodsky in Russian and its English auto-translation. The original line *Odinochestvo est´ chelovek v kvadrate* in Brodsky's poem *To Urania* literally reads: "Loneliness is a person squared". Brodsky himself reconfigures this line into English as "Loneliness cubes a man at random".

It would be irrelevant to ask which of these expressions, Russian or English, is more adequate to Brodsky's poetic thought. Both are necessary to embrace the scope of its metaphoric meaning. Both a square and a cube represent the inescapable self-reflexivity and self-multiplication of a lonely person; they convey loneliness as geometric projections intensified by the dimensional transformation of a square into a cube. For bilinguals, this poem becomes a work of unique art that can be called *stereo-poetry*, which contains more metaphorical levels than mono-poetry. In Brodsky's poem, the *stereo effect* is produced by the figurative relationship between the Russian and English lines: the English "cube" amplifies and strengthens the meaning of the Russian "square". Both the "cube" and the "square" serve as metaphors for loneliness, and at the same time these two words are metaphorically related to each other. Robert Frost famously said that "poetry is what gets lost in translation". By contrast, *interlation* doubles or multiplies the gains of poetry. In addition to metaphors that connect words within one language, a new level of imagery emerges through the metaphorical liaison between languages, producing a surplus of poetic value, not its loss. It can be said that poetry is what is found in interlation.

The author may intend a certain stereo effect, or it can also be achieved through the experience of reading multiple versions of a text. For example, Vladimir Nabokov's autobiography can be read as a *stereo-text* in two languages (English and Russian) and in three consecutive versions: *Conclusive Evidence* (1951), *Drugie berega* (1954), and *Speak, Memory*

(1964). Nabokov himself emphasized that these versions are far from being mere translations, rather they relate to one another as metamorphosis:

> This re-Englishing of a Russian re-vision of what had been an English re-telling of Russian memories in the first place, proved to be a diabolical task, but some consolation was given me by the thought that such multiple metamorphosis, familiar to butterflies, had not been tried by any human before. (1964, pp. 12–13)

Thus, at the crossroads of languages, a new work of *stereo-poetry* or *stereo-prose* is born which can be characterized in Bakhtin's words: "[I]n the process of literary creation, languages interanimate each other and objectify precisely that side of one's own (and of the other's) language *that pertain to its world view*, its inner form, the axiologically accentuated system inherent in it" (1981, p. 62).

Translation as the search for equivalence dominated the epoch of national cultures and monolingual communities that needed the bridges of understanding rather than the rainbows of co-creativity. When languages were enclosed within monoethnic cultures, their combination was perceived as an artificial device. In the past, the deliberate mixture of languages called "macaronic" were mostly used for comic effect. With the globalization of cultures and automatization of translation, the *untranslatability* and *non-equivalencies* among languages come to the foreground as genuine polyglossia. In the proto-global society, a *stereo-poem* written partly in English, partly in French, and partly in Russian could find a tri-lingual audience that would be able to savor precisely the meaningful discrepancies between the three languages in which the poem is created.

In the course of time, *stereo-textuality* may come to be viewed as a distinct form of verbal creativity and not just as an exotic outcome of the growing multilingualism. It is known that stereo-cinema (3D film) reproduces sights and stereo-music reproduces sounds more naturally than their mono predecessors. Although they emerged only recently as technological innovations, stereo-cinema and stereo-music are better accommodated to our perceptive capacities. The same can be applied to our intellectual vision and conceptual hearing. Can an idea be adequately presented in only one language? Or, do we need a *minimum of two languages* to convey the range of thought just as we need two eyes to see and two ears to hear? In the near future, we can envision a set of new multilingual creative activities in the venues of *stereo-poetry*, *stereo-philosophy*, *stereo-aesthetics*, and *stereo-criticism*. They will draw from a variety of languages and capitalize in meaningful ways on different worldviews. Multilingual writing or, to use Bakhtin's words (1981, p. 429), the mutual illumination and interanimation of languages, may become as conventional for the global age as stereo-music and stereo-cinema are conventional today.

# 5

# "     " Ecophilogy: Text and its environment

This chapter is about blank spaces in language and culture and their formative role in texts. I propose a new sign that denotes the absence of any sign and is conveyed by quotation marks around a blank space: "     ". This no-sign can be applied to many subject areas, including philosophy, theology, ethics, aesthetics, poetics, and linguistics. "     " more adequately than any of other terms, such as the Absolute, Dao, the Endless, the Inexpressible, or Différance, designates the ultimate condition of any signification. Each discipline has its own "     ", i.e. certain "unspeakable" assumptions that need to be presented inside disciplinary frontiers, as a blank margin moved inside the medium. "     " allows language to speak the unspeakable.

## Nature as an intra-cultural phenomenon

Medium and Margin, Figure and Background, Center and Periphery—these are the traditional dichotomies of the universe of signs. But, what if their roles were reversed, and, for example, the margin found itself within the medium? The blank margins of this paper on which I am writing would then move to the center of the page, becoming a part of the text and leaving a blank space in its medium. If I designate the boundaries of this blank space with quotation marks, it will look like this: "     ". The usual role of quotation marks is to recognize the usage (incorporation, repetition) of a source external to the given text. However, the text here cites not some other text but its own margin, the environment that makes this text possible, visible, writable, and readable.

"          " as a sign transforms the environment of a text, e.g. its white or blue background as given on paper or a screen, into one of the text's own components—a new sign that functions among other textual signs. Once the blank space is put in quotation marks, the relationship between the inside and outside of the text is reversed, and the outside moves into the inside.

There is a parallel in the relationships between text and non-text, on the one hand, and culture and nature, on the other hand: nature is usually posited as the outside of culture, as its preexisting condition and environment.

Ecology, as an ethical concern and social function, attempts to turn the outside of culture into its inside. National parks, wildlife reserves, and nature sanctuaries become the zones of nature within civilization, protected by civilization from itself. This concern is paralleled in ecologically-conscious philology, linguistics, literary and cultural studies by the same transformation of the text's environment into its interior area, "          ". Here, the inverted commas have the same function as the boundaries of nature sanctuaries have within industrial settings and developed areas. As a result, "          " appears as an island of environmental purity, a sanctuary of non-text within the text.

The turn of the humanities toward ecology is determined by the fact that the object of ecology, i.e. natural environment is actually an *intra-cultural* phenomenon produced by humans. Unlike physics, biology, and other natural sciences, the object of the so-called "human ecology" is not nature, as such, but nature as a human, cultural environment. Those very cultural acts by which humans withdraw from nature transform the latter into their environment. This explains why physics and biology are among the most ancient disciplines, while ecology, as a discipline, emerged only recently. It took several millennia for nature to be transformed from cosmos and organism, as studied by physics and biology, into *environment* as a phenomenon related to culture, studied by ecology. As Boris Groys remarks, "The very term *protection of environment* is paradoxical enough: it is impossible to protect the surrounding, only what is surrounded" (Groys, 1993, p. 174). In other words, whereas culture proclaims itself to be surrounded by nature, culture in fact surrounds nature by enclosing it within the protective space such as wildlife reserves. Nature and culture, the original and the derivative, swap their positions. It is time to elevate ecology to a new reflexive level, where it can realize the secondary, artificial character of its "natural" object and thus become a discipline within the humanities.

As a humanities discipline, the ecology of text, or *ecophilology*, focuses on pure extratextual environment inasmuch as it can be inscribed within a text. Ecophilology can be conceptualized as a discipline that explores the role of textual environments in all kinds of settings and media, from prehistoric cave paintings and graffiti to contemporary electronic media. The main premise of ecophilology can be summed up as follows: writing and " " are set as mutual preconditions; without the latter, writing cannot take place, while without the former, " " cannot be written upon. This way, as a result of a long historical co-evolution, it becomes possible to write " " into the writing itself.

The reversal of the outside and the inside of text is not merely an act of individual self-reflection, but the result of the historical evolution. Textuality first creates its own condition in the form of a clean background and then consciously moves it into its graphical, semantic, and ethical center. Regardless of its material components, the text's environment has a special "sacrificial" quality: it exists for the text to be printed, written, typed, or scribbled upon. For the environment to function properly, effectively highlighting the text against its background, it must completely *disappear* from the field of the reader's perception and let the text take center stage.

In this light, it is not surprising why the textual environment has remained unexplored for such a long time. One remarkable exception is the work by Meyer Shapiro exploring the semiotics of surface in visual art:

> We take for granted today as indispensable means the rectangular form of the sheet of paper and its clearly defined smooth surface on which one draws and writes. But such a field corresponds to nothing in nature or mental imagery where the phantoms of visual memory come up in a vague unbounded void. The student of prehistoric art knows that a regular field as an advanced artifact presupposes a long development of art. The cave paintings of the Old Stone Age are on unprepared ground, the rough wall of a cave; the irregularities of earth and rock show through the image. ... The smooth prepared field is an invention of a later stage of humanity. It accompanies the development of polished tools in the Neolithic and Bronze Ages. ... We do not know when this organization of the image field was introduced; students have given little attention to this fundamental change in art which is basic for our own imagery, even for the photograph, the film and the television screen. (1985, pp. 209–10)

Meyer Shapiro uses different words to label the object of his research, including such descriptive characteristics as "clearly defined smooth surface" and "the smooth prepared field". In its turn, " " is a non-descriptive name for this smooth field of writing, drawing, or painting. It can be presented in any given medium: for example, " " can appear as the white surface of paper or as the bluish surface of a computer screen. What appears within the quotation marks varies from one medium to another, e.g. from the rough surface of a stone to the smooth surface of paper. In each case, however, "        " represents the condition of signification specific to its particular medium. On the white, it is white; on the blue, it is blue. It is consubstantial with its medium, which makes this sign both relative and universal. "        " is the same sign everywhere, in each language, on each surface, precisely because it points to the given surface; it directly manifests "the beyond" of the text through its internal gap.

    Today, "        " can be legitimately inscribed into texts, millennia after texts were inscribed into "        ". In Meyer Shapiro's words, "the clean surface in painting is a late achievement in civilization" (1985, pp. 209–10). Nowhere in nature can we find such smooth and clean surfaces as a sheet of paper. All natural surfaces that helped to convey to us the heritage of early literacy, e.g. a cave, a rock, or the beech-bark writings, were originally marked by nature itself and covered by materials ill-suited for writing. Even the papyruses that were designed for writing still preserve the traces of plant fibers; this way, the handwriting of nature overlaps on to the handwriting of humans, producing interference and "information noise". The development of writing, and later print, required the creation of smooth and, at the same time, durable surfaces capable of preserving cultural markings. The very practice of writing creates its own ideally pure environment, similar to how culture creates a natural environment and gives it the attribute of purity in order to protect it from itself.

# Transgression of language.
## "        " as an index

From antiquity, philosophers and language theorists have looked for a sign that could adequately convey the condition for the very existence of signs. However, even the most universal signs that refer to mystical concepts and express the inexhaustible and vacuous nature of being, e.g. Tao, are not adequate to their intended signifieds. As Lao Tse says at the very beginning of the treatise *Tao Te Ching*, "Tao that can be expressed in words is not a permanent Tao."

    Such general concepts as *essence, being,* or *différance* are only names generated by the play of difference, which must remain unnamable:

> 'Older' than being itself, such a *différance* has no name in our language. But we 'already know' that if it is unnamable, it is not provisionally so, not because our language has not yet found or received this name, or because we would have to seek it in another language, outside the finite system of our own. It is rather because there is no *name* for it at all,

not even the name of essence or of being, not even that of '*différance*,' which is not a name.... This unnamable is not an ineffable being which no name could approach, for example, God. This unnamable is the play which makes possible nominal effects, the relatively unitary and atomic structures that are called names, the chains of substitutions of names in which, for example, the nominal effect *différance* is itself *enmeshed*, carried off, reinscribed, just as a false entry or a false exit is still a part of the game, a function of the system. (Derrida, 1991, pp. 75–6)

Derrida implies that the name *différance* is one of many names drawn in the play of *différance*, which does not have and cannot have one privileged name. Indeed, the word *différance*, no matter how profoundly interpreted, remains only a language sign consisting of the letters of the Latin alphabet. Is language in its search for the foundation beyond itself that makes signification possible, doomed to be locked in the chain of conventional and replaceable names? The semiotic replacements and substitutions that Derrida discusses do not form a closed chain; rather, they are constantly stretched out and overstrained to the breaking point. The life of language is never as full and vigorous as it is on the edge of desemiotization. At the point where the chain of signifiers is torn apart, the precise name for signification is revealed in and through that very extralinguistic phenomenon, "      ", that constitutes the sign of itself. In Lacanian terms, the break in the chain of signifiers can be described as a trauma of language. This trauma constitutes the main event in the life of language: not an addition of still another symbol, but the inscription into language of the condition of its very possibility.

"      " is a privileged name, in which the extra-textual environment, as the condition of signification, becomes its interior part, a link in the chain of signifiers. The oral equivalent of "      " is a pause: an articulate unit of silence. My way of introducing "      " in an oral presentation is a short interval of silence marked by air quotes.

The sign "      " is not symbolic or iconic; it belongs to the indexical type of signs, in the famous triadic classification of Charles S. Peirce. An index is a part or a companion (a cause or an effect) of what it signifies; for example, a smoke is an index of fire, or dark clouds are an index of impending rain. Indexes are ubiquitous in nature, but almost never appear on printed pages, in books, or albums. "      " signifies that empty background which underlies every text and constitutes the very condition of textuality and signification.

It is only partly true that the way out of language and into the world of extra-linguistic entities is merely an illusionary, a 'false exit,' as Derrida asserted (1991, pp. 75–6). In reality, as soon as the textual environment is placed in quotes and transformed into "      ", it becomes enmeshed in the play of language signs. At this point of rupture, language transgresses its conventional boundaries, semiotizing its material environment to the same extent as it desemiotizes and deverbalizes its internal space. Language transcends itself as a meaningful pause in order to *indicate* (as is appropriate for an indexical sign) something that cannot be expressed in words or characters, but which speaks for itself through its silent, inarticulate, non-verbal presence. What is not said *shows* itself in language, or, according to an even stronger assertion by Wittgenstein: "What *can* be shown, cannot be said" (1971, p. 115). In "        " language reveals its beyond—that transcendent region of the world which cannot be said, but can only be shown. We can see "        ", but we cannot say it. While ceasing to speak, language begins to show, operating as an index and pointing to the environment beyond itself.

Thus, language is not a one-dimensional phenomenon; its entries and exits cannot be considered only as illusionary signs of the language game itself. Language ins and outs are part and parcel of its structure, just as doors and windows belong to a building. However, if these ins and outs do not lead anywhere, and if the building is not connected to a street, a square, or some outside space, then such a construction cannot function as a building. By the same token, language cannot perform its role if all its entries and exits turn out to be nothing but decorations or fake props. The condition of signification is created by the environment outside of language, and the definition of language as "a game" is possible only when juxtaposed to "not a game". According to Bakhtin, the most intensive life of culture takes place at its borders, not in its interior areas, "enclosed in their own specificity" (1986a, p. 2). The same is applicable to the life of language, which intensifies at its borders. "        " is the non–sign of such extreme intensity in the dual processes of semiotization and desemiotization, which make language a truly exciting game.

# The ultimate (non-)name.
## "        " in philosophy and theology

As mentioned earlier, even the most universal language signs, used to express the infinite and inexhaustible nature of Being, are not adequate to their intended signified because of their symbolic, conditional, and arbitrary nature. Each of such words is only one among many—a combination of letters or hieroglyphs.

There are many words attempting to designate the ultimate nature of everything: *Absolute*, *Idea*, *Oneness*, *Essence*, *Nothing*, *Infinity*, *Unnameable*, *Tao*, or *Différance*. The constant renewal of such foundational terms in various philosophical systems only proves that no single, verbally articulated concept can serve as an expression of the universal philosophical principle. According to Heidegger: to name the "beingness of being", language must come up with a unique "singular word". Heidegger suggests the Greek ὄν, meaning "Being". (2009, p. 216) But even the most universal verbal signs used to express the infinite, inexhaustible nature of Being are not adequate to their intended signified, because verbal signs are symbolic and arbitrary. The foundation of everything, *Being as such*, cannot be expressed with language signs due to their contingency and relativity. And yet, it cannot remain unexpressed, either, because one of the ultimate aspirations of philosophy is the articulation of the most capacious and all-comprehensive concepts from which other concepts can be derived. Such a sign cannot be within language due to its arbitrariness, and it cannot be outside language, because then it would not be a sign. Such a sign can be only *at the border* of language, both inside and outside—as the non-speakable condition of speakability, the non-verbal condition of verbality.

"      " is adequate for this purpose because, as both a sign and index, it manifests the conditions of both signification and indication.

"      " speaks the most universal language, that of the blank space.

"      " gives a name to the condition for any naming.

"      " is a more adequate and universal term for the Absolute or the Infinite than the words *absolute* and *infinite*, which are composed of certain letters in a certain language.

"      " does not name Being in a contingent and arbitrary way in which all language signifiers are related to their signifieds.

"      " is the foundational (non-)word, the void-word unavoidably co-present with any and all other words, while remaining unexpressed in any single of them. "      " points to the mystery of Being as underlying the being of all words and, at the same time, irreducible to them.

"      " is not just a name for Being; it *is* Being presenting itself in language. It is Being that underlies any text at any given place and moment, where and when you are reading *this text* and contemplating the paper or the screen beneath and between all the words that you are reading. Being is here: "      ".

This blank space, representing the background of any text, is the true Heideggerian *Da-Sein*, "existent in the presence" of these very words, written by me, and being read by you.

Thus, "      " is adequate to what it intends to signify precisely because it does not merely signify it, but indexically manifests the condition of signification by being itself a part of this condition. I call "      " a *(non-)sign* because it emerges at the boundary of text and non-text. It is an indexical sign, but, from the point of view of symbolic signs which constitute language, it is not a sign.

The (non-)sign "      " belongs to the field of *negative*, or *apophatic semiotics* and corresponds to the concept of unknowable, invisible, and undefinable God in apophatic theology. Contrary to cataphatic theology that aims to present God in positive terms, such as *light, strength, reason,* or *perfection*, apophatic theology ascends to God and speaks about God through silence and darkness, through non-visibility and non-speakability. In apophatic terms, this Final Cause (as Pseudo-Dionysius Areopagite called God), can be defined as the "        " of theology.

One can apply "        " as a semiotic concept to any subject area, not only philosophy or theology. Each discipline has its own "unspeakable" conditions and assumptions that need to be presented inside its disciplinary frontiers. At the same time, such conditions must be sequestered from representation to remain transcendent with respect to what they make possible. Hence the need for a negative semiotics: a semiotics of non-signs.

## "        " and ethics

By making "        " the focus of our writing and reading experience, we partially repay to it what we owe it for our capacity to write and read. The fact that the pure field of "        " is created in order to be polluted for the sake of writing and thus destroyed in its purity, emphasizes the sacrificial nature of "        " and invokes the founding myth of the Western civilization about the self-sacrificial Logos. Logos creates its own Other and becomes nothingness, void, so that, through this self-erasure in the blankness of "        ", other words could acquire their shape and meaning.

In this light, the ecology of text reveals its ethical dimension. In general, one can speak about two main ethical relationships: to the parental that precedes and creates me, and to the neighborly that co-exists and has an equal value with me. Hence the two greatest commandments of the Bible: "Love thy Creator with all your heart", and "Love your neighbor as yourself". Similarly, in a double ethical relation to humans, nature can be seen as both their mother (progenitor) and neighbor (environment).

Through "        ", the text fulfills its ethical relationship with what precedes it and is outside it. Writing falls back on to its unconscious, neglected condition in order to make it the focus of its self-reflexive practice. This process can be described by the Russian word *vossoznanie*, literally "reconsciousness", i.e. the reconstruction through consciousness, which involves the ethical recognition and theoretical reconstruction of pre-cultural beginnings in the very unfolding of culture. We can also call this process *"ecognition"*, as the recognition of the ecological premises of all human activities, an attempt to restore and honor the conditions of their possibility. The *ecognition* of "        " is a part of the debt that every writer can return to the condition of the possibility of writing.

The ethics of the relationship between the text and "          " may serve as a model for other aspects of human activities. We write and read texts, but we also speak, eat, love, and breathe. Each activity has its own "          ", its precondition. For example, the precondition for eating is hunger. To honor this precondition, people fast. Fasting is not hunger in its primordial state; fasting is a *sign* of hunger, a *citation* of hunger within the "gastronomic" text of our life. Fasting is the "          " of eating.

A precondition of our life is the instinct of breathing. It is honored in the yogic art of (non)breathing, "          ", a non-sign in the "respirational" text of our life. Yoga develops the kinds of meditation that reveal the "          " of our consciousness by restoring it to its own precondition, i.e. non-consciousness. The yogi is not unconscious as stones or plants are unconscious. The yogi is consciously unconscious, reproducing, or quoting, the "unconscious" in the "text" of consciousness. Meditation can be understood as the search for "          " in the text(ure) of our life, a reverential practice of citing the preconditions of our existence. "          " is textual yoga, a meditation on textuality that restores and honors its precondition. The present text, with many clean zones on its surface, is an experiment in textual fasting and self-purification through the sign of "          ".

Reconsciousness, or ecognition, is a selective and purposeful correlation of each activity with its own self-sacrificial foundation, which suffers a continuous self-erasure in what it founds. Ecognition is the actualization within consciousness (e.g. writing, speech, or action) of its constitutive conditions (e.g. blankness, silence, or stillness). The white that makes the text visible has to be made visible by the text: both exposed and concealed, it is a double gesture of gratitude and reverence.

Thus, "          " allows us to speak ethically about any primary condition without objectifying and verbalizing it in terms of its own consequences. "          " should not be verbalized, lexicalized, phoneticized, or in any other way forcefully appropriated by text. Ethics pressuposes incorporation without appropriation. According to Alain Badiou, "Evil in this case is to want, at all costs and under condition of a truth, to force the naming of the unnameable. Such, exactly, is the principle of disaster" (2002, p. 86). In order to designate the condition of writing, i.e. to name the unnameable, without naming it, I have to write it down, but in a different way than I write down all other words and signs: I have to write it *up* and thus elevate it over the conventional level of writing.

The two attitudes of restoration and elevation converge in the abovementioned Russian word *vos-soznanie*. The prefix "voz-" ("vos-") has two different meanings: one is that of "re-", i.e. *repetition, reconstruction, revival, renewal,* or *resurgence* of the initial conditions; and the other meaning is that of "up", i.e. a movement of ascension, elevation. The Latin prefix "ana-" has the same double meaning: *up* and *back,* or *again.* The word "analysis", derived from the Greek *analyein,* meaning "to unloosen" ("ana" + "lyein", "to loosen, to untie"), actually signifies this double procedure of going back and up, un-loosening and up-loosening. We usually understand "analysis" only in the "backward" sense, i.e. as a theoretical "re-storation" of the initial origin, or the "truth" of a thing. But "ana-" also presupposes an "upward" movement, the elevation of something to a new level of being. "Analysis" is both *re-consciousness* and *up-consciousness*: the reconstruction of what precedes consciousness and makes it possible and simultaneously the ascent of consciousness on to a new level. To "ana-lyze" something means to bring forth its origins and preconditions as the way for its further growth out of itself and beyond itself. In the ecological sense, re/up/consciousness is not merely a return to nature, which would be destructive for culture, but a progressive movement of culture, an act of gratitude and generosity, which nurtures nature by creative means of culture itself.

## "        " and art

"        " played an important role in many visual art movements of the twentieth century. When presented as an unpainted canvas, as background left unfinished in a completed work, the background moves forward and takes the place of foreground.

Kazimir Malevich, the father of Suprematism, may be considered also a founder of margin-into-medium art, i.e. the art that transforms visual margin into medium. His painting *White on White* (1918) is an image of background only slightly contrasted with the background itself, which in its turn may be an image of a larger background that surrounds the painting. The white square is presented within a frame on the background of a larger white square, which is framed on the background of a still larger background stretching beyond the painting itself.

This case of a double visual citation—a citation of a citation—can be compared to the smaller "     " placed within the larger "     ". It is possible to present "     " in different sizes, one within another, like Russian dolls. " "    "    "    "    "    ".

This citation mode—both visual and textual—can be multiplied *ad infinitum*.

A radical experiment of representation of the original blank canvas is found in the *White Paintings* of Robert Rauschenberg exhibited at the Black Mountain College in 1953. The painting exposed its own bare preconditions, usually hidden under layers of paint.

This "void-art" is not limited to an individual work and can include the entire exhibition space. A landmark of such artistic environmentalism can be seen in Yves Klein's notorious exhibition *The Void* at the Iris Clert

Gallery, Paris, in April 1958, which consisted of empty, whitewashed walls. At the opening of the exhibition, the artist handed out specially prepared cocktails that caused drinkers to urinate blue for a week. Klein said that he imagined the white gallery to be like his blue paintings, enveloping visitors in the fields of colored space.

'Emptification' later became the focal point in conceptual art, which is a continuous process of awareness and re-production of the visual "      ". For example, this device plays a very big role in Ilya Kabakov's albums, paintings, and installations. Conceptualism deviates from the traditional art by introducing texts, on the one hand, and emptiness, on the other hand, into visual space, thus going beyond the visual field simultaneously in two directions: extra-language ("       ") and alter-language (words). These polar elements are correlated and balanced, the words pointing to what remains empty and unseen. In Kabakov's painting *At the Big Artistic Council* (1983), the area of words presupposes an area of emptiness; the reader learns about the football game only from the detailed caption, while in place of the image we find only a smooth white surface of the stand (with a hardly perceptible spot in the middle). The detailed description corresponds to the blank canvas. In such trans-visual work, the visual element is bracketed out and functions as an axis of the scales with their dynamic balance between the alter-language and the extra-language elements, i.e. the detailed description and the blank canvas.

A musical manifestation (and manifesto) of "      " is found in the composition 4'33" (1952) by American composer John Cage. The score instructs the performer not to play an instrument for the duration of the piece. Although commonly referred to as *Four Minutes Thirty-three Seconds of Silence*, the composition consists of sounds—the sounds of the environment that the listener hears while the piece is (non) performed. The outside of the text moves inside, once again, framed as a separate piece.

One of the earliest examples of "      " in a literary work is *Poema Kontsa* ("The Long Poem of the End") by Vasilisk Gnedov. This poem concludes his collection *Smert' Iskusstvu* (*Death to Art*, 1913) and consists of one page that, except for the title, the page number, and the publisher's seal at the bottom, is left blank. The poem was performed: "Gnedov would raise his arm and then quickly let it fall in a dramatic gesture, eliciting stormy applause from the audience" (Wanner, 2003, p. 132). Another witness, Ivan Ignatiev, says there was a rhythmic gesticulation of Gnedov's hand from left to right and from right to left, performed so that one movement nullified the other and represented, symbolically, a self-erasure.

A poet, essayist, and Berkeley professor Lyn Hejinian once remarked: "A question has arisen among some graduate students at Berkeley as to why there is nothing in academic arts/humanities scholarship that might be comparable to the 'avant-garde' in the arts proper. That is the question we hope to explore—what might experimental criticism or avant-garde scholarship look like?" (the invitation to a conference titled 'Medium and Margin,' Berkeley, March 2009). In fact, most avant-garde movements, including Futurism, Suprematism, and Surrealism, emerged from avant-garde theories: manifestos, projects, and utopian visions. Avant-garde theory tends to precede and shape avant-garde art.

The avant-garde experiments radically undermine the foundations of all sign systems, overturning the order of subordination between their centers and peripheries. The reversal of the medium and the margin is a textual analogue and prototype of all avant-garde reversals, a signature device of the avant-garde. Thus "        " graphically represents what the avant-garde aims for: marginalizing the center, centralizing the periphery, voicing the mute, and uncovering and advancing suppressed layers of culture. Insofar as the humanities deal with texts and textuality, avant-garde scholarship can be viewed as exploration and intellectual encouragment of "        " and its infinite manifestations across discourses and disciplines.

# Problems of ecophilology

Ecophilology is a discipline that explores the role of textual environments in all kinds of settings and media, from ancient cave paintings and graffiti to contemporary electronic media. In a cursory and interrogatory manner, I will outline some issues of ecophilology.

Ecophilology considers:

The number of printed signs per square meter of living space as a measure of semiotic saturation of space.

The semiotic load of offices, streets, public places, and various cities and countries.

The textual capacity of a space: the number of posters, billboards, slogans, announcements, street signs per square mile or other unit of territory.

The length of texts. The size of a text as an ecological factor.

With the increase of textual production—the "information explosion"—the size of texts that compete for readership needs to decrease. The number of classics, the texts that must be read, increases, thus increasing the number of people—the "uneducated"—who have not read the classics.

Ecophilology also considers the ecology of various genres. For example, fragment and aphorism are ecologically pure genres: tiny texts among vast, virginal—blank—spaces.

Ecophilology is linked to the problems of time and space, or, in Bakhtin's terms, "chronotope". We should remember that "the space of the novel" means both its internal ("described") and external ("occupied") space. How intratextual chronotopes—a system of spatial and temporal imagery—are related to the extratextual chronotopes, the spatial and temporal extension of the text itself displayed in the volume of the book or in the multiplication of volumes of the same work? The ecology of book series, of anthologies, encyclopedias, and complete works—each of these megatextual wholes has its own environmental dimension.

Among the most provocative issues of ecophilology is non-reading as a passive resistance to *semiocracy*, the power of signs. Out of ten messages coming by email, seven or eight end up in the trashcan; to determine which ones, we need an undetermined amount of time. This factor is important. What is the time needed for detection of textual waste, how much reading time is necessary to establish that reading is unnecessary? What increase of semiotic procedures is required for non-participation in semiotic processes? How much do we need to read in order not to read? Minus-time and minus-space of culture.

Ecophilology helps to explain the difference between poetry and prose which derives from the various ways in which they interact with "        ". The variable, broken, zigzag layout of lines is characteristic of poetry, where the relationship between the text and "        " changes from line to line:

All happy families
resemble one another;
every unhappy family
is unhappy in its own way.

Although this text comes from a novel (the first sentence of *Anna Karenina*), it reads as poetry in this layout because the structure of its intentionality is different from that of novels. The variation of blank spaces on the sides of the lines deepens the intensity of the semantic expectation. The potentiality of meaning exceeds the actual meaning. In verse, "        " is much more expansive, occupying the larger part of the page, and is more active: each line has its own zone of "unsaid" and "undersaid." This zone is resilient, now contracting and now expanding, in inverse relationship with the length of lines.

## The paradox of invisibility and white holes

It is more difficult for "        " to manifest itself in literary texts than in visual art, where iconic signs predominate and "        " is visible, like the ground that immediately represents itself on the canvas. We do not *look* at the text in the same manner as we look at the painting: we *read* the text, interpreting and deciphering its meaning as projected beyond the material surface of the text and beyond any horizon of visibility.

Perhaps the most paradoxical aspect of the theory of visuality is the essential *invisibility* of a pure textual background. When we try to stare intently and closely at a computer monitor or a sheet of paper, we experience a strange sensation of unbearable brightness: our eyes hurt, and we instinctively narrow them in order to stop the influx of this incomprehensible energy. Paper itself is not bright enough to make one's eyes hurt, especially since the same impression is produced by dark or gray paper when it is viewed as a blank space for writing, not as a colored object. One is reminded of the inspired description of whiteness in Melville's novel *Moby Dick*:

> But not yet have we solved the incantation of this whiteness, and learned why it appeals with such power to the soul. … Is it that by its indefiniteness it shadows forth the heartless voids and immensities of the universe, and thus stabs us from behind with the thought of annihilation, when beholding the white depths of the milky way? Or is it, that as in essence whiteness is not so much a color as the visible absence of color, and at the same time the concrete of all colors; is it for these reasons that there is such a dumb blankness, full of meaning, in a wide landscape of snows …? (Melville, 1938, p. 253)

The difference between the colorful materiality of things and the transparent semioticity of writing materials, such as paper or a screen, is similar to the difference between seeing and reading. If we look at a white wall or a blue tablecloth, we perceive colors as a part of physical space. We cannot contemplate in the same way, as a material surface, the blank white paper or the blank blue screen that serve as a *background for signs*. Those make up semiotic vacuum, existing at the zero level of signification. We do not look *at* them, we look *into* them—and the more we look, the more we lose the object of contemplation. Whiteness or blueness are no longer colors of the material surface, but the depth of the sign-continuum, which is essentially colorless, for the pure potentiality of signs and meaning is colorless.

When we cease to *look* at a blank page (which is, after all, perfectly visible) and try instead to *read* its blankness, we experience a sort of dizziness. The semiotic vacuum *invites* reading and simultaneously *prevents* it, since the vacuum has no signs to read. It is this cognitive dissonance that is the cause of dizziness. From a blank page or a screen, our vision receives this mixed message: "Look at the text, not at the surface". But it is only the material surface that we find there: no text. We strain and overstrain to see beyond the colored surface into the semiotic void, which is the absent, purely intentional object of reading.

What we read in this blankness is the *intentionality* of discourse as such, its phenomenological *writability* and *readability*, while factually it remains unwritten and unread. If we want to learn *to read*, in the full meaning of the word, we need to learn to read the intentionality of writing, not only its actualization in letters.

"      " causes a semiotic shock in the reader: it is perceived not as a white spot but as a glimpse into semiotic nothingness, a *white hole* that both provokes and denies our intention in reading. The white holes of textuality may be regarded as semantic analogs of the black holes of the physical universe. The so-called vacuum described in physics is not vacuous at all. It holds a tremendous amount of energy in the form of virtual particles, perceived by some scientists as a limitless source of free energy. Similarly, the semiotic vacuum holds a tremendous amount of energy in the form of "virtual", purely potential words and meanings.

If the semantic intensity of a text equals *one*—for an actual sign corresponds to its actual meaning—then, in the reader's perception, the semantic intensity of margins approaches *zero*. For, in the absence of actual signs, there is no expectancy of potential signification. By contrast, the semantic intensity of "      " approaches *infinity*, as its potential significance is textually inscribed in the absence of an actual sign. "      " is a singular event in the life of a text. A singularity means a point where some property becomes infinite; for example, at the center of a black hole, the density is infinite.

"      " as a white hole is a singularity because it represents the potentially infinite environment of a text condensed in one non-verbal sign with its semantic density approaching infinity.

# How to read "      "?

Observe yourself while reading a text full of white holes. Your glance is instinctively drawn to and, at the same time, repelled by them, for, besides the constructive energy, you sense the destructive energy breaking up the text and hindering your perception of semantic coherence. Such is the difficulty of our direct encounter with the intentionality of writing, when it reveals itself in the rupture of the text. Gradually, the reader develops *transtextual* intentionality, paying attention to the boundaries of text, to its margins and internal blanks.

This chapter can be read as evidence of the explosive role of "      " which it attempts to describe. "      " presents a particular difficulty because we do not know how to pronounce it, unlike the pronounceable terms such as *Absolute, Tao,* or *Différance.* As we attempt to pronounce "      ", we catch ourselves filling this hesitation pause with a non-linguistic sound like 'mhm' or 'eh,' which stops abruptly, recognizing its lack of motivation and a failure of full articulation. "      " functions in our internal speech as a mechanism of disruption. The intention to pronounce "      " cannot realize itself in any phonetically motivated form. Thus, "     " is a barrier between the potentiality and actuality of speech. Stumbling over this barrier, we become aware of the automatized process of speech and start to participate in this process consciously: the very impossibility of pronunciation all of a sudden makes us realize our unconscious habit of mute articulation. "     " turns out to be a mechanism of deautomatization, or defamiliarization, not only of a specific text, but textuality itself.

As a rule, we use language unconsciously, and language itself, according to Lacan, presents the structure of the unconscious. In this light, "     ", as an unnoticed textual background, is the meta-level of the unconscious in language: the unconscious of the unconscious. By introducing "     " into a text, we become aware of this double unconscious and acquire a new consciousness of language within language. Through this white hole language exposes to our vision, voice, and consciousness whatever was previously buried in its invisible and mute depths.

From that moment on, our relationship with our own internal speech can be conducted consciously. The pause necessary for the pronunciation of "     " is gradually filled with specific meaning. At first, we look for ways to fill "     " in a traditional lexical and morphological manner, e.g. by searching through synonyms (mostly nouns) and adopting a word that seems more appropriate in a certain context, such as *blank, whiteness, void,* or *emptiness.* Then, we start articulating this word-substitute in place of "     ". However, we soon realize that a substitution appropriate for one context does not fit in another. Slowly, as contexts alternate, "     " is purified in our perception of all synonyms and fillers, and reveals to us its unique meaning in its wholeness, its holeness, its semiotic holiness, as the sign of pure (un)pronounceability, (un)readability, and (un)writability, for which there is no substitute among verbal signs.

# 6

# Semiurgy: From language analysis to language synthesis

## Sign generation and the internet

There are three types of sign activity: combinative, descriptive, and formative.

Most written or oral texts fall under the first heading. Be they the product of Shakespeare, Newton, or an illiterate person, they all consist of words combined in their own way, although the numbers of words and ways in which they are combined in literature, politics, science, or colloquial speech differ greatly.

Books of grammar, dictionaries, linguistic studies and manuals where words and the rules of their combination are described belong to the second type of sign activity. The descriptive mode goes beyond the first, practical level of language, and so functions as a language of the second order (or a meta-language).

The third type of sign activity is the rarest of all three: it does not deal with the use, or description of, signs that already exist, but introduces new signs into language; its focus is sign creation, or *semiurgy* (from Greek *semeion*, meaning "sign", and Greek *–ourgia*, meaning "work"; cf. *dramaturgy, liturgy, metallurgy*). Thus, semiurgy is the activity of generating new signs and their introduction into language[1].

---

[1]The word 'semiurgy' can be found in J. Baudrillard's *Systems of Objects* (1968), and also in the postmodern theory of communication where it is used in a very broad, unspecified way,

It is generally assumed that the creation of words and new signs is a collective, communal, and anonymous process, and that word formation can only be the result of the activity of a nation as a whole. This assumption is only partially true. In fact, word coinage is a private enterprise: someone's mouth utters a new word or a hand writes it down. Shakespeare alone added about 1500 words to English, including *critic*, *generous*, *gloomy*, *hint*, *luggage*, *manager*, and *outbreake*[2].

Ben Johnson is credited with *analytic* and *antagonist*. In 1531, Sir Thomas Elyot in *The Boke Called the Governour*, the earliest treatise on moral philosophy in English, set himself the task of purposely extending the national vocabulary by introducing new words: "I intended to augment our Englyshe tongue wherby men shulde as well expresse more abundantly the thynge that they Conceyued in their hartis (wherfore language was ordeyned)" (Baugh and Cable, 2002, p. 201) Elyot's neologisms included many masterpieces that are now staples of the English language, e.g. *activity*, *audacity*, *education*, *exactly*, *involve*, *mediocrity*, *sincerity*, and *society*.

Of course, the more a language matures, the less malleable it becomes. It is hard to believe that in the twenty-first century anybody could emulate the linguistic exploits of Shakespeare or Sir Thomas Elyot and their abundant gifts to the English language. But even one word successfully introduced into common usage can bring its inventor fame comparable with that of a poet. Such is the case with the humorist and illustrator Gelett Burgess, whose best known legacy is the word *blurb* published in *Burgess Unabridged: A New Dictionary of Words You Have Always Needed* (1914).

We use many other words with recognized authorships: *gas* (a substance), by the Flemish chemist Jan Baptist van Helmont (seventeeth c.); *serendipity* (an accidental discovery), by the English writer Horace Walpole (eighteenth c.); *psychedelic* (mind-altering drugs), by Humphry Osmond, a British psychiatrist (late 1950s); *workaholic* (addicted to work), by Wayne Oates, a Christian pastor and writer (late 1960s); and *Newspeak* (a totalitarian language), by George Orwell (1948).

In Russian, the examples of semiurgy can be found in the famous dictionary compiled by Vladimir Dal, who coined about 14,000 out of its 200,000 words, or in the poetry and fiction of Andrei Belyi, Velemir

---

meaning "sign activity in general", "production and propagation of signs". This includes combinative and descriptive activity, i.e. any semiotic activity.

[2] "In all there are 2,035 'first usage' words ... assigned to Shakespeare. My estimate is that about 1,700 of these are imaginative coinages on his part—an amazing total, by any standard. And even more amazing is the impact of these words on the subsequent development of the language. About half of them fell out of use ... . But that leaves some 800 clear-cut cases, such as *abstemious*, *accessible*, and *assassination*, which achieved a permanent place in English ..." (Crystal, 2007, pp. 140–1; see also: McQuain and Malles, 1998).

Khlebnikov, Vladimir Mayakovsky, and Igor Severianin. At the same time, this type of sign activity is still in the initial stages of its development.

Inventing new words does not mean submitting language to ideological schemes or authoritative planning, as with Newspeak, a fictional language in George Orwell's novel *Nineteen Eighty-Four*. Newspeak is an intentionally impoverished language promoted by a totalitarian state, with a greatly reduced and simplified vocabulary. Although he was aware of the dangers posed by political abuse of neologisms, Orwell believed strongly in the art of word coinage as the means to express the depths of human experience:

> At present the formation of new words is a slow process …, and no new words are deliberately coined except as names for material objects. … [I]t would be quite feasible to invent a vocabulary, perhaps amounting to several thousands of words, which would deal with parts of our experience now practically unmeanable to language. … What is wanted is several thousands of gifted but normal people who would give themselves to word-invention as seriously as people now give themselves to Shakespearean research. Given these, I believe we could work wonders with language. (http://orwell.ru/library/articles/words/english/e_words)

Individual contributions to word invention went unrecorded for millennia, so we can only see the results of centuries of "natural vocabulary selection". Indeed, the evolution of language is, in a certain sense, reminiscent of selective process in nature. According to Charles Darwin,

> We see variability in every tongue, and new words are continually cropping up; but as there is a limit to the powers of the memory, single words, like whole languages, gradually become extinct. … The survival or preservation of certain favored words in the struggle for existence is natural selection. (1871, p. 60)

It is known that the process of adaptation is based on the evolutionary variability of organisms caused by mutations. In the case of language, it is individuals who initiate creative mutations in words. The nation does not have a single mouth to pronounce a new word or a hand to write it down. There is always an individual who does this for the first time, and then the language community accepts or declines the freshly coined word.

There have been cases of several individuals independently and almost simultaneously coining new words, but this coincidence just goes to confirm the rule that the creative impulse comes from an individual, whereas the survival of a new word depends on its reception by, and adaptation to, the overall language milieu. There were times when literature as a field of individual creativity did not exist. Songs and fairy tales were passed down the generations via word of mouth. With the creation of writing, the individual authorship of literary works came into being. Similarly, with the transition to electronic networks, the folk epoch of language formation is ending, and more and more individual authors of words will appear as their individual coinages can be exposed and searched on the Web.

Before the Internet, it was difficult to trace new words back to their origins and to determine their initial meaning or the intention of their authors. With the Internet, however, it is simply a matter of pressing the search button. The Internet also makes it possible, in an instant, to send a new word out to numerous users. New formations catch on instantaneously, their growing usage testifying to their success. The Internet is an ideal medium for the registration and dissemination of new signs: verbal as well as graphic or visual. *The Internet does to language what writing at one point did to literature, i.e. undermines its folkloric foundations, moving it into the area of individual creativity*. Indeed, systematic sign formation, which checks its coinages against an existing vocabulary, becomes possible only through the electronic network.

Today writers or thinkers must have the entire Web at their fingertips. This is not only for searching information sources which can be found at the library (albeit, after more time spent looking), but also for having access to everything that has been written and registered. This allows us to check the novelty of our own sign-creations. The sign maker (or wordsmith) is more interested in what does not yet exist on the Internet than in what it already contains. Only the Internet—as the most comprehensive resource of all existing signs—is commensurable with the task of sign creation. For the transhumanist thinker, who creates new signs and concepts, new genres and disciplines that lead to paradigm shifts in thinking, the measure of novelty of signs is obtained through their comparison with the existing sign systems as they are found on the Web.

One can anticipate that, as time goes on, the *formation of new signs* will become a creative activity more prominent than the combination of the signs that already exist. With new and faster electronic ways of information processing, what at one time was the important activity of combining language signs, will gradually be more or less automatized, its value as a unique human activity reduced not only in the technological, but also the aesthetic and intellectual domains. It will lose its power of estrangement and the effect of surprise—once a prerogative of literature and philosophy. Estrangement, or the deautomatization of language, will more often take the form not of the combination of old signs, but the generation of new ones. Sign givers and sign makers will play as important a role in society as lawmakers. Sign making and law making are complementary types of activity in that the law makes everyone subject to self-restriction, while the new sign creates for everyone a new opportunity for self-expression.

Thus, we need a new discipline that would study methods of the creation of new signs. Three branches are usually identified within semiotics: semantics as the study of relationships between the sign and its meaning, or between the signifier and the signified; syntactics as the study of relationships between signs; and pragmatics as the study of relationships between signs and their users. However, there is no branch specifically devoted to the study of the creation of new signs, i.e. relationships between signs and their absence (the semiotic zero, or sign vacuum). Such a branch could be called *semionics* by analogy with such disciplines as bionics, electronics, avionics, and culturonics.

Semiurgy is the activity of generating new signs and their introduction into language. Semionics, as the fourth branch of semiotics (along with semantics, syntactics and pragmatics) is the discipline that studies the activity of generating new signs. Different areas of science, art, mass communications, and information technologies that deal with the creation of new signs could fall under semiurgy as the practice of sign formation, and semionics as the theory of sign formation.

# Creative philology and the future of culture

Semiurgy cannot be confined to the production of new signifiers; rather, it presupposes meaning formation, or concept construction. Every new word brings about a new meaning, and, with it, a possibility of new understanding and a new action. People's conduct is guided by the meaning of words. We ask ourselves, "Is the feeling we're experiencing love or not love, or is it more accurate to call this feeling *compassion,* or *friendship,* or *lust,* or *respect,* or *gratitude*?" Having decided on the exact word for our feeling, we act in accordance with its meaning, e.g., we get married or divorced, meet or leave, confess our love or lack of love. The Greek language had several words denoting different types and shades of love. We still use some of these words today, such as *eros, mania, philia, agape,* and *storge.* However, in English, as well as in many European languages for that matter, there is only one word, *love,* indiscriminately applied to the Motherland, an ice cream, or a woman. With new formations, derived from the ancient roots and refracted through the prism of prefixes and suffixes, new layers of meanings emerge, including new shades and nuances in the range of feelings, actions, and intentions. Here are some coinages that help to articulate those shades of feelings that escape the current limited vocabulary of love.

**amort** *n* (Lat. *amor,* love + Lat. *mors,* death)—the mixed love/death instinct; the union of Eros and Thanatos, or transformation of one into another; a cruel passion destroying the loved one and/or the lover.

**Amort** is the most common theme of European literature, from *Tristan and Isolde* to Oscar Wilde's *The Ballad of Reading Gaol* ("And all men kill the thing they love…")

**dislove** *v trans* (prefix *dis-* + *love*)—to have a deep negative feeling, attraction-through-aversion to somebody.

**Dislove** is a deeper feeling than "dislike", a matter of personal relationship rather than taste. **Disloving** implies a strong negative emotional connection to its human object.

I **dislove** my ex-husband, I don't dislike him. I would never marry someone I simply dislike.

**equiphilia** *n* (Gr. *aequi*, equal + *philia*, love)—indiscriminate love of many persons or things.

**Equiphilia** may be close to indifference. Equal love to many means no love at all.

Mary has hard time making up her mind. Not that she is indifferent to her admirers but she is now at the point of **equiphilia**.

**lovedom** *n* (*love* + suffix *-dom*)—the world of love, the totality of loving emotions and relationships.

Edward VIII was that rare romantic who challenged society by trading his kingdom for **lovedom**.

Your heart is large enough to love many, but can you find a small corner for me in your **lovedom**?

**philocracy** (Gr. *philos*, loving + *kratos*, power, rule)—the rule of love; love as a governing principle of social and communal life.

**philocrat**—a believer in the power of love, in love-based governance.

**Philocracy** assumes that God, who is Love, is the source of all authority. Hence, love should be the ultimate authority.

**Philocracy** is different from theocracy, which implies the power of organized religion and would be better termed *hierocracy*—government by the clergy, ecclesiastical rule.

**philophilia** *n* (Gr. *philia*, love)—love for love's sake.

Todd is a **philophile**. He does not love anybody in particular; he just enjoys being in love.

**philophobia** *n* (Gr. *philia*, love + *phobia*, fear)—a fear of love and intimacy.

> Stalin had **philophobia**: he never had a deep personal relationship, like friendship or love, with anybody.

**siamorous** *adj* (*Siamese* + *amorous*)—closely connected by a psychic symbiosis based on love.

> Have you seen this **siamorous** couple? They have lived next door for 20 years, and I've never seen them apart.
> —"Your boyfriend was flirting with that redhead". —"It's OK, we're not **siamorous**, I've been flirting with Bob, too".

I suggest calling such brand new words "protologisms" (from Greek "*protos*", meaning "first, original" and Greek *logos*, meaning "word"; cf. *prototype, protoplasm*). The protologism is a freshly minted word not yet widely accepted. It is a verbal prototype, which may eventually be adopted for public service or remain a whim of linguo-poetic imagination. Protologisms and neologisms are different age groups of verbal population. Along with the decrepit, obsolescent archaisms facing death, and strong, thriving middle-aged words that make up the bulk of the vocabulary, we should recognize neologisms as the youngsters vigorously making their way into public spaces, and protologisms as the newborns still in their cradles and nurtured by their parents. Once a protologism has found its way into common usage, it becomes a neologism. Every newly coined word, even if it is deliberately promoted for general or commercial use, has initially been a protologism; none can skip that infancy phase. As it achieves public recognition, it gets upgraded to a neologism; once firmly established in public domain, it becomes "just a word".

Over the last few years, some words that I coined, e.g., "dunch", "cerebrity", "lovedom", "chronocide" or "syntellect", have been gradually turning into neologisms, indicated by tens and hundreds of thousands of Web hits. But the majority of newly minted words are still babies, protologisms, and the word "protologism" is one of them. Or is it? With 40,000 webpages showing it on Google, can we count it as a neologism? Neologisms are a matter of convention and hard to tell from protologisms based on numbers alone. How many leaves does it take to form a heap—ten, 20, 100, or 1,000? I would suggest considering any word a neologism if it is used independently by at least ten authors and found on at least 1,000 webpages.

Innovations in technology, politics, and material culture are usually considered the privileged domains of semiurgy. However, human emotions, attitudes and relationships, as well as philosophical and religious ideas, are also in dire need of new modes of articulation. The twenty-first century with

its spirit of accelerated cultural and intellectual innovation is consonant
with the avant-garde of the twentieth century, when Symbolists, Futurists,
and such experimental writers as James Joyce and Andrei Belyi, favored
the radical renewal of language, both in its vocabulary and grammar. For
example, Belyi wrote:

> Speech that we hear, living and full of images, sparks our imagination
> with the fire of new creations, i.e. new word formations ... . The only
> life responsibility we have is word creation ... . Poetry aims at language
> creativity, while language is the creation of life relations, as such. ... The
> first experience, summoned by the word, is evocation, incantation by the
> word of a never-existing-before phenomenon; the word gives birth to
> action. (1994, pp. 133, 135, 137)

Velimir Khlebnikov, a poet and one of the fathers of transrational language
("zaum" in Russian), advanced a new avenue of creativity that he called
"*iazykovodstvo*", i.e. the cultivation of language, or "linguistry":

> Word creation does not break the rules of language. ... Just as the
> modern man populates the waters of shallow rivers with fish, so does
> linguistry makes it possible to populate language with new life, with
> extinct or non-existent words, the impoverished language waves. We
> believe that they will spark with life again as they did in the first days of
> creation. (1986, p. 627)

While theoretical linguistics can be compared to botany as the study of
plants, practical linguistics or linguistry, can be compared to forestry or
gardening, horticulture, soil cultivation, or arboreal practices[3]. In fact,
linguistic creativity (or creative philology) is the only ideology of our
time that can provide a nation with a sense of identity, linking its past
and future. Hardly any political, philosophical, or religious ideology can
unify today's society. The splits and disorders in a nation begin precisely
at the point where a certain "unifying" national idea is put forth as an
evaluative assumption with the claim for universality. It is not in an idea,
but in language that a unifying national sense can be found, but only when
language develops freely and creatively, with its roots rich in derivatives
and its crown thick. Only language can nourish our consciousness with
common meanings, making it possible for people to understand one
another. We disagree in views and opinions as expressed in acts of speech

---

[3]The term "linguistry" exists in English as a rarely used synonym for "linguistics". I use
"linguistry" in a more specific sense, i.e. to denote transformative linguistics, the practical art
of cultivating and expanding language.

(utterances, sentences, texts), but language unites us. There is nothing more deeply shared for English-speaking people than simple precious words and morphemes, like *co-, in-, un-, -ful, -ous, -ify*, and *-ness*.

Lexicology is not only the study and description of vocabulary, but also the scientific foundation of its enrichment through creative word formation, which expands the original sphere of meanings available to all members of a certain culture. Ludwig Wittgenstein famously pronounced: "The limits of my language mean the limits of my world" (*The Tractatus*, 5.6). Philology is the discipline that not only loves and studies words, but also draws on them for new thought and action by expanding the limits of language. Creative philology expands the world of a certain nation by enriching the pool of its signs and symbols, mental patterns, and modes of activity.

Roman Jakobson noted a remarkable similarity between the genetic program of an organism and the language program of the development of a culture or a society:

> Today's agenda has the study of the temporal programming role of language as a bridge from past to future. It is worth mentioning that in 1966, N. A. Bernshtein, a well-known Russian specialist in biomechanics, in the conclusion to his book had an appropriate comparison between 'the DNK and RNK molecules', which contain the codes that reflect 'the anticipated processes of growth and development', and 'the psychobiological or psychosocial structure of speech as the anticipated model of future. (Jakobson, 1985, p. 395; Bernshtein, 1966, p. 334)

The future can be described in different genres: scientific forecast or hypothesis, fortune telling, prophecy, apocalypse, a utopia, or an anti-utopia, a political or an aesthetic manifesto, or a science fiction. However, the most compact genre of future description is a new word, especially a *futurologism*. A new word does not simply describe something that is possible in the future, but also creates this very possibility by expanding the sphere of meanings enacted in language. By coining a certain word, we make thinkable and therefore possible that which it signifies. What is in language is on the mind; and what is on the mind translates into action. According to Velimir Khlebnikov, "the word governs the brain, the brain governs the hands, and the hands govern the kingdoms" (1928–33, p. 188). One simple word can be the embryo of new theories and practices, just as one seed contains millions of future plants.

The idea of the programming role of language is especially relevant in view of the discipline of *memetics*, formed on the basis of genetics, which can be defined as the genetics of culture. Memes are units of meaning or information, transferable from one mind to another through words, images, catch phrases, and quotes. Memes, as genes or viruses of meaning, are the transmitters of cultural rather than biological information, e.g. slogans, musical tunes, fashions, cook recipes, mathematical formulas, and computer algorithms. In fact, the entire history of humankind can be seen as the evolution of memes, their struggle for survival, dissemination, conquest of minds, and incorporation into material and spiritual culture. From this standpoint, "the function of the language is memes propagation" (Blackmore, 2000, p. 99).

Different levels of language are capable of different degrees of replicability. The word as a separate unit is the undisputed champion among language memes. In fact, the word is the principle meme, the most productive of all infogenes. Travelling from one mind to another, the word sows seeds for future thought and action. The word propagates much faster than a sentence or text. Not even idioms, aphorisms, or catch phrases propagate as quickly and frequently as lexical units. Even the most popular text with millions of copies in print still cannot compete with the most frequent words, which are repeated in all the texts in a given language.

A new word is like a mini-meme; it contains the strongest power of propagation, since the maximal meaning is generated with the minimal sign. Cultures that worship Logos as the Word that was before everything must also pay attention to the Neologism, or anticipation of the new word, still silent in the depths of language, until the moment when it bursts into life. In this respect, I wish to make a plea to all writers, lecturers, orators, linguists, literary scholars and teachers, and journalists. We are all users of language's treasures, drawing from it words and phrases and turning them into the means of our very existence; in this way, language value turns into monetary value. We are all dependent on language for our lives. However, language has no Internal Revenue Service agency, to which each of us must pay back with at least one new word for each thousand or tens of thousands of words we have used. And yet, we still can repay our debt (if only in part), enriching language with new words. Let it be a matter of our professional honor.

## *PreDictionary*

Semiurgy is not limited to the creation of new words; it involves a much more capacious genre—a *PreDictionary* that offers a variety of new words organized thematically, systematically, or alphabetically[4]. Generally,

---

[4]On the theory and practice of semiurgy and on the genre of predictionary see: Epstein, 2011. The predictionary is a very rare genre; nevertheless, one can find several remarkable examples of this genre in the English language: Burgess, 1914; Hitt, 1992; Faith and Adam, 2001; Wyse, 2009. In Russian, this genre is represented by my Internet project *Dar slova: Proektivnyi*

dictionaries, even those that accommodate neologisms, tend to be reactive, i.e. they reflect all words that already exist as part of language. A predictionary is proactive as it contains protologisms—freshly minted words that may make their way into the language and dictionaries of the future.

The term "predictionary" can be understood in two senses: first, as a *pre-dictionary* i.e. a draft, a beginning, or a prototype of a dictionary; and, second, as a *prediction-ary*, i.e. a collection of predictions of would-be words or words to-be, of a vocabulary hopefuls, so to speak. Thus, a predictionary has a goal of predicting and introducing new words (rather than recording those already in use) to be potentially included over time into regular dictionaries.

More specifically, the predictionary has three objectives: analytic, aesthetic, and pragmatic.

1   Analytically, the predictionary looks for gaps and semantic voids in the lexical and conceptual system of the language in order to fill them with new words describing potential things and emerging ideas.

2   Poetically, the predictionary aims to create miniature works of verbal art, micropoems, lexipoems. Filled with drama and intrigue, these novel pieces of language open new avenues for thought and imagination by provocatively juxtaposing available word-forming elements.

3   Pragmatically, the predictionary seeks to introduce new words into the language by providing examples of their usage. Each word is defined and illustrated to show its communicative value and the range of possible applications in typical situations and contexts.

---

*slovar' russkogo iazyka* (Donate-a-Word: The Projective Dictionary of the Russian Language), which has existed since April 2000 as a weekly newsletter with several new coinages in each issue circulated among 6,000 subscribers. To date, 380 issues of the newsletter have come out, containing about 2,700 new words, or "protologisms", some of which have gained wide social usage. Predictionaries can emerge on the scale of national languages, but also in certain professional areas as well. For instance, the first-ever philosophical predictionary came out in Russian: *Proektivnyi filosofskii slovar'. Novye terminy i poniatiia* (A Projective Philosophical Dictionary. New Terms and Concepts), (Epstein and Tulchinsky, 2003). Some of the terms included in this predictionary (but coined much earlier, in the 1980s–90s) have received their recognition and circulation in English, as well, e.g. "hyperauthorship", "inteLnet", "kenotype", "metarealism", "minimal religion", "postatheism", "transculture", "videocracy", and "videology". Each entry in a predictionary is also a semiurgic genre in itself that needs a special lexicographic approach.

# Magic, logic, and aesthetics of the word: The dictionary entry as a genre

Any verbal sign, in addition to its phonemes and morphemes, includes a referent, or a signified, described by its dictionary definition, as well as its actual and potential pragmatic use (according to Wittgenstein, the meaning of a word is its use in speech). Thus, to fully introduce a new verbal sign into language we need a dictionary entry. This would include the word with its definition and examples of usage.

The dictionary entry, as a semiurgic genre, is an important form of semiotic discourse that comprehensively describes a verbal sign as a unity of the signifier, the signified, and the context/usage.

The dictionary entry has barely been subject to linguistic study[5]. There is, however, a short article titled "The paradox of a dictionary entry" by Natalia Shvedova, an outstanding Russian linguist. It is noteworthy that the paper has no reference section, since there is no "prior art". According to Shvedova, the "dictionary entry is a linguistic genre that tells not only about the word itself, but also about its various linguistic environments: contextual, classificational, derivational, phraseological, and functional" (2005, p. 420). Shvedova sees the dictionary entry as a model of the entire language universe: "The macroworld of language appears through the microworld of a word, as if condensed in it. A word as a unit of language represents the entire language" [Ibid.]

The dictionary entry is a complex form, including various grammatical and stylistic markers, and etymological and historical references. However, three elements are essential to a dictionary entry: (i) the headword itself; (ii) the definition; and (iii) phrases that show how the word is used in typical contexts. Here are two examples, one from a conventional dictionary, and another from my *PreDictionary*:

**happiness,** *n.* [from *happy*]—good luck; good fortune; prosperity; a state of well-being; a pleasurable or enjoyable experience.
*All happiness bechance to thee in Milan!*—W. Shakespeare.
*I had the happiness of seeing you.*—W. S. Gilbert

**happicle,** n. (happy + diminutive suffix –icle, as in "particle," "icicle")— a particle of happiness, the smallest unit of happiness; a single happy occurrence or a momentary feeling of happiness.

---

[5]Sidney I. Landau provides a study of the dictionary work in *Dictionaries: The Art and Craft of Lexicography* (1989); chapter 3 (pp. 76–119) is most relevant to our discussion. The book is a helpful survey, but does not elaborate on the dictionary entry as a linguistic genre in its own right.

*Happicles make life worth living, even in the absence of one big happiness.*
*There is no happiness in this world, but there are happicles. Sometimes we can catch them, fleeting and unpredictable as they are.*

Three branches of semiotics embrace the three main dimensions of a sign: (i) syntactics describes the elements (phonetic, morphological, or lexical) of a sign, or a sign sequence and relationships between them; (ii) semantics describes the meaning of a sign, including any concepts and objects to which the sign refers; and (iii) pragmatics deals with the sign's uses and communicative functions.

The dictionary entry covers all these three aspects: the headword represents a syntactical unit (a set of morphemes and phonemes); the definition addresses the semantics (describes the sign's meaning); the examples reflect the pragmatics by indicating the appropriate situations and contexts where the sign is typically used.

Thus, the dictionary entry comprehensively reproduces a semiurgic act with its syntactic, semantic, and pragmatic dimensions. The creation of a new word as a sign demands much more than simply combining phonemes and morphemes in a way never used before; it also requires an explanation of its meaning and the provision of potential context(s) for its usage. Designing dictionary entries that introduce new words rather than dealing with existing ones goes beyond a purely academic pursuit. "A good dictionary thrives on the brilliance of its definitions. They have to be clear, succinct, relevant, and discriminating. They can also be elegant, humorous, quirky, and memorable. Definitions ... involve imagination and creativity, just as any other literary genre" (Crystal, 2007, p. 33).

A projective dictionary, or predictionary, is a form of especially intensive and creative semiurgic activity—a form of "linguo-fantasy",or "lexifiction". In a traditional dictionary, which is designed to define and clarify words found in texts, the reference pattern can be described as a *text—dictionary—text* sequence: we encounter a word, look for its definition in the dictionary, and then go back to the text. Projective dictionaries do not refer to any actual texts since the words in such dictionaries have never been used before. Such words relate to the language as a system, so the sequence for the reference pattern would be *(pre)dictionary—language—possible text* (one that could include a new word taken from that projective dictionary).

For example, the word *conaster* refers to the English lexicon (rather than any existing text), specifically, to those words derived from the Latin *aster* (meaning "star"), especially to the motivating word *disaster* (literally, "away from stars"). Naturally, any examples used in a projective dictionary would be made up by the author, since there is no existing text to quote them from.

**conaster** n (Lat. *cum*, meaning "with" + Gr. *astron*, meaning "star")—literally "with star", the exact antonym for "disaster" (literally "away from stars"); the fortunate outcome of an almost imminent disaster.
*There were several conasters in my life that I cannot recall without thanking God for his undeserved mercy.*

Semiurgy is a holistic activity that integrates the magic, science, and art of sign creation. A semiurgic act limited to syntactics alone (i.e. combining phonemes and morphemes into a signifier) would result in magic spells, incantation and glossolalia (speaking in tongues), often as part of mystical or religious practice. For example, reciting an unintelligible mantra would plunge the believer into an ecstatic or meditative state. What is meaningless for some may be a holy language for others.

A semiurgic act limited to semantics alone (i.e. generating concepts and ideas) would fall into the area of intellectual, philosophical, or scientific creativity.

A semiurgic act limited to pragmatics alone would be verbal art, such as poetry or prose, i.e. the art of combining words in the most expressive and beautiful way.

But, in a true semiurgic act, all of these aspects come together to make up the microcosm of the dictionary entry: the newly crafted word is the magical element; the definition is the scientific and logical component; and the example is the artistic and aesthetic component. What we call the dictionary entry is, in fact, a miniature manifestation of the entire semiosphere.

Word magic usually needs no clarity or definition of its meaning; in fact, the incoherence may even contribute to a mantra's effect. Similarly, verbalizing scientific concepts may not require artistic expression. Used separately, the three kinds of semiotic activity may interfere negatively with one another and the intended goal, i.e. the magic of the word, the scientific accuracy of the concept, and the artistry of speech. Only a semiurgic act combining sound, meaning, and usage would be a comprehensive manifestation of the semiosphere.

Three identities coexist in a semiurge: a magician conjuring up a new word from the depths of language; a scholar carefully defining the word's unique meaning; and a writer plotting a situation that would require the usage of the new word.

The process of sign creation can start anywhere and proceed in any direction, not necessarily following the '*word > meaning > usage*' path. For example, a situation or a concept may emerge and call for a new word. As soon as one of the semiurge's three identities has initiated the process, the other two must be involved as well: the magician would ask the scholar for a definition, and the writer for a plausible context. Or, the scholar may request a word for a new concept from the magician, and a convincing example of usage from the writer. The three elements are inseparable in any dictionary entry, which, for this very reason, is the most comprehensive genre that unites the magic, the logic, and the aesthetics of the word.

# Philosophy and language synthesis

Every new discipline or method of thinking, from the quantum physics to Hegelian philosophy, develops its own vocabulary. One cannot imagine, for instance, the quantum mechanics without such neologisms (words or word combinations) as *quantum, photon, quark, spin, super-conductivity, uncertainty principle,* and *matter-wave dualism.* From the standpoint of linguistics, the development of every discipline equals the continuous growth of its vocabulary as a system of signs that not only describe the phenomena of that field, but also pave the way for new ways of thinking.

Sign creation is especially important in philosophy, which searches for terms, concepts, and categories that could free our thinking from the prison of everyday language and common-sense prejudices. To think means to create a new language of intellectual wonderment and estrangement, a language that is orthogonal to common sense and critically cleansed of all clichés and meanings corrupted by everyday use. A philosopher quite often fails to find necessary words in the existing language and so coins new words or assigns new meanings to the old ones, e.g. *idea* (Plato), *thing-in-itself* (Kant), *Aufhebung* (Hegel), *Ubermensch* (Nietzsche), and *Zeitigung* (Heidegger). The language of Plato, Kant, Hegel, Nietzsche, or Heidegger is rich in neologisms expressing fundamental categories of their thought that did not fit into the existing vocabulary. Philosophy creates new terms and significations the same way that economy creates new goods and values.

In the Anglo–American philosophy of the twentieth century, the linguo-analytical approach predominated. Philosophy's main task was proclaimed to be the analysis of everyday, scientific, and philosophical language with its grammar and logical structures. At the same time, both the synthetic aspect of utterances and the task of producing more substantive and informative judgments were practically ignored.

The philosophy of language synthesis, or constructive nominalism, may be seen as a twenty-first century response to the tradition of language analysis. Insofar as the subject of philosophy—universals, ideas, or gener-alizations—is present in language, the task of philosophy is *to expand our mental vocabulary and grammar, to synthesize new words and concepts, lexical fields, and syntactical rules. The philosophy of language synthesis helps society to increase the volume of the speakable, conceivable, and thinkable, and, therefore, of the doable and accomplishable.* Thus, from language analysis, which was its focus in the twentieth century, philosophy is moving toward linguistic and conceptual synthesis—a program that was boldly unveiled in G. Deleuze and F. Guattari's books *A Thousand Plateaus: Capitalism and Schizophrenia* (1987) and *What is Philosophy?* (1996):

> [P]hilosophy is the discipline that involves *creating* concepts. The object of philosophy is to create concepts that are always new. ... In fact, sciences, arts, and philosophies are equally creative, although only philosophy creates concepts in the strict sense. ... They must be invented, fabricated, or rather created and would be nothing without their creator's signature. ... Plato said that Ideas must be contemplated, but first of all he had to create the concept of Idea. What would be the value of a philosopher of whom one could say, 'he has created no concepts; he has not created his own concepts?' (1994, pp. 5–6)

Language synthesis is a philosophical trend aimed at the synthesis of new terms, concepts, and judgments on the basis of their language analysis. Every act of analysis contains the possibility and condition of a new synthesis. Where there is a possibility of breaking a judgment into elements, there also exists a possibility of new judgments, a new combination of elements, and, therefore, a new domain of thought and speech. For instance, the judgment "stupidity is a vice" can be treated analytically, in the spirit of G. Moore, i.e. as equivalent to such judgments as "I have a negative attitude towards stupidity", or "Stupidity creates negative emotions in me". The synthetic approach to this judgment, however, positions it as a potential foundation for other, alternative and more informative, "wondrous" judgments (cf. Aristotle's idea expressed in *Metaphysics* about philosophy born out of wonderment). Analysis, as such, is intellectually trite and empty unless it provokes attempts at a new synthesis.

Let us create a possible sequence of synthesizing questions and alternative judgments regarding the statement "Stupidity is a vice". Is stupidity always a vice, or can it be considered, in certain cases, a virtue? If intelligence can be exercised for a sophisticated justification of a vice, then can innocence serve as a justification of stupidity? If stupidity is sometimes used as a means to a virtuous goal, can it then itself be considered a virtue? Mikhail Saltykov-Shchedrin, a prominent Russian satiric writer of the nineteenth century, coined a remarkable moral term that has come into general usage in Russian: "*blagoglupost*'" (*blago* + *glupost*', meaning "virtuous + stupidity"), which can be conveyed by the English neologism "virtupidity". "Virtupidity" is well-intentioned stupidity, high-sounding nonsense, or pompous triviality.

Let us take our interrogation to the next level. If stupidity, even only in an ironic sense, can be a virtue, can baseness or meanness be virtuous, as well? Or, rather, can virtuousness be mean and base? Can we speak not only of "virtupidity", but also "benemalence" (from Latin *bene*, meaning "well" and *malus*, meaning "bad"; cf. "benevolence" and "malice") as "well-intentioned meanness?" "Benemalence" appears at first sight to be a dubious oxymoron. Lack of intelligence can go hand-in-hand with good intentions, but can the same be said about the malicious and perverse intentions? Can one betray, rape, and blaspheme while having good intentions? The answer is "yes", as evidenced by the examples ranging from The Grand Inquisitor in Dostoevsky's *The Brothers Karamazov* to the exemplary pioneer Pavlik Morozov, a Soviet official hero who became notorious for denouncing and betraying his father.

Thus, as a trivial subject of analysis, the judgment "stupidity is a vice" can set up grounds for a synthesis of non-trivial, thought-provoking judgments and new word formations such as "virtupidity" and "benemalence". Language synthesis can be formally operationalized by the symbol ÷ as the sign of logical bifurcation, i.e. an alternative emerging from the analysis of the above-mentioned judgment. The elements of the judgment which precede the sign ÷ are viewed as variables, whereas their alternatives or variations that follow are the new judgments:

Stupidity ÷ is a vice.
Stupidity can be ÷ a vice (but may not be).
Stupidity can be ÷ virtue (under certain circumstances).
One of the conditions of virtue is a good intention.
Stupidity can be the product of good intentions: "Virtupidity".
Meanness can be the product of good intentions: "Benemalence".

Every element of any judgment can be questioned and substituted by another one, generating a new judgment. For instance, if the elements *a*, *b*, and *c* can be isolated in a judgment as a result of analysis, their synthesis generates the combinations *acb*, *bca*, *cba*, and *bac*, i.e. a new thought, a mental object yet to be cognized, requiring interpretation, and a new act of analysis to be followed by a new synthesis. Gottfried Leibniz considered the art of synthesis to be more important than that of analysis. For him, synthesis is defined as the algebra of qualities, or *combinatorics* "which deals with forms of objects or formulas of the Universe, i.e. *the quality* in general, or the similar and dissimilar, for formulas are the result of the combination of the initial elements *a*, *b*, *c*, etc., and this science is different from algebra, which manipulates formulas as they apply to *the quantity*, or the equal and non-equal" (1984, p. 122).

Below, I give another example of synthesizing a new concept from its analysis. *Definition* is an important term in philosophy and linguistics; analytical philosophy, for instance, requires a strict definition of all terms and concepts. However, are all concepts to be subject to definition? If every term in the definition must itself be defined, where should we stop?

The scholastic philosophers claimed that the most general concepts (the so-called *generalissima*) cannot be defined, since there is no greater category under which they may fall. For instance, we cannot define God, being, unity, essence, or other similar concepts. Locke suggested that individuals, too, cannot be defined, nor can the names of the simplest concepts. Wittgenstein argued (1994) that for terms such as *game*, *number*, and *family*, there is no clear boundary that can be used for their definition; rather, one has to understand the *use* of the term. In all these cases, is it possible, or indeed necessary, to define that which cannot be defined? If we are still required, in the name of linguistic meticulousness, to define some indefinable terms, might there be a definition that would demonstrate precisely the impossibility of a definition?

I call such a self-subversive definition, which infinitely postpones the very possibility of definition, an *infinition*. The term *infinition* is a blend of *definition* and *infinity* (both from Latin *finis*, meaning "a boundary") and signify "indefinite definition". *To infine* means to suggest many possible definitions and to recognize that all of them fail to define the complexity or fluidity of the subject. *Infinition* is for the humanities what the transcendental number, with its infinite expansion expressed by a non-periodic decimal fraction, is for mathematics: an endless approximation to, and escape from, discrete definition. The term *infinition* is an example of a linguistic synthesis based on the analysis of the concept of definition:

1  The starting point, thesis: definition is a concise description or explanation of the meaning of a word, term, or concept.

2  Analytical dissection, or logical bifurcation: a word or a concept can be definable or indefinable, i.e. not capable of being precisely described.

3  Synthesis: infinition is a definition of something that is indefinable.

Infinition is an incomplete and unfinalizable definition, an infinite process of defining something that cannot be fully or precisely defined, an endless list of possible definitions.

Certain fluid concepts in their emergent state are subject to infinition—infinite dispersal of their meaning—rather than to definition. We can find many examples of infinitions in philosophy and religious thought. For example, Lao Tse never gives a definition of Tao, but only multiple infinitions: "The Tao that can be trodden is not the enduring and unchanging Tao. The name that can be named is not the enduring and unchanging name" (*The Tao Te Ching*, ch. 1, 1–2). Pseudo-Dionysius the Areopagite offers infinitions of the Cause of Everything. "We therefore maintain that the universal and transcendent Cause of all things is neither without being nor without life, nor without reason or intelligence; nor is it a body, nor has it form or shape, quality, quantity or weight" (*Mystical Theology*, ch. 4). Jacques Derrida never defines his method of deconstruction, but only *infines* it in numerous passages.

A concept can be infined by:

1 Directly indicating that the concept cannot be fully defined;

2 Putting forward multiple definitions that succeed and erase one another and have no end, thus amounting to a long infinition;

3 Providing a self-contradictory, paradoxical definition that points out to the mutually exclusive properties of the concept (such as *perfection* and *evolution*).

The necessity of infinitions can be logically inferred from Gödel's *Incompleteness Theorem*. The most foundational concepts of any philosophical system, such as God, Being, Absolute, Spirit, Beauty, or Love, are not definable within these systems. Each discipline has its own primary concepts, such as *wisdom* in philosophy, *soul* or *mind* in psychology, and *word* in linguistics, which are subject to infinitions.

In principle, analytical and synthetic procedures are reversible. Every analysis that isolates certain elements of a judgment can be transformed into a synthesis, i.e. the recombination of these elements and the formation of alternative judgments, and also of new terms, concepts, sentences, disciplines, methods, and worldviews. Thus, the level of synthesis correlates with the level of analysis that precedes it and makes it possible. Accordingly, all analytical philosophy can be interpreted and revised by using the language of synthesis. Wherever separate elements of a judgment can be isolated, their new combinations are also possible. Each new combination describes a state of affairs which does not exist, but which is possible as part of various discourses, worldviews, futures, virtual worlds, and alternative fields of knowledge. Every language synthesis introduces a new mental state, which searches for its further implementation in new theoretical, political, scientific, and technical practices.

Synthetics must not be seen as a departure from the analytical and critical functions of philosophy; on the contrary, syntheticism is their legitimate extension and transformation.

In the analysis-synthesis procedure, the following stages can be singled out:

1 Analysis: The structure of a text or a discourse, its elements;

2 Criticism: Conceptual and verbal constraints and biases, ideological construction of a text;

3 Synthetic stage 1—combinatorial: Various alternative recombinations of elements; gaps and lacunae that are not realized, yet can be inferred from the text or discourse;

4   Synthetic stage 2—interpretative: Semantic interpretation of
    new sign combinations, search for their referents, denotative
    and connotative components; mental states and transformation
    of meanings, which can find their place in complementary and
    alternative discourses;

5   Synthetic stage 3—constructive: Constructive and experimental
    work on implementing such alternatives, formation of new terms,
    discourses, disciplines, cultural styles and practices.

The synthetic transformation and deepening of analysis might draw the
Anglo–American philosophy, where analytical tendencies dominate, closer
to Continental philosophy, which is known for its synthetic traditions and
aspirations.

The philosophy of synthesis combines two traditions that appear to be
incompatible: Nietzsche's philosophy of life and Wittgenstein's philosophy
of language, the most ambitious and radical versions of vitalism and
linguism. Syntheticism, then, is a form of *linguo-vitalism*—an increase in
the vitality of language itself, an expansion of the discursive frontiers of
the humanities in order to embrace the maximum of what can be thought
and said. The will to power specific to language is the multiplication of
speakables and thinkables.

According to the analytical tradition, philosophy is a *critique of
language*; it is aimed at the study of language games, at clarifying word
meanings, concepts, and rules used in ordinary speech, science, the arts,
or professional areas. Following this assumption, philosophy itself is just
one language game, among many others. As such, it has a further goal,
which is precisely to conduct its own language game with the utmost vigor
and breadth, constantly revising and updating its rules, thought-images,
and conceptual framework. According to Wittgenstein, language neither
tells the truth about the world, nor really reflects the facts or atoms of the
universe. Instead, it plays by its own rules that are different for various
discourses and types of behavior: "Here the term 'language *game*' is meant
to bring into prominence the fact that the *speaking* of language is part of an
activity, or of a form of life" (Wittgenstein, 1994, p. 11). For Wittgenstein,
language is not only a reflexive instrument, but also the play of life and,
as such, the expansion of life into the sphere of signs. *Play* and *life* are the
key concepts connecting Wittgenstein and Nietzsche: life should play in
language just as it does in nature or history.

Philosophy, then, as a meta-language that describes and refines the
"natural" language, is aimed not at the "truthful" analysis of language, but
at playing its own language game with an increasing intensity. Language
as a game contains in itself the refutation of pure analytism and presents
philosophy with a new task of synthesis. Philosophy no more tells the

truth about language than language tells the truth about the world. Instead, language extends the boundaries of what can be thought and said. Nietzsche's vitalism rescues Wittgenstein's analytism, endowing it with power, valor, and courage. The philosophy of synthesis manifests the will for power: not of a superman over the world, but of a superlanguage over the world of meanings.

# 7

# Scriptorics: An introduction to the anthropology and personology of writing

## Scriptorics and grammatology. From writing to the writer

I propose *scriptorics* as a new discipline dedicated to the study of the writing human—*Homo Scriptor*. One might ask, of course: Isn't the study of the history of writing already a part of linguistics? Isn't grammatology, a discipline that appeared in the second half of the twentieth century, specifically focused on writing? Didn't Derrida's famous book *Of Grammatology* (1967) put writing at the heart of humanistic study? It might even be possible to speak about the dictatorship of writing over the entire field of modern humanist knowledge; *to dictate*, after all, means "to say or read aloud in order to be recorded or written by another". To transform the oral word into the written one is a great dictatorial power, and grammatology endows writing with absolute priority over voice.

However, grammatology in its poststructural form is open to criticism precisely because of its intellectual dictatorship of writing. An alternative to grammatology is found in scriptorics. A key difference between these two disciplines is highlighted by their very names. Grammatology is derived from the Greek *gramma*, which is the participle from *grapho*, meaning "I write", and refers to something written. Scriptorics, in its turn, is derived from the Latin *scriptor*, meaning "a scribe", and refers to the writing person. *Gramma* refers to what is recorded, i.e. letters or written characters left on paper or a screen. *Scriptor*, in its turn, refers to the subject who writes and to what takes place between a writing person and paper or a screen. Thus, grammatology can be conceptualized as the science of *writing*, whereas scriptorics is the study of the *writer*, i.e. those for whom the activity of writing constitutes their very way of life and worldview. Scriptorics draws from anthropology, ethology, psychology, and the personology of writing. It focuses on writing as a human activity, whether by an individual subject or large groups of people, and also on human attitudes to writing, whether existential, national, or religious.

The activity of writing is based on a number of social and existential motivations. For example, Petrarch wrote: *Scribendi vivendique mihi unus finis erit* ("I will stop living when I stop writing"); for him, writing equalled living. At the other end of the scriptorics spectrum, we find one of the characters created by Nikolai Gogol—Akaky Akakievich Bashmachkin, for whom living equalled rewriting or hand-copying documents. There is but one thing in common between Petrarch, the genius of the Renaissance who left after his death many volumes of creative work, and Gogol's *little man* who left after his death only an ink-pot and a pen—and that is writing: for both men, it was a way of life that gave meaning to their existence. And yet, how strikingly different were the goals and driving forces behind their dedication to writing!

The key tenets of scriptorics are found in such questions as 'Who writes?' and 'For what purpose?' These questions are of practically no interest to grammatology, which virtually ignores the role of the writer. In grammatology's view, those who write, unlike those who speak, are not really present in their work; only traces are left, which are in fact traces of the writer's disappearance. Writing turned out to be an ideal object for deconstruction because, unlike oral speech, it renders writers and objects that surround them absent from their work. According to Derrida,

> All dualisms, all theories of the immortality of the soul or of the spirit, as well as all monisms, spiritualist or materialist, dialectical or vulgar, are the unique theme of a metaphysics whose entire history was compelled to strive toward the reduction of the trace. The subordination of the trace to the full presence summed up in the logos, the humbling of writing beneath a speech dreaming its plenitude, such are the gestures required by an onto-theology determining the archaeological and eschatological meaning of being as presence, as parousia. (1998, p. 71)

Archaeology views traces as the remnants of some constructs and events of the past, while eschatology views them as the anticipation of some final events, which will bring about being in its fullness when the signifier becomes one with the signified. According to Derrida, all such views are nothing but the metaphysical projections of writing in general, which presents itself only in its traceability. Thus, grammatology itself becomes impossible as a positive discipline since, as a form of writing about writing, it only leaves traces, which by their nature are subject to self-erasure.

Scriptorics takes over exactly where grammatology leaves off. Self-erasure constitutes the very being of the writer as a process of kenosis, in which humans *empty themselves out* in the act of writing. However, the writer, while absent, is still present in writing as vividly and powerfully as he or she is in living voice and gesture. Does writing not reveal as much about the scriptor as oral speech does about the speaker? Empirically absent, writers are present in writing, albeit as different subjects capable of self-manifestation in the forms of their absence. Writers die in their writings just as actors and actresses die in their characters. Writing turns out to be stronger and richer than voice, not because the author is absent in it, but because the author makes bloodless (and sometimes bloody) sacrifice to the text (cf. the relationship between blood and ink). While accepting the definition of writing established in grammatology, scriptorics takes it further by posing the following questions: "Who is the subject that is absent in writing?" and "Why do subjects substitute their life in flesh and blood by traces removed from their bodies, voices, and gestures?"

The revolutionary significance of grammatology consists in turning our attention from the writer to writing. The significance of scriptorics consists in reversing this trend and shifting our focus back—from the writing to the writer.

# The anthropology of writing

To address the anthropological nature of writing, let us look at three main forms of life. Animals are different from plants in that they discover space by freely moving from "here" to "over there". In their turn, humans are different from animals in that they discover time by going beyond not only "here", but also "now", by discovering "then" and "after that". Memory, imagination, language, and culture, in general, are all different ways for humans to overcome the limitations of their present. For humans, the past lives in their memory, and the future in their imagination. We feel the neurosis of temporality when we become anxious that time may be completely reduced to the present. Thus, the significance of a trace is formed in humans' attempts to flee from the prison of their present moment.

There are many different traces left in space by animals, which is evident in the richly developed terminology of hunting and zoology, cf. *nibbling, digging, dragging*, etc. One can also mention such traces of animal activity as holes, dens, nests, and beavers' dams. There is even a special branch of zoology called *ichnology*, from the Greek *ichnos* meaning "trace". Criminologists, archaeologists, hunters, naturalists, and paleontologists often resort to this science of traces. Much of the information about many ancient organisms was obtained by studying their traces.

Both animals and humans leave behind not only their energetic aura; their presence lingers in such traces as molecules, vibrations, or smells. The totality of all such material emanations of living beings into the outside world can be called *ichnosphere*. It would be interesting to explore, by means of modern technologies, this entire ichnosphere, which encompasses human traces not only in the world of physical objects, but also in the perception and memory of other people—from the traces of handshakes and intimate embraces to the influence of human personalities on others. There are people with a big and shiny ichnosphere, and then there are those with a smaller ichnosphere; but no one is "traceless".

Animals usually leave traces as a result of their natural activities: running, digging a hole, or building a nest. For humans, however, *ichnographia* (writing by traces) becomes the core of their existence; it is not simply the result of their life processes, it is their very goal. Moreover, while animal traces are spatial, human traces are also temporal; humans want to be survived by their traces left in time. Ichnographia is caused by the neurosis of temporality as humans strive to break through time to eternity, to live in the future for the present and in the past for the future. In other words, humans place themselves ahead of, or behind, the actual moment of their existence in the present time. Humans do not leave traces only by living their life; rather, they live their life in order to leave traces of themselves. Whereas natural, instinctive traces are what humans and animals have in common, ichnographia sets humans apart as the creatures that overcome time.

There are people obsessed with traces—*ichnomaniacs* such as Qin Shi Huang, a Chinese emperor whose mausoleum is guarded by a life-sized terracotta army. But, the most time-resistent material of all is the written word; in this sense, everyone who writes can repeat after Horace: "Exegi monumentum aere perennius, / regalique situ pyramidum altius ..." ("I have created a monument more lasting than bronze, / and higher than the royal site of the pyramids ..." Odes, Bk III, xxx)

To escape from the present—such is the anthropological motivation behind writing as a process of leaving traces. Unlike the spoken word, the text exists separately from its author to whom it becomes unfaithful at any moment with whoever happens to be closer—a reader, a critic, or an interpreter. The most human characteristic is one's ability to become alienated from oneself. Humans forget themselves in what they write and, at the same time, create something by which they are remembered. The absence of the one who writes in what is written is as significant and human(e) as the presence of the one who speaks in what is spoken. To be human is to *simultaneously* create the forms of self-expression and self-erasure, to be here-and-now and to be elsewhere and afterwards.

Let me refer to the ideas of Michael Polanyi—a British epistemologist and scientist known for his concept of personal knowledge. Contrary to positivism as the ruling methodology of science in the first half of the twentieth century, Michael Polanyi argued that any form of knowledge, no matter how "factual", contains a tacit subjective assertion. For instance, if it is written in a textbook that the Earth rotates around the Sun, this statement contains a personal attitude of the author of the textbook to the fact stated. The subtext of this seemingly trivial statement could be read as follows: "I am confident that this is so; I believe it necessary to inform you about this; you need to know this fact". According to Polanyi, "The concept of commitment postulates that there is no difference, except an emphasis, between saying '$p$ is true' and 'I believe $p$.' Both utterances emphatically put into words that I am confidently asserting $p$, as a fact" (Polanyi, 1962, p. 333).

If one follows this logic, then one can find in *any* written message the following hidden personal assertion: "I am now with you even though I am not here. I have overcome distance and time so I can pass to you, and everyone reading this, something that I consider necessary for you to know. What I want to pass to you is so important that my voice and physical presence are not powerful enough, and for this reason, I resort to writing. I want this writing to be passed on to others independently of me, even after I am gone". Such is the implied premise of a written message, especially in its printed form. One might say that this is an anthropological, not individual, premise of written communication as it applies to all those who write, regardless of their personal intentions.

The act of writing implicitly contains the meaning of sacrifice, one's self-erasure for the sake of the other. It is substitution that lies at the basis of the sign, as argued by René Girard (1987) in his theory of the roots of semiosis going back to the earliest sacrificial rituals. The guilt of those performing such rituals is transferred to the innocent victim. The primary act of signification evolves in the rituals between the sacrificed, who serves as the signifier, and the sacrificer, who serves as the signified:

> The imperative of ritual is therefore never separate from the manipulation of signs and their constant multiplication. ... Driven by sacred terror and wishing to continue life under the sign of the reconciliatory victim, men attempt to reproduce and represent this sign; ... and it is there that we find the first signifying activity that can always be defined, if one insists, in terms of language or writing. (Girard, 1987, p. 103)

In the light of such understanding of writing, the conscience of those who write can never be completely clear; they always have something to hide because they are aware of substitution, which may take the form of a pen or computer keys penetrating the "innocent" surface of a white sheet of paper or a computer monitor. What is sacrificed in such acts of writing? It is the one who writes, for any scriptor is split into the victim and the vicitimizer. All scriptors sacrifice a part of their present life to some other time and space so that their writing could find its reader and will thereby be resurrected. As scriptors, we all die in our writing, thus punishing ourselves for a life that has been unworthy or unfulfilled. This way, we redeem our sin of temporality, trampling death by death. By killing an innocent victim, in this case the clean surface, white paper, the writer purifies oneself and thus gains the grace of living through future generations. Writing is both repentance and self-punishment, and those who write, no matter how sinful their life may have been, constantly, and mostly subconsciously, subject themselves to this ritual. They burn letters on themselves like a tattoo on a victim's body, which is the oldest form of writing.

Therein lies the profound anthropological meaning of writing. Sacrifice as redemption of guilt calls for new and newer signs; it requires the substitution of the guilty by the innocent, the signified by the signifier. Such is the never-ending relay race of writing, in which the one who writes is substituted by what is written. This sacrificial meaning can be traced in the creative pangs of writing. It can be found in the metaphors of the pen as a weapon. There are many testimonies to that effect; here is one by Jean-Paul Sartre: "For a long time I took my pen for a sword; now I know we are powerless. No matter. I write and will keep writing" (1964, pp. 253–4). The pen is but a sign substituting the sword; however, such substitution is crucial in the history of writing as a sacrificial activity. It is felt in the psychological difficulty of making the first mark on the blank page or screen. The sacred power of substitution is not effective unless the victim is pure and innocent.

Gradually, the human victim was replaced by the animal victim; the animal skin was then replaced by the parchment made from it; the parchment replaced by papyrus and then by paper, both made from plants; and now paper replaced by the screen. Such constant replacements are inherent to the very nature of writing. Whatever the tone of one's writing—ironic, critical, or aggressive—the meaning of writing as a formal act is always sacrificial. One sacrifices one's very skin as it turns into paper; one sacrifices one's eyes as they turn into a computer screen; and one sacrifices one's fingers as they turn into a keyboard. One dies here and now for the sake of the Other, to appear on the other end of writing wherever the reader is found.

Scriptorics makes a contribution to anthropology by presenting humans as sacrificial signs of themselves and, by that virtue, creators of external signs. Because of their nature of "being-instead-of-themselves", humans set off a chain reaction of replacements, turning the world into a semiosphere, a constant interplay of signs and meanings. Thus, to view writing without any relation to those who write is to miss its essence and to neglect the crucial link between semiotics and anthropology. The sign can be itself only insofar as it is not itself; a person can be oneself only insofar as he or she is not oneself.

# The personology of writing

In addition to the anthropological premise, writing is also characterized by the psychological and personological motivation. Following the German psychologist Wilhelm Wundt, the Russian psychologist Lev Vygotsky emphasized a key difference between written and oral speech: " ... [T]he mental functions which form written speech are fundamentally different from those which form oral speech ... . It is not a simple rendition of oral speech in written signs ... . Written speech is the algebra of speech, the most difficult and complex form of intentional and conscious speech activity" (1993, pp. 204–5). In algebra, there are no concrete numbers or units of measurement; instead, one finds abstract symbols that can be substituted by any number. Similarly, writing is abstracted from concrete situations of oral speech and the presence of signifieds as well as the speaker. "The situation of written speech ... requires a double abstraction from the child: an abstraction from the auditory aspects of speech and from the interlocutor" (Vygotsky, 1993, p. 203). It is the abstract character of written speech that makes its motivation difficult for children to understand: " ... *the motives that would cause one to resort to written speech are even less accessible to the child when he begins to learn to write*" (Vygotsky, 1993, p. 203).

Six- or seven-year-old children do not yet see any personal need for writing taught in elementary school; everything that they want to express can be expressed through oral speech. When does the need for writing first appear in human development? This need arises when the period of the "golden childhood" comes to an end, i.e. when the child is about to enter adolescence. At this turning point, the child loses a sense of immediate unity with the outside world and becomes aware that such unity is irrevocably gone and cannot be brought back. As a result, the young adolescent is overcome with an acute awareness of fleeting time, feels lonely and separated from everyone else. This usually occurs between the ages of 11 and 14. It is at this time that one often starts keeping a diary, feeling thc need to express oneself in writing in order to compensate for the lost connection with one's friends, parents, and the world in general. Thus, the psychological motivation for writing appears much later in life than its technical skills acquired in school; it appears together with self-reflexivity when one is split into the subject and the object. Writing is a sign of this split, when one no longer expresses oneself through voice, but recreates oneself outside of oneself, as it were, objectifying oneself in text. "My text" can be seen as the "I-outside-of-myself", the "not-I" that I can write and rewrite, defying the power of time and constraints of space.

Let me quote one of the first entries in Anne Frank's *Diary*, which reveals very well the relationship between one's motivation to write and a certain stage in the development of one's personality:

> I feel like writing, and I have an even greater need to get all kinds of things off my chest. 'Paper has more patience than people.' I thought of this saying on one of those days when I was feeling a little depressed and was sitting at home with my chin in my hands, bored and listless, wondering whether to stay in or go out … . Now I'm back to the point that prompted me to keep a diary in the first place: I don't have a friend. Let me put it more clearly, since no one will believe that a thirteen-year-old girl is completely alone in the world. And I'm not … . No, on the surface I seem to have everything, except my one true friend … . This is why I've started the diary. To enhance the image of this long-awaited friend in my imagination, I don't want to jot down the facts in this diary the way most people would do, but I want the diary to be my friend, and I'm going to call this friend *Kitty*. (June 20, 1942). (Frank, 1997, pp. 6–7)

Thus, the crisis of adolescence becomes the personal motivation for writing, which tends to happen five or six years after one is exposed to these skills in the first year of formal education. This new motivation is associated with the "'complex of the teenager" and the neurosis of passing time, when one feels the need to put on paper everything that can no longer be expressed immediately through oral speech. To preserve one's being in the alienated world, one turns to writing as an alienated and "abstract" form of communication; from this standpoint, writing can be seen as the speech of a lonely person. The absence of the writer in what is written is not a mark of depersonalization; on the contrary, it is the most acute and adequate form of expressing one's personality.

# The future of writing

The process of writing is not just a solitary human activity; the entirety of humankind progresses by increasingly putting its being into various forms of writing, predominantly electronic ones. *To be* means *to write*; as a result of creating signs, the scriptor transcends one's body and becomes a part of the global semiosphere. By spending more and more time at the computer, and thus converting their own being into writing, people become professional scriptors. Imprinted with letters and digits into the World Wide Web, virtual cities, stores, banks, universities, books, publishing houses, clubs, and professional communities all become our very substance as well as the horizon of our being. There is a growing class of people who write, or scribe, or type, or publish. This class needs its own class self-consciousness, which eventually may be found in scriptorics.

But, are humans themselves not imprinted into this world according to the rules of their genetic code? Can it be in the genetic code that we should look for the original motivation for writing, which turns the world into a universe of characters? Perhaps the written source of everything living can be found in the genetic code, according to the scientific view, or the Word that created the world, according to the view presented in the Bible. We subconsciously feel that we ourselves have been inscribed into the world, so we try to verbalize and articulate our being further into a system of characters and digits that somehow correspond to those signs in which our being was written in the first place. In this light, it is not surprising that (genetically) *written* organisms become, through the cultural activity of humans, (textually) *writing* organisms; in other words, humans turn the world into writing from which they themselves came into being. Perhaps a human being can be viewed as a bilingual *geno-scriptal* dictionary, which translates from the language of genes into the language of writing. As humans become aware of their own nature as a biologically written message sent to future generations, they see in their foundation the Logos, which first created the world and then humans themselves.

Writing and print increasingly turn into direct means of industrial production. If one is to believe the technological projections for the not too distant future, in the next several decades plants and factories will come to function as nanoprinters producing any materials and objects according to required specifications. *To produce an object will mean to write it and print it out.* In the foreseeable future, everyone will be able to print out 3D objects of the real world from their home computer: from items of clothing to furniture to robots. It will become possible to print out entire houses, streets, cities, or, for that matter, an entire planet, as long as there is someone who needs that object and there is an address to which it can be sent. It will be enough to put into a computer the complete information matrix of any desired entity, which can then be produced from any material, be it air, soil, garbage, or dust, since everything is assembled from particles and atoms.

The relationship between writing and the world is inversely proportional: as writing grows in its powers to embrace more and more of the world, the world of writing itself shrinks to the size of memory chips taking up less and less space. I always carry a 16 GB flash drive with me: everything that

I have written, including different versions of many works, takes up only half of that space, still leaving enough memory to store everything that I will ever write. It is somewhat humbling to hear the entire output of your creative life rattle together with a bunch of keys in your pocket. However, with gadgets becoming smaller and smaller, each person will be able to carry the entire humankind in a pocket, everything ever written in all languages. Perhaps, one will not even be carrying it in a pocket, but in one's brain as a microchip.

As predicted by Ray Kurzweil, a famous cyberinventor and futurist, even the human body may undergo a similar reduction in size and fit into a flash-drive, along with its complete description and assembly guide. According to Kurzweil, the human organism is a pattern of information that remains invariant throughout one's life while its material substance constantly changes. The information of such a pattern, therefore, can be translated on to any other substance, e.g., a computer's hard drive or a flash drive, so that unlimited copies can be printed out and sent through communication networks. And so "we will ultimately be able to upload this pattern to replicate my body and brain to a sufficiently high degree of accuracy that the copy is indistinguishable from the original" (Kurzweil, 2005, p. 383).

There will be no need for the body itself; why bother with this cumbersome, vulnerable, and perishable shell if the patterns of all its information can be carried out in just one microchip? Perhaps in the future, it will become a form of hedonism to have a body, and only a selected few will be allowed this luxury. After all, biological bodies require food, heat, energy, transportation, and many other material resources. Would it not be more convenient for the suprarational humankind of the future to keep most of its intellectual resources in the compact form of microchips or intelligent molecules, rather than full-fledged bodies? As there are now paperless offices and banking systems, in the future all these enterprises may become bodiless as well.

There is a direct theoretical link between grammatology, with its premise of the disappearance of humans in writing, and the futurology of self-acting computer programs. Such is the eerie image of our civilization as a self-sufficient world of "writing without writers". With the explosive development of the universe of writing, and simultaneous reduction of its corporeo-material substance, it becomes clear that grammatology can generate not only its own (anti)metaphysics, but also its (anti)eschatology. If writing as "the origin of the origin" (Derrida) can produce, and even do without, the writer, perhaps humans will one day simply disappear as a result of the increasing dehumanization of the universe of signs. Poststructuralism prepared the intellectual ground for technological poshumanism. According to Roland Barthes, "the modern scriptor is born simultaneously with the text, it is in no way equipped with a being preceding or exceeding the writing, it is not the subject with the book as predicate" (Barthes, 1977, p.

145). On the contrary, the scriptor should be viewed as the text's predicate. It is the text that "writes the scriptor" rather than the other way around; in other words, the scriptor is generated by the text.

Thus, the axioms of grammatology open up new perspectives of the posthuman technological evolution in its truly eschatological scope. This scope goes beyond the traditional, pre-Derridian eschatology, which conceptualized the end of history as the realization of all signs, writings still to be actualized in the fullness of being. The perspectives opened up by grammatology point to a future when being turns into signs no longer in need of any signifieds objects or signifying subjects (humans). Kurzweil predicts that by the end of the twenty-first century the world will predominantly be inhabited by intelligent computer programs moving from one machine to another through electronic networks. Such programs will be able to physically manifest themselves in the form of robots while having control over a large number of their programmable *robodies*. What used to be traditionally considered "the subject" is to dissolve in information flows through electronic networks.

When confronted with such grammato-eschatological visions, it should never be forgotten that anyone who writes is still larger than writing, which is a result of the author's sacrificial self-erasure. Generally speaking, there is an internal contradiction in the notion of a creator, because it is only through absence that a creator is present in all creations. A creator is at the same time less and more than oneself, striving towards zero while disappearing in creations, as creator-0, and also striving towards infinity through creations, as creator-$\infty$. Grammatology focuses on the 0-status of the creator, showing how those who write become smaller and smaller compared to their creations until finally disappearing in them. Scriptorics focuses on the creator-$\infty$, highlighting the growth of the writer towards new forms of subjectivity.

The subject matter of scriptorics includes not so much real-life human subjects putting a pen to paper or tapping on a computer keyboard, but rather those forms of suprasubjectivity or transsubjectivity that come into being as a result of writing. Scriptorics deals with (a) real-life human subjects and their concrete acts; (b) human subjects as creators of their own empires of writing; and, most importantly, (c) similarities and differences between such subjects, one striving towards zero in relation to texts, and the other one striving towards infinity.

Franz Kafka observed this multi-layered structure of subjectivity in his own writing: "I write differently from what I speak, I speak differently from what I think, I think differently from the way I ought to think, and so it all proceeds into deepest darkness" (1977, p. 10). Scriptorics recognizes this "I" underlying every act of writing, but it also recognizes the differences inherent in multiple "I's", the deepest darkness of subjectivity. The latter is lost in both the existentialist reduction of the writer to his or her ego and in the grammatological elimination of the writing subject. Whereas grammatology can be said to have anticipated the tendencies of the dehumanization of information technologies, scriptorics may be destined to map out new possibilities for their (re)humanization at the level of the supraempirical subject.

# By way of a conclusion: The return of a (different) subject

Most decisively, the subject was expelled from the humanities by post-structuralism in the area of philosophy of writing. Scriptorics brings the subject back to the same territory of writing along with its increased role in the new humanities paradigm. Today we witness a growing appreciation of writing as part of human self-identification. Furthermore, there is an increased interest in the most subjective, intimate written genres as forms of self-knowledge and self-creation, such as a personal diary, a blog and a vlog, a confession, a memoir, an autobiography, a life story, and any other individual empires of writing created by their "emperauthors". The fact that an average person today enjoys a multiplicity of online avatars and nicknames does not annul the problem of the subject. Instead, the problem of hyperauthorship, the excess of simulated and fictitious authors over the actual writing personality, is made more intriguing because subjects can never be fully objectified, i.e. identified with one of their empirical instantiations that appear on the Internet. [1] According to Ray Kurzweil, "in virtual reality we won't be restricted to a single personality, since we will be able to change our appearance and effectively become other people. Without altering our physical body (in real reality), we will be able to readily transform our projected body in these three-dimensional virtual environments. We can select different bodies at the same time for different people" (2005, p. 314). The multi-layered structure of a human subject will find increasingly more adequate representation in the growing number of virtual and progressively real-like avatars. Every human being will become a complex multividual in the future, just as in the past the writer's world was complex with its multiplicity of fictional characters

It must be emphasized that the return of *Homo Scriptor*, as witnessed today, only in part repeats the events of the 1930s–60s, when the existential philosophy, as represented by Heidegger and Jaspers, Sartre and Camus, restored the subject's rights and rejected the essentialism of such trends as idealism, materialism, and positivism. In this light, it is important to

---

[1] On the problem of hyperauthorship see Epstein, 2008; 2012.

separate scriptorics not only from the grammatological understanding of writing without the subject, but also from the existentialist understanding of the subject as presence. What distinguishes the modern day personology from the personalism and existentialism of the 1930s–60s is its understanding of the person as non-presence, i.e. a process realized through sign system and especially writing that cannot be identified with any choice of self in a situation outside of writing.

According to existential philosophers such as Jean-Paul Sartre, one can make one's choices with the help of a sword or a pen, through courage or cowardice, heroic feats or illness, or by political or aesthetic engagement. Scirptorics as a new personology of writing is broader that this existential position and, at the same time, more subtle. The subject of writing is not simply an individual looking at a sheet of paper or a computer screen; this subject is not really present, at home, at work or at battle, and so cannot be subject(ed) to empirical or existential verification. Scriptorics looks at any scriptor as the *transsubject* incorporating a multitude of persons that play with, and compete against, one another. For example, Alexander Pushkin as the transsubject, known to us through his biographies as well as all his written creations, incorporates numerous persons that substitute him, while absent or else partially present in real life, e.g. heteronyms or hypoauthors such as Ivan Belkin, John Wilson, Ippolito Pindemonte, the narrator of *Evgeni Onegin*, or the lyrical hero of *The Bronze Horseman*. The transsubject is the person put in numerous quotes, the hyperauthor of all his hypoauthors, the subject of all his substitutes, and the face of all his masks. The transsubject has more in common with Gilles Deleuze and Felix Guattari's creator of *conceptual persons* than Jean-Paul Sartre's *existential subject*.

We are only beginning to learn how to properly speak about the transsubject—about, for instance, the Shakespearean or the Tolstoyan as subjective categories of writing itself. We are still learning how to overcome the two familiar modes: the biographical and existential language of the *subject outside of the writing*, and the grammatological language of the *writing outside of the subject*. It is important to realize that the subject of writing returns in its absence, having passed through the looking glass of quotes and substitutions.

# PART THREE

# Humans and machines

# 8

# The fate of the human in the posthuman age

## Humanology and technology

### Technohumanism vs posthumanism and antitechnicism

There are three major positions regarding the meaning of technology in human life and the technological perspectives of humanity.

One is *posthumanism*: the belief that human beings, as a biological species, will be superseded and archaized by intelligent machines. To cite Ray Kurzweil, "By the 2030s the nonbiological portion of our intelligence will predominate, and by the 2040s … the nonbiological portion will be billions of times more capable" (2005, pp. 201–2). Thus, biological humans are to be outnumbered and increasingly ruled by artificial intelligence as the most advanced form of civilization.

Another position is *antitechnicism*, as represented by a well-known tradition of Western thought, which is nostalgic of the past and suspicious of the future and is exemplified by philosophers such as Jean-Jacques Rousseau and Martin Heidegger. This view regards technology as subversive of humanity while defending humanism against the onslaught of soulless and ontologically empty technology.

The third position, which I find to be the most adequate one, is *technohumanism*, i.e. the belief that, by creating machines in many respects surpassing human capacities, our species is expanded rather than merely superseded. For technohumanism, technology is a mode of affirming humans through their self-denial. Great achievement demands great sacrifice.

I will draw a parallel from aesthetics. When an artist creates a character so vivid that it appears to exist independently from the creator, as a living entity of its own, it is the artist's triumph rather than defeat. Creativity is an act of self-giving. The creation of artificial beings, which may exceed the human capacity for calculation, problem-solving, mathematical and perhaps even poetic creativity, is not a denial or a defeat of humans, but rather their greatest triumph. Technohumanism provides a way of upholding humans as a species through technology as an artistic creation of the highest order.

## Technohuman and superhuman

Nietzsche's heroic and tragic dream of the Superman exemplifies this third position of human self-creation:

> I teach you the Superman. Man is something that is to be surpassed. What have ye done to surpass man?

> All beings hitherto have created something beyond themselves: and ye want to be the ebb of that great tide, and would rather go back to the beast than surpass man? ...

> The Superman is the meaning of the earth. (Nietzsche, 2008, p. 47)

We can envision this Superman as a technologically and genetically enhanced human, a self-creation of a techno-species out of a bio-species. When Nietzsche claimed that "All beings hitherto have created something beyond themselves", which beings did he have in mind? Flies? Goats? Tigers? It is a unique capacity of human beings to create things beyond themselves, e.g. paintings, sculptures, or poems, which are more permanent, powerful, and beautiful entities than their mortal creators themselves.

This idea is already present in D. S. Halacy's book *Cyborg: Evolution of the Superman,* published in 1965. The cyborg, as a technologically enhanced human, represents the peak of this creative capacity. The cyborg is not simply an artificial object, but also a new *subject*, in which a new being capable of learning and intellectual growth is manifest. There is no contradiction between technohumanism and humanism because the most human feature of humans is to transcend and technologize themselves.

# Technohuman and panhuman

Now that humans expand their abilities to the world of inanimate objects and instruments, they become more human than ever before, truly *panhuman*. The term "panhuman" (*vsechelovek* in Russian) was coined by Dostoevsky and used only once in his speech on Alexander Pushkin, referring to the comprehensive and all-responsive genius that embraces qualities of various national, cultural, and psychological types. Dostoevsky's own panhuman characters, like Nikolai Stravrogin in *The Posessed* or Dmitry Karamazov in *The Brothers Karamazov*, combine the low and the high, the good and the evil, the saint and the sinful, the angel and the beast—all polarities of human nature and everything that lies in between.

In the context of electronic and biogenetical technologies, the notion of *panhuman* acquires a new meaning: the holistic entity that combines properties of a universal machine with the properties of a human individual—a *humachine*. This term first appeared in the cover story of *Technology Review*, MIT's magazine of innovation, entitled *Humachines*. The word was coined to describe the symbiosis developing between humans and machines:

> A first example of a humachine begins with a Canadian teenager, Steve Mann, tinkering with imaging and computing systems that can be worn on his body. His first effort is a burdensome rig that blisters his feet when he wears it – and causes people to cross the street when they see him coming.... Today, Mann is a professor at the University of Toronto, having worn computing gear of his own design virtually every day for the last 15 years. (*Technology Review*, May–June 1999)

I believe it would be more precise to call this relatively superficial type of gear a "corputer", blending "corpus" (the Latin for "body") and "computer". A *corputer* is a corporeal computer, i.e. an electronic prosthetic device that, through many interconnected microchips and artificial neurons, becomes a part of the human body. It could be easily projected that in the future computers will be transformed into corputers and integrate with human bodies. A "humachine" suggests a much deeper level of integration between biology and technology: the resulting entity is half-human and half-machine.

At any rate, we usually view the process of such computerization as the transfer of human functions to machines, but a different understanding is possible: the history of civilization as a process of the humanization of machines, from the wheel to the computer to the human-like intelligent robot. From such a viewpoint, with the accelerated pace of cybernetic technologies, the phenomenon of humanity does not disappear. On the contrary, human beings overcome their biological limits, perceiving and transforming the world in those dimensions where previously only machines were able to penetrate. A microscope, a video camera, a computer—all of these devices will gradually become parts of the human organism.

Of course, the question arises whether such technologically enhanced, potentially ubiquitous, and perennial human beings will remain human in the traditional sense? Will they laugh, suffer and feel anguish, longing and inspiration? Or, will they be ashamed of their human ancestors, just as humans are ashamed of their bestial and brutal instincts. Will the technologically enhanced human beings be more or less human than they are in the present condition?

In comparison with the depth of contradictions in a new bio-techno species, the struggle in the soul of the Dostoevskian panhuman may appear shallow. Can one possess the speed of light or the mobility of a wave while still preserving homesickness? Can we view fat cells in the internal organs and still enjoy the touch by another being? Can we know "everything" about others, including the details of their intestines and genome, and still be in love with them? Is it possible to be informationally transparent to others and, at the same time, preserve a feeling of mystery and shame? In other words, is it possible to be fully a machine and fully a human being without one suppressing the other?

There are potential new tragedies in the proud aspirations of future humans for technically endowed freedom and power. As Martin writes, "The sin of the hero of Greek tragedies is hubris, leading him to ignore warnings from the gods and thus invite catastrophe. We now have new stories for Greek tragedies, grander and stranger than those of ancient times" (2007, p. 272). The source of tragedy, however, is not only the will of humans to transcend the biological boundaries of their species, but the objective contradiction between the constituents of this enhanced being—between the human-like and machine-like qualities of technohumans as mortal creatures embracing the potential for immortality.

If we see a future human being in this perspective, as a possibility of a new harmony and a new adversity in the relations between the human organism and mechanism, between the born and the created, then we should acknowledge that we are just distantly approaching this gigantic technohuman figure that would exceed the scale of Shakespearian and Dostoevskian tragedies.

# Anthropology, the humanities, and humanology

A new map of the three main areas of human studies can thus be drafted, made up of anthropology, the humanities, and humanology.

Anthropology studies humans as a biological species, whose uniqueness is built into their cultural evolution. The objects of anthropology are the physiological, racial, ethnic, genetic, and cultural properties of *Homo Sapiens*, its origins and transition from nature to culture. Anthropology deals mostly with the early, primitive, syncretic forms of culture, in its connection to, and contrast with, nature.

The humanities study humans as the creators and masters of the cultural, semiotic universe. The humanities deal with the purposeful endeavors of humans in various developed and specialized cultural areas, such as philosophy, literature, art, history, or psychology. Hence the very term *humanities*, being plural, indicates the variety and differentiation of human capacities.

Finally, humanology (or techno-humanology) studies humans as part of the technosphere, which is created by people, but which outgrows and controls them. If anthropology studies the distinctive features of humans among other living creatures, especially higher primates and hominids, then humanology studies their distinctive features in comparison to other intelligent beings, such as cyborgs, robots, and their gendered varieties, e.g. androids and genoids. Humanology is a mirror-image of anthropology since both disciplines deal with humanness in a liminal position: the latter focuses on humans evolving from nature, while the former focuses on humans evolving into artificial forms of life and intelligence.

Another occasionally used name for this new disciplinary field is "posthuman studies", which, in my view, is less appropriate than *humanology*. "Post-" seems to suggest that humans have receded into the past. However, as I have discussed in the first chapter ("From 'Post-' to 'Proto-:' Toward a New Prefix in Cultural Vocabulary"), the phenomena described as "post-" can be properly reinterpreted in terms of "proto-" as the anticipation of the future rather than successors of the past. The word "posthuman" sounds like "posthumous" and has similar underpinnings. It appears dubious, if not inadequate, as a term to denote the process of technological enhancement of humans. The term *humanology* suggests that humans will not be replaced, to use the old defeatist language, but instead supplemented and enriched by technological intelligence. Humanology looks at humans at the threshold of this double transformation as they are giving their intelligence to machines while gaining new possibilities through this sacrifice. *Humanology* has a double meaning: a) the study of humans; and b) the synthesis of "human" and "logos", the human beings and the world of information understood as instantiation of Logos (the Greek term for "word", "speech", "account", "thought", and "reason"). Thus, humanology is the study of humans enhanced and transformed by Logos.

Humanology is a discipline that studies the (self-)transformation of humans in an advanced technological society. Humanology explores human specifics in the artificial environment where machines undertake many functions previously performed by humans, such as labor, calculation, and management. Studied in this light, humans are only one of the inhabitants of the noosphere as the sphere of reason and thought, along with cyborgs, robots, computer–based intelligent beings (artilects), and self–controlling programs capable of creating their own physical bodies. Humanology arrives at a methodological point of observation from which it can consider humans in the framework of non-biological forms of intelligence, as an element of a more comprehensive paradigm.

Strikingly, the globalization of humankind, i.e. the unification of nations in technological, economic, and cultural integrity, occurs simultaneously with the specification and even "nationification" of humankind, as one of the subspecies of intelligent beings. Such an inscription of humans into a larger class of beings both narrows and expands their significance while highlighting their unique role. Earlier, as a non-systematic phenomenon, humans were both the only subject and the sole object of the humanities. By approaching humans as a member of a larger set, humanology enriches our discourse on humanity, and therefore constitutes itself as a new discipline at the border of the traditional fields of the humanities.

# Humanology and ecology. The human environment

As technology, machines and computers move into the traditional domains of human thinking and action, the human being is perceived more and more as something rare, strange, irregular, and surprising, with an additional flavor of nobility and distinction, like a fine old wine. A more advanced technical civilization is necessary in order to start seeing humans as part of the ecological system. In the past, we used to assign only plants and animals to this ecological system. The body manifestations, such as touch and handwriting can now be viewed as belonging to the *paleonoic* era of civilization, when humans mostly functioned as natural beings.

Handwriting is but one small example of a recently formed humano-logical area; it is a remnant of the "wild culture" in a world of computerized word processing. A hand accustomed to pressing keys with ready-made characters all of a sudden rediscovers its own humanness in the motion of writing. Earlier, the act of writing was not usually perceived as intrin-sically human because it was charged with the function of information transmission. In the computer age, however, humans have delegated this function to a machine, and so handwriting is rather seen as an exotic display of human corporeality. Writing is a process of the revelation of the personality, an intimate *mani*-festation of psycho-motoric qualities of the writer. It is a ritual of the hand, a variety of the art of dance performed by one limb, not the entire body. The phenomenon of writing that has been around for millennia becomes an object of humanology only now, precisely as a result of its redefinition as an outdated method of written communication, an instance of the tactile and gestural capacities of the human body, a relic of a proto-informational civilization.

Now that we have caught a glimpse of distant technological development, we can look back from that panoramic perspective at our proto-digital habits and identities as isolated relics in the civilization of the future. Already in the eighteenth-twentieth centuries, primitive tribes and archaic cultures became an object of ecological attention and nostalgic sentiment. Gradually, modern humans, born in the pre-Internet era, will also move into the focus of ecological concern and preservation projects. It is possible that a "human kingdom" will be progressively transferred to artificially protected territories similar to publicly maintained nature parks, which are the only place for wild, unspoiled nature. Such isolated preserves, or human life sanctuaries, may acquire refined and fantastic forms as non-computerized havens of "natural civilization".

In accordance with this historical shift, the new discipline of humanology relates to the humanities much as environmental studies relate to the natural sciences. Physics and biology explore *nature as such*, whereas environmental studies treat it as part of a milieu transformed by humans. Similarly, the humanities study *humans as such*, while humanology approaches humans as part of a technologically transformed milieu. From this angle, humans are a *biospecies*, coexisting and interacting with emerging *techno-species*.

The technization of human capacities occurs in conjunction with the archaization and ecologization of humans themselves. Humanology is both the *ecology of humans* and the *anthropology of machines*, i.e. a study of the mutual redistribution of their functions. Humanology studies what happens to humans after their functions are taken over by thinking machines, as well as what happens to machines in the process of their intellectualization and humanization. Thus, humanology has a dual subject: the human outside the machine, and the human integrated into the machine.

Accordingly, humanology can be divided into *eco-humanology*, dealing with the specificity of humans irreducible to machines, and *techno-humanology*, dealing with human functions capable of being transferred to machines.

# Humanology and theology

## Human creative potential and technotheism

The vision of new, technically or biologically enhanced (super)humans does not need to be atheistic, as conceptualized by Nietzsche or by other theorists of posthumanity, including N. Katherine Hayles, who announced the end of humans as "autonomous beings exercising their will through individual agency and choice" (1999, p. 286). Technohumanism sits well both with an individual agency and the Judeo–Christian view of God creating human beings in his image and likeness, and endowing them with free will and even the capacity to rebel against him. This freedom can be further disseminated from God's creations to the creations of his creations, i.e. artificial intelligence in its diverse forms. The very process of creation, as it is presented in Judeo–Christian theology, includes the self-alienation and the self-emptying will of the Creator bringing to life somebody who is able to resist his power and to challenge his authority. God's kenosis—his self-exhaustion in humanity—further extends into humans' kenosis, i.e. their self-exhaustion in technology[1]. From this theo-technological point of view, humans continue God's work.

Thus, by no means does the recognition of the autonomy of machines, programs and techno-species signify antihumanism or depreciation of humans. Humanology relates to the posthuman as theology relates to atheism. For an atheist, the human autonomy means that "God is dead" just as for a militant posthumanist, the autonomy of artificial intelligence means that "the human is dead". However, from a theological perspective, such a "death of God" is the evidence of his infinite creative power, including his capacity to empty himself sacrificially in his creations. In the same way, the human being, while disappearing and exhausting oneself in the increasingly autonomous techno-creations, acquires in them a new dimension, sometimes sublime, and sometimes degrading, when the creation falls away from the creator. The humanities need to embrace the perspective of the kenosis, or creative disappearance, of humans. Along with a-theology that examines the kenosis or radical disappearance of God, we can envisage *a-humanities* that explore the human dimension in its radically alienated or degraded forms, such as colonies of computer viruses. Thus, humanology crosses over the boundaries of the humanities that have dealt with the *human, all too human*: the human itself is problematized in this new theoretical model.

---

[1]The ancient Greek word κένωσις (*kenosis*) means "emptying", from κενός *kenos* "empty". The word is used in Christian theological contexts, for example, in Philippians 2.7: "Jesus made himself nothing (ἐκένωσεν *ekénōsen*) ..." or " ... he emptied himself ..."

# Information technologies and an argument for the existence of the supreme mind

The logic of scientific-technical progress suggests to us, on the evidence of our own increasing possibilities, that the Universe has a Maker. It is much easier for us today, on the basis of contemporary scientific data, to believe in the Supreme Mind than it was for our less knowledgeable ancestors. I use the word *argument*, not *proof*, because the existence of God, strictly speaking, cannot be proven, just as incomparably simpler mathematical truths cannot be proven, in keeping with Gödel's *Incompleteness Theorem*. It can be shown, however, that the existence of the Maker not only does not contradict scientifically observable facts, but can also be logically derived from those facts with a very high degree of probability.

Technology is usually considered to be a sphere with the most radically atheistic outlook on the world. Indeed, if humans are able to rearrange the universe with their reason and energy, where does that leave the Maker? Why does He do nothing? How is His will manifested? Human activity, ever increasing throughout history, seems to leave less and less space for the Maker's activities. The Tower of Babel is being rebuilt, people keep climbing towards the sky, and, it would appear, there is no force which could bring down that tower of scientific technical progress, except for those forces which are unforeseen and therefore impossible to manage, such as natural catastrophes.

But let us ask: "Why should the success of technology disprove the existence of the Supreme Mind?" Why, on the contrary, should it not render even more realistic the possibility of such an all-powerful mind, which earlier seemed completely unthinkable to people who possessed only primitive tools? How can one, for example, explain to a farmer or a lumberjack that God can read all human thoughts? Or that a person, having died and turned to dust, can still outlive one's body and preserve the entirety of one's personality, the immortality of the soul? In days of old, technology was material, e.g. the axe, the plough, the hammer, and the sickle. In fact, the intellectual technology was only developed in the life of our generation, with the invention of computers, the electronic network, and simulated worlds. I personally found it easier to believe in the supernatural Mind after becoming acquainted with the possibilities of the artificial intellect (even though these still remain rather primitive, represented by computers and early corputers). If we are able to create something that resembles ourselves to such an extent, does that not increase the likelihood that we were ourselves created?

Unlike our ancestors, we understand how information can be gathered on a multitude of people within a small electronic device, and how our thoughts and habits can be calculated and predicted by powerful servers that accumulate information. For example, I type a word, and the computer knows in advance, even better than I do, which word I intend to type, on the basis of the frequency of the words I have used before. Or, when I use a search on Amazon.com, it offers me various items for sale that are connected, in a highly associative manner, with something that I searched for several months ago. The computer memorizes what I have forgotten, it knows what I want, it suggests what I can or must do, and it becomes a collocutor of my mind. For instance, recently I searched for a book by a certain author, and today Amazon offers me a different book by another author on a related issue. The whole worldwide network (or noosphere, or infosphere, or the world electronic databank) encompasses my intellectual demands and habits with increasing thoroughness, sending them back to me with some comments, offers, and associations, which become an active part of my mind, filling in the holes in my knowledge, memory, and, to a certain extent, my imagination. Given time, the network will find out about my sensory characteristics and habits, including my favorite smells and tastes. I will communicate with the network by using my voice, touch and gestures, which will also become part of the infinitely growing and, in its own way, creative memory of syntellect—the integrated intellect of people and machines.

Now, based on the experience of communicating with the latest technology, it is much easier for us to imagine how the Creative Mind can communicate with every living entity, read human thoughts and respond to them. To a ploughman who saw only the direct influence of one material object on another, it would be incomparably more difficult to imagine that whatever is secretly happening in his soul can become public and that "even the very hairs of [his] head are all numbered" (Matthew 10:30). How is it possible to number all the hairs of so many people? And how can one fathom all their thoughts? Where can one find such an all-seeing and omniscient spirit? How can it be everywhere and in everyone? Of course, a ancient peasant could simply take someone's word for this, without any explanation or proof, but for my contemporaries, such a notion of an all-seeing and omnipotent mind is no longer a matter of faith; it is the subject of an entirely reasonable, probable and well-founded assumption (again, I avoid the word *proof*). We now know how compact the means of storing information are, how a grain of matter can accommodate not only a plan of the future tree, but also—if the matter in question is electronic, e.g. a computer chip, a quantum system, and the like—thousands and millions of books, city plans, or information about all people, states, planets, etc. All information about the Universe and its every particle can potentially be stored in an electronic grain the size of a mustard seed.

Even such an erudite scientist as Richard Dawkins refutes the existence of God on the grounds that this hypothesis would entail an all-too-complex, all-encompassing mind:

> God, capable of incessantly controlling and adjusting the state of each and every individual particle of the Universe, cannot be simple. His existence in itself requires a grandiose explanation. Even worse (from the point of view of simplicity) – other nooks and crannies of God's gigantic consciousness are simultaneously engaged following the activities, feelings and prayers of each individual human being, and also of all the extraterrestrials who possibly inhabit this galaxy and a hundred billion others. (2006, p. 215)

It is difficult for Dawkins to believe in such supernatural ability. But why does he not pay attention to the computer on his desk, which can find in a second what thousands of people, many of whom lived thousands of years before us, thought about any subject whatsoever. All it takes is to type a word and press a key. The Internet as we know it was created only two decades ago. It is easy to assume that, in the Creator's realm, during the course of the 13–14 billion years of the existence of our Universe (not to mention the unknown eternity before its coming into being), there could have appeared machines more perfect than the desk computer. Besides, God does not really need to regulate "the state of each and every individual particle of the universe": there are precise physical laws of the mutual influence of particles to take care of that. In a good laboratory, it is not necessary for a technician to constantly monitor all the details of a research process and regulate them manually.

If we can get information about the living and the dead in a mere moment by logging on to the Internet, what is strange about the fact that the Supreme Mind can hold inside itself the designs of not just our universe, but also the countless myriads of other universes, and can penetrate the greatest secrets of every person, the past and future of all sentient beings?

Primitive people could not understand how someone, who had died and vanished corporeally, could live on inside an invisible, intangible substance called "the soul". One could only believe in that by relying on speculations and promises that the soul would reach other worlds and find its place in heaven or hell. But to us, the coevals of CD-ROMs and electronic networks, it is much easier to comprehend rationally the difference between information and its material carrier. In the blink of an eye, information can be recorded from one disk on to another, from an old memory into a new one, or transmitted by cables or wireless signals. Does this not make the belief in the immortality of the soul, or (to use the language of the electronic era) the indestructibility of the informational matrix of a person, perfectly legitimate based on the data supplied by information science?

In ancient times, when the physical world was so domineering and unfathomable, it was hard to believe in the omnipotence of words that in some mysterious way determine the color of one's eyes and hair, hereditary diseases, and temperament. But does not contemporary genetics, which discovered the laws of heredity guided by the language of genes, confirm, in its own way, the fact that "in the beginning was the Word", i.e. that informational patterns precede corporeal existence and determine its properties?

For more than a century now, we have known of invisible rays that can be transmitted over infinite distances; we have known of the speed of light, and, more recently, of the dark matter and dark energy making up the greatest part of the Universe. And what of those mysterious black holes, possibly leading to parallel worlds? And what of the vacuum in which virtual particles are begotten? Or the Big Bang that led to the creation of our universe? And what of the astonishing balance of all the physical parameters of this universe, right down to their billionth parts, making possible our existence in it as sentient beings? Why should not science, relying on these physically verifiable facts, find a common language with theology?

# Cognitive faith

In the past, people believed in the religious image of the world in spite of its oddness and unreality. Why now, when it is becoming increasingly plausible, should we believe in it less? Is it only because we know more? In no way does this knowledge contradict faith: rather, knowledge absorbs and clarifies it. As a result, the vision of the omnipotent Engineer, the creative Word, and the immortal soul, which could earlier only be a matter of faith and superstition, now becomes incomparably more plausible. The religious development of humankind does not move from faith to disbelief; it moves from faith to knowledge. The time has come to speak of the *religiosity of knowledge*, not only of the religiosity of faith. The religion of knowledge is not a religion that bows to knowledge, but a religion that finds out from science, with increasing verifiability, about the things that the religion of old could only take on trust. I would say that the time has now come for *cognitive religion*, where cognitivism will play the same role that once was played by fideism, which holds faith superior to reason in discovering truth. Science and technology will not be the enemies of cognitive religion; they will not even be indifferent to it as an ostensibly "different culture" that has nothing to do with religion. Instead, science and technology will form a synthesis with religion since reason is increasingly in agreement with faith.

If reason abolishes faith at all, it is only to the extent of absorbing its content, becoming the believing reason. The scientific thesis, which holds that the Big Bang led to the creation of the universe *ex nihilo* is the object of not only physical, but also religious knowledge. The anthropic principle, which confirms that the universe was created so that humans could live in it, is religious knowledge as well. Separating information from its known material carriers, and allowing for an infinite diversity of these carriers, which transmit information about humans by extra-biological means, is a thesis of religious knowledge. Another thesis of religious knowledge is the idea that intelligence could in principle be implemented not only in biological neurons, but also in artificial devices, such as computational processors. One could go on for some considerable time enumerating all the ways in which religious faith enters the realm of contemporary science and turns into knowledge, at least approximately. That which people believed in the old days, we can now almost know, according to the words of St. Paul about how guessing will turn into knowledge: "For now we see through a glass, darkly; but then face to face" (1 Cor. 13.12).

Earlier, in times of the hammer and the hoe, the only thing left for people to do was to believe in the supernatural as a fairy tale, a marvel, or a myth. Technology brings the supernatural closer to us, makes it more natural to reason and thus rationally explicable. What lies in-between is no longer an abyss that can only be overcome by a leap of faith, but a high mountain that reason may gradually climb (even though it might never reach the top). We are apprentices who can, for the first time, assess the techniques of the Master's work—not to penetrate its secrets, but at least to understand where to look for them. In this respect, the history of science and technology constitutes a preparatory workshop where we gradually master the craft of engineering new worlds.

One widely discussed recent hypothesis on the artificial nature of our own world belongs to Nick Bostrom, a philosopher and the Director of the Future of Humanity Institute at the University of Oxford. He finds it plausible to think that we are living in a computer simulation:

> You are almost certainly living in a computer simulation that was created by some advanced civilization. What Copernicus and Darwin and latter-day scientists have been discovering are the laws and workings of the simulated reality. These laws might or might not be identical to those operating at the more fundamental level of reality where the computer that is running our simulation exists (which, of course, may itself be a simulation). In a way, our place in the world would be even humbler than we thought. (Bostrom, 2006, pp. 38–9)

According to Bostrom, it is highly probable that we exist in a virtual reality simulated by our technologically advanced descendants who, in a certain number of generations after us, will achieve the level of a superpower and superintelligence. However, this reasoning contains a fundamental flaw because the alleged civilization of the future that simulates us itself descends from us as simulations. There is a sort of circularity involved in this argument: we produce those posthumans who produce us. The proposition to be proved is assumed in one of its premises. If the world in which we produce our offspring is a simulation, then the source of this simulation cannot come from the same world, even in its future condition. To avoid this circularity, we have to admit the existence of another realm of being that is beyond our world of simulation, in the same way as the gamer and the gamer's computer belong to a different level of reality than the one simulated in the game. Bostrom himself acknowledges such a possibility, with all its theological implications:

> These simulators would have created our world, they would be able to monitor everything that happens here, and they would be able to intervene in ways that conflict with the simulated default laws of nature. Moreover, they would presumably be superintelligent (in order to be able to create such a simulation in the first place). An afterlife in a different simulation or at a different level of reality after death-in-the-simulation would be a real possibility. It is even conceivable that the simulators might reward or punish their simulated creatures based on how they behave. (The Simulation Argument FAQ—http://www.simulation-argument.com/faq.html)

As technology advances, humankind will find it increasingly difficult to manage without the notions of the Supreme Master of all computer games and simulations, designated as galaxies, planets, and the laws of nature in the language of the denizens of those simulations and the avatars of those games, in which the Author conferred upon everyone the gift of free will and the unpredictability of chance. As the virtual worlds that we create become increasingly authentic and lifelike, along with our own avatars within them, we will come to recognize more and more the features of such virtual reality around us and inside ourselves.

# The theological paradox of technical advancement

If I can create an artificial mind or an artificial life that resembles me so very nearly, this increases the likelihood of my having also been created, and of the natural life and mind also being the products of artful engineering. This is not proof in the strict sense of the term, but rather a growing probability that the natural world as we know it, and we too, were created, just as virtual worlds are created by us and populated with our avatars.

We can recall Pascal's famous wager with its probability argument: If there is no God, then I, following the path of religion, deprive myself of a small amount of transient earthly goods. If, on the other hand, God does exist, I thereby obtain the infinite goods of immortality and heaven. This makes it more profitable for me to bet on God's existence.

In our case, it is not more profitable, but *more reasonable* to bet on God's existence, for the more the world manifests itself as our creation, the more likely it is that we were created ourselves. If we are capable of creating virtual worlds that are practically no different from the real one and possess the same sensual qualities, then what prevents us from positing that the physical world itself is a simulation? Insofar as only the artistic-conditional likenesses of the real world existed, for example, in the form of verbal descriptions and visual images, the difference between human hand-made creations and the "real" universe was evident. It was more reasonable then to assume that the universe had not been created, since it was difficult for the mind to imagine such power of creation. But if the ontology of our simulated worlds begins to approach the ontology of the "real" world in its complexity and sensory verisimilitude, then the creatability of this real world becomes increasingly probable.

It is more and more difficult to think of the world without the Maker— such is the conclusion of the entire technological evolution of humankind. The fact that we shall be able to become designers of life and reason (which is where contemporary technology is gradually taking us, albeit without any guarantee of success), will most directly point to the existence of the Designer, although traditional faith does not really need any proof of that kind.

Generally speaking, the more superior the mind becomes, the more able it is to recognize the superiority of another mind. Humility is not just a moral virtue, but an intellectual one as well. As human power to create an artificial mind and change the paths of evolution increases, we begin to come to terms with the idea of a power that created ourselves.

As a result, we will be compelled to recognize the evidence of the Engineer, the Designer, the Simulator, or the Gamer, i.e. the Somebody above us. This recognition may make spiritual and ritualistic forms difficult to imagine at present. This religious knowledge may be coupled harmoniously with traditional faith. Techno-theism may visit the temples of its ancestors in order to pray there, or it may turn them into museums. However, it cannot be questioned that science and technology possess enormous spiritual potential. Science discovers the laws of existence, while technology demonstrates the power of reason capable of creating a new existence on the basis of those laws. Based on these important testimonies of science and technology, it is difficult to resist a conclusion that the laws of existence were created by an even more powerful mind.

# The universe is much bigger

I side with Carl Sagan, a prominent astronomer, author, and science populariser. Sagan was of the opinion that religion loses a lot by not accepting the achievements of contemporary science:

> How did it happen that in none of the popular religions did its followers, having taken a closer look at science, notice the following: 'Why, everything has turned out much better than we thought! The universe is much bigger than our prophets claimed—more magnificent, elegant, complex.' Instead, they repeat monotonously: 'No, no and no! Let my god be a small one—that's the kind that suits me.' If a religion—no matter whether it is old or new—praised the magnitude of the Universe that contemporary science has discovered, it would provoke rapture and command respect never even dreamed of by traditional cults. (1994, p. 52)

But why does the biologist-atheist Richard Dawkins, who sympathetically quotes Sagan, react with his own 'No, no and no!' to each most sophisticated, magnificent, and non-dogmatic form of religion? Why do all those atheist naturalists repeat over and over again: 'Let my world be material only— that's the kind that suits me?' Why are they so unwilling to admit that, parallel with the visible matter, there also may exist a world that can never be adequately seen from the outside, but can only be experienced from the inside—the world of love, wisdom, sadness, conscience, repentance, desperation, and hope? Why do these materialists narrow their world far more than the most primitive believer, who still admits the existence of other worlds, miracles, and God's love and mercy? Why do they narrow their horizon down to natural selection and the "selfish gene" as the cause and bearer of all those aspirations, feats, and discoveries that make humans such fascinating, fantastic, creative, and self-sacrificing beings? Why do they address the question 'Why?' to believers only and not to themselves? What stops the propagators of scientific atheism from looking more closely at religion and seeing that science also loses a great deal by renouncing their possible joint action? Let me paraphrase Sagan's passage quoted above:

> Why, everything has turned out much better than we thought! The universe is much bigger, more diverse, and more spiritual than claimed by our materialist prophets, who recognized only matter given to us in our perceptions. This universe, the creation of the Supreme Creator who can address me personally and at the same time create myriads of worlds, who knows everything about me and loves me, who can do anything, but does not want to restrict my freedom, who has placed me to live in this world, but has revealed to me the paths leading to other

worlds as well—this universe is incomparably more magnificent, elegant, and complex than can be imagined by any atheistic chemist or biologist, who allows only the existence of a scanty, tiniest part of a wondrously diverse cosmos.

Those who live in the twenty-first century should present such arguments to the learned opponents of religion whose atheistic views were shaped by the materialism and positivism of the nineteenth century. Let us patiently wait for a response, hoping that, in the century of technohumanism, a new mutual understanding of science and religion can be achieved. The more powerful humans become as the inventors of technology, the architects of the world, and the engineers of simulations, the more humble they find themselves in the presence of the Supreme Master.

# 9

# The art of world-making and the new vocation for metaphysics

*Numerous universes might have been botched and bungled*
*throughout an eternity, ere this system was struck out; much*
*labor lost, many fruitless trials made, and a slow but continual*
*improvement carried out during infinite ages in the art of*
*world-making.*

DAVID HUME

Never before have industry and technology, or even business and advertisement, been as metaphysically loaded as they are today. While in New York City, I noticed the following signs:

- Be the master of your destiny. Likewise, your bill payments.
- Dreaming is good for the soul. Relax a little. Credit can help.
- Dance through life. Walk through the station (in subway).
- Transfinitive aposterior apopheosis is warranted with the telephone URC.

Such "metaphysical" advertisements do not so much appeal to the practical qualities of things as to abstract concepts such as "destiny", "dream", "life", and "transfinitive apopheosis" (whatever that happens to mean)—that is to say, they appeal to the opportunities these things provide for individuals to change their life and enter a different world.

Metaphysics is commonly defined as the most general branch of philosophy that deals with the nature and structure of the world as a whole. Of all the humanities, metaphysics appears to be the least practical discipline as it addresses the broadest questions regarding "being as such" or "the first causes of things". Thus, metaphysics can serve as a useful testing ground for the examination of the practical applications of the humanities. If metaphysics can be used as an engineering tool and a site for practical construction, then the humanities in principle have the potential to change that which they study.

The foundational unit of metaphysical thinking is a *world as whole*. This sets metaphysics apart from more specific, positivistic disciplines discussing particular aspects of the world. In order to be positive and practical, a discipline has to compare various manifestations of generic laws and properties: for example, various substances and elements (chemistry), organisms (biology), or languages (linguistics). Metaphysics, however, has had at its disposal only one world—the one in which we live. Respectively, philosophers debated over what constitutes the beginning or the first principle of this world. Is it composed of water or fire (Thales or Heraclitus)? Which is preeminent—a universal or an individual (Realism or Nominalism)? Is the world ideal or material in its foundations (Hegel or Marx)? These philosophies, however brilliantly espoused and internally coherent, all remained speculative in that they simply extracted various qualities from the same single world and hypostasized them into general principles, while the world itself remained unchanged.

Now, with the discussion of parallel physical worlds, and with the proliferation of digital virtual worlds, we can look at the range of possible applications of metaphysics differently. Here is one of many examples—an experiment in creating an augmented reality that promises to erase the difference between the real and the virtual:

> Called a *Virtual Cocoon*, the round-room device provides a far more realistic delivery of virtual experiences via total sensory input. This device positions the occupant in a chair before a nearly 360 degree screen where s/he becomes completely immersed in not only a visual and audio presentation encompassing almost the full view, but also one where the occupant has skin sensations, smells and tastes … . A mock-up of the device is on display today at Pioneers 09, which is an EPSRC showcase event held at London's Olympia Conference Centre. (Hodgin, 2009)

Similar to the way in which metaphysics deals with the "worldness" of the world, the virtual cocoon offers to our senses a different but holistic world that can have its own metaphysics. Jon Turney writes: "One ultimate vision of IT future is access to virtual worlds which are as rich as, or richer than, the everyday world" (2010, p. 305). The metaphysics of such multiple virtual worlds may be more fascinating and sophisticated than that of the single world in which we live. This new metaphysical domain embraces the entire *metaverse*.[1] The metaverse is created by the convergence of virtually enhanced physical reality and physically embodied virtual space; it includes the totality of all simulated and augmented realities. We can imagine how the field of metaphysics can expand immensely to embrace these newly created worlds, each potentially endowed with its own laws and universals.

Of course, the majority of the virtual worlds (VWs) that we have been able to observe until now in various computer games are metaphysically unspectacular in their dutiful imitation of the laws of the existing world. Gamers and their avatars have so far been pursuing mundane goals by building replicas of the real in the virtual. Technologies of simulation are currently at a stage similar to that of cinema in the first years after its invention. For example, early films showed a running horse, a garden scene, a locomotive approaching a station, and other simple fragments of real life. Similarly, current VWs are simplistic extensions of our trivial experiences of walking, flying, buying, and dating, in full accordance with the empirical laws of our three-dimensional world.

Jon Turney (2010, pp. 306–7) identifies three types of computerized worlds: 1) mirror worlds that are ultra-detailed models of actual worlds, such as Google Earth; 2) augmented realities where information comes through artificial devices, such as glasses or wired contact lenses; 3) immersive virtual environments, or fully realized virtual worlds, where you can send your computer-controlled avatar. As information technology progresses from mirror worlds to immersive worlds, which encompass self-contained universes in them, metaphysics will get a better ground for the realization of its world-forming visions[2].

With that in mind, why not turn our thoughts to the next possible stage, when virtual technology will be able to produce something like Tlon, a world from Jorge Luis Borges' story *Tlon, Uqbar, Orbis Tertius*? In order to

---

[1] The term *metaverse*, meaning *meta–universe*, was coined by Neal Stephenson in his science fiction novel *Snow Crash* (1992).

[2] According to a recent article in *The Economist*, "Games developers say that technology is pushing back the frontiers of their business in a way that is simply not open to, say, books or radio. They point to improving graphics, better artificial intelligence and bigger worlds featured in their products" (Cross, 2011). "Better artificial intelligence and bigger worlds …"—these are the key factors for the future converegence of e-games and metaphysics.

describe this world in its worldness, which is based in thought only, Borges
has to resort to philosophical arguments and refer to thinkers of the past:

> Hume noted for all time that Berkeley's arguments did not admit the
> slightest refutation nor did they cause the slightest conviction. This dictum
> is entirely correct in its application to the earth, but entirely false in Tlon.
> The nations of this planet are congenitally idealist. Their language and
> the derivations of their language – religion, letters, metaphysics – all
> presuppose idealism. The world for them is not a concourse of objects
> in space; it is a heterogeneous series of independent acts. ... [T]he men
> of this planet conceive the universe as a series of mental processes which
> do not develop in space but successively in time. Spinoza ascribes to his
> inexhaustible divinity the attributes of extension and thought; no one in
> Tlon would understand [this] juxtaposition. (1983, pp. 8–9)

We can see how the philosophical ideas of Hume, Berkeley, and Spinoza
turn out to be indispensable when considering what would make one
world, Tlon, so different from our familiar Earth. This example shows how
certain metaphysical assumptions, idealistic in this case, are incorporated in
the construction of possible worlds and thus may have a direct impact on
the virtual technologies that produce these worlds. Inventors of computer
games must first of all set metaphysical parameters for the virtual world
in which action will take place. To that end, the following questions must
be addressed: "How many dimensions does the world contain?", "What
is the nature of time and space in it, and do they constitute one indivisible
continuum?", "What are the relationships between subject and object, and
cause and effect?", "How many moves or hits is each avatar allowed?", and
"What constitute the conditions for each avatar's death or disappearance
from the game?"

What is thus brought to light is a new relationship between philosophy
and the advanced technologies that I call *onto-technologies*, because they
change the foundations of being, and the structure of existence and the way
in which we experience it. In the past, technology was preoccupied with
material particulars, while taking care of concrete human needs, such as
food, shelter, and transportation. Philosophy, in its turn, was preoccupied
with big ideas, the first principles, essences, and universals. Technology
used to be utilitarian, while philosophy was speculative. Today, technology
and philosophy are moving ever closer towards each other: the power
of technology is extended to the fundamental properties of the Universe,
while philosophy becomes increasingly active in its ability to define and
change these properties. Technologies of the late twentieth and especially
the early twenty-first centuries are no longer applied tools, but fundamental
technologies making transformative advances into the micro- and macro-
worlds, including the structure of the brain and DNA. Such advances make

it possible for us to penetrate into the very foundations of being, potentially changing its original parameters or setting up parameters for new kinds of being. *Onto-technology* has the power to create a new spatio-temporal continuum, a new sensory environment and modes of its perception (like in the virtual cocoon), along with new kinds of organisms and new forms of intelligence. Nano-technologies provide the means for the production of any object of desirable qualities and proportions from the quantum bottom of matter. Humans are becoming increasingly skillful and successful in the art of *world-making.* As a result, technology is now moving not away from, but *towards,* metaphysics; this way, the two of them are meeting at the very core of being, where the principles and universals traditionally considered the prerogative of philosophical study can be found.

A new synthesis of philosophy and technology is taking the form of *techno-sophia*—a *technically-armed philosophy* or *philosophically-oriented technology. Technosophia* establishes the first principles not only in theoretical thought, but also in practical action through alternative forms of matter, life, and mind. With the recent breakthroughs in physics, cosmology, genetics, and computer technologies, the *worldness* as the primary interest of metaphysics is now expanded into a multiverse in its multiple forms and alternative branches. With the advent of the multiverse, metaphysics ceases to be a discipline that speculates about the foundations of one world. Instead, it becomes a practical discipline of constructing worlds with various properties, laws, and universals.

In fact, each virtual world is a world unto itself, from the most primitive action game to *Second Life,* the design-your-own-avatar online world launched in 2003, and populated by millions of people who can participate in individual and group activities, creating and trading items of virtual property. Today, we can imagine, and even technologically construct, different worlds, for example, the Thalesean and Heraclitean worlds, or the Spinozian and Hegelian worlds. These "watery", "fiery", pantheist or panlogical worlds have their own metaphysical truth and value. Why should we exclude one for the sake of another and reduce the wealth of *worldness* to one single world?

In fact, in the construction of a virtual world, programmers, engineers, and web designers should all follow in the footsteps of the philosopher, who, as a Demiurge of this particular world, formulates its foundational laws to be technologically enacted into material reality by other specialists later on. If a philosopher withdraws from this foundational act of thinking "world-wise", then a computer specialist, a software engineer, or a game designer will inadvertently take upon themselves the role of a philosopher, because a world, even within a primitive game, cannot exist without a certain philosophy as a system of laws and universals. But, of course, web wizards or game designers are not philosophers; that is why the worlds produced in their workshops are metaphysically so plain. Those who are

genuine philosophers by vocation and education must fill this huge professional niche formed by the accelerated processes of world-making across so
many disciplines and occupations.

Some university departments of computing and informational technologies have recently started collaborating with history departments in
producing games with historical content, e.g. games set in the Elizabethan
era or World War II. One can foresee philosophy departments following
their example and engaging in strategic decisions about the nature of virtual
worlds in the making. Virtual worlds become more and more intrinsically philosophical as information technologies become more advanced
and broaden the scope of their application from material details to the
*worldness* of the world.

*Virtualism*, i.e. the theory and practice of constructing virtual worlds and
beings, promises to become a direction in philosophy that appears to be
much more potent and congruous with the advanced technologies of today
than any other philosophical "-ism" of the past. Virtualism is a philosophy
of emerging worlds that can be projected metaphysically and then implemented by using new information technologies, nano-technologies and
bio-technologies.

In this light, the technological progress prepares a new role for the
philosopher as a *metaphysical engineer* or a *world designer*. In the past,
the philosopher pronounced the last word about the world, consum-
mating it in thought; for instance, Hegel was fond of repeating the
maxim that "the owl of Minerva spreads its wings only with the falling
of the dusk" (1967, p. 13). In the world of tomorrow, the philosopher
will more closely resemble a lark or even a rooster, proclaiming the first
word about something that has never existed before, but which may come
into existence. The twenty-first century introduces, at least potentially,
alternative varieties of life and intelligence, such as the enhancement of
brain capacity with the help of artificial devices and the exploration of
holes and tunnels in a space and time continuum. Philosophy, therefore,
is no longer mere speculation about the first principles, but an experiment
in the conceptual production of multiple worlds—be it the creation of a
computer game or a parallel universe with the quality of worldness.

The twentieth century was an age of grandiose physical experiments.
In its turn, the twenty-first century might become a testing ground for
metaphysical experiments related to the problem of free will, the role of
chance, and the paradoxes of twins, doubles, and clones. Michio Kaku, for
example, sees the issue of our doubles, or clones in the parallel quantum
worlds, as one of the great ethical and metaphysical concerns:

Are *we* responsible for our clone's actions? In a quantum universe, we
would have an infinite number of quantum clones. Since some of our
quantum clones might perform acts of evil, are we then responsible for

them? Does our soul suffer for the transgressions of our quantum clones? (2006, p. 353)

Similar problems may emerge with our digital avatars, biological clones, or the new power of the brain-computer interface. For instance, am I responsible for the actions of an individual who is genetically identical to myself and who has been cloned by my own will? Or, with the creation of wireless links between human brains and external electronics, how can my uncontrollable thoughts impact the surrounding world? If my brain is enhanced by the prostheses that transmit the energy of neural signals directly to mighty factory-like machines, this enormously increases my responsibility for the contents of my thinking as compared with the time when it was impenetrably constrained within the cranium.

Today, the foundational principles of existence, formerly considered predetermined and unchangeable, are being questioned and transformed into metaphysically loaded models of world-like realities. Notably, not a single aspect of the philosophical heritage will be lost or neglected in this new technosophical field. All knowledge proceeding from all past systems and schools of thought can be employed in the conceptual design of alternative worlds.

Metaphysics applied to the art of world-making is just one example of how the humanities can find a new vocation in the age of advanced technologies.

# 10

# Information trauma and the evolution of the human species

## The gap between humans and humanity

Over two centuries ago, in 1798, Thomas Malthus published *An Essay on the Principle of Population, as it Affects the Future Improvement of Society*, in which he formulated the law of disproportion between the population growth and the available resources of food. According to Malthus, population grows in geometric progression, whereas the increase in the supply of food is merely arithmetic. He predicted a demographic explosion, which indeed took place... in the twentieth century, especially in the Third World countries, causing food shortages, starvation, and social tensions.

The intensity of this crisis decreased by the end of the twentieth century as a result of of new technological developments in agriculture and more effective means of birth control and family planning. However, today the world faces a new disproportion—no longer demographic yet potentially as explosive. This new disproportion is between the collective producer of information and its consumers; in other words, between humanity and human beings.

Various thinkers, such as Vico and Malthus, Hegel and Marx, Oswald Spengler and Pitirim Sorokin, have attempted to formulate what might be called "the basic law" of human history and development. My modest proposal for a basic law can be formulated as follows: *Individuals fail to keep pace with the evolution of our species.* In other words, *humans are lagging far behind humanity.* This law does not pretend to be universal; I offer it only to explain some contradictions and paradoxes of our times. The development of individual human beings is limited by their biological ages, whereas the social and technological development of humanity as a whole has no time limitations. The increasing age of *Homo Sapiens* as a species is not accompanied with a commensurate increase in the life span of individuals. With each new generation, therefore, individuals have to cope with an increasingly heavy load of knowledge and experience accumulated by their ancestors.

The progression from Marxism to existentialism to poststructuralism, despite their wide differences, makes it clear how the gap between human species and individuals has widened. For Marxism, all individuals share the same reality in the form of labor and resources of human consciousness. This common possession of humanity, despite the perversity of private ownership, can eventually be reappropriated through social revolution. In their turn, by the early and mid-twentieth century, existentialists regarded alienation as *inherently* human and thus irresolvable by any kind of reform or revolution. Existentialists see individuals as doomed to freedom and loneliness, losing their authenticity in society, which imposes unsuitable roles upon everyone. While Marxism still tried to bridge the gap between individual and human species, existentialism found the abyss between them impassable. Finally, in the late twentieth century, post-structuralism dismissed the very idea of reality: there is nothing to be alienated *from*. Reality is not temporarily *alienated* from us (as argued by Marxists) or eternally *alien* (as argued by existentialists); instead, reality is delusional, fabricated and infinitely deferred. In poststructuralism, the idea of humanity as a species is rejected and replaced by an array of local social and cultural constructs. Each race, gender, age, place, culture, and individual creates its own reality. The words *mankind, humankind,* and *humanity* rarely appear in poststructuralist texts without scare quotes, question marks, or cancellations. Placing *humanity* and *reality* in scare quotes, however, was perhaps no more than reality taking revenge on humans, i.e. individuals grumbling about a civilization that needs them less and less. The alienation of reality from the individual and its subsequent "disappearance" are the two stages in the process by which reality—the sum total of information accumulated by humanity—becomes increasingly inaccessible to individuals.

The development of information and information technology has accelerated exponentially. In the past 30 years, more new information was produced than in the previous 5,000 years. A single daily edition of the *New York Times* contains more information today than an average person in the seventeenth century encountered in a lifetime. The world's largest libraries double their resources every 14 years—in other words, they grow about 130 times larger in the course of each century. [1]

In the early thirteenth century, the library of the Sorbonne was considered to be the largest one in Europe: it contained 1,338 volumes. According to recent calculations cited in the *Encyclopedia Britannica*, the number of books published in Europe in the sixteenth century doubled every seven years. Thus, by the year 1600, only a century and a half after Gutenberg's first printing press was in operation, about 35,000 books had been printed, with the total number of copies estimated at 20,000,000. Other calculations show that, in the twentieth century, the global volume of literature in science and technology grew at about the same speed, doubling every seven or eight years (Large, 1984). Since 1970, with the growth of computer technologies, the number of bits of information transmitted has doubled every 1.1 years (Kurzweil, 2005). While in 5,000 years of its existence, humankind has created about 5 exabytes of data (1 exabyte = 1,073,741,824 gigabytes), in 2006 alone this figure had reached 280 exabytes. With the spread of high-resolution user-generated content, the amount of information created by humankind in one year is expected to exceed 1,000 exabytes. Traffic networks will grow by tens and hundreds of times. Meanwhile, the average life expectancy in the last 400 years has only doubled, growing in the arithmetic, not geometric, progression. Thus, the volume of data is increasing, while our ability to adjust to this information environment is decreasing.

# Postmodern symptoms

Postmodern sensibility, while famously open to everything, perceives everything superficially. The postmodern individual appreciates surfaces and signifiers, traces and simulacra, while resisting depth and meaning. Postmodern culture is a culture of fast and fleeting touches and appearances. In other words, postmodern culture shows the symptoms of an acutely traumatic experience. It is usually assumed that superficiality precludes tragedy; in the case of the postmodern culture, however, a tragic or traumatic experience may have induced our low sensitivity to meanings. According to the theory of trauma, which is among the most dynamic

---

[1] I take these striking statistics from Richard Wurman's book *Information Anxiety*. The very concept of information anxiety as introduced by Wurman suggests the disproportion between our craving for information and our capacity to absorb it: "Information anxiety is produced by the ever widening gap between what we understand and what we think we should understand. Information anxiety is the black hole between data and knowledge. It happens when information doesn't tell us what we want or need to know" (1989, p. 14).

current divisions of cultural studies and psychology, trauma has two distinct features: first, trauma is brought on by experiences so difficult and painful that one is unable to assimilate them and therefore must repress them; and, second, the effect of trauma is delayed and unfolds in a sequence of reactions not directly connected to its source. Such delayed reactions are often inadequate, absurd, and monotonous repetitions that appear meaningless as they re-enact a repressed memory. In the words of Michael Herr,

> it took the war to teach it, that you were *as responsible for everything you saw as you were for everything you did.* The problem was that you didn't always know what you were seeing until later, maybe years later, that a lot of it never made it in at all, it just stayed stored there in your eyes. (cited in Caruth, 1996, p. 10)

A striking example of how postmodern sensibility has developed in response to cultural trauma is Russian conceptualism, which from the 1970s–90s was preoccupied with clichés of totalitarian ideology. The Soviet state incessantly bombarded citizens with stereotypes that traumatized the consciousness of several generations. These stereotypes later surfaced in the poetry and visual art of Russian postmodernism, whose aesthetics was purposefully mechanical, distant, and insensitive. A "concept" (*kontsept* in Russian) is a unit of conceptual art, a cliché, or a scheme intended to demonstrate its own semantic and affective emptiness. Such concepts as 'Proud Muscovites, "a humanistic militiaman", "a communal apartment", or "the evil and stupid Reagan" regularly appeared in the art of Ilya Kabakov and Eric Bulatov, and in the poetry of Dmitry Prigov, Lev Rubinshtein, and Timur Kibirov—the most popular conceptualists of the late Soviet and post-Soviet periods.

A traumatized consciousness works with surface images impressed on the retina or the eardrum without really affecting the mind and the heart, which are represented in conceptualist art as the signs constructed out of, or modelled on, statements like "the party is the mind, the honor and the conscience of our epoch"[2]. It is noteworthy that conceptualism did not appear during the decades of the most aggressive ideological pressure on the public mind (1920s–50s); it appeared later, when the Soviet ideology was no longer taken seriously. A delayed rehearsal of images and concepts accumulated through the eye and the ear, while repelled by the membrane of consciousness, is typical of trauma. When ideology is perceived as a truthful reflection of reality, its semiotic construction is concealed; however,

---

[2]In his celebrated phrase, Lenin called the Bolshevik party the "Mind, Honor and Conscience of our Epoch". The phrase became a widespread propaganda slogan, especially in the Brezhnev era of stagnation. (Editor's Note).

as perception comes to be split off from attention, understanding, and trust, the constructedness of that reality becomes traumatically obvious. The senses are overwhelmed with signs and images, but the intellect can no longer admit and processes them.

A similar traumatic situation emerged in Western culture as a result of the increasing assault of mass media on the senses of at least two recent generations. For instance, the experience of watching television with its hundreds of channels can be paralyzing: its excessive diversity can be as traumatizing as repetition and monotony. Screens, monitors, texts, graphs, and images multiply, inundate, and influence people, but there is nothing behind them. By the turn of the 1960s, in the East and the West alike, the information trauma of one kind or the other had already helped to shape the postmodernist mentality, which processes sense data on the level of signifiers because that level is the only one with which it can cope.

Postmodern images are the residual traces of the pressure exerted on our senses by ideology and the media. Postmodern art disseminates signifiers without any critical charge or depth. Even the theoretical concepts of poststructuralism, such as *trace* or *différance* in Derrida's writings, can be seen as evidence of trauma. The trace differs from the sign in that the former is not representational and has no connection to the signified, which is always deferred, postponed, and never manifested "as real". *Différance* as deferral is typical of traumatic response, which blocks every access to the original stimulus. Trauma itself is a trace of the original, while the original is regarded as lost or, rather, never existent. In sum, the trace is understood as non-referential—related to other signs rather than to any signified. Following this logic of deconstruction can be fatal, for example, in case of following the traffic lights, as signs, and ignoring the actual traffic.

One reason why America, otherwise so pragmatic a society, has so eagerly embraced postmodern theory is that the information explosion has occurred in the US on a larger scale than elsewhere. Average Americans, who spend one-third of their lives in front of a television and/or a computer screen, are ready to take the flickering of signifiers for an ultimate reality. Sophisticated poststructuralist terms such as "the chain of signifiers", "the play of signifiers", "simulacra", and "hyperreality" reflect a mentality that, traumatized by an excess of information, no longer believes in the "signifier–signified" axis, having lost both the intuition of depth and the will for transcendence.

The postmodernism—euphoric, playful, and permissive—is often said to be oblivious of tragedy. However, euphoria can also be the consequence of a trauma that retains its pain unconsciously. Trauma is healed anesthetically: since the pain does not subside, the sensitivity to it is numbed. The traumatized consciousness glides easily over the surface of things and into the bliss of thoughtlessness. In this condition, one is stimulated and intoxicated by diversity for its own sake—a feast of unending differences.

# Negative reference

Jean Baudrillard, among other theoreticians, holds that postmodern mentality has abandoned reality and all referential connection with it. However, reference does still occur—though negatively. The nerve endings in a human hand are capable of feeling an object and transmitting an adequate impression of it. If a hand were to lose its sensitivity, it would fail to feel an object, yet the referential connection to it would not be lost. For example, a frostbitten hand is the evidence that the frost causing the trauma to the hand is real. As Cathy Caruth points out, "the attempt to gain access to a traumatic history . . . is also the project of listening beyond the pathology of individual suffering, to the reality of a history that in its crises can only be perceived in unassimilable forms" (1996, p. 156). While, in one sense, interrupting the referential process and rendering further experience of reality distorted or even impossible, trauma still permits *negative* reference when reality can be indicated through a failure to register it. Various physical handicaps (blindness and deafness, notably) may prevent a person from developing an undistorted image of the world, but the body may still bear witness to the accident that has incapacitated it. Burned skin may not feel heat, and blinded eyes do not see light, but burned skin and blinded eyes still convey adequately the reality of an explosion. Indeed, insensibility may reflect the event behind the interruption of the senses more truthfully than any representation of that event. Would not loss of vision be a more adequate evidence of a nuclear attack than its meticulous observation? Speaking at the opening of a Holocaust archive, Geoffrey Hartman (1996) said this on behalf of its victims: "My mind forgets, but my body keeps the score. The body is bleeding history."

Trauma theory can stimulate insights into the theory of cognition and genesis of culture. According to Kant's famous agnostic postulate, we cannot perceive reality as it is, cf. his concept of "things-in-themselves". In that sense, we are all epistemologically handicapped and perhaps traumatized. Could it be that things-in-themselves have a shell-shocking quality that incapacitates cognition? We cannot rule out that culture resulted from a prehistorical trauma splitting reality into things-for-us (signifiers) and things-in-themselves (signifieds), the latter hidden from our senses. Signifiers may be the scars preventing us from immediate perception of signifieds yet referring to something absent from the here and now. If we can access reality only through signs, it may be that they are the marks of insensitivity inflicted long ago upon our senses.

From this perspective, postmodernism signals the emergence of mature self-awareness on the part of a handicapped culture. Only by accepting that our knowledge is constructed and insurmountably semiotic can we come to terms with the limitations of our condition, which helps to explain why cripples, prostheses, organs without bodies, and bodies without organs are so prevalent in postmodern discourse: "We must, in short, consider our limbs, hands, toes, breasts . . . in themselves, severed from the organic unity of the body . . . we must, in other words, disarticulate, mutilate the body" (de Man, 1984, p. 19). Our handicapped culture requires, more and more, that we rely on external devices and technological enhancements in order to integrate us as individuals into its grand informational systems. Between my hand, which presses a key on a computer keyboard, and my eyes, which look at the monitor, there are dozens of hardware and software mediators: wires, gigabites of electronic memory, and multitudes of microprocessors. The body itself appears as a more or less effective natural surrogate for more perfect wires and microprocessors; the body has become prosthesis for prostheses. In the fragmentary, aggregate body of postmodern theory, all our parts can be disassembled, enhanced with prostheses, and reassembled in a different order. Gilles Deleuze and Felix Guattari maintain in *Anti-Oedipus: Capitalism and Schizophrenia* that the dismembered body is a revolutionary challenge to late capitalist civilization. However, our state of affairs is more likely just the opposite: the information culture dismembers us, separating eyes from hands, ears from legs, and consciousness from the body. The human being is not the head and brains of the information culture, but rather its beheaded victim. We are now facing the challenge of *reassembling* the human being, disassembled and disabled by postmodern culture.

To assess the panhuman informational resources required to bridge the gap between humanity and individual humans, we can take Nietzsche's idea of the *Übermensch*. For this Superman is an individual actually commensurable with the entire species. But Nietzsche's Superman would be universal and unified in ways that would impede the specialized and prosthetized future that postmodernism predicts and prefers. Every move toward integration and wholeness meets with strong opposition from postmodern intellectuals who view such tendencies as potentially threatening us with ideological intolerance and, ultimately, totalitarianism.

# Specialization and disintegration

One can imagine a time when only exceptional individuals—superhumans equipped with supercomputers—can keep up with the information age. Sooner or later, however, even they will fall behind, and civilization will rush ahead uncontrollably and incomprehensibly. One way to decrease the gap between humans and humankind is to compress the material that needs learning: this way, the volume of information accumulated by humankind can be absorbed within an individual life span. Voltaire noted the already increasing significance of anthologies, digests of excerpts, and encyclopedias as the summaries of knowledge that the previous generations had received in extensive and raw form. Today, fewer and fewer people read the classics (even the classics of the eighteenth and nineteenth centuries, such as Voltaire and Rousseau): instead, we learn about them mainly from screen versions, or from articles and (occasionally) lectures. The reading list of modern classics, for example, now includes Proust, Woolf, and Nabokov, whereas the canon for our great-grandparents would have extended from Voltaire and Austen to no one later than Tolstoy. At the same time, our life span has not increased sufficiently to compensate for the expanded reading list. If we could miraculously increase the average life span to a thousand years, we could leisurely read Tolstoy and Homer in the original, and university courses could dedicate ten years to the study of antiquity alone. As matters stand, however, in postmodern education even of the most elite varieties, criticism and theory increasingly predominate over literature and metadiscourses over primary sources.

To meet the intensifying needs for compression, high technologies have been developed for the storage and transmission of information. Since this process simultaneously complicates and compresses, it can be termed "involution" as opposed to, but parallel with, evolution. Anything that humanity develops historically, humans condense symbolically. In 1937, inspired by the "involutionary" potential of microfilm, H. G. Wells wrote optimistically that

> there is no practical obstacle whatever now to the creation of an efficient index to all human knowledge, ideas and achievement, to the creation, that is, of a complete planetary memory for all mankind. And not simply an index. . . . It foreshadows a real intellectual unification of our race. The whole human memory can be, and probably in a short time will be, made accessible to every individual. (1938, p. 58)

Yet, even involutionary technologies and techniques themselves are subject to evolutionary proliferation. Criticism, for instance, condenses literary material, but the material of criticism itself increases incessantly; even the critical literature in a relatively narrow subject area is by now impossible to keep up with, let alone master. Metalanguages proliferate, and new languages of higher discursive levels are being created upon them.

Involution still lags behind evolution, with further fragmentation of cultures and specialization of subcultures. Individuals identify less and less with humanity at large, and more and more with a local culture or a narrow

discipline. By the end of the twentieth century, the problem of multiculturalism had become central to both intellectual and political discourse:
a variety of subcultures claimed the status of fully developed and self-
sufficient cultures, without any connection to the universal culture or any
comprehensive idea of humanity. The ideas of humanity and universality
became as ridiculous among postmodern intellectuals as they had been in
Marxist party cells at the turn of the twentieth century. According to such
divisionary logic, there are men and women, hetero- and homo-, white
and black, people with income above and below the average, and dwellers
in large and small cities, whereas the human being, as such, is a harmful
myth or naive abstraction promoted by utopians and totalitarians. In much
the same way, all forms of human knowledge and activity are becoming
increasingly particularized. It is still possible to be a specialist in Leibniz or
Hegel today; one simply needs to read a few hundred books by and about
them. In a century or two, however, even such narrow specialization will
be considered inadmissibly broad. As a result, there will be specialists on
Leibniz's or Hegel's individual themes or works.

The main result of the disproportion between a panhuman culture and its
individual reception may eventually be information trauma so extreme as to
occasion mental illness. R. Buckminster Fuller, a thinker and scientist of a
rare Renaissance kind, went so far as to speculate that information trauma
could result in human extinction. In the introduction to *Synergetics*—his
magnum opus—Fuller wrote:

> Advancing science has now discovered that all the known cases of
> biological extinction have been caused by overspecialization, whose
> concentration of only selected genes sacrifices general adaptivity. ... In
> the meantime, humanity has been deprived of comprehensive under-
> standing. Specialization has bred feelings of isolation, futility, and
> confusion in individuals. It also resulted in the individual's leaving
> responsibility for thinking and social action to others. Specialization
> breeds biases that ultimately aggregate as international and ideological
> discord, which, in turn, leads to war. . . . Only a comprehensive switch
> from the narrowing specialization and toward an ever more inclusive
> and refining comprehension by all humanity—regarding all the factors
> governing omnicontinuing life aboard our spaceship Earth—can bring
> about reorientation from the self-extinction-bound human trending, and
> do so within the critical time remaining before we have passed the point
> of chemical process irretrievability. (Fuller, 1975, pp. xxv, xxvii)

The dangers of the information explosion are as real as the demographic
ones predicted by Malthus. Malthus pointed out the disproportion between
the biological and economic productivity of humankind, indicating the
threats involved. Humanity as a whole still has a better chance of competing

with itself successfully compared to an individual human being competing with humankind.

# A century of new catastrophes?

It is clear that the main resources of common wealth are now informational rather than industrial or agricultural. Paradoxically, in the sphere of material production, consumption is much easier and faster than manufacturing, whereas in the realm of information the situation is reversed. In other words, the consumption of information by individuals lags drastically behind the production of information by humanity. With concerted efforts, humanity can feed itself; but can it understand itself, however great the efforts made? Can an individual mind ever encompass what the mind of the species creates? Given the possibility of failure, individuals will continue to diversify and specialize: they will narrow their scope until the words *humans* and *humanity* have almost nothing in common.

Among the first to see this kind of diversity as disintegration was a German philosopher Wilhelm Windelband:

> Culture has grown too much for an individual to view it as a whole. This impossibility harbors a great social danger. . . . The awareness of universal connectedness that should dominate the whole of cultural life is gradually lost, and society is threatened by the danger of falling apart into groups and atoms, linked by external need and necessity rather than by spiritual understanding. . . . Unable to penetrate into the depths, the specifics, and the contents of other areas of knowledge, a contemporary man is satisfied by superficial dilettantism, skimming the cream from everything without touching the essence. (1915, pp. 254–5)

Given our current taste for surfaces and diversity, we naturally dismiss this warning, written in 1878, about an impending "great social danger". If more than a century and a quarter have passed without any incident, surely we must be safe. But then we think again: passed without any incident? Were not the world wars and revolutions of the last century consequences of the conditions that Windelband described? Is it accidental that a nation that had for many years led in the progress of humanity also initiated both world wars? As Max Horkheimer and Theodor Adorno said of the nazification of Germany, "the progress toward the new order has been carried out largely by people whose consciousness progress has left behind—bankrupts, sectarians, fools. The 'dialectics of Enlightenment' had turned those in Germany who could not keep up with it toward a violent simplification" (2002, p. 174).

One can only speculate about what catastrophes may yet ensue as epiphenomena of the information explosion. It is easy for the Internet smart alecks to unite in contempt for those who cannot handle traffic on the information highway. And yet, Horkheimer and Adorno's caution is still apt:

> One of the lessons of the Hitler period is the stupidity of cleverness ... . Clever people have always made things easy for barbarians, because they are so stupid. It is the well-informed, farsighted judgments, the prognoses based on statistics and experience, the observations that begin: 'I happen to be an expert in this field,' it is the well-founded, conclusive statements which are untrue. Hitler was against intellect and humanity. But there is also an intellect which is against humanity: it is distinguished by well informed superiority. (2002, p. 173)

Among the "idiots of progress" are some who are formidably intelligent and cunning. Those left behind are led by the *professional* idiots of progress who are not infrequently geniuses and who, on behalf of the idiots they lead, can make quick work of any smart aleck. For instance, as Horkheimer and Adorno note, "those who came to power in Germany were smarter than liberals and more stupid" (Horkheimer and Adorno, 2002, p. 174). This insight about stupidity and intelligence in Nazi Germany is applicable to Bolsheviks in Russia as well. The Hitlers, Lenins, and Stalins may fail to understand dialectics and the products of the Enlightenment, but the intelligence of such people is adequate to their task. Now that the main types of wealth and capital are more informational than material, we can expect revolutionary unrest among those who are informationally deprived. Informational impoverishment may prove to be even more explosive than material poverty. The revolutions of the twentieth century would appear to be mere street pranks in comparison with those that may take place in the twenty-first century.

Societal disproportions, if ignored, will sooner or later find cataclysmic outlets, as demonstrated by the experience of the twentieth century, when the brown plague and the red plague ran their course, taking millions of lives. Such cataclysms are usually followed by periods of sobering up, during which peaceful resolutions are sought. Slowly, the demographic crisis is also being resolved, though not without millions of starving and starved as its own victims. The most pronounced disproportion of all is now upon us and should be treated as promptly and as seriously as possible. The overwhelming majority of us are becoming more and more idiotic in relation to our species' accumulated knowledge. In the nineteenth century, the materially dispossessed were called *proletarians*. In the twenty-first century, the growing new class of dispossessed can be called *infoprols*.

However counterintuitive it may seem, informational wealth is more difficult to distribute than material wealth. In order to feed five people with one piece of bread, we must divide it into five parts, and each person will have sufficient food. In order to transmit one idea to five people, one cannot simply divide it; on the contrary, the idea will in a sense multiply by five, differently perceived by each individual. Informational capital increases easily, and, as a rule, no deficit occurs when information circulates. However, its circulation occasions a new problem—that of inconsumable excess. A mind unable to process information and grasp a given idea is a deprived and potentially destructive mind. Incomprehension is a graver predicament than undernourishment: a hungry person can be fed, but an informationally deprived one is like a starving person without any digestive system. The informational deficiency is internal. The lack is not of informational resources to distribute, but of the intellectual ability to consume them. In various degrees, everyone is informationally deprived because, as individuals, we all lag behind the advancement of our common knowledge, which is both everyone's and no one's. This disproportion, unlike that between the rich and the poor, to some degree separates everyone from all. Consequently, the wrath of this growing majority can be vented only on itself.

# Para-informational society

There are some who believe that the dangers I am describing are illusory because computers can solve the problem of any informational excess. The Internet, after all, permits us to access and sort through a vast amount of data very quickly, so no matter how much information we produce, computers should be able to help us store, organize, and use it. But, by moving to solve one set of problems, the computer has brought on a set of new ones. With the Internet, each consumer of information becomes potentially also its producer. Further, the information produced in this way tends to be of very inferior quality, yet must still be taken into account. In the past, the deficiency of printing materials limited the author's access to publication by imposing professional, editorial, educational, and stylistic standards. Manuscript culture, over the previous centuries, had created its own rigorous criteria of selection of information; it was mostly the Holy Scriptures and canonical literary works that were copied. The criteria of print culture have been less rigid but still usefully exclusive. With the spread of digital literacy, most selective criteria for publishing have become obsolete. The sound waves of the Internet are now everywhere, but these sounds are mostly noise. Though the production of information is accelerating, the capacities for its transmission are growing even faster, and the widening gap between them might be termed informational noise. The catastrophe of the information explosion is that many people cannot absorb the information that they need, whereas the catastrophe of informational noise is that at least as many people can spread information that is not needed.

To filter out all noise is a practical impossibility. Since most of us have ten fingers, we are en route to developing a para-informational society, in which any meaningful phrase that is uttered drowns quickly in insignificant sound. The result is close to Borges's *Library of Babel*, a universal treasury/dumpster that contains everything that ever was, will be, or can be written:

> For every rational line or forthright statement there are leagues of senseless cacophony, verbal nonsense, and incoherency . . . . Infidels claim that the rule in the Library is not 'sense', but 'nonsense', and that 'rationality' (even humble, pure coherence) is an almost miraculous exception. (2000, pp. 22, 32)

Can this development be called "progress"? The literacy of an all-encompassing library does not differ much from the illiteracy of the Bronze Age. In order to produce Shakespeare's plays or Tolstoy's novels, it took humans several millennia of language and literary refinement. It would take millions of years to locate these plays or novels in a true Library of Babel, one containing all possible combinations of signs. Paradoxical as it may seem, it is easier to create something out of nothing than to locate something amid everything. This rule of thumb is equally valid for scientific research, as observed by John Naisbitt, a leading analyst of social megatrends:

> Uncontrolled and unorganized information is no longer a resource in an information society. Instead, it becomes the enemy of the information worker. Scientists who are overwhelmed with technical data complain of information pollution and charge that it takes less time to do an experiment than to find out whether or not it has already been done. (1982, p. 24)

No industry can contaminate the natural environment as noxiously as our words can pollute the informational one. To build an ecologically dirty factory or machine in real space is expensive and time-consuming. Yet, the purity of virtual space is as precious as that of the natural environment. What we take in from the Internet is impressed upon our brains, occupying megabytes of our personal memory. If the individual lags disastrously behind humanity at large, a way must be found to protect mental space, and that is a task for the "ecology of consciousness".

The dregs of verbal entropy grow in geometric progression, as does the growth of information itself, and both are clogging mental space. The effect is an intellectual numbness that Orrin Klapp described as boredom:

> While we tend to think of boredom as arising from a deficit of stimuli (information underload), it also (and, in fact, more commonly) arises from excessive stimulation (information overload). Information, like energy, tends to degrade into entropy—into noise, redundancy, and banality—as the fast horse of information outstrips the slow horse of meaning. (see Wurman, 1989, p. 38)

In this chapter, I have tried not to move beyond the limits of alarmist discourse. The foundations of secular alarmism, as opposed to religious alarmism, e.g. the biblical prophets, were laid by Malthus at the end of the Enlightenment, and received a powerful new impetus from ecologists and pacifists in the second half of the twentieth century. Alarmist discourse should be distinguished from revolutionary and utopian discourse, although their elements sometimes overlap, as in Marxism. Alarmist discourse warns of a possible danger, but does not point to a specific remedy, nor does it necessarily envision the possibility of deliverance. Two hundred years after Malthus sounded his alarm about the perils of deficiency, an alarm ought to be sounded about the perils of informational excess. Fortunately, the pessimistic prophecies of Malthus have not been fulfilled, so we have reason to hope that the informational crisis too will be overcome. Hölderlin writes that where danger is, there arises salvation also (see Haverkamp, 1996, p. 48). We can add that only those who do not take pleasure in facing danger deserve salvation.

# 11

# Horrology: The study of civilization in fear of itself

Political terrorism has been practiced for 150 years, since the 1860s in Russia. However, today, its global scale and unpredictability indicate a new possible state of civilization that goes far beyond terrorism itself; this new state can be called *horrorism*. Terror is usually defined as violence, or threats of violence, used for intimidation and coercion; often, terror is carried out for political purposes. In its turn, horror as a painful and intense fear, dread, or dismay is caused by terror. Etymologically, horror is derived from the Latin word *horrere*, meaning "to bristle with fear". It would be more appropriate to relate terror and horror not as an act and a reaction to that act, but as the actual and the potential. Horror is caused by the possibility of terror even more than by actual terror. It is known that illness can cure at least one thing—the fear of getting ill. Horror is incurable because it is not the fear of illness, but the illness of fear itself.

In the second half of the twentieth century civilization was haunted by the threat that it posed to its natural environment. The twenty-first century, from its very beginning, underscored the threat that civilization poses to itself. A discipline that might emerge in the humanities in response to these new realities is *Horrology*, which explores civilization as a system of traps and self-exploding devices, making humankind a hostage of its own creations.

The name of the proposed discipline—*Horrology*—is no less horrible and hideous than its intended meaning. The term *horrology* is precise in its onomatopoeic way, with the bone-chilling roars of the two *r*'s and moans of the three *o*'s. *Horrology* is the study of the self-destructive mechanisms of civilization, which make it susceptible to all forms of terrorism, including its biological and technological forms. Horrology explores how any accomplishment of civilization can be used against it, as a means for its subversion. So many forms of technology can put humanity at risk that practically any of them deserves its own horrological study. For example, after 9/11, it is possible to speak of the horrology of aviation and the horrology of architecture (or sky-scrapers). Consider also the threat posed to civilization by future technologies such as self-replicating machines and nano-devices, as described in the "hell" scenario by Bill Joy, a cofounder of Sun Microsystems, and rendered by Joel Garreau in his book *Radical Evolution*:

> Robots more intelligent than humans could reduce the lives of their creators to that of pathetic zombies. ... Nanotechnology holds out the possibility of the 'gray goo' end-of-the world scenario, in which devices too tough, too small, and too rapidly spreading to stop, suck everything vital out of all living things, reducing their husks to ashy mud in a matter of days .... Unlike nuclear weapons, these horrors could make more and more of themselves. Let loose on the planet, the genetically engineered pathogenes, the superintelligent robots, the tiny nanotech assemblers and of course the computer viruses could create trillions more of themselves, vastly more unstoppable than mosquitoes bearing the worst plagues. (2005, p. 139)

An archetype of such endless and self-destructive productivity is the magic pot from the famous fairy tale by the Brothers Grimm: the porridge that came pouring out of it began to fill the kitchen, the house, the yard, the street, the town, and potentially the entire world. The more productive a system, the more potentially destructive it becomes in the age of advanced technologies—these "magic pots" of today. As an example, it is possible to speak of horrology of the Internet, focusing on the spread of viruses in computer networks. Viruses do not spread in telephones or TV networks; it is much more powerful electronic connections that fall easy prey to such *misorganisms*, to use the same prefix as in the words *mistake* and *misunderstanding*. As was shown with the newest Macbook laptops, a hacker can hijack the firmware to render a lithium-ion battery useless so it no longer holds a charge, or worse, turn off the temperature management to make it potentially explode. In other words, a laptop potentially becomes a bomb ready to explode in our hands.

The year of 2001 turned out to be a furtive step through the back door into the third millennium rather than a grand entrance through its front gates. Behind this back door is a stairway to the top of a skyscraper, which may collapse at any moment. The higher the skyscraper of civilization soars, the more fragile it becomes under its own weight. The inauspicious beginning of this new epoch cannot be attributed solely to the battle of Islamic fundamentalism with the Western civilization. At the height of its evolution, civilization posits a danger to itself. A passenger plane becomes a rocket, and a letter becomes an agent of chemical warfare. The postal service, medicine, computers, aviation, water-reservoirs, and bridges—any of these means can become a weapon for civilization's destruction. Symbolically, on 9/11, the terrorists did not use anything besides the targets themselves as their weapons. This "math of terror" shows how adding together various elements of civilization—in this case, airplanes and skyscrapers—amounts to their mutual subtraction, or destruction. This accounts for the unusually "efficient" terrorist act, which provoked a shocking statement by Karlheinz Stockhausen, a German composer and a leader of the European musical avant-garde:

> Asked at a press conference on Monday for his view of the events, Stockhausen answered that the attacks were 'the greatest work of art imaginable for the whole cosmos.' According to a tape transcript from public broadcaster Norddeutscher Rundfunk, he went on: 'Minds achieving something in an act that we couldn't even dream of in music, people rehearsing like mad for 10 years, preparing fanatically for a concert, and then dying, just imagine what happened there. You have people who are that focused on a performance and then 5,000 people are dispatched to the afterlife, in a single moment. I could not do that. By comparison, we composers are nothing.' (see Lentricchia and McAuliffe, 2003, p. 7)

Such an aesthetic apology of terror is certainly terrifying by itself. For his cynical statement, the great German composer was ostracized, his concerts in Hamburg were cancelled, and his reputation suffered a blow. What Stockhausen failed to acknowledge is that civilization prepared this "artistic" act of terror against itself, making it practically feasible and aesthetically impressive. The terrorists needed the airplanes and Twin Towers of the World Trade Center, so symbolic of the material values and achievements of Western civilization, to commit such a "beautiful" evil. Western civilization could only have been beheaded so "scenically" because it had raised its head so high.

The terrorists did not simply destroy the New York cityscape, but in their own way completed it. The view of New York forever imprinted in the memory of future generations will not be the glaring Manhattan with the Twin Towers, nor will it be the gaping Manhattan after their collapse; it will be the Manhattan of September 11, precisely between 8:45 am and 10:29 am, with the silhouette of the airplanes as if forever collaged on to the silhouettes of the towers. This is the exact image of civilization in its dramatic chiaroscuro. The profound archetypal pattern of this event demonstrates that terrorism, in its "highest achievements", is inseparable from civilization, or, in other words, that civilization is harboring terror deep within itself.

This self-destructive potential of the hyperactive Western civilization was clearly foreseen by Johann Wolfgang von Goethe in the early nineteenth century. Though often misrepresented as social utopia, the second part of his *Faust* testifies to quite the opposite. The activity of Faust as a social reformer and "civilization builder" culminates in his constructing a new city at the shore that is forcefully won from the sea. Faust dreams of settling a new world "on acres free among free people", and with this last effort he savors his "striving's crown and sum":

> I might entreat the fleeting minute:
> Oh tarry yet, thou art so fair! (*Faust*, lines 11581–2)

However, Mephistopheles, who had instigated Faust to this feat, makes a sarcastic note behind the back of his blind and half-deaf patron:

> For us alone you are at pains
> With all your dikes and moles; a revel
> For Neptune, the old water-devil,
> Is all you spread, if you but knew.
>     You lose, whatever your reliance—
>     The elements are sworn to our alliance,
>     In ruin issues all you do. (*Faust*, lines 11544–50)

Such is Goethe's vision of the master terror, whose executor turns out to be "the sea devil" Neptune himself, or Mephistopheles' brother. Terror is not a chaotic destructive action against civilization, but an ironic accomplishment of the latter's own catastrophic potential. Whatever Faust strives to build is designed for ruin. The city on the "free acres" won from the sea is, in fact, a generous gift from Faust to the sea's devil. Civilization constructs itself in the forms most condensed and suitable for its subsequent destruction, according to the law of dangerous beauty that is the result of the combined efforts by Faust and Mephistopheles. A human creative genius and the devil eager to support his endeavors form an indivisible pair.

It is noteworthy that Karlheinz Stockhausen, apologizing for his notorious comments mentioned earlier, follows Goethe's hint and points to Lucifer as a major inspiration behind 9/11 events:

> After further questions about the events in America, I said that such a plan appeared to be Lucifer's greatest work of art. Of course I used the designation "work of art" to mean the work of destruction personified in Lucifer. In the context of my other comments this was unequivocal.

I cannot find a fitting name for such a 'satanic composition.' (Personal communication from Professor Karlheinz Stockhausen, http://www. stockhausen.org/message_from_karlheinz.html)

Ironically, under the guise of protection and comfort, freedom and efficiency, civilization gathers us together in one palace of "good and light", exposing us to one precise and sweeping blow.

Just as a computer network brings forth viral epidemics that can cause its paralysis, so too our entire civilization casts a gigantic shadow that threatens to eclipse it. *Horrorism* is the state of a civilization in fear of itself because any of its achievements can become a weapon for its own destruction. Even white powder and nail files can be perceived as a potential threat. The associative fabric of our post-9/11 life is woven from metaphors of death.

Following 9/11, the American people were advised by the US government to lead their normal life, continue with their business, while, at the same time, being particularly vigilant and careful. That ambiguous recommendation was met with many sneers and complaints. How is it possible to reconcile "normal life" and "vigilance" with "pervasive danger?" But these complaints are prompted by mindsets of the previous times, more relaxed and innocent. The mature civilization of today enters a zone of extreme risk that increases with each new stage of progress. The formula for the future is this: "Business as usual plus the *horrification* of the entire way of life".[3]

If the fear of pollution—civilization's threat to nature—haunted the second half of the twentieth century, then the twenty-first century may fall prey to the horror—the threats of civilization to itself. Ecology, as the primary concern of humanity, is succeeded by horrology that explores civilization as a system of traps and self-exploding devices, and humankind as a hostage of its own creations. Horrology as a dicipline is the reverse of all other disciplines that study civilization. It is a negative science of civilization: hence nega–technology, nega–architecture, nega-sociology, nega-politics, and nega-aesthetics as branches of horrology. Everything studied by other disciplines as positive attributes and structural properties of civilization, horrology studies as a growing possibility of its self-destruction.

---

[3] The formula is a reference to Lenin's famous slogan: "Communism is Soviet power plus the electrification of the whole country". Lenin considered electrification crucial for the industrial transformation of Russia, literally bringing "enlightenment" to workers and peasants in every town and village. This slogan was later often rephrased in Soviet times (for example, "telephonization" or "chemification of the whole country") to emphasize the USSR's drive towards modernization. (Editor's Note).

# PART FOUR

# Humans and humans

# 12

# Universics: From relativism to critical universality

## Intellectuals and universality

The twentieth World Philosophical Congress in Boston (1998) was the last one of the twentieth century. Intended to summarize the trends and achievements of the century-long intellectual search, the congress was symbolically titled "Paideia", which in Greek means "harmonic development". Its slogan was "Philosophy as an instrument for educating humanity". However, the common message of many plenary speakers, including Martha Nussbaum, Ioanna Kuçuradi, Karl-Otto Apel, Israel Scheffler, and Leon Olive was precisely the inability of contemporary philosophy to achieve the goal of educating humanity, even by means of its most recognized trends, such as analysis, hermeneutics, poststructuralism, and deconstruction. By the end of the twentieth century, philosophy seemed to have lost the dignity of universal reason—the basis of its self-esteem—that is necessary for teaching and edifying. The contemporary philosopher is less like an exhorting preacher and more like a repentant sinner who does not believe in oneself, and is incapable of securing the trust of non-philosophers. Western philosophy feels obliged to disavow its former claims of universality along with such concepts as *humankind*, *truth*, and *objectivity*. The very idea of "humanity as a collective (universal) subject" (Lyotard, 1996, p. 503) has become either suspicious or irrelevant in the postmodern age, which prefers to define culture in terms of ethnicity and gender. This anti-universalist stance is dangerous because it can easily be co-opted for the opposite cause:

if universality is fiction, then there is no intellectually justifiable way to limit the power of any particular group which aims to expand its political and cultural dominance at the expense of others.

"Away with objectivity and long live solidarity"—this neo-pragmatic approach, formulated by Richard Rorty in his famous article "Solidarity or Objectivity?" (1985) is characteristic of many trends in contemporary Western philosophical thought. But, if solidarity were the criterion of truth or even a substitute for truth, what would be the role of Socratic reflection and debate in contemporary society? What would be the place of philosophy in a totalitarian society where solidarity clearly triumphs over truth? The fact that all people are in solidarity about something does not automatically make their opinion true. We know all too well from the lessons of the twentieth century that collective madness, and even national madness, is possible. By sacrificing the categories of truth and universality, philosophy renounces its critical role in society; it stops being Socratic and instead becomes an ideology that serves the interests of certain groups involved in the struggle for the position of power.

Michel Foucault has expressed his anti-universalist stance in the most resolute terms:

> It seems to me that what must now be taken into account in the intellectual is not the 'bearer of universal values.' Rather, it's the person occupying a specific position—but whose specificity is linked, in a society like ours, to the general functioning of an apparatus of truth. In other words, the intellectual has a three-fold specificity: that of his class position (whether as petty-bourgeois in the service of capitalism or 'organic' intellectual of the proletariat); that of his conditions of life and work, linked to his condition as an intellectual (his field of research, his place in a laboratory, the political and economic demands to which he submits or against which he rebels, in the university, the hospital, etc.); lastly, the specificity of the politics of truth in our societies. (1996, p. 380)

This suggests that the entire "three-fold specificity" of intellectuals is defined by politics and nothing else. But, what makes intellectuals different from any other representatives of a given class or political and economic positions? Is it not intellectuals who are capable of critically approaching their own class identities and rationally problematizing the conditions of their life and work within a given society?

Intellectuals are so valuable for society precisely because of their trans-social mentality and imagination, i.e. their capacity to keep distance from those particular identities to which they belong by birth, gender, employment, social stratum, or ethnic tradition. To use Mikhail Bakhtin's term, it is the position of "being beyond" (*vnenakhodimost'*) that allows intellectuals to be critical of existing conditions. Intellectuals who simply identify themselves with certain political attitudes turn out to be ideologists. In fact, Foucault's definition applies not to intellectuals, but to *ideologists* who take on certain social roles and use reason in instrumental ways in order to promote a specific political agenda. The denial of universal values reduces reason to a utilitarian tool. How can an intellectual criticize society while being completely defined by, in Foucault's words, "his class position (whether as petty-bourgeois in the service of capitalism or 'organic' intellectual of the proletariat)"? (1996, p. 380). This brings to mind Lenin's idea of literature as a "cog" in the party machine—the idea that came to justify the huge repressive apparatus of Soviet Ideology:

> Down with non-partisan writers! Down with literary supermen! Literature must become *part* of the common cause of the proletariat, 'a cog and a screw' of one single great Social-Democratic mechanism set in motion by the entire politically conscious vanguard of the entire working class. Literature must become a component of organised, planned and integrated Social-Democratic Party work. (Lenin, 2008, p. 22)

The submission of intellectuals to the demands of a party discipline signals the end of universality and, in fact, the end of their intellectual vocation as critics of contemporary society. "One cannot live in society and be free from society. The freedom of the bourgeois writer, artist or actress is simply masked (or hypocritically masked) dependence on the money-bag, on corruption, on prostitution" (Lenin, 2008, p. 25). This famous statement governed Soviet cultural policy for many decades. However, it is precisely the *freedom from society* that enables intellectuals, by holding themselves at a distance from any existing political class or party, to be the strongest proponents of the universality of reason and critics of present conditions.

Universal values shape the two most important responsibilities of intellectuals: first, to criticize any specific set of social rules and practices, and second, to reconcile those who belong to different or opposing groups. Critique and reconciliation are two complementary aspects of universality, its forces of negation and affirmation. Universality is not something static and immutable; on the contrary, it is the most explosive kind of intellectual energy that undermines the stability of all established positions. Philosophy can be truly critical only if it refuses to identify itself with any particular social order or political interest, thus expressing the spirit of *critical universality*.

## Universality against totalitarianism

The contemporary refutation of universality emerged in response to the catastrophes of World War II, German Nazism, and Soviet Communism.

The classical, though fragmented manifestation of this view is found in Max Horkheimer and Theodor Adorno's Dialectic of Enlightenment (1947), in which the Enlightenment is blamed for the spirit of domination that led eventually to the rise of totalitarian myths and acts of brutality and irrationality.

We now must re-examine the alleged connection between the idea of universality and the crimes of totalitarianism. If we agree that the universals of "reason", "truth", and "knowledge" were indeed the offspring of the Enlightenment, then by no means can we blame the latter for the horrors of Communism or Nazism. How can universalism be implicated in the fight of the proletariat against bourgeoisie, and in the attack of Nazism against Jewish and cosmopolitan culture? The communist doctrine, as practiced in totalitarian societies, dramatically digressed from early Marx's universalist vision of the human species as a whole; only in his later works did this vision become one of class struggle, beginning with the *Manifesto of the Communist Party* (1848), where Marx and Engels state: "The history of all hitherto existing society is the history of class struggles." The doctrines of class and national superiority have nothing to do with the idea of universality. Rather, these historical lessons of the twentieth century prompt us to think about universality as the first and foremost victim of totalitarianism, both in its class and race varieties. These lessons invite us to be suspicious of any social, racial, and nationalist denunciations of universality.

The dismissal of universality under the pretext of its complicity in the crimes of Nazism and Communism only shows the historical blindness of those European intellectuals who had never experienced the reality of Communism or Nazism themselves. Is there any connection between Lenin's and Stalin's forms of Bolshevism, which systematically destroyed entire social and ethnic groups, and the ideal of universality? None, except that some Western intellectuals of the 1920s–50s, such as Romain Rolland, Bernard Shaw, Leon Feuchtwanger, Alexandre Kojève, Andre Breton, Louis Aragon, and certain Frankfurt neo-Marxist thinkers, were so disillusioned by the crisis of liberal democracy in the West that they preferred to see something universal in Soviet Communism. Alexander Kojève, to take one example, applied the Hegelian vision of Napoleon to Stalin as manifestation of the Absolute Spirit in the middle of the twentieth century.

Thus, the universal had to pay twice for the same aberration of vision because, within half a century, many European intellectuals succeeded in reversing its value from positive to negative. While Stalin was initially praised as an embodiment of the universal spirit of the Enlightenment, later universality came to be suspect due to its associations with Stalinism and the Gulag. While, for the leftist intellectuals of the 1920s–30s, Communism and the so-called "proletarian internationalism" were rational ways by which to construct an all-human classless society, for the postmodern generation the rationalism of the Enlightenment was compromised by its connection with Communism. Yet, there has never been any real connection between such obviously incompatible worldviews. If we wish to learn anything from the history of the twentieth century, with its myths of class and race and other ideological obsessions, we must shift our focus from the denunciation of universalism to an appreciation of the need for its revival.

# Universalism and postmodern pluralism

Postmodern pluralism was generous in asserting the intrinsic value of any existing culture and tradition. According to Jean-François Lyotard, any consensus can be only local and partial, and its language and values are incommensurable with the language and values of other discourses:

> ...[A]ny consensus on the rules defining a game and the 'moves' playable within it *must* be local, in other words, agreed on by its present players and subject to eventual cancellation. The orientation then favors a multiplicity of finite meta-arguments, by which I mean argumentation that concerns meta-prescriptives and is limited in space and time. (1996, p. 504)

Lyotard argues that "consensus has become an outmoded and suspect value" (1996, p. 504), insisting on its local and temporary limitations, i.e. on the plurality of consensuses.

If we accept this view, then the next logical question would be how to achieve consensus among different consensuses. The question of universality does not disappear, it simply moves on to the next level. This must continue until all consensuses, all forms of rationality, and all groups find for themselves some meta-consensus that would include, as a minimum precondition, an *agreement to disagree* peacefully.

After the fall of the Berlin Wall and the World Trade Center towers, we can see how utopian the idea of blissfully isolated local consensuses was. In the contemporary world of growing globalization and new polarization, the interaction of various consensuses is inevitable, and one needs at least to have an agreement about the ways to disagree. The multiplicity of finite consensuses must include the rituals of negotiations and reconciliation. In other words, the right to disagree must once again be recognized by all participants as a universal and not just local value.

The question of universality is especially relevant for the political dilemmas of the twenty-first century, emerging in the war between civilization and terror. Lyotard assumed that the incommensurability of values and discourses should become the foundation for a new cultural order: "A recognition of the heteromorphous nature of language games is a first step in that direction. This obviously implies a renunciation of terror, which assumed that they are isomorphic and tries to make them so" (1996, p. 504).

It is instructive to note how in 1979 Lyotard conceptualized terror, which, in our time, became one of the factors determining political and everyday life. For Lyotard, terror is based on the pretension towards an isomorphic structure of "language games", i.e. social and cultural values. The practice of terrorism, however, demonstrates quite the opposite: the insistence on the incommensurable and irreconcilable. The experience that goes far beyond language games demonstrates that terror results not from isomorphism, but from heteromorphism, i.e. the idea of absolute heterogeneity and incompatability of various cultures and religions. The idea that consensus has become an outmoded and suspect value does not help to renounce terrorism, but only encourages it.

We see that no localities remain isolated in the age of globalization. What becomes the principal issue today is how the local consensus achieved within one particular group—amongst, for example, militant Islamic fundamentalists or militant Basque separatists—may fit into a metaconsensus with other ethnic, religious, and political groups. Can we avoid metanarratives in our attempt to build this metaconsensus? The idea of local discourses, incommensurable and simultaneously peaceful, presents a vision no less utopian than the idea of an absolutely homogeneous world-state governed by the rules of pure reason. It is only commensurability and translatability among discourses and values that may keep various groups peacefully negotiating their place and role in the global civilization. In no way must the lessons of postmodern multiculturalism be forgotten or neglected; instead, they should be incorporated into a broader, more tolerant, demanding, and simultaneously more responsible culture of agreement, i.e. a culture of critical universality.

In his critique of the Enlightenment and modernity, Lyotard famously pronounced that we had paid too high a price for our nostalgia for the whole and universal, and called to "wage a war on totality" and "activate the differences" (Lyotard, 1984, p. 82.). Indeed, today we cannot allow any metanarratives to impose on us their totalitarian logic. At the same time, the world now faces the opposite danger: its possible disintegration into numerous local narratives along religious and civilizational lines. Thus, Lyotard's famous pronouncement should be rephrased as follows: "We have paid too high a price for our nostalgia for fragments: so we cannot now allow our differences to tear apart the world."

## Apophatic, or critical universality

This raises again the issue of critical universality or, in this case, self-critical universality. Every consensus and every discourse must be critical about its own rules and abandon any hegemonic claims. The ethical motive of new transcultural thinking must be humility and not pride.

The philosophy of the twenty-first century still has the task of elaborating the criterion of *critical universality* in order to distinguish it from the old, pre-critical type of *universality* as well as the *critical* attitudes of post-Kantian philosophy that undermined the value of universality. The universality of pre-critical, pre-Kantian epoch proceeded from the category of *identity* in two senses: first, the self-identity of reason, allegedly possessing some immutable truths, and second, the identity of reason and reality, allegedly exemplifying the transparent laws of reality open to cognition. The critical epoch that followed the Kantian revolution in philosophy, while demonstrating the opaqueness of reality for rational comprehension, taught us to think in categories of difference, revealing a great diversity of historical, national, and ethnic reasons, or types of rationality.

At the same time, the death of universality is fraught, as a result of critical limitation and differentiation of reason, with outbreaks of racism, nationalism, fundamentalism, and other power seeking "-isms", for which some varieties of postmodern philosophy inadvertently offer justification. The liberal denouncers of "humanity as a fiction" may be shocked by the non-liberal practical consequences of their theories in the religiously and ideologically divided world. If we think that every culture and every tradition, even that of cannibals, is justified and self-valued, that view will only lead to the epidemic of parochial "-isms" that may exterminate humankind itself.

This proliferation of "prides" was described in the epilogue of Dostoevsky's *Crime and Punishment*, in Raskolnikov's dream:

> Some new sorts of microbes were attacking the bodies of men, but these microbes were endowed with intelligence and will. Men attacked by them became at once mad and furious. But never had men considered themselves so intellectual and so completely in possession of the truth as these sufferers, never had they considered their decisions, their scientific conclusions, their moral convictions so infallible. Whole villages, whole towns and peoples went mad from the infection. All were excited and did not understand one another. Each thought that he alone had the truth and was wretched looking at the others, beat himself on the breast, wept, and wrung his hands. They did not know how to judge and could not agree what to consider evil and what good; they did not know whom to blame, whom to justify. (Translated by Constance Garnett, pp. 488–9).

We can diagnose this "terrible new strange plague" as a loss of the universal.

It is now the time to understand that the critical post-Kantian epoch, with its pluralistic effects sufficiently tested by postmodern multiculturalism and other "multis", may lead, in fact, to the extension of the concept of universality, not to its exclusion. Universality must not be reduced either to the generality of one canon or to the plurality of isolated and self-sustained canons, but should proceed to the next stage, where the difference itself may become a starting point in the movement towards a new, critical universality. In this sense, universality represents the capacity of each culture and each ideology to criticize itself, recognizing its own limitations in an attempt to build new trans-cultural and trans-ethnic communities. The critical universality of the early twenty-first century prompts us to treat each culture as incomplete and "deficient" (rather than self-sufficient): every culture needs to transcend its own set of values and to enrich itself with elements from other cultures. Instead of a parade of prides, we need a meeting place for humilities. Each culture has a huge potential of desires and possibilities that can be fulfilled only through communication with other cultures (see the section "From Multicultural to Transcultural" in Chapter 3).

Critical universality, unlike the idealistic or positivistic universality of the past, does not provide us with a pre-established system of values. Rather, it proceeds from our dissatisfaction with what we are and what we have; it emerges in the process of our distancing ourselves critically from all existing political, ethnic, and cultural identities. To the extent that each local culture has admitted its own "deficiencies" and failures, it contributes to the rebirth and growth of the universal. The universal is not a place of comprehensive and immutable truths, but a space for concessions among cultures. We should think about universality in *apophatic* rather than cataphatic terms: we know what it is *not*, not what it is. This apophatic type of universality is captured in "not" as a response to any claims of a culture to being universal.

Thus, the transition at the turn of the twenty-first century from the old-style universality to a cultural relativism does not imply the ultimate collapse of universality; rather, this transition reflects the evolution of universality from a cataphatic mode to an apophatic one. We have found as unsatisfying all positive definitions of universality shaped by modernity and the Enlightenment, just as the theology of the Middle Age found it unsatis-fying to define the Cause of Everything solely in positive terms. Through the mystical theology of Pseudo-Dionysius the Areopagite, both Western and Eastern Christianity began to consider God as One who cannot be cognized and defined. Dionysius talks about the unsurpassable darkness and silence of God, who can be approached only through the most profound and authentic way of non-knowing and non-speaking:

> Since it is the Cause of all beings, we should posit and ascribe to it all the affirmations we make in regard to beings, and, more appropriately, we should negate all these affirmations, since it surpasses all being. ... One is supremely united by a completely unknowing inactivity of all

knowledge, and knows beyond the mind by knowing nothing. ... We would be like sculptures who set out to carve a statue. They remove every obstacle to the pure view of a hidden image, and simply by this act of clearing aside they show up the beauty that is hidden. (Pseudo-Dionysius, 1987, pp. 136, 137, 138)

If we agree that the idea of universality was the primary cause and engine of modern Western history, then we must reconsider our recent postmodern past as a lesson in *negative* universality that operates by "clearing aside". The negative universality cannot be authentically defined in positive terms, but presupposes critically distancing itself from all of its dogmatic affirmations, as well as from uncritical pluralism that speaks in the language of secular polytheism and worships the gods of classes, nations, races, genders, and disciplines. Critical universality is the apophatic philosophy of the secular age, more sensitive to, and therefore more critical of, what is not universal than what the universal actually is. We need to reexamine the relativism that dominated our cultural theories and practices in the 1970s–90s as a transitional point rather than the end in the history of universality.

# Plurality as an aspect of universality

According to postmodernist uncritical pluralism, every discourse is intrinsically good and justified as long as it is based on a local consensus and does not claim its applicability to a different consensus. In his book *The Differend: Phrases in Dispute* (1988), Lyotard does not offer any criterion for evaluating different positions in a dispute when he develops his theory of incommensurability. No discourse is better or worse, higher or lower, than any other discourse. With critical universality as an emerging cultural paradigm, we can incorporate pluralism into a consistently evaluative mode of thinking. Plurality in this sense does not mean that every culture or every discourse is unquestionable, or, in another formulation, beyond good and evil. Instead, plurality itself may serve as a criterion of evaluation, depending on how intrinsically pluralistic a certain culture or a discourse may be.

For example, there are three cultures: A, B, and C, each relying on a local consensus. Based on passive, uncritical pluralism (sometimes called "relativism"), the very fact of being a culture, as an expression of certain community and consensus, makes the existence of all three cultures equally justified. Now let us look at how these cultures are pluralistic within themselves. Culture A recognizes and embraces those values that are characteristic of cultures B and C; it allows, for example, the religions and temples of B and C to prosper peacefully within their own territories. Culture B recognizes the values of C, but rejects all elements of culture A. Finally, culture C resolutely rejects cultures A and B and can be considered purely monolithic or monodiscursive. From a pluralistic point of view, are these three cultures equally justified and valuable? It is precisely the criterion of pluralism that makes it possible for us to recognize culture A as more universal than culture B, and culture B as more universal than culture C. This *creative pluralism*, in contrast to passive pluralism, does not merely accept the diversity of discourses as they are, but distinguishes among them on the basis of their internal plurality and openness to the values of other cultures. This pluralism is creative because it attempts to *pluralize* each culture and to diversify it internally, making each culture more universal by accepting the values of other cultures and elaborating the modes of negotiation and reconciliation among them.

The openness to others always presupposes the capacity to distance oneself and to look at one's own identity through the eyes of others. Universality is impossible without this self-reflexive and self-critical component. In fact, the more internally pluralistic and self-critical a culture is, the more universal it is.

## Universal vs general. Universics

Pluralism itself, therefore, can be viewed as an aspect of universalism. The universal has often been perceived as a synonym of the *total*, *common*, and *general*, i.e. as a characteristic of all people, cultures, or epochs. However, this understanding of *universality* mistakes it for *generality*, whereas in fact these are two very different concepts.

*Universal* literally means "around one": the word is derived from the Latin *unus* and *versus* (a participle from the verb "vertere", meaning "to turn"). It is a category that applies not to all entities of a certain class, but to one single entity, which possesses the qualities of many entities. If the *general* is a quality that is common to many objects, then the *universal* refers to one object that contains or displays many qualities. A master key, for example, can be called *universal* if it opens all doors in a given building. It is also possible to say "a universal genius" or "a universal mind", meaning that a given individual is creative and fruitful in many areas. The work of one writer can display a variety of genres and styles and exemplify a microcosm of the entire national literature; this way, Shakespeare, Goethe, and Pushkin are deemed to be *universal creators* in relation to those themes, heroes, and genres of English, German, and Russian literature, respectively, prefigured in their works. At the same time, the expressions "a general genius" or "a general mind" are meaningless because *general,* unlike *universal,* cannot be applied to a single individual. *The uni-vers-al is the vers-atility of the uni-que, leading to the multifaceted nature of the singular.*

Thus, not only does universality not neglect the individual and the particular, it recognizes the individual's inherent potential for diversity. The demand for pluralism dominating cultural theory since the 1970s can lead to a very superficial multiplication of differences, unless it embraces the value of universality as the capacity of a single individual or a single culture to be different from itself and to incorporate the multiplicity of others. Creative pluralism is a way *to,* not from, universality.

In this theoretical perspective, we need to demystify the category of the universal and to separate it from naïve metaphysics. We need a new discipline that would study the universal as a quality of individuals, in distinction from metaphysics that traditionally focused on generalities. We can call this discipline *universics,* using the productive suffix found in the formation of the names of other disciplines, such as *physics* or *aesthetics.*

In metaphysics, *universal* is a general term that is applied to many individuals or many single cases, such as *beauty, materiality,* or the *ideal.* However, every individual also belongs to many universals and thus contains universality. Even such a simple entity as a grain of sand can be viewed as an intersection of such universals as *firmness, dryness, whiteness, smallness, lightness, and discreteness.* Each individual is a community of universals, a micro-universe. The task of universics is the analysis not so much of universals, but of the universality of individuals in their internal diversity. The object of universics may be a human, a planet, a plant, a building, a cloud, a blade of grass, or a grain of sand, inasmuch as this individual object presents a universe, i.e. a combination and interaction of various universals (qualities, properties). Only singular objects and person-alities, such as Leonardo da Vinci, possess universality.

In contrast to the dogmatic universalism that imposes one ideal or canon on all cultures and individuals, critical universlism presupposes internal diversity of individuals in their dialogical openness to others. In the secular age, the concept of critical universality may become a major force that challenges both fragmentation and totalitarianism and ensures the survival of humanity as a species.

# 13

# Micronics: The study of small things

As I wrote in chapter one, the avant-garde movement of the early twentieth century was dominated by hyperboles. In its turn, the proteism of the twenty-first century has a propensity towards litotes (from Greek *litos*, meaning "small" and "meager"), congenial to those nano-technologies that reduce the scales of industry and cybernetics to the size of an atom or a quantum. In fact, it is possible to identify four major kinds of technology that are shaping our future: (1) biotechnologies (including genetics); (2) nanotechnology (including molecular self–assembly); (3) information technologies (including computering and robotics); and (4) neuroscience (including brain-related technologies). All of these technologies have one feature in common: delving into the world of micro-objects. As Jon Turney puts it, "One interesting feature tying all four of these upcoming technologies is that they all involve working with very small stuff.... . Potentially, there are lots of ways they can converge, and some official reports just refer a general "nano-bio-info-cogno" (NBIC) technology as the thing to watch" (2010, p. 90).

The humanities have their own interest in the study of small things. This field of study that can be called *Micronics* has a considerable chance of becoming the center of transdisciplinary consciousness and the principal point of interaction between the humanities and the sciences in the twenty-first century. In this chapter, I first offer an overview of the diverse "micro" interests across various humanistic areas, and then I clarify what unites them.

Ever since antiquity, science has been searching for the smallest units of the universe: atoms, elementary particles, quanta, and one-dimensional "superstrings". The analysis of a whole by dividing it into elementary units was considered the most reliable method of cognition. Aristotle believed that "[a]s in other departments of science, so in politics, the compound should always be resolved into the simple elements or least parts of the whole" (Aristotle, 1916, p. 25). Francis Bacon proposed in his *Novum Organum* that "one has to look for the nature of this great State, i.e. universe, and of its government both in any primary combination and in the smallest parts of things" (1826, p. 109).

In the twentieth and twenty-first centuries, as a result of discoveries in quantum physics and progress in computing and genetic technologies, it becomes clear that the small abides by its own physical, biological, aesthetic, and even theological laws. It is a more or less accepted view that we can never reduce the properties of large systems to the properties of their constituent elements. However, it is equally fallacious to believe that the qualities of small entities can be derived from their larger wholes. The distinction in size is not purely quantitative; it is qualitative. To use Hegel's term, it is a "measure" by which quantity becomes quality. We can see that today many disciplines have begun to consider micro-objects in their respective fields. For example, microbiology investigates the smallest (mostly one-cell) organisms, such as microbes, bacteria, viruses, amoebas, and infusoria. Quantum physics studies the laws of movement and interaction of microparticles (as opposed to the laws that govern the macroworld). Microsociology explores the interpersonal relationships in small groups, such as families, sports teams, task forces, university departments, and military squads. Microeconomics investigates the activity of the basic economic units, such as companies, firms, and enterprises. Microelectronics is occupied with the construction of mechanisms and tools of miniature size. Nanotechnology, as the most advanced discipline of this kind, deals with objects approximately one billionth of a meter in size that obey the laws of quantum mechanics (see Amato, 2000; Schumacher, 1989).

However, it is not solely the province of the natural and social sciences to impart qualitative meaning to the size of an object, but of the humanities too. Some cultures, such as Japanese and Korean, develop the aesthetics and poetics of smallness and prioritize the miniature as a form of literary and artistic expression. The category of the small also plays an important role in many religions. Zen, for example, teaches concentration on the minute elements of experience that escape rational understanding in the system of broad and general categories. Christianity turns to the model of the "least of those" and the "little ones" who are humble, meek, and child-like because "theirs is the kingdom of heaven". In the gospels, the "mustard seed" and the "eye of the needle", the ultimate images of smallness are used as metaphors for the heavenly kingdom. In such cases, the law of reversal is applied: the least will become the greatest, and faith the size of a mustard seed can move mountains. This theology of diminution corresponds to the psychology of *umilenie*, the Russian word for an emotional state brought on by the impression of smallness and weakness as if it were its opposite—strong and powerful. There is a Christian sentiment in this touching and tender experience, inspired by something outwardly fragile, humble, and yet spiritually triumphant. Jesus Christ's attitude to children, whose weakness and meekness open the Heavenly Kingdom to them, exemplifies this feeling of *umilenie* as tenderness or melting of the heart.

One of the greatest Christian theologians, Nicholas of Cusa, wrote about the coincidence of the absolute maximum and absolute minimum. One can say the same about the Absolute with equal certainty: it is infinitely great and infinitely small.

According to Jewish Hasidism, a spark is the only current manifestation of God's presence in the world that is accessible to people. The Kabala reveals, that during the creation of the world, the divine light dispersed into the smallest sparks, which descended to the depths of lower worlds in order to infuse the attraction to the higher worlds into earthly things. These sacred sparks, imprisoned in dark matter and seeking liberation and a return to their divine primary source, can be found disseminated in the most mundane, everyday things, for example, in a loaf of bread or a drop of water (Buber, 1975, pp. 53–4).

Nineteenth century Russian literature had a special fascination with images of "little people", beginning with Akaky Bashmachkin[1] from Gogol's *Overcoat*. These "slighted and insulted" men and women hold the lowest position in society and have neither the courage nor intelligence to defend themselves against the powers that be. These characters embodied the social and humanistic concerns of Russian writers: smallness as a sign of the trampled, but not abandoned, human dignity.

While the ethics of smallness focuses on such qualities as humility and meekness, the aesthetics of smallness appreciates the richness and subtlety of detail. In Russian literature, Boris Pasternak is a master of poetic micronics. His images extend to the limits of minimalism in the depiction of the material world. He portrays flashes of the minute particles of the ordinary captured in a drop of water or a grain of sand.

Micronics has its own reach into language. For example, Russian is very sensitive to the category of smallness and has many suffixes to form diminutives from nouns. The suffixes, such as "ok", "chik", "ik", "itsa", "k", "ink", "ushk", "ashk", "onk", "on'k", and "en'k" can be

---

[1]In *The Overcoat*, Nikolai Gogol, a great Ukranian-born Russian writer of the nineteenth century, tells the story of Akaky Akakievich Bashmachkin, a poor but virtuous copyist toiling within St. Petersburg government bureaucracy. With *The Overcoat*, Gogol is said to have introduced into Russian literature the theme of "little people" ("malen'kie lyudi") with its humanitarian concerns and sympathy for the downtrodden. "We all came from Gogol's 'Overcoat'", a phrase usually attributed to Dostoevsky, highlights the significance of the theme of 'little people' in Russian literature. (Editor's Note).

combined, further intensifying the degree of smallness. For instance, from the diminutive word *mal'chik* (a boy), two diminutives of the second order are derived, *mal'chishka* and *mal'chonok* (a little boy). From these, the diminutives of the third order are then formed, *mal'chishechka* and *mal'chonochek* (a tiny boy).

The culture of postmodernism develops its own sensibility to the notions of the minor and the minority. For example, Deleuze and Guattari (1986) elaborated the concept of *a minor literature* in opposition to the big canons of established classics.

All of these "micro" areas of different disciplines can be united by the meta-discipline of *micronics*. The fast growth of micronics can be explained by two factors. First, the sharpness of human vision increases as the eye becomes equipped with more and more complex devices, penetrating deeper into the world of matter and energy, time and space. Second, gradual miniaturization of all objects occurs in the processes of expansion of the physical universe and the accelerated growth of civilization. Both the history of humanity and the history of the universe involve a process of relativistic diminishment of their constituent parts. As the world becomes larger, everything becomes smaller relative to the world, thus joining the ranks of micro-entities.

This process was allegorically described by Goethe in the parable *The New Melusine*, in *Wilhelm Meister's Years of Travel* (1821–9). The story, which is about a beautiful princess from a family of dwarfs, illustrates that nothing in the world is permanent:

> [A]ll that was one great must become small and decrease, so we too are in the position that we have continually been decreasing and growing smaller, and before all others the royal family which has succumbed to this fate in the first place because of its blue blood. (1982, p. 46)

Such decreasing is the fate of all material and ideal singularities in the expanding world of physical mass and information.

# Quantum metaphysics

A similar fate of diminishment befalls the grand "aristocratic" metaphysical categories of the most pure and ancient origin: *being, spirit, ideas, and substances.* The theoretical need emerges for *micrometaphysics, micro-ethics, micropsychology, and microaesthetics* in order to comprehend the changing scale of personalities and things in the growing world. According to Theodor Adorno, this shift in scale calls for a transition from metaphysics to *micrology*:

Enlightenment leaves practically nothing of the metaphysical content of truth... That which recedes keeps getting smaller and smaller, as Goethe describes it in the parable of New Melusine's box, designating an extremity. It grows more and more insignificant; this is why, in the critique of cognition as well as in the philosophy of history, metaphysics immigrates into micrology. Micrology is the place where metaphysics finds a haven from totality. (1992, p. 407)

Historically, the sharpness of vision in metaphysics increases so it can see separate trees, where previously it only saw a forest. The new metaphysics, focusing on a thing in its singularity and the minimal units of meaning, is similar to physics, seeking the indivisible quantum units of matter and energy. Thus, similar to "quantum physics", one can call this new range of philosophical inquiry "quantum metaphysics". This is a metaphysics of the smallest elementary thinkables, including extra-conceptual and extra-linguistic, unnamable singularities. This is not a metaphysics of spirit or being, but a metaphysics of a garden and a tree, or a kitchen and a plate. The main intuitions of quantum metaphysics were first clearly expressed by Duns Scotus in his doctrine of individuals as the sole real existents in distinction from universals. From this point of view, whiteness or tallness do not exists but certain things, such as a wall or a hat, happen to be white or tall...

Any word or concept can become the point of departure for quantum metaphysics; in fact, any word in any language may serve as its ground concept. For example, the primary metaphysical concept can be "a hair" as the smallest tangible interval between things (metaphysics of "thinness") or "an umbrella" as a moving and folding cover for a lonely human being under the open sky (metaphysics of "shelter"). Each word contains a certain meaning, which may become the focus of a certain metaphysics, the same way "cogito" became the foundation for the "mega" metaphysics of Descartes, or "life" for the "mega" metaphysics of Nietzsche. Of course, such compact "chamber" metaphysics can encompass only a very limited range of phenomena related to the original micro-concept. For example, the metaphysics of a desk includes such related terms as *a chair, paper,* and *a desktop computer.* Small metaphysics are not metaphysical in the traditional sense because they contain no assumptions about the extra-sensual, invariable, and all-encompassing foundations of the world. They are constructed as a metaphysical gesture that relinquishes its metaphysical pretensions by offering itself only as a sign of discursive play.

As a philosophical discipline, quantum metaphysics offers multiple interpretations of the same microunits of meaning. While *miniaturizing its object,* quantum metaphysics simultaneously *possibilizes its method.* For instance, microphysics reveals the probabilistic nature of elementary particles; similarly, micrometaphysics reveals the probabilistic nature of micro-concepts. Words with micro-meanings display their capacity to function within multiple metaphysical systems, which is why their location can never be pinpointed. For example, *paper* can be the object of such intersecting metaphysics as a metaphysics of a surface, a metaphysics of whiteness, a metaphysics of flatness, or a metaphysics of writing. One should particularly note the role of grammar morphemes and words with grammatical meaning, such as prepositions, conjunctions, particles, prefixes, and suffixes as the quanta of sense with the largest range of metaphysical interpretations. The analysis of such elementary units of meaning as "on" or "of", "-ness", or "-dom" opens one of the most fascinating venues for the future of metaphysics.

The grand metaphysics of general concepts, such as Reason, Being, Idea, and Matter, is determined by the category of the necessary because it encompasses an infinite number of the most diverse objects and represents them in terms of identity. The world of large masses as presented by macro-physics appears just as deterministic. The shift from macro-physics to micro-physics reveals the probabilistic world of micro-particles within the world of determined macro-objects. In the same way, the shift from macro-metaphysics to micro-metaphysics reveals the probabilistic world of meanings, challenging the laws of logical necessity.

The terminological system of the metaphysics of the small naturally gravitates toward nouns with very concrete and material meanings, such as *a table* or *a leaf*. One may even wonder if they belong to the philosophical, presumably the most generalizing, approach. Mikhail Bakhtin dispels such doubts:

> In the first place, every science begins with unrepeatable single phenomena, and science continues to be linked with them throughout. In the second place, science, and above all philosophy, can and should study the specific form and function of this individuality. (1986a, p. 108)

Bakhtin's term *"nepovtorimaia edinichnost'"* ("unrepeatable singularity") does not seem to indicate a class of objects denoted by a specific word; rather, it refers to the individual object itself, which is of an even higher rank of singularity that cannot be verbally marked. In this sense, for example, "the apple" refers not to the concept of "apple", but to this singular apple itself. This raises the following question: "Is there a metaphysics of extra-verbal, sub-semiotic singularities, which have so far been completely ignored by the metaphysical tradition?" Even the most concrete word still refers to a whole class of objects and is thus a generality. The word "crumb" is a semantic giant among individual crumbs, myriads of which are designated by the same word.

When we think of the metaphysics of a single blade of grass, its actual, tangible presence in the philosophical text is necessary for the construction of this complete micro-metaphysics. A singular thing that is inscribed, or rather pasted, into a treatise becomes its first and ultimate metaphysical term, in which the signified coincides with the signifier. The duality of a verbal sign (the signifier in its distinction from the signified) is thus removed in the treatise about a particular blade of grass: only this very blade, not the common expression "a blade of grass", can represent itself as the ultimate micro-metaphysical object.

Such singularity is the unattainable limit of thinking, which both attempts and fails to reach pure actuality, "thisness", as the ultimate object of quantum metaphysics. "Thisness" (*haecceitas*) can be defined as a pure singularity divorced from all general qualities and predicates that it could share with other singularities; the property of being "this" and nothing else (see Adams, 1999). For example, the general qualities of a blade of grass are its being green, long, thin, sharp, and flexible. These qualities must be bracketed as soon as we approach it as *haecceitas*, ontologically different from all other blades of grass in the world—situated here and now, in a unique relationship with other objects and humans. *Haecceitas* is the ultimate temptation for metaphysics and its crucial self-test: can it grasp something beyond the nominative capacity of language? Can it bring the unnamable and unthinkable back to its own territory? What is left for thinking at the "zero" point where no general concepts and categories can be applied? How can we think "thisness" if it is only here and now, irreducible to any class of objects, common properties, or even to its name like "a blade of grass"?

Singularities are pariahs in the caste society of grand metaphysics; the most tangible things turn out to be metaphysical untouchables. To transcend metaphysics, while still remaining on its own ground, it is necessary, first, to develop a new language of singularities that would include proper names, both for individual animate beings and inanimate entities, and second, to move even further into the non-verbal realm of tangible, trans-semiotic singularities. Will it be possible to weave things, as such, into the texture of philosophical writing so that words and categories can be interspersed with the real-life objects?

Theodor Adorno saw our involvement with non-thinkable beings as the ultimate, yet unattainable goal of philosophy:

> Philosophy, indeed theoretical thought in general, suffers from an idealistic prejudgment because it deals only with concepts, never directly with what these concepts refer to … Philosophy cannot paste an ontic substratum into its treatises. It can only talk about it in words, and in so doing it assimilates that substratum, whereas it should want to keep it distinct from its own conceptuality. (1986, p. 365)

And yet, is it really true that philosophy cannot "paste an ontic substratum into its treatises"? In the end, all philosophical treatises are somehow pasted in the ontic substratum of the world. Even the manuscript of Hegel's *Science of Logic* rested at one point on his desk next to his inkpot and pens. If things can surround a treatise, then why can't a treatise surround things, inscribing them into its contents?

The idea that things are ontologically incompatible with writing is based on the archaic association of writing with a certain material (paper). In our time, electronic forms of writing transcend any localization of any material objects in space, making them a potential part of the text. One can imagine digital treatises that would unfold around a singularity, e.g. this blade of grass, this tree, or this house. This ontic substratum, introduced into electronic texts yet irreducible to words, would be meaningful exactly through its presence in the here and now.

# Philosophy beyond textuality

Philosophy's role can be quite different from the currently prevailing form of verbal discourse that keeps it at a distance from singularities. Instead of philosophical texts, we can encounter *philosophical events* transcending textual semiotic borders and venturing into the territory of singularities. Yury Lotman defines an event in semiotic terms as crossing a border established by a code of a given culture: "An event in a text is the shifting of a persona across the borders of a semantic field. ... The less probability that a given event will take place (i.e. the greater the information conveyed by the message concerning the event), the higher the rank of that event on the plot scale" (1977, pp. 224, 228). A literary narrative includes the description of such events as the crossing of a border, for example, between the realms of the dead and the living, the states of war and peace, the capital and the province, the low and the high social classes, and so on.

The most significant border in culture lies between text and non-text. However, the crossing of this border cannot be fully enacted within the textual boundaries only, for it requires the trans-semiotic acts of "embodied thinking", which does not mean that the border is eliminated and the difference is erased. On the contrary, the eventfulness of thinking is based on the radical disparity between words and things. In a philosophical event, a word as an indexical gesture calls for the demonstration of an object precisely because they are essentially different, and because one cannot be substituted for the other. A similar relationship of trans-semiotic rupture between words and things can be found in René Magritte's famous painting that presents a pipe with the inscription "This is not a pipe". Indeed, in the painting, there is no pipe, as such, only its depiction.

However, if the inscription "This is a pipe" were under a real pipe, the obvious truism of this statement would immediately reveal the radical distinction between the textual sign that can refer to any and every pipe in the world, and the singularity of that particular pipe. The apparent semiotic connection between the word and the object demonstrates their ontological difference, when the border between a common word and a unique object can never be completely overcome. The paradox of this inscription is that it names a thing without saying anything about it. At the limit of truthfulness of language, we discover its complete failure in the face of the concrete and the unique; in Wittgenstein's words, "What *can* be shown, cannot be said" (1971, p. 115). *This* pipe is only one representative of the whole class of pipes, and thus functions as litotes (understatement) in an ironic play with its *common* name. Juxtaposing words with things is an instance of artistic micronics: the sign is ironically diminished by its attachment to only one of its countless possible signifieds.

This micronic technique is used consistently in the installations of Ilya Kabakov, which are usually classified as *conceptual art* that displays objects alongside texts. But what is primary and what is secondary in such juxtapositions—words or objects? It is equally possible to consider Kabakov's installations as a material environment accompanied by text, or as *indexical writing* that demonstrates its own signifieds as if pasting them in the text. The indexical signs are simultaneously a part of language and the participants in extra-linguistic communication, accompanied by objects to illustrate the meanings of words, such as "this", "that", "here", and "there", indicating something outside of language.

Such are the inscriptions or labels under different art objects, signs on public or commercial buildings, directions for usage of any product, or guides for museums and parks. These signs contain indexical intentionality, as if an invisible index finger were pointing to certain material objects in space. The same indexicality can become part of a philosophical text. In fact, many of Kabakov's installations, such as *The Palace of Projects* or *A Fly with Wings*, present a philosophical or quasi-philosophical text in which an ontic substratum is pasted. For example, Kabakov's installation *A Man Who Flew into Space* presents an ontic substratum in the form of a room full of enigmatic tools and garbage pasted into the textual narrative of a mad inventor who launched his spaceship through the roof to the sky.

Overall, the juxtaposition of things and words in their ironic interplay is the focus of Ilya Kabakov's metaphysical art:

We are talking about a more profound, determining significance of the text for any visual depiction, where behind the various types and forms of participation of the text in visual works ... stands the narrative which exists and 'works' on all levels, in the creation of these works as well as in the 'understanding' of them. ... I have always had this quality— to connect any visual perception with an internally spoken text—a

distinctly spoken monologue would always arise inside of me right along
with the examination of anything in life and in art. Without this text or
commentary formulated in my consciousness, contemplation for me was
incomplete, experienced insufficiently strongly. And this did not mean
that words 'covered' what was standing before me, that 'vision' was
replaced by words. No, it remained sharp and tense, and the more it was
concentrated, the more naturally and inevitably it would engender, 'lead'
a text. (2000, p. 237)

Kabakov stresses that textuality and visuality in his works intensify and
instigate each other. His indexical writing is definitely oriented towards
litotes, for it presents things as inferior to the words that signify them. Not
all indexical writing, however, is necessarily based on litotes. For a long
time, hyperbole dominated indexical writing, projecting a self-aggrandizing
image of its transformative power. For example, the classic utopian
writing of Marx, Nietzsche, and Nikolai Fedorov is indexical in nature: it
presupposes a certain material environment as a result of its transformative
action in the form of a communist society, the dance of a Superman, or the
resurrection of the dead. Each word serves as a signal to a world-shaping
practice, which is supposed to absorb and increase the semantic power of
the word. This hyperbolic dimension of a utopian discourse leads to the
full embodiment and removal ("sublation") of a sign in the subsequent
transformation of the world.

The indexical writing based on litotes, on the contrary, is not overwritten
by its practical implementations, but rather demonstrates the incommensurability of word and deed, the latter being inferior to the former. The fact
or the singularity is always more narrow, negligible, or distorted when
compared to the meaning of the word that designates it. For instance, in
Kabakov's universe that reproduces the ideological excess and material
scarcity of Soviet reality, the store sign "Meat" does not refer to meat,
as such, but rather to bleak samples of this substance, inadequate when
compared to its "grandiose" name.

This explains why Ilya Kabakov's installations are often related—reflec-
tively and ironically—to projects based on utopian writing. Moreover, his
objective is to transform hyperboles into litotes, while remaining within the
bounds of indexical writing. One of the 65 projects constituting the *Palace
of Projects* ironically highlights Russian philosopher Nikolai Fyodorov's
idea of resurrection of all the dead:

[T]he only worthy goal of a living person can be the resurrection of all
the people who have died in the past.... In this project death is understood as something that shouldn't be, as something which delivers misery
and injustice to all of humanity, which can be overcome if all of those
living concentrate all their efforts on it. This theory was given the name

'The Philosophy of the Common Cause' and received widespread notice in philosophical and intellectual circles of Russian society of that time (the end of the nineteenth – beginning of the twentieth c.). ... Russian thought has always revolved around searches for ideas of a common meaning of life for all humanity, as a unified whole. (1998, project 35)

In Kabakov's installation, this sublime vision is illustrated by a 150 × 80 × 110 cm metal frame-table covered with plywood. A plastic case with earth scattered into it up to a height of 10–13 cm is placed on the table. About 50 little white figures are cut out of paper and vertically stuck into the ground in such a way that they touch it only with their feet without sinking into it. These tiny figures of the "resurrected" people in a plastic case ironically set off the verbal grandiosity of this project. In this installation, a small object is not hyperbolically projected into the future as the predicted resurrection of all the dead, but accompanies the text as a materially insignificant, ironic illustration of the grand vision. The word and the thing together form a grotesque couple, like Don Quixote and Sancho Panza. The scale relations are important here: the installation works as a semiotic machine, which materially enlarges and semantically diminishes the text in the system of its displayed signifieds. Kabakov's artistic micronics exemplifies what Adorno called "the pasting of ontic substrate into a philosophical text".

The last words of Adorno's *Negative Dialectics* programmatically invoke the possibility of "material" philosophy beyond words and thoughts, but to be found in things themselves:

Represented in the inmost cell of thought is that which is unlike thought. The smallest intra-mundane traits would be of relevance to the absolute, for the micrological view cracks the shells of what, measured by the subsuming cover concept, is helplessly isolated, and explodes its identity, the delusion that it is but a specimen [of a general concept]. There is solidarity between such thinking and metaphysics at the time of its fall. (1992, p. 408)

The fall of metaphysics does not mean its end, but rather its break into a variety of small metaphysics, and its move beyond the boundaries of texts into the space of singularities. The new metaphysics is pluralistic and transverbal, grounded in litotes while reaching beyond thought itself[2].

---

[2]On the metaphysical significance of unique things in their distinction from words see: Epstein, 1995, pp. 253–89.

# 14

# From body to self: What is it like to be what you are?

## Partying with the body

At the turn of the twentieth century our attitude towards the body underwent a radical change. Today, more than ever, medical and sports underpinnings can be found in every area of social life. Up to a quarter of all leading US newspaper headlines and websites are dedicated to medicine (including diet and nutrition) and sports, which are both aimed at healing and strengthening the body. Never before has science penetrated so deeply into the body's mysteries, its nuclear-molecular build-up, mechanisms of aging and heredity, and the biochemistry of the brain. At the same time, something eerie is being revealed as the body approaches a unique point in its biological evolution. Once that evolutionary boundary is crossed, the body, medically and genetically modified and standardized, may lose such characteristics, inherent to it, as wholeness, uniqueness, individuality, irreproducibility, and spatial-temporal boundedness. As a result, the body may become a perfect instrument of organic nature in its metabolic exchange with the technical milieu.

A similarly radical change occurred in our view of the physical world at the turn of the nineteenth century. With the physical discoveries of Marie and Pierre Curie, and their philosophical interpretation by Ernst Mach, energy as the ultimate substrate of the universe displaced matter, causing the latter "to disappear". In the middle of the twentieth century, N. Wiener, J. Newman, and C. Shannon published their works, and the famous Macy conferences on cybernetics took place in New York, pushing the foundational level of the world even further away from matter into the realm of information. Today, matter (including living matter) is viewed more and more often as an object of data storage and transmission, with the body being one of the most compact ways to package information. In terms of information density and plasticity, however, the protein body is inferior to texts and codes that function on a silicone or quantum basis. As a result, the body comes to be treated as the first, "naïve" prototype of informational machinery. In the noosphere, consciousness, breaking through the slow evolutionary process of nature, can start operating directly in texts and codes, no longer in need of the body as an inter-mediary. Furthermore, the body itself comes to be subjected, more and more often, to reading, interpretation, virtual representation, and genetic decoding. Meanwhile, such "old" ways of perceiving the body as touch and sensual pleasures become more rare. Baudrillard writes in his book *The Ecstasy of Communication*:

> ... the human body, our body, seems superfluous in its proper expanse, in the complexity and multiplicity of its organs, of its tissue and functions, because today everything is concentrated in the brain and the genetic code, which alone sum up the operational definition of being. (1988, p. 18)

What previously had been an intellectual challenge soon became the dogma of many new scientific ideologies and cultural movements. N. Katherine Hayles, a well-known authority in virtual reality and human aspects of cyber-technologies, describes this new dogmatic worldview as follows:

> ... the body is primarily, if not entirely, a linguistic and discursive construction. Coincident with cybernetic developments that stripped information of its body were discursive analyses within the humanities, especially the archeology of knowledge pioneered by Michel Foucault, that saw the body as a play of discourse systems. Although researchers in the physical and human sciences acknowledged the importance of materiality in different ways, they nevertheless collaborated in creating the postmodern ideology that the body's materiality is secondary to the logical or semiotic structures it encodes. (1999, p. 192)

Although she herself insists on the irreplaceability of the embodied forms of consciousness, Hayles admits that theory today is largely "posthuman" because "the posthuman view privileges informational pattern over material instantiation, so that embodiment in a biological substrate is seen as an accident of history rather than an inevitability of life" (1999, p. 2).

With the prospective merger of living organisms and computers, complete "informatization" of the body seems to be merely a task that will one day be solved by technology. If consciousness is but an informational matrix that can easily be planted in the silicone or quantum basis, what does the body bring to consciousness besides its limitations? If cyborgs are posthuman, one can view the body as a proto-informational resource and a proto-thinking machine. According to the prediction made by Ray Kurzweil,

> By the end of the twenty-first century, there won't be a clear difference between humans and robots. What, after all, is the difference between a human who has upgraded her body and brain using new nanotechnology and computational technologies, and a robot who has gained an intelligence and sensuality surpassing her human creators? (2000, p. 148)

Hans Moravec is even more radical in his vision, taking the robot—a consciousness integrated into artificial machines—to be superior to any organism constructed on the protein basis, no matter how perfect:

> ... protein is not an ideal material. It is stable only in a narrow temperature and pressure range, is very sensitive to radiation, and rules out many construction techniques and components. ... a genetically engineered superhuman would be just a second-rate kind of robot, designed under the handicap that its construction can only be by DNA-guided protein synthesis. Only in the eyes of human chauvinists would it have an advantage.... . (1988, p. 108)

Thus, in light of the new theories of artificial life and AI, the body is semiotized, devitalized, and treated as an informational machine capable of simulating any biological function better than nature itself. The Latin root "vit-", meaning "vita", "life", is replaced more and more often by "vitr-" ("in vitro", i.e. "in artificial environment") or "virt-" ("virtual", "imaginary", "simulated").

Medicine and sports focus on the body's most semiotic manifestations, or digitalized corporeality. For medicine, the body is devitalized as an object of symptomatic and analytical procedures; for sports, it is mechanized in the form of meters, kilos, or seconds. Paradoxically, terrorism is the only contemporary movement that takes the body seriously, though destructively, assigning it with religious or political missions. However, for terrorists, too, the body turns out to be a figure of political language, a rhetorical device of an ultimatum. Thus, the body today is a subject of informational-biotechnical decoding and transmission, a matter of professional businesses and careers, such as sport, fashion, and pornography, or a stake in political struggle. In all these cases, the body is but a sign.

It can be that, two or three generations from now, the intelligent beings of the future with their neuro-extensions and artificial limbs, immersed in the ecstasy of safe cybersex including virtual-tactile contact and multi-sensual orgies, will have completely turned the physical body over to medical workers, bio-restorers, video-technicians, programmers, and, of course, sportsmen. However, the interest in the body in sports, advertising, and pornography will continue to grow as the body itself is relegated to the biological past of humankind. Hence the almost rhetorical question asked by Arthur Kroker and Marilouise Kroker: "If, today, there can be such an intense fascination with the fate of the body, might this not be because the body no longer exists?" (1987, p. 20). We witness this commotion around the body—in sex, sports, and fashion—precisely because of its gradual disappearance and the growing means of its simulation. The body will fall out of use just like the horse or the steam machine did in the age of electricity. As a result, the body will start to be forgotten as a source of deep and intimate experiences, a site of human self-consciousness and the bedrock of civilization with all its human values.

Even if the body does not completely fall out of use, replaced by computer databases and artificial neuro-electronic organs, the twenty-first century can still do to it what the twentieth century did to things. To quote R.-M. Rilke:

> Even for our grandparents, a 'house,' a 'well,' a familiar tower, their very clothes, their coat was infinitely more intimate; almost everything all was a vessel in which they found what is human and added to the supply of what is human. ... Filled with human spirit and taking part in our life along with us, things are now disappearing and can't be replaced. We may well be the last ones to have known such things. We are responsible not only for preserving their memories (which would not be enough and would be unreliable anyway) and their human and sublime value. ... Our task is to stamp this provisional, perishing earth into ourselves so deeply, so painfully and passionately, that its being may rise again, 'invisibly' in us. We are the Bees of the Invisible. (Rilke, 1935, pp. 335–6)

For Rilke, the crisis of our personal involvement with things that took place in the industrial age was translated into the creative task of interpreting and saving every individual thing. Similarly, today we face the task of saving memories of the body in its human dimension. To paraphrase Rilke:

> Our task is to stamp this mortal, vulnerable flesh into ourselves

so deeply, so painfully and passionately, with such intellectual and emotional responsibility, that its being may rise again, 'invisibly' in us.

Parting with the body may pave the way to a new, embodied philosophical thought, which for centuries has ignored corporeality, driving it out of its speculative language. Philosophy's mission is to think differently, challenging the dominant systems of thought. When our civilization was dependent upon the natural life of the body, with its reproductive and labor functions, philosophy wanted to leave the body behind, soaring high into the realm of abstractions, universals, and ideals. It is only now, with the prospect of a post-corporeal, proto-informational civilization that philosophy could perhaps take on the mission of saving the body in the totality of its meaning and value, with corporeality permeating every unit of its language.

An example of such a philosophical approach to the body is found in George Lakoff and Mark Johnson's work, most explicitly in their book *Philosophy in the Flesh: The Embodied Mind and its Challenge to Western Thought*, where they write: "We can only form concepts through the body. Therefore, every understanding that we can have of the world, ourselves and others can only be framed in terms of concepts shaped by our bodies" (1999, p. 555). The authors argue that the language used by philosophy is overwhelmingly metaphorical, shaped by the images of our embodied experience: left and right, high and low, back and forth, unity and difference, progress and regress, and so on. Their argument is persuasive, but, at the same time, it is reversible, i.e. if all concepts are derived from embodied experience, does this not mean that our bodies can be conceptualized? If that is, indeed, the case, then all of those abstract categories that Lakoff and Johnson view as bodily metaphors can serve to transform the body into a storage of information and a set of conceptual units. The "philosophy in the flesh" signals the *philosophization of the flesh* rather than the "embodiment" of philosophy, and belongs to the same trend of semiotization of the body that was described above.

# Rethinking the self

What makes the body irreducible to any concept? What prevents the body from any objectification, either in medical research or in images of mass media? These questions point to the perception of the self and, in fact, any experience as completely subjective. It is not sufficient to say that any kind of cultural activity, such as philosophy, proceeds from embodied experience, because the body can be easily externalized and appropriated by any language of science and entertainment. What cannot be externalized and is therefore doomed to muteness, is the experience of being a self within one's own body—being the one who I am. A deeper truth than the embodiment of thinking is the realization that the body itself is the *embodied self*. It is *selfness*, rather than bodyness, that cannot be objectified because it belongs to the irrevocably subjective experience.

*What is it like to be a bat?* This is the title and main question posed by Thomas Nagel in his famous article (2000). First published in *The Philosophical Review* in 1974, the essay continues to be discussed and reprinted in anthologies as a unique manifesto against reductionism, physicalism, and materialism in our understanding of the mind. Nagel insists that behind any subjective experience, there is a certain reality that cannot be described in any terms but those of the experience itself. Nagel chooses the bat, with its webbed wings and use of echolocation, as an example of the special difficulty presented to human understanding:

> If the subjective character of experience is fully comprehensible only from one point of view, then any shift to greater objectivity—that is, less attachment to the specific viewpoint—does not take us nearer to the real nature of the phenomenon: It takes us farther away from it. (2000, p. 399)

Whatever the results of a biochemical analysis of the bat as an organism may be, being a bat does not mean being studied underneath a microscope. Being a bat means flying, flapping wings, sensing the sonic responsiveness and permeability of darkness, and swinging on branches.

Similar objections to reductionism can be made, according to Nagel, in other areas of cognitive activity, including sensory perception. For example, sound can be observed from a physical standpoint with an acoustic instrument as an elastic wave moving through air. However, in order to describe sound objectively like this, one needs to observe it from a different point of view (or, rather, point of hearing) than that of a human being. For sound to be described as sound in terms of how it is experienced (loud, soft, distant, near, etc.), it needs to pass through the ear. The subjectivity of perception is inseparable from the reality of the experience itself. Everything that occurs in the sphere of experience is related to someone's subjectivity; the objective presentation of any experience would necessarily entail a form of subjective projection and introspection. In other words, only a bat knows what it is like to be a bat.

According to Nagel (2000), cognitive science has yet to refine the technical means and objective language for the description of subjective experiences. Furthermore, "does it make sense to ask what my experiences are *really* like, as opposed to how they appear to me?" (2000, p. 402). The reality of the experience is my own experience and nobody else's.

I will offer my own answer to Nagel's question of whether we can know what it is like to be a bat. My answer is partially (not completely!) affirmative: yes, we can. I would like to preserve Nagel's anti-reductionism, but separate it from his skepticism and epistemological pessimism. We can comprehend what it is like to be a bat without conducting any laboratory research on its physical and chemical make-up: such a method, in fact, can only tell us what it is like to be a dead, dissected bat.

First, let us turn our attention to how the question is posed. "What is it *like* to be a bat?" In his essay, Nagel does not analyze the form of his question, which relies on the comparative conjunction "like", and yet this conjunction is very important. When speaking of the other's experience, we enter the realm of how it compares to ours. Modern cognitivism is based on the premise that any thought, even strictly logical thought, is intrinsically metaphorical because the brain, as a part of the body, refracts all concepts through the prism of somatic experience: upper—lower, near—far, etc. (Lakoff and Johnson, 1999). This is especially true for the comprehension of individual experiences belonging to foreign bodies, and even more so to species different from ours, because then all concepts go through two- or three-fold metaphorical refraction. The knowledge of the external world is refracted through the prism of our internal experiences, while the knowledge of the other's inner world is refracted by the two prisms of one's own internal and the other's external existence. Metaphorical "likeness" is inherent in the formulation of the question. Thus, we cannot say what it *is* to be a bat, but we can say what it is *like* to be a bat, if we can imagine ourselves flying, and feeling the supple oscillation of the air through our whole bodies ("sound-air" corresponding to "body-ear"). True, it is not the same thing as *being* a bat, but the question only asks to establish a measure of *likeness*.

A less metaphoric, but similarly valid answer to Nagel's question is also possible. What is actually being discussed: What it is like *for a human* to be a bat, or *for a bat* to be a bat? Nagel is more interested in the latter question, which leaves no room for imagination, conjecture, or metaphor. Of course, I can pretend that I have webbed hands, poor vision, eat bugs, and spend my days hanging by one leg from a beam in the attic. For Nagel, however, this endeavor misses the point:

> Insofar as I can imagine this (which is not very far), it tells me only what it would be like for me to behave as a bat behaves. But that is not the question. I want to know what it is like for a bat to be a bat. (Nagel, 2000, p. 394)

In response to this more difficult question, or rather from the impossibility of answering it, one can hear a motif of cognitive pessimism in Nagel's essay. Since we are not bats ourselves, it is not for us to know what being a bat is like.

Here, a line of reasoning absent from Nagel begs for further inquiry. What is for humans equivalent to the bat's experience of being a bat? Obviously, it is the experience of being a human, i.e. oneself. "Being oneself" is the common ground between humans and bats, not only as kinds of organisms, but also as individuals. Each living being experiences selfhood. This experience may manifest itself at various levels, from the primitively sensual to the higher intellectual, from the instinctive, self-preservation urges to self-awareness. One feels one's own hand or paw differently than the others'. When we mechanically raise a finger to our mouth and bite a nail, we feel very differently than if others were to have offered up their nail for us to bite. We would shudder, becoming frightened or upset, and blood would rush to our face. We don't feel any discomfort in constantly swallowing saliva, but if we were made to spit it up into a cup and then drink it back down, we would most likely gag even though nothing had happened to the saliva since being poured in a clean cup in front of us. It has merely taken on the appearance of something external, cooled from our body temperature. Something alive, as opposed to dead, is that which tells itself apart from not-itself.

There is a great variety amongst species and different individuals of the same species, e.g. between the elephant and the hare, myself and the mouse, myself and John, or this mouse and that mouse. Yet, what all these species and individuals have in common is the fact that they feel what it is to be *oneself*. Through this subjective experience, we can approach the closest prime root of being what we are.

Any number divided by itself always equals one. This is true of any number's relation to itself. Similarly, each of us is unique, and this singular relation to one's own self unites us. The very subjectivity of experience is the basis of universality—not because it can be objectified, studied by physics, chemistry, or neurology, but because experience can be shared with others and, to a certain degree, communicated.

*Universal* does not mean objective or externally observable. Experience can be conveyed commonly only on the basis of its subjectivity. Nagel sees this as a hurdle to generalization, since the description of an experience presupposes the singular point of view of the one experiencing it. However, the experience is not simply a subjective property of one individual, but the relationship between the observer and the observed. In experience, these coincide in one subject; the relation is oneself to oneself.

Strange as it may seem, Nagel's second, more difficult question is easier to answer than his first. What it is like for a *human* to be a bat requires imagination and mental projection, by putting oneself in place of another species. However, to answer what it is like for a *bat* to be a bat requires no conditional projection of oneself on to another. It is the same thing as asking, "What is it like for a bat to be itself?" Clearly, this question can be answered from personal experience, i.e. from what it is to be oneself. (This experience includes differentiating oneself from another, near from far, related from unrelated, one's experiences of pain, hunger, calm, movement, pressure, freedom, touch, and listening.) The answer no longer requires any metaphor, since there is nothing more literal and direct than the experience in relation to itself, i.e. self-identity (A is A).

The first question, what it is like for me, a human being, to be a bat requires anthropomorphism: I can put myself in a bat's place only by transferring some of my human qualities on to it. Imagining myself hung in the air, swallowing insects, and using echolocation, I make myself the subject of an experience foreign to me. This substitution involves metaphorism (picturing myself as not myself) and anthropomorphism (turning a bat into a human being). To answer the second question, what it is like for a bat to be a bat, another cognitive strategy is undertaken, which can be called "ipseism", from the Latin *ipse* ("self", "oneself", and "per se"). The bat's sense of being a bat cannot but correspond to our own familiar sensation of being ourselves.

# Ipseism: Subjectivity and universality

Ipseism, as a radical alternative to physicalism, may help to answer Nagel's larger question: how can exclusively subjective experiences, inseparable from the individual, be described in general terms? Physicalism proposes the description of mental events in the language of physics, chemistry, and neurology, which register the occurrences of cognitive processes in nervous impulses and signals between brain cells. But these impulses or chemical reactions, observed from the outside, contain nothing of what is actually being experienced internally, such as sensing light or sound, hunger or fullness, fear or anxiety, joy or wonder. The universality of experience should be approached not from the outside, by replacing the subject of an experience with an external observer, but by exploring the internal correlation between the subject and the object of the same experience, since they coincide. Ipseism, unlike physicalism, looks for the objective foundations of experience from inside its subjectivity. Such experience is universal, not in the sense that it can be placed within some externally observable parameters, but in that it is innately common to all living beings, inherent in their self-feeling.

One more line of reasoning is possible, also absent from Nagel. I as a subject and I as an object are not completely identical. I cannot know what it is like for a bat to be a bat because I do not even know what it is like *for myself to be myself*. At the core of myself, I always sense somebody else. Between myself and myself, there is always an existential gap. The self I know or sense is always falling into the past; as an object of self-observation, I am always lagging behind myself as a subject. What I am saying should be put in parentheses as something said by *him*, who I was a moment before completing my utterance. Insisting, as Nagel does, that every experience is perceived only from a certain subjective point of view is an over-simplification: the point of view itself is constantly slipping, and that which is now mine will in a moment be another's, to whom I can refer only in the second or third person (similar to the saliva which tastes differently when poured into a glass and then swallowed back). This kind of self-alienation is familiar to anyone reading one's own diary, which appears as if written by another person.

This incommensurability of one to oneself, with constant self-alienation, is a common topic in philosophical anthropology.[1] Self-referential loops are always left hanging loose, incapable of becoming knots. This incompleteness of self-perception is an intrinsic property of life: the capacity to grow and to exceed oneself. A living loop meant to co-relate myself and myself has ends that can never meet. The selfness is given not as self-identity, but as the difference between self and self.

This is why "I" as a subject and "myself" as an object of the same experience are designated by different pronouns, personal and reflexive: "ego—ipse", "I—self". It is impossible to say: "I feel me" because "me" (as the accusative case of "I") presupposes another's point of view, e.g. "He looked at me". Only the other can know or feel "me", whereas I can only know "myself". Thus, the concept of *ipse* must be approached dynamically: *I* as the subject and *myself* as the object of experience are separated by a certain gap or hiatus.

This way, the entire epistemology of experience seems to run into a dead end. How is it possible for us to perceive what it is to be a bat if we cannot fully perceive what it is to be ourselves? In the depth of our experience we always find somebody else, another "self" different from "I". Yet, it is precisely in this dead end that we find an escape from this predicament. I am capable of feeling *myself as the other*. By the same token, I am able to perceive *the other as myself*. The cognitive and ethical aspects of personality are interconnected. Cognitively, I experience *otherness in myself*, while ethically I experience *selfness in others*.

The very question asked by humans—"What is it like to be a bat?"—shows the ethical subtext of a cognitive issue: we want to know what it is for another, even a non-human being, to be what it is for itself. Selfness, therefore, is inscribed into otherness just as otherness is inscribed into selfness. The experience of self-alienation is the precondition necessary for finding one's own self in another. Thus, the ethical dimension is born from

[1] See the sections "The Humanities and Sciences" in the Introduction and "The Rehumanization of the Humanities" in Chapter 3, "Mikhail Bakhtin and the Future of the Humanities".

our cognitive habit of recognizing the other within ourselves. All of ethics, arising from this principle, can be distilled to the golden rule: "Love your neighbor as you love yourself, do unto others as they would do unto you". In you, I see somebody like myself: I recognize some kind of selfness, while remaining the other.

Now we can fully appreciate the ethical underpinnings of the question Thomas Nagel raises in cognitive terms, "what is it like to be a bat?" Who is asking this question and why? What kind of concern necessitates this mode of questioning? Why is a representative of one species so intrigued by the inner state of the other species? Though Nagel's question does not readily allow for a direct answer, the question itself appears to be the answer to another, more essential question: "What is it like to be a human?" To be a human means to emerge out of self-containment and immerse oneself into the being of the other, as if it were one's own. To be human means to ask what it is like to be a bat.

# 15

# Differential ethics: From the golden rule to the diamond rule

The selfness of otherhood, as we perceive it in other personalities, is the foundation of the ancient golden rule, which requires that we relate to others as we do to ourselves. The golden rule was most famously formulated by Jesus in his Sermon on the Mount: "Whatever you wish that men would do to you, do so to them" (Mt. 7.12). Similar instructions can be found in Confucianism, Hinduism, Buddhism, Jainism, and Islam. For example, to Tsekung's question, "Is there one word that can serve as a principle of conduct for life?", Confucius replied, "It is the word *shu*— reciprocity: Do not do to others what you do not want them to do to you" (see Wilson, 1995, pp. 114–15).

The golden rule assumes that there is reciprocity of human wills. My earlier discussion of the problem of selfhood in bats and humans was based on the same assumption. Now I want to take a further step by demonstrating that the selves of a moral subject and a moral object are deeply different; as a result, the criterion of uniqueness must be added to the criterion of universality. In addition to the golden rule based on the idea of the universal self, we must recognize certain principles of moral behavior based on the uniqueness of each personality. Morality includes the right and duty of everyone to be different from everyone else. Following the metaphor of the golden rule, I propose a tenet that can be called the "diamond rule", formulated as follows: "*Do that which others need and **no one else** can do in your place*". The image of a cut and polished gemstone alludes to the idea of a uniquely shaped human personality as a moral agent.

# Courage deferred

It is unlikely that, in the history of the late twentieth century, one could find a more significant example of courage than the life of Aleksandr Solzhenitsyn, who, as an isolated individual, challenged the vast authority of the Soviet communist system. However, had he used his courage impulsively, as an immediate and unquestioning bravery, Solzhenitsyn would have hardly lived to see its result in the fall of Communism.

The first chapter of *The Gulag Archipelago*, "The Arrest", contains an episode in which the author, an army officer, is arrested in 1945 from his post on the line of combat on the Baltic Sea and taken by special convoy to Lubyanka, the infamous KGB headquarters in Moscow. At the time, Solzhenitsyn cannot find enough courage to resist, or even to shout and warn his fellow citizens:

> So why did I keep silent? Why in my last minute out in the open, did I not attempt to enlighten the hoodwinked crowd?
>
> Every man has handy a dozen glib little reasons why he is right not to sacrifice himself....
>
> As for me, I kept silent for one further reason: because those Muscovites thronging the steps of the escalators were too few for me, *too few*! Here my cry would be heard by 200 or twice 200, but what about the 200 million? Vaguely, unclearly, I had a vision that someday I would cry out to the 200 millions.
>
> But for the time being I did not open my mouth, and the escalator dragged me implacably down into the nether world. (1973, pp. 17–18)

Solzhenitsyn acted prudently, yet his conscience continues to torture him. It is difficult to find a point of balance between the two virtues of prudence and courage that serve two different purposes: preserving one's life and giving it to others.

The fact that this great author still blames himself for keeping silent cannot be morally evaluated from within that episode of several decades ago. Instead, it must be judged from the perspective of Solzhenitsyn's entire life. In ethical judgments, time goes back, and the future illuminates the past. One can judge Solzhenitsyn's silence in 1945 only having heard his cry in 1973 in the publication of *The Gulag Archipelago*. If his desire of shouting the truth to 200 million people had remained merely a well-intended fantasy, permanently silencing the voice of conscience, we might judge him differently today. However, today we know that the silence that allowed Solzhenitsyn to save his life and strengthen his voice for the future was a necessary and morally justified choice.

We are confronted here with an ambiguous situation. Is it possible to postpone the moment of truth? There is a great moral risk in such *deferred courage*. First, will you have enough courage to do later that which you cannot do now? Secondly, will circumstances still require your courage, or will your act lose its value as society becomes less oppressive? The very act of courage that costs millions in hard times will cost a penny if conditions change. In Aristotle's words, "courage is revealed not at any time, but at the time when fears and dangers are the closest" (2001, p. 1191a). Deferred courage resembles a deferred payment: in both cases, interest accumulates. Contrary to the prevailing use of this term in the philosophy of deconstruction, deferment is not just an indefinite postponement; it is an accumulation of expectations and meaning, a silent growth of values not revealed before, so that the deferment can be justified by their growth. The cost of deferment can be great, and in Solzhenitsyn's case it paid off.

# Duality of virtues. Stereo ethics

There are two goals in life and, accordingly, two poles among virtues: self-giving and self-preservation. The first includes courage, generosity, and selflessness, i.e. readiness to act for the sake of others by renouncing one's own interests. By contrast, the second entails prudence, caution, and thriftiness, i.e. an impulse to cultivate and expand oneself. Lacking the former set of virtues, one fails the human community; lacking the latter, one has nothing to sacrifice and to give to others. This duality comprises life's inescapable and tragic contradiction. In this context, the term *contravocation* may be more appropriate than "contradiction": *contravocation* (from Latin *vocare*, "to call") refers to two moral voices that sound in a human soul with equal strength. *Contradiction* is a logical category in which two discourses rise in opposition to each other; in its turn, *contravocation* is an ethical category in which conscience appears as if torn apart by equally justified purposes, i.e. by the duality of virtues. Thus, any individual's life has two dignified vocations that can never be fully reconciled with each other.

One finds a tacit contravocation even in the commandment "You shall love your neighbor as yourself". How can I love my neighbor if I don't love myself, if I cannot transfer to another that sensation of uniqueness, infinite importance, and precious singularity that I learn initially from the experience of being myself? But, in loving myself, do I then commit adultery by engaging in a love affair with my neighbor? If one follows this commandment, there arises a love triangle ("I—me—my neighbor"), and one cannot help but suffer from jealousy.

Such are two ethically demanding realities: the community of others "given" to me, and my own gift that I must protect and increase. As a rule, moral responsiveness and vocational self-fulfillment are bound to conflict with each other, affecting the pendulum-like movements of conscience. There are unique personalities for whom "gifts" and "givens", self-realization and self-sacrifice, coincide: people endowed with *ethical vocation* and *professional responsiveness*. I will mention only one: Janus Korczak (1879–1942), the Polish-Jewish writer and educator who volunteered to be deported by the Nazis with the children of his orphanage and died with them at Treblinka. However, for most people, vocation and responsiveness are two different calls. They cry for unification, yet defy it.

It is impossible to know ahead of time which of these two calls will turn out to be the winning one; any situation involves a zone of total risk. One can give oneself almost for free, without yet having become something, or one can preserve and cultivate oneself throughout one's entire life, without ever living up to an act of giving oneself. For instance, a curly-haired boy of 15 may give his life for the workers' cause or for the Islamist cause, which can turn out to be the cause of demagogues or assassins—something unworthy of the boy's heroic sacrifice. Or, a renowned writer in communist China or Soviet Russia would wait all his or her life for the right moment to speak freely and fearlessly, but, in the end, leave nothing except many volumes of works written in the submissive genre "at your service".

Aristotle stated one of the most influential postulates in the history of ethics: virtue is the middle point between two vicious extremes: "excess and defect are characteristic of vice, and the mean of virtue; for men are good in but one way, but bad in many" (*Nicomachean Ethics*, 1106b; 2001, p. 959). This postulate appears to be the counsel of common sense: don't be a coward and don't be a daredevil. What lies in the middle between these vicious extremes is mature, prudent, and wise courage.

However, is it always possible to find a place for one single virtue between two extremes? If a surplus of fear is cowardice, and a lack of fear is recklessness, then between them there are two middles, two virtues: the virtue of *courage*, which stays further away from fear, and the virtue of *prudence*, which is further away from recklessness. The scope of moral behavior is not fixed in one central point of "correct action", but rather is described by a large interval *between* courage and prudence. Similarly, *two* virtues can be found between the vices of miserliness and wastefulness: *generosity*, which is further from miserliness, and *thrift*, which is further away from wastefulness.

There are no concepts in our language to precisely designate one "virtue" on such a four-step scale. There is a large interval for free action—a moral continuum, a wave function of the good—that exists between complementary pairs of virtues: between generosity and thriftiness, courage and prudence, and *joie de vivre* and temperance. Just as there are stereo films and stereo music, which convey three-dimensional images of objects and sounds, there is *stereo ethics*, based on the duality of life's purposes, neither of which presents the singular correct moral choice. Stereo ethics combines different moral perspectives, just as sight combines two different projections of an object for us to perceive the world realistically in three dimensions.

Generosity and thriftiness, courage and prudence can be called *co-virtues*. They are as necessary for ethics as the right and left hands are necessary for the human body, or the right and left hemispheres for the brain. Any virtue degenerates into a vice unless it acknowledges its counter value; for example, generosity without thriftiness turns into wastefulness, while thriftiness without generosity. turns into miserliness. A vice is precisely the rejection of stereoscopic vision.

# Wisdom and conscience

There are two "super-virtues" regulating the relationship between co-virtues: *wisdom* and *conscience*. *Wisdom* is the meta-level of moral consciousness, which measures and correlates the values of self-sacrifice and self-preservation as one is seeking the most worthy path of self-realization. Wisdom whispers the words of courage during moments of weakness and gives prudent advice during moments of recklessness.

*Conscience* also regulates the relationship between co-virtues so that, leaning towards one of them, we do not fall into the extreme of vice. Conscience reminds a thrifty person about generosity lest he or she become miserly; it reminds a generous person about thriftiness lest he or she become a spendthrift. Conscience makes one grieve and suffer because one cannot achieve a complete balance between virtues. There is a virtue of courage and there is a virtue of prudence, but *Virtue as such* is unattainable. While wisdom is the *affirmative* side of morality, searching for unity and harmony of virtues, conscience is the *critical* side of morality, reminding us of the impossibility of such harmony and causing the pangs as a result of such impossibility. Wisdom rises above contradictions and conciliates them; conscience is afflicted by *contravocations and* cannot resolve them. While wisdom is an organ of joy, conscience is an organ of suffering, which is healthy when it is in pain.

Like co-virtues which wisdom conciliates but conscience cannot, wisdom and conscience themselves constitute two meta-ethical co-virtues. It is not easy to follow Aristotle's advice and "aim at what is intermediate" between them (2001, p. 958). Wisdom says one thing; conscience, the other. The former rejoices, while the latter aches. No single middle point exists between virtues, which constantly split, requiring a new choice, a new doubt, and a new repentance. In the final analysis, there can be no wise solution completely releasing us from the remorse of conscience.

# The diamond rule

From the perspective of stereo ethics, we can rethink the golden rule as the most ancient embodiment of moral wisdom, based on idea of the reciprocity of human wills.

It should be noted that the golden rule has also been used within the systems whose proponents destroyed themselves as well as others, while following the same law of moral equality. For example, the golden rule is quoted in *The Declaration of Human Rights* by Maximilien Robespierre, the leader of the Jacobins, who executed thousands of his compatriots and was then also executed himself. Another French revolutionist, Gracchus Babeuf, the leader of "the plot of the equal", also based his ideas on the golden rule, while trying to prove that the supremacy of an individual talent and initiative is but a chimera and a masked lie. Of course, we cannot blame an ethical maxim for its abuse; yet, the very form of the reversibility of the object and the subject of moral acts must be revised in the light of the revolutionary and totalitarian movements of the eighteenth—twentieth centuries with their postulates of equality. The ethics of the identity of moral subjects and objects should be supplemented with the recognition of their profound difference.

In the so-called "Axial Age" (eighth—second centuries BCE), when, according to Karl Jaspers (1977), the foundations of universal, super-tribal, all-human morals were laid, the emphasis on differences among individuals could have undermined and destroyed these foundations. At the basis of the golden rule lies the reversibility of moral subjects: you should put yourself in somebody else's place, treating others as you wish them to treat you, or act so that your behavior could serve as a standard for all. This is the very essence of the classical understanding of morality: you are an object of the same actions that you perform as a subject.

Today, however, it is obvious that only the ethics of comprehensive differentiation can save us from relativism, which is a negative reaction against the universal norms of traditional morals. A person cannot completely identify with someone else, and, as a consequence, people start to act as if their subjectivity were immoral or antimoral.

It is precisely this irreducibility of the individual to the general that may become a source of new moral energy flowing into the world, but not along the old, dried-up channels. The highest value lies in my distinction from others, as well as their distinction from me. Mikhail Bakhtin, in his *Philosophy of Act*, introduced an ethics of *dutiful uniqueness* (*dolzhenstvuiushchaia edinst-vennost'*): "That which I can do cannot ever be done by anyone else. The uniqueness of actual existence is *per force* necessary. This fact of my non-alibi in the actual reality lies at the basis of the most concrete and unique necessity of act" (1986b, p. 112). Thus, the unique possibility—that which only a given person can accomplish—is elevated to the rank of necessity.

Marina Tsvetaeva, a great Russian poet, who, as an *émigrée,* had to earn her living by day-to-day labor, confessed: "I am not a parasite because I work and I want to do nothing but to work; but to do my own work, not somebody else's. To make me do somebody else's work is meaningless, because I am not capable to do any work except my own work and dirty work (to carry heavy things, etc.)" (2002, p. 241). "One's own work" is an important concept: it refers to the work that is entrusted to me and that nobody can fulfill better than I. Other people could translate poetry, write weekly reviews, or carry heavy things better than Tsvetaeva could. But, writing poetry was her work, her duty, and her vocation. Morality is not isolated from individual gifts. The faithfulness to one's gift is the most demanding duty.

The apostle Paul taught about the diversity of spiritual gifts: one is granted faith, another, the word of knowledge, yet another, the gifts of healing or speaking in tongues (Cor. 1: 12.4–11). This diversity of gifts lies at the basis of *differential ethics,* which can be summarized in the following formulation: *The best action is that through which the maximal capacity of one matches the maximal need of the other/s.*

There is something I can do better than anybody else in the world. Granted, there are people who can play the violin better or write better poems than I. But no one can take care of my mother, or of my child, or my friend, or of my garden better than I. For the vast majority of people, the focus of their moral irreplaceable activity is the sphere of their work and families; this, however, does not make the uniqueness of their vocation less significant.

A violinist is of the greatest benefit to people not when, mobilized to the work front, he takes up a shovel or an ax, but when he wields his bow. Certainly, a violinist could be of practical help to society cutting trees for firewood or digging vegetable patches, but, as a rule, the majority of differently gifted people can cut trees and dig. Only in difficult times, for example, when human resources are in short supply and the ability to cut trees or to dig becomes a unique gift, is the violinist morally obliged to do that which no one else can do. Here, his obligation is not social anymore, but precisely ethical: he acts not for the society as a whole (represented by the government or the law), but for the cold, the hungry, and the perishing.

Thus, I propose a postulate that does not annul the general character of the golden rule, but rather sets a diamond stone of the individual gift in its "golden frame": *Do that which anyone, including yourself, could wish for and which no one else but you can do.*

Ethics represents a dynamic equilibrium between the normative and the individual; moreover, in the "diamond-golden" rule, it is precisely the individual difference that becomes the basis of commonness—the "categorical imperative".

The double criterion of morality proposed here is a measure of the compatibility of unique gifts and common needs. Solzhenitsyn could have cried out at that metro station, but then anyone could have done the same as long as they had enough air in the lungs to do this. Society needed such a cry, but, in order to reach millions of people across the planet, it was precisely Solzhenitsyn who was needed; yet, not the Solzhenitsyn of 1945, but rather the Solzhenitsyn of the 1960s and 1970s, after eleven years in the Gulag, and many years of literary work. In order for that cry to provoke a global response, another historic scene and a different actor were needed.

Morality is neither a measure of individual abilities nor a measure of social needs, but rather a variable measure of their correlation. For this reason, ethics cannot be reduced to aesthetics or psychology, which deal with individual gifts. By the same token, ethics is not reducible to social demands or historic conditions, which define a measure of necessity in certain actions of an individual.

Thus, two questions form a moral criterion: 1) Would you wish to become an *object* of your own actions? and 2) Could anyone but you be a *subject* of your actions?

From this perspective, the best action is that which corresponds to the *needs of the largest number* and *the capacities of the smallest number* of people. It is such an action whose subject would like to become its object and, at the same time, it is such an action that can only be performed by that subject. The first criterion is the "golden" universality of a moral act, while the second criterion focuses on its "diamond-like" uniqueness. Ethics requires that both criteria are present:

> *Act in such a way that you yourself would like to become an object of your actions, but no one else could be their subject.*

It is moral to do for others that which no one else except you can do: to be *for-others*, but not *like-others*. To be moral is to nurture one's selfhood while conquering one's selfishness.

# PART FIVE

# The future of wisdom and creative theory

# 16

# What is "the interesting"?

## What is interesting about the "interesting"?

The "interesting" is a complex trans-disciplinary label often applied not only to works of literature, art, and sciences, but also to real life phenomena—persons, events, actions, relationships, and so on. In its evaluative scope, the interesting is hardly less universal than the "beautiful" or the "truthful", and it seems to have become even more popular in our day. While in the past a literary or scholarly work was generally valued for its truthfulness and beauty, or usefulness and instructiveness, in the twentieth and twenty-first centuries it is a work's primary evaluation as "interesting" that paves the way for its further assessment, including critical analysis.

Furthermore, the concept of the "interesting" not only introduces the discussion, but often concludes and crowns it as well, through statements such as "In spite of a number of flaws, this article in interesting in that it …", or "The outlined merits of this works make it possible to explain the interest that the work generated in the reading public". The interesting is simultaneously our initial, intuitive evaluation of the quality of a work and the resulting synthesis of all its analytical definitions.

In some cases a work devoid of internal interest may present an external interest, reflecting surprising tendencies in public tastes, literary markets, or publishing policies. A mediocre collection of poetry or an incompetent work of scholarship may be interesting as a symptom of certain intellectual or social trends. A dull book that has been published by a prestigious publisher or has achieved inexplicable success with the public creates a paradox and sometimes even a scandal; it attracts interest not to itself, but to the situation as a whole—this seems to be the case, for instance, with some TV reality shows. We can call "*exteresting*" such phenomena that appear to be interesting exactly because they are *devoid of any intrinsic interest*. Thus, it would be useful to discriminate between a work that is interesting in itself, and one that is *exteresting* as part of an external situation, of a larger social or intellectual context. This latter case is often described by the expression "interesting as"; for instance, a work may be interesting *as* evidence of the degradation of public taste or *as* indicative of a crisis in the writer's creativity. There are interesting people and books, but there are also interesting *situations* that involve boring people and tedious books as focal elements.

There is a clear discrepancy between the growing popularity of the interesting as an evaluative term and the lack of its theoretical exploration. Thousands of volumes have been written on *truth* and *beauty*, while one can hardly find a single volume on the *interesting*. Thus the lines between the rigorous application of the term *interesting* and its colloquial use or even misuse become blurred, and this evaluative word is often applied unreflectively or euphemistically. To say that something is *interesting* is a convenient way to say something pleasant about a work without giving it any substantive consideration. "That's interesting!" often sounds as an empty remark, meaning everything—and nothing in particular. Such exclamations can serve as an excuse for evading further discussion, or as a signal to change the topic, rather than an introduction to the issue of what makes this thing interesting

My own interest in the interesting comes from the fact that I have found this concept relevant to practically all the disciplines with which I have been engaged in my theoretical pursuits, from literary theory to cultural studies to linguistics to philosophy. Though my primary impulse here is to discuss interesting ideas and theories, that is, the application of this concept in intellectual endeavors, I see no reason why the universal value of the interesting shouldn't be addressed as well, including its relevance for the discussion of literary works or human personalities. My intention here is to clarify the meaning of the term "interesting" without sacrificing the breadth of its current usage both within and outside of academia. The art of definition, after all, combines two complementary imperatives: (1) the term must be defined as narrowly and specifically as possible; and (2) all the various areas and contexts of its usage must be covered as broadly as possible.

The category of the interesting can be questioned on the basis of its subjectivity, since different people are interested in different things. Yet, while the concepts of the beautiful and the good are susceptible to the same line of criticism, few critics question the relevance of aesthetics and ethics as sciences of the beautiful and the good. Our question is not what is interesting to various people, but what constitutes the category of the interesting itself. In other words, the task is not to enumerate "what is interesting" the way Sei Shonagon did in the lists that form her *Pillow Book*. Our question is rather: "What is the interesting *itself* as a cultural concept?" One person might be interested in ice hockey and another in soccer; one person might be interested in philosophy and another in literature; one person might be interested in Hegel and another in Nietzsche. At the same time, all these people find something interesting, albeit in different phenomena, and it is this very category of the interesting that interests me. Here, I will perform a simple phenomenological reduction, bracketing out all subjective and objective factors—that is, who takes interest in particular things and why— in order to focus on the phenomenon of the interesting as such.

# The modality of the interesting

The ascent of the interesting among evaluative terms can be attributed in large part to the deep transformations in the epistemological field initiated by Thomas Kuhn's groundbreaking book *The Structure of Scientific Revolutions* (1962). According to Kuhn, it is not the acquisition and accumulation of new facts, but rather a change of vision, new lenses on the eyes of the professional community, that causes revolutionary shifts in scientific paradigms. The postmodernist critique of the concepts of truth and reality contributed further to the search for alternative criteria in the evaluation of ideas and texts. These new criteria stressed the heuristic value and transformative potential of an idea, its capacity to break the established configuration of knowledge rather than to expand its correspondence to external reality (I return to this point below in my response to Deleuze and Guattari's critique of "truth"). What makes an idea (a theory or a text) interesting is its provocative stance, its challenge to the norms of "normal" science.

Though this kind of radical epistemology appears to be postmodern and post-Kuhnian, it also reminds us of the classical notion of *wonder*, or *surprise*, postulated by Aristotle as a cognitive trigger providing the motivation for philosophizing. We are surprised by something that challenges our expectations and the rules of our reasoning. The surprising appears to be highly improbable. In our response to this challenge, we must attempt to bridge the gap between reason and surprise, at once rationalizing the improbable and extending the limits of rationality. It is this internal tension between reasonable expectation and the cognitive value of the unexpected or unexpectable that undergirds the category of the interesting.

I would like to propose that the interesting is related to the modal categories of the possible and the impossible, the probable and the improbable. The oscillation between these two and their mutual transformation constitutes the phenomenon of the interesting. Thus, what makes a certain theory interesting is its presentation of a *consistent and plausible proof* for what appears to *be least probable*. In other words, the interest of a theory is *inversely proportional to the **probability** of its thesis and directly proportional to the **provability** of its argument*. This criterion can be applied to such different fields as religion, history, and physics. For example, the probability of a human being's resurrection after death would appear to be extremely small, and it is in part for this reason that the Christian narrative, consistently arguing in favor of resurrection, has been the focus of interest for a significant part of humanity for two millennia. The probability of the old man Fedor Kuzmich being the same person as Tsar Alexander I is very small, so any historical evidence in support of that theory would present great interest. Similarly, among the most interesting theories of the twentieth century are those of relativity and quantum physics, the conclusions of which challenge common sense to the extreme, leading to a situation in which the ultimate improbability nevertheless seems to possess scientific provability.

Thus, *as the probability of a thesis increases and its provability decreases, a theory becomes less interesting*. The least interesting theories, meanwhile, are those that: (1) prove the obvious; (2) speculate about the improbable without solid proof, or, worst of all; (3) fail to prove even the obvious. *The interesting is the relationship of provability to probability—* that is, *a fraction where the numerator is the reliability of the argument and the denominator is the validity of the thesis*. The degree of the interesting grows both with the increase of the numerator and with the decrease of the denominator. On the other hand, as the probability of a thesis increases or its provability decreases, a theory becomes dull.

We now see that the category of the interesting emerges as the measure of tension between wonder and understanding, or, in other words, between the alterity of the object and reason's capacity to integrate it. On the one hand, an object offering a proliferation of wonders without any reasonable explanation diminishes its potential to be interesting because we give up all hope of rationally integrating such a phenomenon. On the other hand, the evacuation of wonder that guarantees an easy triumph for reason undermines our interest as well. If wonder involves the measure of improbability, then reason provides the measure of provability.

The same double criterion of the interesting would hold for a literary text. An interesting plot development is one that is perceived, on the one hand, as inevitable, and on the other, as unpredictable. As in a scientific theory, the logic and consistency of fictional action must be balanced by its provocative novelty. Voltaire's famous saying, "All genres are good except for the dull ones", is also applicable to scientific genres and methods. The dull is the opposite of the interesting and is characteristic of research in which, like a story that goes nowhere, the conclusions repeat the premises, and nothing unpredictable happens in between.

For the purposes of my analysis of the interesting, short utterances, rather than long narratives, would perhaps be most suitable. Such utterances as "A table is an item of furniture" or "The Earth revolves around the Sun" are true but trivial, because the truth they describe is well known and self-evident. On the other hand, such utterances as "A table is an agricultural tool" or "The Earth revolves around Jupiter" are false, yet this does not make them any more interesting. Errors and falsities may be as boring and trivial as plain truths.

Which utterances, then, are most interesting? Those which express truths, but the least evident and predictable ones. Aphorisms, in particular, exemplify the interesting as such, producing a revolution in our consciousness by undermining common-sense truths and affirming apparently unpredictable and nevertheless true ideas. Take the famous saying attributed to Heraclitus: "You cannot step twice into the same river"—a profoundly interesting statement precisely because it denies the obvious fact that one can enter and cross the same river many times. (But, we learn to ask: "Will the river be the same?", "Will it be filled with the same water?"). Or take Henry David Thoreau's aphorism: "Men have become the tools of their tools". The conventional relationship between men and tools is reversed in this statement, but the reversal does not make it false; on the contrary, it suggests a deeper truth about economic alienation and the psychological subjugation of men by their tools.

Among aphorisms, there is a special variety called "paradoxes"; the etymology of the term (Greek *paradoxon*: from "para-", *beyond*, and "doxa", *opinion*) suggests the way that paradoxes are understood to conflict with expectation. Oscar Wilde was, famously, a great master of them. "Action is the last refuge of those who cannot dream", he proposes, reversing the conventional view that dream is the last refuge of those who cannot act. In some cases, a paradox becomes an end in itself, a pure reversal of a plain idea, and does not bring forth a deeper truth. But in fact, any good, memorable aphorism is more or less paradoxical, because it conflicts with our established opinions and defies truisms in order to find the truth at the very edge of common sense. And it is precisely this edge that sets the parameters of an interesting object of whatever kind—text, theory, situation, or individual.

## The interest and the profit

It is instructive to trace how the modal meaning of "interesting" in its contemporary usage ("curious", "attracting attention"), a meaning which in English dates only from the late eighteenth century, has evolved from the earlier sense of the word "interest" as a financial term. Since the fifteenth century, "interest" has signified "compensation for loss", "interest in money lent", and "money paid for the use of money and the rate of such payment". Raymond Williams, in his famous dictionary of conceptual etymology, remarks:

> [i]t is exceptionally difficult to trace the development of interest [from an economic term to] the now predominant sense of general curiosity or attention. ... It remains significant that our most general words for attraction or involvement should have developed from a formal objective term in property and finance. ... It seems probable that this now central word for attention, attraction and concern is saturated with the experience of a society based on money relationships. (1985, pp. 172–3)

The development of "interest" from its early financial sense to its contemporary evaluative usage can be explained precisely by the notion of the high value attached to the low probability of profit. There is a clear conceptual connection between the modal definition of *interesting* and *interest* as a term of lending and investment. Both refer to the notion of a higher return under the condition of higher risks. *The least probable profit results in the highest rate of interest.* An idea is more interesting, that is, it generates a higher interest, if its assumptions are less probable. The less predictable a narrative is, the more interesting, i.e. engaging and fascinating, it is. Similarly, higher financial interest is reaped from a more risky investment: the probability of its return is lower, thus the potential gain should be higher.

Our interest in a certain book or a theory is an intuitive anticipation of a possible profit from an intellectual investment. We invest our time, our labor, indeed, a portion of our life in consuming an intellectual product, in the hope that we will be rewarded by multiple gains and eventually receive more than we had invested. If a book or a theory is based on familiar assumptions leading us to obvious conclusions, that is, if they simply return to us what we already know, then they are not worthy of investment as they do not generate interest—in both the financial and cognitive senses of this term.

Looking even deeper in the origins of the term, the word "interest" derives from the Latin *inter esse*, "to be between; in the interval". In Russian, meanwhile, "interesting" can be synonymous with "pregnant"; one can say, for example: "She is in an interesting state". Although she herself is one, there is another entity within her. This, indeed, is precisely the situation of the interesting; it is a form of pregnancy, of potentiality, of surplus. In more general terms, it is that which fits into the gap between two extremes: between evidence and wonderment, between logic and paradox, between system and chance, between order and freedom, between self and other. The interesting occurs *between* thesis and antithesis, if (a) they are both relevant for the situation; (b) their synthesis is impossible; and (c) the victory of either side is precluded. As soon as one of these extremes overpowers the other, though, interest disappears, lapsing into detached respect or listless indifference. Oddity and madness are not interesting in and of themselves, but only in that kind of madness that has its own method, "a mind of its own", or, conversely, in an idea that contains some madness within it. We might rephrase Niels Bohr's aphorism: Your theory is crazy, but it's not crazy enough to be interesting.

In contemporary scientific discourse, the concept of the interesting is utilized in reference not only to the theories, but also to the objects of research.. According to the principle of "maximum diversity" developed by the physicist Freeman Dyson, "the laws of nature and initial conditions are such as to make the universe as interesting as possible. As a result, life is possible but not too easy. Always when things are dull, something turns up to challenge us and to stop us from settling into a rut" (1988, p. 298). As soon as life becomes dull and balanced, something unpredictable occurs: comets or meteorites strike the Earth, a new ice age arrives, wars break out, or computers are invented. This constant introduction of diversity leads both to an increasingly stressful life and to more complex and interesting modes of cognition. Experts in the theory of chaos—that is, the theory of this kind of unpredictability—often use the term "interesting" to denote what is non-linear or unsusceptible to simplification and prediction (see Horgan, 1997, p.197).

# The interesting, the truthful, and the potential

As mentioned earlier, the concept of the 'interesting' gained momentum with the postmodernist deconstruction of "truth" in the 1970s–90s. Gilles Deleuze and Felix Guattari sharply contrast the interesting with the outdated paradigms of knowledge as an approximation to an external reality:

> Philosophy does not consist in knowing and is not inspired by truth. Rather, it is categories like Interesting, Remarkable, or Important that determine success or failure. ... a concept must be interesting, even if it is repulsive. ... [T]hought as such produces something interesting when it accedes to the infinite movement that frees it from truth as supposed paradigm and reconquers an immanent power of creation. (1984, p. 82)

Thus the *interesting*, according to Deleuze and Guattari, provides an alternative to the truthful. The interesting is what repels and resists, breaking positive conventions of knowledge and contradicting both factual evidence and public taste. I would argue, though, that such a concept of the interesting, deriving only from the "infinite movement" and "power of creation", is overly romantic and as narrow, in its own way, as the rationalist conception of truth.

It is no wonder that poststructuralist views on the irrelevance of truth have offended the majority of scientists and drawn their sharp criticism. Usually the merit of a scientific theory is measured by three interconnected factors: truthfulness, correctness, and verity. Theory is truthful when it corresponds to external reality, correct when it is free from internal contradictions and veritable when it is verified by tests and experiments. Of course, these three criteria are necessary but insufficient conditions of being interesting; they lack the dimension of surprise or improbability. On the other hand, wonderment without any search for proof and evidence also becomes empty.

The interesting is constituted not merely in opposition to truth, after all, but in its juxtaposition of the truthful and trustworthy with the improbable and wondrous. The romantic is interesting when it discloses its rational side, and vice versa. Edgar Allen Poe and Jorge Luis Borges deserve, perhaps, to be considered among the most interesting writers for the way that they rationally decode the mysterious; at the same time, this decoding does not abolish the sense of mystery in their work, but rather intensifies it. Similarly, in scientific inquiry, thought that resists facts and despises evidence is as trivial and boring as thought that relies solely on facts without rising above them. The interesting is what comes in between two *mutually exclusive* and *equally indispensable* aspects of the phenomenon. If poststructuralism, as represented by Derrida, Deleuze, and Guattari, among others, tends to dismiss truth as a feature of an outdated episteme and renounces its conceptual status, then the next intellectual paradigm will *restore the value of truthfulness within the broader category of the interesting.* The truth regains its significance as *unpredictable and impossible truth*, a surprise at the unknown rather than an acceptance of the known.

However, if an author attempts to surprise readers by all possible means, the interesting, pursued for its own sake, may well be perceived as "predictably interesting" and therefore turn into the boring. The interesting not only evolves from the unpredictable and surprising, but it has to retain these qualities in the process its own manifestation, i.e. to be spontaneously and unexpectedly interesting. Otherwise, as an end in itself, it degenerates into an artificially enforced *interestism*, which is quickly recognized and fails to arouse genuine interest, instead dulling our attention and curiosity. *Interestism* is a contortion of the interesting, a quick discharge of its resources, an intellectual coquetry, a spasm, an explosion of the unexpected that comes too early, aborting our expectations. In this case, interesting content is condensed into certain short passages while the text as a whole lacks energy and intrigue. In fact, a good writer often needs to sacrifice an interesting fragment in order to build up a momentum of expectation. This accumulation of trivial instances, each one puzzling in itself, helps to direct interest towards an unexpected development (of thought or action) that is yet to come.

The most interesting books are usually written not for the sole purpose of being interesting, but to explore the world and human nature, to engage in emotional and intellectual self-expression, to invent new stories or create original images. Such is the dialectic of the interesting: it reaches its goal more effectively in deviating from it. Ironically, the interesting has to be independent of those "consumers" whose interest it aspires to arouse. This "disinterestedness" of the interesting originates from the same paradox that we have discussed earlier, namely, the combination of provability and improbability. This implies that the interesting itself should not be overwhelmingly and straightforwardly interesting, but should stand out from the contrastive background of the non-interesting, as a surprise rather than a predictable pattern. The interesting usually sparks and glimmers rather than shines brightly and evenly. What interests us deeply is interesting only to the extent to which it does not seek to cater to outside interests. It grips us, rather than submits to our desires. Ignoring this paradox and attempting to arouse interest from the very start and without interruption, *interestism* often ends in failure, obliterating wonder by making it routine. Only on a superficial level can it be said that "pleasing" the consumer or the reader should lie at the very core of the interesting. Martin Heidegger mentions such cases of "interestism" that lack their own center and therefore lead to indifference:

> Interest, *interesse*, means to be among and in the midst of things, or to be at the center of a thing and to stay with it. But today's interest accepts as valid only what is interesting. And interesting is the sort of thing that can freely be regarded as indifferent the next moment, and be displaced by something else, which then concerns us just as little as what went before. Many people today take the view that they are doing great honor to something by finding it interesting. The truth is that such an opinion has already relegated the interesting thing to the ranks of what is indifferent and boring. (1968, p. 5)

How might we relate such an account of the "interesting thing" to the question of an interesting person? We know that even the most talented people are sometimes so full of their own personalities, bright ideas, and deep emotions that they leave no space for anyone else to communicate and participate creatively. Strangely enough, they thus become akin to superficial people—"indifferent and boring", like Heidegger's "interesting thing"—who have nothing substantial in them and cannot lead the listener or the reader anywhere. Just as there is the tragedy of a *poor* man who has nowhere to go (consider Dostoevsky's Marmeladov[1]), there is the tragedy of a *dull* man who has nowhere to lead. Some people are like fountains, emanating their rich contents; others are like cotton wool, so entirely dry that nothing can be squeezed out of them. Finally, there are a few—and these are the most interesting personalities, existing between the polarities of interpersonal communication—who, like sponges, can both absorb *and* emit.

The interesting involves us in the "inter-being" of external objects, but the root of the "inter-esse" is within ourselves. There is an interior relation between my actuality and my potentiality: I can be unpredictable and surprising to myself. The interesting functions as a kind of mediator between me and myself, to the extent to which I *may be* different from what I *am*. In fact, what we find interesting in the world around us are those things that enrich our life with a range of possibilities. Even trivial interests reflect a discrepancy between the actual and the potential self, between what one is and what one can be. For example, a person interested in athletic activity does not simply exercise her body; she actually exercises her alterity, her capacity to surprise herself. She is finding her different self as an "athlete", exploring the possibility of becoming faster and stronger than she is. The interesting plays a central role in this person's self-potentiation, in her self-definition as a potential being. Whatever our external interests are (professional, social, or recreational), our engagement in a variety of activities reflects our desire to wonder at and be puzzled by ourselves, to experience something in ourselves that is, as yet, unknown and undiscovered.

There is a certain dynamic between individuals and interests: one individual can have multiple interests, just as one interest can be shared by many individuals. In this respect, interests are similar to universals, the general concepts of metaphysics. Interests can be characterized as *universals-for-individuals*, as opposed to the traditional *universals-in-individuals* that traditionally belong to the realm of philosophy. In this conventional sense, universals are objective attributes of an individual (be it person or thing) and do not depend upon the individual's consciousness or desire. Such universals as *nation, class, temper, mind*, and *language* (understood as the ability to think and speak) cannot be considered interests. But reading, science, art, politics, and sport can be viewed as universals-*for*-individuals and therefore as interests in that they are matters of conscious

---

[1]In Dostoevsky's novel, *Crime and Punishment*, Marmeladov is a minor character whose life is destroyed as a result of drinking addiction. Full of desperation and anguish, Marmeladov is tortured by the idea of "having nowhere to go" and is eventually trodden by horses. Marmeladov is often viewed as a double of Raskol'nikov, the main character of the novel, who also tries to function in a bleak world but cannot fit into society. (Editor's Note)

choice. Unlike traditional universals that establish our identities, interests are dynamic: they do not relate to properties but to intentions of their subjects.

The interesting interlaces truth and wonder, the obvious and the incredible, the actual and the possible, increasing the intensity of their interrelationship. Now and then one side starts to prevail over the other; the obvious is scrupulously argued or the incredible bluntly asserted. In these cases, the interesting tends to be lost, lapsing into the boredom of easy consent or the frustration of disbelief.

# 17

# Philosophy's return to wisdom

## Philosophy vs wisdom?

No consideration of the future of the humanities can avoid the theme of wisdom as the ultimate goal of spiritual life and intellectual pursuits. This technological age is characterized by a disparity between knowledge and wisdom, with the accumulation of scientific knowledge taking precedence over our understanding of values and goals. As James Martin writes in *The Meaning of the 21ˢᵗ Century: A Vital Blueprint for Ensuring our Future*,

> A serious problem of our time is the gap between skill and wisdom. Science and technology are accelerating furiously, but wisdom is not …. Skills need detailed, narrowly focused study of subjects that are rapidly increasing in complexity, whereas wisdom needs the synthesis of diverse ideas. (2007, p. 292)

Of all the disciplines counted among the humanities, it is philosophy that most directly deals with the concept of wisdom: the very term "philosophy" literally means "love of wisdom". Over the last several centuries, however, philosophy has devoted itself to wisdom least of all. This is especially true of any school of contemporary philosophy: American, Continental, radically social, analytical, hermeneutical, structuralist, or poststructuralist. Very rarely have philosophical analysis, deconstruction, neo- and post-Marxism, feminism, phenomenology, or communication theory have displayed any focused interest in wisdom, or Sophia as the original object and objective of the discipline.

According to the *Oxford Companion to Philosophy*, "although wisdom is what philosophy is meant to be a love of, little attention has been paid to this essential component of good lives in post-classical Western philosophy" (1995, p. 912). This disappearance of Sophia from philosophy could itself become a subject of a philosophical inquiry. In *The Routledge Encyclopedia of Philosophy*, this problem is presented as follows:

> In ancient times, wisdom was thought of as the type of knowledge needed to discern the good and live the good life. Philosophy takes its name from it (philosophia means love of wisdom). But wisdom is little evident as a subject of contemporary philosophical discussion. It is interesting to ask how the concept of wisdom has come to vanish almost entirely from the philosophical map. (1988, p. 752)

Indeed, in the majority of contemporary philosophical encyclopedias and dictionaries, the concept of wisdom is either absent or has a very low profile. Similarly to psychology that has completely abandoned the concept of "soul", philosophy has abandoned the concept of "wisdom", although historically the two disciplines were built around these core notions.

In the twentieth and twenty-first centuries, the search for wisdom has been conducted mostly outside of the limits of academic philosophy, e.g. in the realms of spirituality, esoterics, or higher knowledge. This search for wisdom can be called *sophiophilia*, or a genuine love of wisdom, distinct from philosophy as a disciplinary field. Sophiophilia absorbs the practical wisdom of the ancients, as found in the Books of Job and Solomon's Parables, Confucius and Lao Tse, and, more recently, Montaigne and Pascal, Goethe and Leo Tolstoy, Kierkegaard and Nietzsche. While philosophy has abandoned wisdom and turned into a rigid discipline which limits itself to the systemic organization of notions and a logical analysis of language, sophiophilia searches for new and non-academic venues of living-through-thinking.

In this regard, the following questions arise: "Can we define such a vague and elusive concept as 'wisdom'?", "'Why has philosophy in its historical development increasingly distanced itself from 'wisdom'?", and "'Is it possible for philosophy to return to wisdom?" If yes, how will philosophy change in the light of this "sophian" approach?

# On the history of wisdom

Wisdom is commonly defined as something different from both practical skill and theoretical knowledge. The Greek word *sophia* originally referred to craft skills. For example, in Homer one finds sophia "in the hands of an expert carpenter" who "is well versed in all his craft's subtlety" as he is cutting "a ship's timber" (*The Iliad*, 15, ln. 410–12). This concept was gradually transferred from the practical field to the field of ethics, and later to the theoretical field covering the knowledge of general principles. The famous seven wise men (*sophoi*), often mentioned in Greek classical texts, are wise "in general"—not in any specific area, but in all matters related to governing a society and directing one's life toward a high purpose. Socrates, as presented by Plato, takes knowledge, not skills, to be the origin of wisdom. Those artists and state officials who know how to handle their craft yet cannot explain its principles and cannot account for their actions, cannot be considered wise. Lysias as an orator, Homer as a poet, and Solon as a legislator are all highly skilled in different areas of verbal craft. However, what makes them wise is not their skills, but their ability to speak and theorize about their skills:

> *Soc.* ... if their compositions are based on knowledge of the truth, and they can defend or prove them, when they are put to the test, by spoken arguments, which leave their writings poor in comparison of them, then they are to be called, not only poets, orators, legislators, but are worthy of a higher name, befitting the serious pursuit of their life.
> *Phaedr.* What name would you assign to them?
> *Soc.* Wise, I may not call them; for that is a great name which belongs to God alone, – lovers of wisdom or philosophers is their modest and befitting title.
> (Plato, 1956, pp. 327–8)

In other words, philosophy comes to be viewed as a cognitive activity of reflection over products of creative craftsmanship. Finally, for Aristotle, theoretical and self-contained knowledge of the "first principles" becomes the main attribute of wisdom:

> [T]hat which is desirable on its own account and for the sake of knowing it is more of the nature of Wisdom than that which is desirable on account of its results, and the superior science is more of the nature of Wisdom than the ancillary... (2001a, p. 691).

Wise people pursue knowledge for its own sake and not for the sake of some practical purpose. Strange as it may seem, it was this convergence of wisdom and science that led to the gradual disappearance of wisdom from the pursuits of philosophy, beginning with the Skeptics. Skeptics started to doubt that the first origins and causes could be known by limited human intellect and identified wisdom with the ability of refraining from judgment, avoiding dogmatism and striving toward quietude (*ataraxia*). As a result, wisdom ceased to be necessary for both science, which is based on theoretical research, and ethics, which does not require any theoretical knowledge.

While for Skeptics wisdom is subject to theoretical doubt, for early Christians wisdom loses any religious and ethical value; the good life that leads to salvation is a matter of faith, not wisdom. For example, Paul condemns wisdom as a useless or even harmful tool of sophistication and theorizing: "For the wisdom of this world is foolishness before God. For it is written, 'He is the one who catches the wise in their craftiness' and again, 'the LORD knows the reasoning of the wise, that they are useless'" (1 Cor. 3.19–20). This way, wisdom came to be marginalized in the spiritual history of the West. As theoretical wisdom, it yielded its ground to science; as practical wisdom, to faith.

It was the secularization of European society in the age of the Enlightenment, on the one hand, and the Kantian critique of the metaphysical foundations of science, on the other hand, that brought wisdom back to life, though not on the scale of recognition it had enjoyed in the time of the Bible and classical antiquity. For Kant, "wisdom, theoretically regarded, means the knowledge of the highest good and practically, the suitability of the will to the highest good" (1949, p. 233). Wisdom is a category of practical reason in its ability to not only comprehend a higher good, which consists in the synthesis of virtue and happiness, but also to embody this good in one's own behavior.

With the Romantics and Schelling, wisdom takes on supremacy over knowledge and truth for it allows one to understand truth's change-ability and intellect's limitation. The heart of the matter is that the idea of philosophy, as knowledge that truly reflects the essence of its object, collapsed in the post-Kantian epoch. The category of opinion regained its authority, which had been undermined by Socrates and Plato. In antiquity, knowledge was considered opposed to opinion, similar to the relationship between objective truth and a subjective point of view. With Kant's critique of pure reason, knowledge was progressively assigned the status of opinion. Kierkegaard, Schopenhauer, Marx, and Nietzsche only intensified this epistemological scandal. In their philosophies, knowledge is presented as a manifestation of biological and social forces aspiring to power, or as an existential insight. In Nietzschean cognitive perspectivism there are no facts, only interpretations. Thus the question arises: if all knowledge is no more than an interpretation or an opinion depending on the subject and context of a judgment, which opinions should be preferred to others and on what grounds?

# Wisdom and intelligence

Wisdom as a *search for the best opinion in the absence of precise knowledge* is once again becoming one of the central concerns of philosophy. Having failed to become a rigorous discipline of objective knowledge, philosophy returns to its conceptual and etymological roots found in the meaning of Sophia.

A wise opinion allows us to pursue our interests in agreement with others. Wise persons do not do to others what they do not want to be done to them; instead, they try to do for others what nobody else could do in their place.

If a passive quality of will is called patience, and an active one is called courage, then wisdom is the ability to distinguish between contexts in which these qualities can be applied, that is, to distinguish between the circumstances which should be suffered and the ones that should be reformed. The expression of wisdom, variously attributed to Reinhold Nieburh or Johann Christoph Oetinger (see Platt, 1992, p. 276), is famously formulated as follows: *God, give us the serenity to accept the things we cannot change, courage to change the things we can, and wisdom to know the difference.* In other words, wisdom, which mediates between the virtues of patience and courage, helps us to accept what we cannot change, and to change what we cannot accept.

Wisdom has something in common with intelligence, for both are the opposites of stupidity. Stupidity is a failure to observe the boundaries of things, mistaking one thing for another and acting in one realm by the rules of another one. The fool of fairy tales, for example, cries at a wedding party and dances at a burial procession. In its turn, intelligence is the discriminating capacity of the mind recognizing the boundaries that exist in the world. Wisdom, however, should be distinguished from intelligence. A wise person is usually intelligent, but an intelligent one is not necessarily wise. Wisdom is an *intelligence that understands its own boundaries* and can deliberately choose to act according to the heart or the body, to the soul or the spirit, instead of the mind. To pat on a shoulder of a suffering person is wiser than to give an edifying lecture like the one that Job's friends lavish on him. In a way, wisdom is more intelligent than intelligence itself. Wisdom understands the limitations of intelligence, which is restricted by desires, passions, volition, and absurdity. Wisdom can weigh and balance intelligence and non-intelligence, or various kinds of intelligence, such as logical, or emotional, or social intelligence, and give preference to one over another according to the demands of the situation. For example, what for intelligence may appear as madness can be justified by wisdom.

While intellect is given to humans by nature, and intelligence is gained by education, wisdom is acquired through self-education and self-knowledge. Intellect can be found in children, and intelligence in adults; wisdom, however, is usually a privilege of the old age. As noted by John Kekes,

> Growth in wisdom and self-direction go hand in hand. They are tasks for a lifetime, hence the connection between wisdom and old age. The old man can be stupid, but a wise man is likely to be old, simply because such growth takes time. (1983, p. 286)

Intelligence may be mathematical or political, limited to a discipline or an area, such as chess, computers, or business. Wisdom, on the other hand, encompasses the entire spectrum of human behavior, though it is still possible for a wise person to be wise in one instance and unwise in another. As such, wisdom is a way of living; it is the discriminating capacity of the mind knowing how to exist, not simply the knowledge of what exists. Wisdom is the unity of logic and ethics, an art of thinking which leads to virtuous living.

The *logic of wisdom* consists in the ability to distinguish between things, establishing for each entity its own measure and law. The *ethics of wisdom* consists in the ability to correlate things, matching the advantages of some with the demands of others, e.g. connecting A, which lacks B, with B, which lacks A. Wisdom acts as a sword while bringing peace: with the sharp edge of its logic, wisdom separates things while simultaneously reconciling them ethically.

The development of philosophy with the increasing specializations of its branches, such as logics and ethics, ontology and epistemology, led to the gradual loss of wisdom as philosophy's central and holistic category. However, while wisdom lost its priority for individual philosophers, it still held its own in philosophy and even gained from the epochs of its oblivion. Even post-classic Western philosophy, which cared very little about wisdom, in its own way prepared its return. The Kantian critique that limited the realm of knowledge in order to expand the realm of faith was, in fact, a new exercise in wisdom. Wisdom delimits the domains of knowledge and faith and does not claim to know that which can only be taken by faith; at the same time, wisdom does not limit itself to a belief if the object of this belief can be reliably known. Hegel, who constructed his dialectics of a thesis and an antithesis as an art of transcending the limitations of opposite opinions, paved another path to wisdom. Kierkegaard, who inscribed all abstract metaphysical concepts within the concrete existence of an individual and reconnected the absolute "Thou" of God with the "I" of a believer, did as much for wisdom as did Hegel.

# Wisdom, vanity, and vain wisdom

Philosophy is truly wise because it does not stop at the concept of wisdom, but instead causes imbalance of its constituents in order to see the very quality of wholeness constantly tested and restored at a new level. Wisdom unites one-sided ideas, while making sure their unity is not one-sided. Wisdom is the ability of human intelligence to transcend the sensual heterogeneity of experience, but also to give priority to living particulars over chimerical abstractions of the mind. For this reason, wisdom discerns vanity not only in ordinary life, but also in itself, under the guise of sophistry or *vain wisdom* (cf. the Russian word *suemudrie*). I understand vanity in its Biblical sense—as an excessive, futile, and pointless activity, unworthy of serious effort (*vanitas vanitatum*). Vanity is the main opponent of wisdom, just as stupidity is the main opponent of intelligence. If stupidity is the failure to distinguish between things and to grasp their measure, then vanity is the dependency of our will upon those things that our intelligence recognizes as unworthy and insignificant. Vanity is the stupidity of will, which fails to discriminate between the importance of things, confusing their rank and order. An intelligent person can be a victim of vain pursuits, and it is precisely one's intelligence that sometimes provokes one to indulge in futility, criticizing things unworthy even of criticism and attempting to improve things better left the way they are.

Wisdom is the intelligence of intelligence, or the ability to handle one's intelligence intelligently. Vain people devote themselves to a lesser task than they are capable of handling, or else they demand more than they need. Wisdom keeps intelligence from arrogance and from wasting itself on petty things. However, wisdom itself is susceptible to vanity when it overestimates itself and does not condescend to the level of simple concerns of everyday life. Since there is nothing above wisdom that can humble it, it can accomplish this on its own, calling this self-arrogance *vain wisdom*. Such self-humiliation is characteristic of Socratic wisdom: "He among you is the wisest who, like Socrates, knows that his wisdom is really worth nothing at all" (*Apology* 23b, tr. Church, rev. Cumming).

Vain wisdom, on the contrary, asserts itself as wisdom and acts as a model and an example. As Ralph Emerson notes in his essay *Experience*, "The wise through excess of wisdom is made a fool" (1883, p. 68). Vain wisdom is the wisdom that places itself above other virtues, such as faith, love, hope, courage, kindness, and joy. While exposing the futility of all aspirations and arrangements, vain wisdom does not recognize a higher wisdom that might be above people and yet unknown to them.

Even the wisdom of Ecclesiastes becomes vain when he proclaims that all is vanity: "What befalls the fool will befall me also; why then have I been so wise? And I said to myself that this also is vanity... so I hated life because what is done under the sun was grievous to me; for all is vanity and a striving after wind" (Eccl. 2.15, 17). Only later does Ecclesiastes renounce this arrogant wisdom, which despises all human efforts and labors, and comes to justify the ordinary course of human life in the eyes of God. It is only when his wisdom ceases to denounce the vanity of everything that it stops being vain and opens itself to merriment and the affirmation of life: "A man's wisdom makes his face shine, and the hardness of his countenance is changed" (Eccl. 8.1); "Go eat your bread with enjoyment, and drink your wine with a merry heart; for God has already approved what you do" (Eccl. 9.7).

This unity of wisdom and joy is further explored in Spinoza:

> To make use of things, therefore, and to delight in them as much as possible (provided we do not disgust ourselves with them, which is not delighting in them), is the part of a wise man. It is the part of a wise man, I say, to refresh and invigorate himself with moderate and pleasant eating and drinking, with sweet scents and the beauty of green plants, with ornament, with music, with sports, with the theater, and with all things of this kind which one man can enjoy without hurting another. (1949, p. 223)

The first step of wisdom is to elevate itself above the futility of human affairs and to mourn their transitoriness. The second step of wisdom is to elevate itself over its own detached and haughty contemplation and to accept and to bless the earthly tasks entrusted to humans by God. Such is the rhythmic dance of wisdom, moving from sadness to joy.

# New encounter of wisdom and philosophy

The wisdom of our age is not one of contemplative tranquility. It is both tragic and comical because it is aware of the impossibility and absurdity of comprehensive wisdom. The wisdom of our time must learn to survive without any sages. In Gabriel Marcel's words,

> probably it is time to relinquish a traditional idea of a certain privileged being, who allegedly and inalienably possesses a certain quality of Being. The sage, so understood, risks to appear to us today a mundane and undoubtedly ludicrous reincarnation of a saint .... Wisdom ... is not so much a condition, as a goal. (1991, p. 358)

Wisdom cannot be identified with readily accessible knowledge; rather, wisdom is the constant effort of thought required to be on the boundary of knowledge and non-knowledge, action and non-action. Wisdom is simultaneously a search for knowledge and renunciation of knowledge, a movement from a humble Socratic minimum of knowledge (*I know that I know nothing*) to the hypothetical Platonic maximum of knowledge (*I do not know what I know*). We know more than we can ever imagine ourselves to know, and so our inborn knowledge far exceeds our subjective experience.

The nature of wisdom, however, includes self-unawareness and self-oblivion. Only vain wisdom believes itself to be wisdom. This is why philosophy, as love for wisdom, easily forgets about wisdom even though it never stops serving it. Perhaps this ability of wisdom to forget itself made it possible for philosophy to forget about wisdom Although in the second half of the twentieth century philosophy almost erased wisdom from textbooks and dictionaries, but nevertheless it preserved wisdom as the unintended premise of its pursuits. Phenomenology, existentialism, analytic philosophy, structuralism, and deconstruction—all of these schools of philosophical thought, while partly blinded by the passions of reason, still paved the path to wisdom.

Is it not wise to return from speculative abstractions "to the things themselves", and to trust their own mode of manifestation before our consciousness (phenomenology)? Is it not wise to return to the existence of the individual preceding any rational consciousness (existentialism)? Is it not wise to delimit our language tools from the nature of things themselves, and not to take the rules of word combination for the laws of the universe (analytic philosophy)? Is it not wise to turn from understanding phenomena as separate to understanding their structural interconnections, whereby each element of the whole is meaningful only in its relation to all other elements (structuralism)? Is it not wise to seek in words a deeper meaning than the writer consciously has imparted to them and to find contradictions where the writer has sounded clear to oneself (deconstruction)?

A philosopher is not always a sage, and sometimes philosophy nearing wisdom on one side, departs from it on the other. A philosopher who strictly follows a certain "-ism" is often blind to the whole. In general, any "-ism" taken to exclude all other opinions and directions of thought is a sign of theoretical stupidity and methodological obsession. A wise person, while sympathizing intellectually with all "-isms", does not affiliate oneself with any of them.

Thus the fulfillment of philosophy as a unified project cannot be achieved in any single "-ism" as one "truest" direction; it must move toward Sophia, which lies beyond all "isms". A rare attempt toward that end is the work of the American phenomenologist Dorion Cairns, one of the closest disciples of Husserl, who uses the phenomenological method in contradiction to Husserl's own idea of philosophy as rigorous science. Cairns attempts to bring philosophy back to wisdom, as an integrative experience of knowledge in its agreement with the art of a good, useful, and happy life (Cairns, 1984).

The concert of wisdom is both *pre-philosophical and trans-philosophical*. The beginnings of wisdom are to be found in Solomon, Lao Tse, Confucius, and Heraclitus. Is it possible that now, at the beginning of the third millennium, we witness the moment of philosophy's possible transformation back into wisdom? This does not mean, of course, that the history of philosophy as an academic discipline has been wasted time for wisdom, or that it should simply backtrack to its ancient sources, i.e. to the wisdom of the Greeks, the Bible, and Eastern sages. Wisdom has gained and learned a lot; most importantly, it has learned that the task of wisdom is to learn and not to instruct. According to Gogol, a wise man is the one who

> grasps the marvelous sweetness of being a disciple. Everything becomes a teacher to him, the entire world instructs him; the most insignificant person can be a teacher to him. From the most simple advice, he will extract wisdom; the most stupid thing will reveal to him its wise aspect, and the entire universe will open itself up to him as a book of learning. (1986, p. 220)

The movement of each discipline may consist in the progressive oblivion and subsequent restoration of its foundational concepts. This way, someday psychology may re-embrace the concept of the soul, and philosophy will re-embrace the concept of wisdom. Sooner or later, philosophy will come to understand that all its opposing trends are but the manifestations of wisdom, battling, first and foremost, stupidity and futility, as well as its own arrogance and vanity. It is only when philosophy returns to Sophia as its core, that the labor of love, signified by the very word *philo-sophia*, can be consummated. Then, all divergent sections of philosophy, i.e. ontology, epistemology, logic, ethics, and aesthetics will rediscover their internal connections in the concept of wisdom, as the beginning and the goal of all philosophical disciplines and directions.

Thus, any philosophical conception or system can be read as encoded wisdom, its parable or allegory. Such is the *sophian* approach to philosophy. Realism and nominalism, empiricism and rationalism, materialism and idealism will eventually be understood as various aspects of wisdom and modes of its humble self-discernment. Philosophy that will speak the language of all these movements as complementing one another, will cross the borders of an academic discipline and establish itself as *sophiophilia*, in direct relationship with *Sophia* as its own beginning. All lines and projections of philosophy that have diverged from the starting point of naïve wisdom will converge anew at the point where philosophy becomes wiser and stronger through its trials.

# 18

# Logos and Sophia: Sophian disciplines

## "-logy" and "-sophy"

Philosophy is one among various sophian disciplines (from *sophia*— "wisdom"), which view the objects of their study as related to the holistic vision of the universe. In this sense, the *sophy-disciplines* can be distinguished from the *logy-disciplines*, which study their objects within narrower methodological frameworks. The "-logy" in their names is from *logos*, meaning "word", "reason", "concept", or "account". One can identify a sophian counterpart for almost each logy-science, e.g. *archaeosophy* as the counterpart of archaeology; *psychosophy* as the counterpart of psychology; *geosophy*, of geology; *biosophy*, of biology.

Sophian disciplines attempt to recover the primary holistic nature of the object lost in the historical differentiation of logy-disciplines. For example, while the concept of the "soul", or "psyche", is considered pre-scientific or non-scientific in contemporary *psychology*, it remains central to *psychosophy*. Karl Jung's ideas of collective unconsciousness and psycho-mythic archetypes or Stanislav Grof's ideas on the transpersonal nature of the psyche fit more into the field of psychosophy than into psychology as a contemporary empirical academic discipline. *Technosophy*, which is distinct from scientific technology, explores the spiritual, cultural, and religious meaning of *techné*. *Physiosophy* contemplates the wisdom of the organism, its purposeful and meaningful design, through which the human character and destiny are realized.

Sophian disciplines are not merely sub-categories of philosophy because they study their objects more systematically, developing their own specific concepts and concrete terminology. Therefore, we must distinguish between the *philosophy of nature*, created by Hegel, and *biosophy* and *geosophy*, elaborated, for example, by such scientists as Ernst Haeckel and Vladimir Vernadsky. Sophian disciplines form a realm of transition from the generalizing principles of philosophy to the scientific, empirical, and analytical methods of logy-disciplines.

Sophia, or wisdom, is not actual knowledge, but rather the potentiality of the mind unrestrained by any scientific data or religious dogmas. Wisdom relates to knowledge as the potential does to the actual. While the logy-disciplines dissect objects into their constituents, sophian disciplines approach their objects as the constituents of higher wholes. For example, ethnography and ethnology describe the structure, genesis, history, and culture of (mostly primitive) ethnic groups, whereas *ethnosophy* connects all empirical characteristics of ethnicity with so-called national character and historic destiny. J. G. Herder opened the field of ethnosophy in his unfinished *Outlines of a Philosophy of the History of Man* (1784–91). Oswald Spengler's celebrated book *The Decline of the West* is, in fact, a treatise in ethnosophy in that it generalizes gigantic ethno-historical formations and their representative symbols and figures, such as the Arabic magic culture or the European Faustian culture. Among Russian thinkers, N. Danilevsky, L. Gumilev, and G. Gachev have made substantial contributions to this field. In contrast to ethnography and ethnology, *ethnosophy* mostly studies highly developed and diversified societies, while their various aspects are explored by a number of special disciplines, such as political history, linguistics, sociology, economics, and literary and art history. The task of *ethnosophy* is to bring together all the multiple aspects of a certain national culture—its underlying principles, intuitions, archetypes, and pra-phenomena—in order to define the place of each ethnos in the general evolution of humanity.

*Archaeosophy*, in distinction from archaeology, does not study ancient artefacts; instead, it focuses on the quasi-archaic formations that surround us even today, such as idol worship or the cult-status of political figures, pop stars, myths and superstitions, crypts and mausoleums as the contemporary reincarnations of archaic tradition. *Archaeosophy* deals with the ancient-like phenomena, regardless of the time of their actual origin. Such antiquated formations are characteristic of both modernity and postmodernity. It is the task of *archaeosophy*, not archaeology, to study the archaic in Pablo Picasso, James Joyce, Thomas Mann, or Communist and Nazi political mythologies.

Similarly, there are different approaches to the study of the Earth. Geography describes what is *on* the Earth, e.g. landscapes, climates, states, and borders. Geology looks deeper *inside* the Earth at its tectonic plates, soils, strata, magma, and the mantle, or mineral resources. However, it is possible to look even deeper—into the essence and the noumenal design of the Earth. Plotinus in *Enneads* (6.7.11) raises these important questions:

But earth; how is there earth There: what is the being of earth and how are we to represent to ourselves the living earth of that realm?

First, what is it, what the mode of its being? …

Take the most earthy of things found shaped in earth and they exhibit, even they, the indwelling earth–principle. The growing and shaping of stones, the internal moulding of mountains as they rise, reveal the working of an ensouled Reason–Principle fashioning them from within and bringing them to that shape: this, we must take it, is the creative earth–principle … Realizing thus that the creative force inherent in our earth is life within a Reason–Principle, we are easily convinced that the earth There is much more primally alive, that it is a reasoned Earth–Livingness, the earth of Real–Being, earth primally, the source of ours. (Plotinus 2004, p. 691)

Thus, alongside geography as the description of the Earth's surface, and geology as the study of the Earth's depth, there may also be a discipline devoted to the intelligible essence of the Earth: namely, *geosophy*. Vladimir Vernadsky's ideas (1926) about the living matter that comprises and organizes the mantle of the Earth belong to *geosophy* rather than geology. The Gaia hypothesis advanced by James Lovelock in 1979 and highly influential among ecologists also falls under the heading of *geosophy*. In this view, the Earth is a single living organism that regulates its life functions by effecting changes to the environment and climate.

We can distinguish the corresponding "-logy" and "-sophy" sets:

| | |
|---|---|
| physiology | physiosophy |
| ethnology | ethonosophy |
| geology | geosophy |
| biology | biosophy |
| psychology | psychosophy |
| cosmology | cosmosophy |
| sociology | sociosophy |
| technology | technosophy |
| ideology | ideosophy |

One of central projected disciplines in the transhumanities would be *biosophy*. Unlike biology, a natural science that studies life and living organisms, biosophy would be a humanistic discipline devoted to the life and living properties in culture, mind, and spirit. I believe the property of "being alive" is independent of any material carrier, which can be biological or non-biological, e.g. textual, conceptual, or electronic. Some personalities, thoughts, texts, paintings are more alive, full of life than others. What is it that makes a certain idea, a theory, a work of art or literature a "'living entity", whereas another idea or a work is dead or stillborn? Some criteria for "being alive", in opposition to "being dead", include openness to others in the form of interpersonal or intertextual connections, a multiplicity of meanings and possible interpretations, and potential for structural growth and intellectual change.

The categories of "dead" and "alive" are particularly applicable to labor. Karl Marx distinguished "living labor", as the force of living workers, from "dead labor" or "past labor", accumulated in tools, factories, and goods. According to Marx, "Capital is dead labor, which, vampire-like, lives only by sucking living labor, and lives the more, the more labor it sucks" (*Capital*, vol. 1, ch 10, section 1). Such living labor, in distinction from "dead capital", is definitely a target of biosophical study addressed to the "living" in the broadest sense. The same can be said about the distinction between accumulated, "disciplinary" knowledge, and thinking as the living labor of mind, which crosses the borders of existing disciplines. The project of the transhumanities pursues the goal of changing the ratio of intellectual labor in favor of the living over the dead (see Chapter 20, "The Mass of Knowledge and the Energy of Thinking"). Today, with the spread of intellectual and information technologies, the living thinking is quickly winning over dead knowledge ("gnawledge"), just as living labor is winning over the "past labor" objectified in the manufactured goods of civilization. An electronic network is in principle more alive as a medium of intellectual communication than a traditional book that accumulates certain knowledge in a static form.

Biosophy is especially important for the future of artificial intelligence as a means of ensuring that such an "artlect" can produce a living thought and not just a certain amount of knowledge. I believe that if human creators can make their poems or sculptures come alive, then thinking machines could be even more alive since they are capable of *autopoiesis*, or *self–creation*, which is one of the most widespread definitions of life in biology.

The sophiosphere is overarching all other spheres that surround our planet: the geosphere, biosphere, technosphere, semiosphere, ideosphere, psychosphere, and noosphere. Through sophian disciplines, including philosophy, wisdom is infused into all levels of organization of the living and thinking matter.

# Practical Sophias. Polysophianism

That many established academic "-logy" disciplines are now discovering their "sophian"' underpinnings is one indicator of a growing sophiosphere. The sophiosphere is also being expanded by numerous sophias found in various practical activities and crafts. In modern English (especially

American English), the word "philosophy" has a much wider usage than its equivalents in other languages. In Russian, for instance, "philosophy" has a high-flown, bookish, and academic ring to it; it is not perceived as a word of everyday language. In English, however, "'philosophy'" is not just an academic discipline, but also a general system of principles for guidance in practical affairs which makes it closer to the initial meaning of "sophia" in Greek, for example, in Homer, who spoke of the carpenter "well skilled in all manner of craft (*sophiês*) by the promptings of Athene" (*Il.* XV, 411–12). According to contemporary American usage, a gardener may have a philosophy of saving a tree in your backyard. A soccer coach has a philosophy of planning the best strategy of defense or attack. A housewife has a philosophy of preparing a Thanksgiving turkey. A teacher has a philosophy of dealing with unruly students. And at a local dry-cleaner's, they will share with you their own philosophy of cleaning and drying clothes.

Thus, there are as many philosophies in the world as there are different kinds of human practical affairs, for people can master any activity only by reflecting upon its "first principles". Sophia, then, can be seen as the wisdom of striving toward a balance between a subject and an object, measured according to the inner nature of things. Sophia combines reason with skill, as theory and practice are constantly being turned into one another. Philosophy, in its turn, as love of sophia, inspires us to engage in various activities, not as mere dilettantes, but as knowledgeable professionals faithful to our crafts.

Philosophy, as an academic discipline and a special way of thinking, is different from countless philosophies found in various practical activities and crafts. A philosopher is one who reflects upon the foundations of such activities as "being human", "living in this Universe", "being born and dying", and "learning and believing". A philosopher, in effect, is a specialist in the most universal human activities. This specialty, however, is just one among many other philosophies, because sophia, as reflection upon the beginnings and ends of an activity, can be found in many other practices. Understood this way, sophia not only does not depart from, but rather returns to, its original meaning. Originally, "sophia" used to refer to practical crafts; for instance, as Homer spoke of the carpenter. It was only later that sophia was transferred from the sphere of practical affairs into the sphere of theoretical contemplation to include the knowledge of general principles of the universe. The time has now come for sophia to return to its roots, embracing again all professional crafts and practical arts. In this light, the usage of "philosophy" in American English is not a form of its debasement; rather, it takes this concept back to its very source, the notion of wisdom as practical art. All modern philosophy can be seen in that light, too. Having reached an impasse of self-analysis, i.e. analyzing its own language, philosophy can now turn to practice, instead of merely reproducing teachers of philosophy.

Philosophy must undergo a transition to *polysophianism*, the way the concept of culture at one point underwent a transition to multiculturalism. Such a transition would prove wrong the diagnosis/prognosis of the "end" of philosophy, put forth by R. Rorty, J.-F. Lyotard and other thinkers (cf. Baynes et al, 1986; Bruns, 1999). It may be true that philosophy has lost its connection with reality and no longer has any significant impact on social affairs. However, all that can be compensated for by the realization of the existence of multiple sophias (note the plural) found in the wisdom of carpentry, gardening, etc. Every craft, art, or sport has their own "wisdoms", which may not claim to contain the most universal and powerful knowledge, but are still the forms of self-reflection by their masters.

Once we recognize the existence of multiple sophias, we embark on a new path leading from "a work" and "a doctrine" toward the sophiosphere as an all-embracing sphere of wisdom. The sophiosphere, on a par with biosphere (J.-B. Lamarck), noosphere (Teilhard de Chardin and V. Vernadsky) and semiosphere (Yu. Lotman), embraces everything that is wise in human activity, craft, language, and thought, all of which are interconnected. While the Internet contributes to its rapid growth, a sophiosphere is also taking shape as a logical step in the historical development of philosophy itself from aphorism and parable to a treatise and system of knowledge, and then to the sphere of sophia itself.

Once we start thinking in terms of a sophiosphere, we must look at the goals and methods of philosophy differently and think of it as linguo-architecture and ideo-architecture, i.e. as an activity which creates a mental and verbal environment. This kind of activity is different from simply creating a work of art or a theory. It is different not least because an individual work of art is discrete while a sophiosphere is continuous. The philosophical ideal during the times of Gutenberg was creating an individual treatise as a perfect work. The internet has radically changed the criteria of creative activity: now the goal is to create an intellectual environment rather than a finished product. If we interpret architecture in broad terms, as the construction of an artificial environment, then a single creation, as a unit of such constructive activity, can be taken to correspond to an isolated building. Polysophianism, as a new philosophy, tends to create a continuous environment, which combines different arhitectural elements, such as ideas, projects, theories, and images, in various ways.

The philosophical systems of the past appear today as part of a pre-urban phase in the history of human thought, resembling isolated structures hanging over the void of the wilderness: Descartes' fortress over here, Kant's castle over here, and Hegel's citadel over there. In the past, isolated constructions were built, graceful and majestic, only to be replaced with the new, more durable ones.

Today, instead of building isolated structures, we must create a sophio-sphere as an environment of those logical spaces and passages which often exist beyond the level of our awareness and yet in which we live, the way people live in a complex urban environment. This does not mean getting rid of the old constructions; those still remain, but they are now connected by a myriad of passages, hanging bridges, stairways, and multi-level galleries, looking less desolate in their grandiosity than before. Authors of a sophiosphere, as donors of a sophionet, constantly create and maintain a conceptual environment, unforeseeable for the authors themselves as it reaches beyond their individual horizons.

# 19

# The philosophy of the possible and the possibilities of philosophy

## Beyond modern and postmodern

For every "after" there is a "before". Every time span has its own past and its own future. We live not only after August 6, 1945 in Hiroshima, but also after September 11, 2001 in New York City. These events represent, respectively, the culmination of two paradoxically similar epochs: modernist and postmodernist.

Modernism was characterized by a belief in the triumph of meta-narratives and an attempt to transform the world by the force of grand ideas and all–encompassing political ideologies. The atomic bomb, with its immense destructive power, releases vast quantities of energy from relatively small amounts of matter; in a certain sense, it illustrates the explosive effect of the projection of sweeping ideas upon living reality.

Postmodernism involves the free play of signs and demonstrates the illusive and delusive nature of reality and all that it signifies. The terrorist hijackers who destroyed the Twin Towers in New York City on 9/11 did not possess any serious weapon comparable to the atomic bomb; they were armed with box-cutters (toy weapons, in fact), and, allegedly, with fake bombs. They were not real pilots or masters of flight, but only imitators. They utilized the signs and tools of Western civilization in order to give them a different meaning, using constructive force in a destructive way by crashing *aircrafts* into *skyscrapers*. The perpetrators destroyed two of the most majestic products of Western civilization—the symbolic domination of the sky and the earth. The mirror symmetry of twin towers has added to this effect of duplicity. The activity of the hijackers was that of substitution and falsification, with no substantive material of its own.

The tragic events in Hiroshima and New York City symbolically sum up the modernist (atomic) and postmodernist (simulative) projects. Today we can envision the emergence of a new age of creative philosophy that is called to exclude any violence against the fabric of being and to be respectful of the world, while facilitating multiple possibilities of other, alternative worlds.

In the past, the dead-end of modernist thinking was complicit in the developments leading to the catastrophes of World War II, totalitarianism, and imperialism. Modernist philosophy was daringly and dangerously creative in its peculiar way, presented in the "imperative mood". Karl Marx proclaimed in his eleventh thesis on Feuerbach: "The philosophers have only *interpreted* the world in various ways; the point is, to *change* it" (1967, p. 402). As we know, the practical result of communist transformation of the world was catastrophic. As a safeguard against such activist philosophy, postmodernism offered an alternative to modernist meta-narratives, but failed to advance it in a creative way, stuck instead in playful hypercriticism and a "negative" attachment to the past. Postmodern philosophy reduced creativity to critical deconstruction and refutation of modernist concepts, such as *reality, truth, presence, author*, and *originality*.

Is there any future for *constructive* philosophy that would avoid the deficiencies of both modernist and postmodernist theories and the temptations of both totalitarian meta-narratives and relativistic hypercriticism? As argued at the beginning of this book, we witness a fundamental shift in contemporary culture from postmodernism and other varieties of "post-", such as post-structuralism, post-industrialism, and post-utopianism, to a new cultural formation based on the ideas of "proto-". This new sensibility of proteism accentuates the beginnings of new things rather than the endings of old things, and the prospective rather than retrospective modes of theoretical thinking. Proteism challenges both modernist and postmodernist projects and requires a new modality in philosophy: we must start thinking in the subjunctive rather than imperative mood, constructively rather than deconstructively, and synthetically rather than analytically.

This new methodology in philosophy and the humanities can be called *potentiation*, which, as a logical extension of "proto" culture, is based on the proliferation of virtual and alternative realities in the contemporary world.

THE PHILOSOPHY OF THE POSSIBLE

*Potentiation*, as traced back to the ideas of Nicholas of Cusa, Leibniz, and Schelling, demonstrates that each concept, theory, or discipline has its alternative, which can appear as a primary object of consciousness when viewed from a different perspective. Instead of focusing critically on a given text or a discourse, *potentiation* (or possibilization), inscribes each concept in a broader frame as only one among many possible concepts. This methodology of *potentiation* leads philosophy from the description of the world as it is, to the task of projecting multiple possible worlds, thus enriching the scope of *thinkable* and *beable* realities both ontologically and epistemologically.

# Philosophy in the imperative mood: Criticism and activism

The evolution of modern philosophical thought can be explained in terms of modalities usually defined as types of propositions in their relation to existence. The three main modalities are widely recognized: *actuality*, *necessity*, and *possibility*. I apply this approach within the context of influential philosophical theories of the possible, including the discussions regarding the nature of possible worlds by Nicholas Rescher (1975) and David Lewis (1979). I argue that the "possible" is irreducible to any single mode of actualization. In contrast to the traditional definitions of the possible in terms of realism, nominalism, or conceptualism, I proceed from *possibilism*, which maintains that the possible is a foundational category applicable to various aspects of reality, language, and thought (see Epstein, 2001).

Philosophy has passed through two large epochs in its development: metaphysical and critical/activist.

In its metaphysical epoch, philosophy tried to explain the world and establish certain indisputable truths about the essence of things, mainly, God, nature, and humankind. Philosophy searched for the essence of objects of philosophical contemplation, ignoring any subjective conditions and preconditions of their perception. Of course, this metaphysical orientation remains to this day, as an unreflective, complacent identification of thought with its subject.

The second epoch, beginning with the Kantian revolution in philosophy, limited the possibilities of theoretical philosophy. Such possibilities were drastically narrowed because reliable knowledge of the world, as it exists by itself, was denied. At the same time, during this epoch, the view of philosophy as praxis expanded dramatically: philosophy's role went beyond the task of explaining reality to include that of its transformation. Philosophy as a project of changing the world became a fundamental impulse for such thinkers as Fichte, Saint-Simon, Fourier, Comte, Feuerbach, Marx, Schopenhauer, Nietzsche, Sartre, and Marcuse, as well as for American pragmatists.

In essence, the majority of the socio–political movements of the twentieth century were inspired by the philosophical ideas that became a "material force" (Marx) in the minds of the masses. Philosophy, as a field of practical activism, is supposed to lead to the embodiment of various great ideas, such as that of a classless society (Marx), an omnipotent superman (Nietzsche), a non-repressive civilization (Marcuse), or an open society (Popper).

It is important to recognize the unity of radical criticism and indefatigable activism as the two philosophical extremes of this epoch. Their separation was delineated in Kant's philosophy as a clear-cut delimitation between the spheres of pure and practical reason: the question "What can I know?" was separated from the question "What should I do?" Philosophy needed a better understanding of the continuum of reason between science and ethics. However, these spheres were juxtaposed and developed independently in the history of philosophical thought, the sphere of cognition became increasingly limited and the sphere of action ever more greatly expanded.

Hypercriticism has thoroughly purged philosophy of naive speculations, targeting such illusions as religion, ethics, ideology, love of neighbor, freedom of creativity, and truthfulness of cognition. Meanwhile, activism has filled the void, which was increasingly eating away at the fabric of philosophical knowledge, with a revolutionary transformation of the world and justification of violence, paradoxically complemented by scientism and technocratic rationality.

At first glance, it seems that these extremes rarely come into contact with each other. For instance, what can purely academic language studies by British analytical philosophers have in common with the rage of "militant materialism" inside the Gulag? Stalin would have never understood the *Tractatus Logico-Philosophicus*, nor would he have recognized its author as a real philosopher, just as Wittgenstein would never have considered the chapters on dialectical and historical materialism from *A Short Course in the History of the VKP(b)* to be a philosophical work[1]. Yet, Wittgenstein and Stalin both belong to the same critical-activist philosophical paradigm.

These two extremes have at times coalesced into a single movement of thought. Marx's criticism of ideology as the illusions of an estranged consciousness was supplemented with the development of Marxist ideology in the form of revolutionary consciousness. Stalin and Wittgenstein moved so far apart from each other at particular instances that the link between them almost threatened to disappear—yet the fundamental interconnectedness remained. After all, if a thinker is allowed to describe only bare facts, then the

---

[1] *A Short Course in the History of the VKP(b)* (*Kratkii kurs istorii VKP(b)*), where *the VKP(b)* stands for *the All-Union Communist Party (Bolsheviks)*, was published in 1938. The Course provided an official interpretation of the history of the Party and incorporated the main ideological premises of Marxism-Leninism. (Editor's Note)

connection and the significance of these facts must be given from the outside, e.g. by the will of a figure who determines the course of history. Paradoxical as it might be, the very logic of the *Tractatus Logico-Philosophicus* paves the way for the philosophy expressed in *A Short Course in the History of the VKP(b)*. Crudely put, if the existence of God cannot be ontologically proven and is deemed a "pseudo-problem", then, from that point forward, society will deify whatever the political vanguard may consider appropriate and useful for its purposes. Everything that criticism has castigated theory for as unverifiable and unreliable knowledge, activism has added to its practical strategy and to its tactics for the revolutionary transformation of the world.

Hypercriticism and activism have worked together as poles of a new circuit of philosophical energy, although most often they have not recognized their mutual conditioning. While the connection between philosophy and reality had been purged, the connection between philosophy and practical action still had the potential to grow.

Today, this second epoch in philosophical development has come to an end. Both the critical and activist tendencies had exhausted themselves by the end of the twentieth century. Marxism-Leninism, the most powerful activist philosophy of the twentieth century, is now in ruins. Philosophy as an activist endeavor aimed at changing real circumstances, has lost all its power.

The critical bias in philosophy is apparently close to exhaustion as well. The very substratum of metaphysics, on which its philosophical criticism could be based, has already dissolved, revealing a void. During the past two centuries, Western philosophy has seen wave upon wave of ever more refined and radical criticism. The first such wave was the Kantian critique of pure reason. Then Schopenhauer and Nietzsche heaped criticism on the system of ideal values, discovering a will to life and to power at their base. Marx and Engels criticized all ideological, "transmuted" forms of cognition, discovering in them the basis of the system of social relations and the process of material production. Existentialism, beginning with Kierkegaard, criticized the entire history of Western metaphysics for giving preference to common ideas and essences over individual existence. Freud heaped criticism on all of civilization, calling it a repressive system for suppressing primordial instincts and unconscious impulses.

These kinds of philosophical criticism almost undermined the basis of philosophy itself, since the only positive remnants of the destroyed illusions were not of philosophical nature at all. Material production, which, according to Marx is the first reality, clearly belongs not to philosophy, but to politics and economics. The instinct to live, rising up out of the ruins of Christianity in Nietzsche, is ultimately a biological phenomenon. Freudian criticism of civilization led to the primacy of psychology and psychoanalysis in the humanities. In time, that leading role would shift to linguistics, since criticism of metaphysics led to the analysis of language as the focus of all philosophical problems. Philosophy wanted to regulate language in such a way as to erase any trace of its own presence in it, rendering language to produce only clear-cut judgments that could be accessed by empirical verification. It turns out that, in the critical age, philosophy's sole purpose is to present itself to the scientific worldview as a discipline that is speculative and, moreover, obsolete.

Finally, deconstruction became the last, "ninth wave" of criticism. For postmodernism, it is even impossible to regulate language philosophically. No rationality exists in nature that could compel language to do correct, meaningful work because language is nothing but eternal wandering, a collection of slips of the tongue and misinterpretations. But, any assertion contains ambiguity or aporia, and so the language that we use to deconstruct philosophical language is itself subject to deconstruction; this way, we discover that language consists of metaphors and self-defeating expressions. Philosophy has a persistent habit of leaving on paper unknown meanings that are unclear and indefinable. The philosophy of deconstruction claims to be nothing other than the deconstruction of philosophy itself. If logical positivism came to the conclusion that philosophical propositions could not be actually verified and confirmed, then the theory of deconstruction arrives at the conclusion that philosophical propositions cannot even be adequately expressed and interpreted. Not only do they not designate anything true, they do not even designate anything definite.

It was far from accidental that the activist and critical philosophies arrived at their logical completion at the same moment in history: at the same time as Gorbachev's *perestroika* (literally, "reconstruction") finalized the movement of philosophical activism, Derrida's deconstruction finalized the movement of philosophical criticism. All philosophical attempts at practical action, beginning with Plato's *Republic* and ending with Lenin's *The State and Revolution*, have turned out to be detrimental both to reality and to philosophy itself. The precise meaning that critical philosophy set out to find has turned into slippery cells in a semantic grid of empty forms. Thus, the philosophy today must radically revise its assignment and find its new creative calling.

# The modality of the possible and the method of potentiation

The change of large philosophical epochs is primarily a change of modalities, which are much more profound and fundamental than any differences in the content of thinking. Thus, the two propositions, "there is a God" and "there is no God", while opposite in content, are formally included in the same indicative modality that asserts or denies God as a fact of reality. Thinkers of the pre-critical period could hold the most diverse opinions about the essence or the origin of the world, but their thinking still unfolded in the indicative modality, reflective of what exists. The Kantian revolution established the imperative modality for thought, which defined how reality and thinking should delimit and transform each other.[2]

At present, philosophy, having exhausted the indicative and imperative moods, is opening up within itself a third modality—the modality of the possible. This is perhaps the only way out of the impasse into which philosophy has been drawn by attempts to narrow its theoretical authenticity and expand its practical applicability. It has become clear that philosophy is neither a reliable method for understanding reality, nor a productive method of changing it. Philosophical thinking, as distinct from scientific thinking, is not rigorous and, unlike technological or political thinking, it does not correspond to anything concrete in existence. *Up to this point philosophy has tried to explain or to change the world, while its proper work is to expand the thinkability of the world and to make multiple worlds possible.*

Our further elaboration on this new paradigm should include the problem of *universals*, treated from a possibilist perspective that challenges both the nominalist and realist solutions. Contrary to the famous principle of *Occam's razor*, which states that entities should not be multiplied beyond necessity, I consider the task of philosophy to be the multiplication of entities (or thinkables) according to possibility. In Russia, this principle has been jokingly called "Epstein's stubble" (as opposed to "Occam's razor")[3]. Philosophy's goal is not—or no longer—to explain or to change the existing world (these are the goals of the sciences and of ideologies, respectively), but to make it thinkable and to posit it in terms of possible worlds.

This new task of philosophy corresponds to the explosive "proto-" tendencies, outlined earlier in the book. The philosophy of the possible focuses on the *potentiation* of the real, i.e. a gradual transition from actuality to potentiality, both in ontological and epistemological projections. *Potentiation is the growth of the degrees of the possible in reality itself*, the process of transformation of facts into probabilities, theories into hypotheses, statements into suppositions, and necessities into alternative possibilities. All reality is permeated by possibilistic constructs as it passes *from the "is" mode to the "if" mode.* The strongest degree of *potentiation* is the transformation of the impossible into the possible.

---

[2] The pre-critical type of philosophy continued to exist even after Kant. It simply began to be perceived as "pre-Kantian", archaic in style, and more amateur than professional. Critical philosophy will exist in the third millennium in exactly the same way: it will be recognized as the preparatory stage for post-critical, constructive, possibilistic thinking.

[3] For more information about the concept of "Epstein's stubble" see the following links:
http://www.lomonosov-fund.ru/enc/ru/magazine:0136512
http://kitezh.onego.ru/topia/zametki_ru.htm
http://censura.ru/articles/epstein.htm

Thus, *proteic* civilization is shifting from the paradigm of the realization of possibilities to a new one. The possibilization of reality presupposes an excess of the possible over the actual, the proliferation of possibilities rather than their reduction to one mode of actuality.

Nicholas of Cusa (1401–64) was the first thinker to construct a systematic metaphysics of the possible and, in so doing, to reverse the relationship between the potential and the actual. In a number of treatises, such as *On the Possibility-Being (De Possest), The Hunt for Wisdom* and *On the Summit of Contemplation*, Nicholas of Cusa laid the basis for "potentiology". In his search for the most substantial entity that can be revealed to the mind, he approaches the category of *Posse*—the intrinsic potentiality of all things. *Posse* is the Latin for "can be" or "to be able" and is found as the root in such words as "possible" and "possibility", "potency" and "potential". According to Nicholas of Cusa,

> The summit of contemplation is *Posse* Itself, the *Posse* of all *posse*, without which nothing at all can be contemplated. Indeed, how could it without *posse*? ... Nothing exists except that which can be. To be, therefore, does not add to the *posse* to be. So a human being does not add anything to the *posse* to be a human. ... Nothing can be prior to *Posse* Itself. For how could it without *posse*? So nothing can be better, more powerful, more perfect, simpler, clearer, more known, truer, more sufficient, stronger, more stable, easier, and so forth, than *Posse* Itself. (1997, p. 300)

Thus, the being of a person adds nothing to the possibility of being a person. On the contrary, as it proceeds from the possible to the actual, there is a certain diminution of being. Only God is completely what He can be; in Him, absolute possibility coincides with absolute reality. Other types of beings and existences can be lower than they are because their actuality is inferior to their potential. The exceeding of the actual by the possible is a source of movement and change in the world.

According to Aristotle, all that is eternal exists in actuality, while the possible is impermanent: it can be or not be. For Nicholas of Cusa, conversely, everything actual is subject to change, for it does not include within itself all of its possibilities, and only the "possibility in and of itself" embraces the fullness of the eternal: "both the *posse* to be and the *posse* to be this or that presuppose *Posse* Itself" (1977, p. 298). Possibility stays ahead of all possible doubts and questions addressed to it, since it makes them possible, and so it acts as knowledge within the very lack of knowledge: "there is nothing more certain than *Posse* Itself, since doubt cannot do otherwise than presuppose it, nor can anything be conceived more sufficient or more perfect" (Nicholas of Cusa, 1977, p. 298). If the transition from the Creator to a creation comes about by fragmentation of the possible into the diversity and mutability of the existent, the mind seeking the essential beginning and the foundation of everything, proceeds in the opposite direction—from actual existences and particular realizations of the possible to the possible in and of itself:

> For what could satisfy the longing of the mind other than *Posse* Itself, the *Posse* of every *posse*, without which nothing whatever can? Indeed, if something other than *Posse* Itself could be, how could it without *posse*? … There can be no other substantial or quidditive principle, either formal or material, than *Posse* Itself. (Nicholas of Cusa, 1977, pp. 298, 303)

Thus, at the beginning of modernity, the first philosophical apology for the possible was born. Leibniz subsequently developed the category of the possible in depth, associating it with the question of freedom of will. In his correspondence with Arnault, Leibniz advanced the idea of a multitude of possible Adams, a concept that was alien to his correspondent. It would seem that Adam, as the first man, would, more than any other creation, be singular. But, since Adam was created by the free will of the Creator, there could have been other Adams as well. This possibility is revealed to the mind of the philosopher, while the mind of the dogmatic theologian proceeds from the existence of one biblical Adam:

> But when I speak of several Adams I do not take Adam for a determined individual but for some person conceived *sub ratione generalitatis* … and so there might be several other disjunctively possible Adams. … Everything that is actual can be conceived as possible … . In order to call something possible, it is enough merely to be able to form a concept of it when it is only in the divine understanding, which is, so to speak, the realm of possible realities. … If we wished absolutely to reject such pure possibles we should destroy contingency and freedom, for if nothing is possible except what God has actually created, whatever God has created would be necessary, and, in willing to create something, God could create only that thing alone, without any freedom of choice. (Leibniz, 1969, pp. 335–6)

Thus, for Leibniz the modality of the possible is rooted in the multiplicity of possible worlds created by the free will of God.

Later *potentiation* as an alternative to Kant's critique was introduced into philosophy by F. W. J. Schelling under the name *construction* or *constructing*:

> Unless construction is introduced into philosophy as a rigorous method, we can neither overcome the narrow constraints of Kant's critique nor move forward in the direction of the positive and apodictic philosophy, as outlined by Fichte. The study of philosophical construction is

positioned to become in the future one of the most important chapters of scientific philosophy; we must admit that a lack of the proper notion of construction prevents many of us from contributing to the development of philosophy. (1856–61, vol. 5, p. 125)

This study of construction by Schelling introduces a new stage of thinking that follows Kant's critique, but, at the same time, goes beyond those critical functions by means of which post-Kantian philosophy limited itself. While criticism puts limits on theoretical reasoning, constructive possiblism transcends them. Schelling emphasizes that construction is potentiation and creates only potential objects. Thus, reality itself can be determined only within a broader concept of absolute possibility. In other words, reality is seen as potentiality, as a special kind of thinkability, in its radical distinction from thinking as such. Schelling gives the name of *potencies* to those ideal definitions, which reveal in the variety of specific phenomena the ultimate whole as the goal of philosophical thinking and aesthetic contemplation. Between innumerable entities found in the empirical world and the absolute as understood by Schelling, there are *potencies* of multiple orders and levels, where the actuality is transformed into potentiality, the finite into the infinite. Thinking, according to Schelling, is progressive *potentiation* of its object, the ascension from lower to higher *potencies*: "All internal integrity of transcendental philosophy is based only on constant potentiation of self-contemplation, from the first and simplest potency of self-awareness and up to the highest aesthetic potency" (Schelling, 1856–61, vol. 1, p. 630).

If criticism limits the domain of theoretical reason, then *potentiation* proceeds from within these limits and overcomes them, unifying the theoretical and practical capacities that were strictly separated by Kant. But, unlike the pre-Kantian naïve or dogmatic unity, *potentiation* is a conscious production of a self-reflective unity, aware of those boundaries that it aims to transcend. Such is the creative impulse of reason, which seeks adventures by breaking beyond the purely theoretical realm of contemplative and speculative knowledge. All boundaries are set in order to be crossed, generating thought-events and intensities in an area in which, before Kant, there had been only a homogeneous space of uncritical ideas.

The adventurous thinker of today is quite different in kind from an old nomadic metaphysician. The thinker of today is keenly aware of the boundaries to be crossed and the risks to be taken. Hence the audacious and impassioned nature of possibilist thinking, which has the courage to overcome epistemological challenges, while simalteneously realizing that they cannot be completely overcome. The adventurous thinker not only knows—following Socrates and Kant—how much he or she does not know, but also, taking this paradox further, he or she also does not know how much he or she already knows and can know in the future. It is with this not knowing that the adventurous thinker sets out on a journey.

Possibilistic thinking dares to overcome cognitive obstacles that it knows cannot be overcome, and thus brings the impossible into being. Invention is a true adventure of the mind, the *eventfulness* of thinking, which can be defined as transgression of a border between conceptual fields, demarcated by their analytical distinction. A true event of thinking always crosses the borders of established, necessary, and even possible concepts, breaking into the realm of the impossible. As defined by Yury Lotman,

> An event in a text is the shifting of a persona across the borders of semantic field. ... The less probability that a given event will take place (i.e. the greater the information conveyed by the message concerning the event), the higher the rank of that event on the plot scale. ... The movement of a plot, an event must be seen as crossing the forbidden boundary, established by a 'plotless' structure. ... It is precisely what is asserted as impossible by a 'plotless' structure that constitutes the content of a plot. A plot is 'a revolutionary element' in relation to the 'picture of the world.' (1977, pp. 224, 1988, 228)

Jacques Derrida sees such eventfulness of thinking as the core of the new humanities: "There is no future and no relation to the coming of the event without experience of the "perhaps". What takes place does not have to announce itself as possible or necessary; if it did, its irruption as event would in advance be neutralized. The event belongs to a *perhaps* that is in keeping not with the possible but with the impossible" (2001, p. 54).

Methodologically pure and consistent philosophical strategies, such as idealism or materialism, are deployed in a homogenous continuum of thought. We can envision, however, a philosophy based on the complexities of *event* and *invent*. Both these English words are derived from the same Latin root *venire*, with the original meaning "come out" and "come in". Thus *eventfulness* and *inventiveness* of thought become a measure of philosophical potency. How much of the impossible is possibilized by the event of thinking? The most eventful, inventive, and simply *interesting* texts are those that provide the strongest possible arguments for the least probable ideas. The improbability, rather than verification or falsification, is the criterion for the productivity of thinking, as discussed in more detail earlier in Chapter 16, "What Is 'The Interesting?'"

In this light, the development of philosophy is not a succession of schools and movements, but the acceleration of events of thinking, which are more and more condensed in time. By applying the method of potentiation, philosophy can discover the thinkability of the unthinkable, which takes us beyond Marx's dilemma of explaining or changing the world. Philosophy neither reduces the world to a structural unity nor intervenes in history; instead, it creates its own *history of thought-events* and *cosmosophy of possible worlds*.

# From analysis to synthesis and from deconstruction to potentiation

Nietzsche laid down the creative task of philosophy when he wrote: "Philosophers must no longer accept concepts as a gift, nor merely purify and polish them, but first *make* and *create* them and make them convincing" (1968, p. 409). In this light, the creative task of philosophy is neither to explain nor to change the existing world; rather, it is to broaden and multiply the worldness of the world and its thinkability and conceivability that cannot be reduced to any existent world or any actual object in it.

In their later works, Giles Deleuze and Felix Guattari see the main function of philosophy as the transition from analysis and criticism to conceptual creativity:

> The philosopher is the concept's friend; he is potentiality of the concept. … More rigorously, philosophy is the discipline that involves *creating* concepts. … The object of philosophy is to create concepts that are always new. Because the concept must be created, it refers back to the philosopher as the one who has it potentially, or who has its power and competence. It is no objection to say that creation is the prerogative of the sensory and the arts, since art brings spiritual entities into existence while philosophical concepts are also 'sensibilia.' In fact, sciences, arts, and philosophies are equally creative, although only philosophy creates concepts in the strict sense. Concepts are not waiting for us ready-made, like heavenly bodies. There is no heaven for concepts. They must be invented, fabricated, or rather created and would be nothing without their creator's signature. … Plato said that Ideas must be contemplated, but first of all he had to create the concept of Idea. What would be the value of a philosopher of whom one could say, 'he has created no concepts; he has not created his own concepts?' (1994, pp. 5–6)

Deleuze and Guattari anticipate the transition from the descriptive and analytical functions of philosophical discourse to its creative and synthetic functions. The linguo-analytical tradition, dominant in the humanities and the philosophies of the twentieth century, was characteristic, to varying degrees, of Continental structuralism and poststructuralism as well as of Anglo–American analytical philosophy. That tradition focused on the study of ordinary, scientific, and philosophic language, and its semantic, grammatical, and logical structures.

*Potentiation* both continues and overcomes that tradition: it shows why it is necessary not only to study language and culture, but also to expand them by synthesizing new words, notions, lexical and conceptual fields, grammatical rules, genres, disciplines, discursive practices, and entire new cultures.

*Potentiation* challenges the traditional predominance of the actual (or real) over the potential in the ontology of Aristotle and Hegel. Potentiation can be seen as a positive, *constructive* deconstruction. As such, *potentiation* both inherits the method of deconstruction and moves beyond it. Deconstruction, at least in its conventional form of academic poststructuralism, is mostly understood as the undoing and decomposing of structures, which, according to Jacques Derrida's own intention, was not meant to be a negative operation: "Rather than destroying, it was also necessary to understand how an 'ensemble' was constituted and to reconstruct it to this end. However, the negative appearance was and remains much more difficult to efface" (Derrida, 1991, p. 272).

The humanities, according to one of Derrida's last statements on "the future of the profession", need to incorporate the subjunctive mood and become the "thinking of the 'perhaps,' of that dangerous modality of the 'perhaps' that Nietzsche speaks of and that philosophy always tried to subjugate. There is no future and no relation to the coming of the event without experience of the 'perhaps'" (2001, p. 54). Consequently, Derrida emphasizes the transformative tasks of the humanities, which are to lead them beyond pure scholarship ("study and analysis" of what already exists) and into the creative practices of making impossible possible:

> I just said that one must 'study' or 'analyze.' It is necessary to make clear that such 'studies,' such 'analyses,' for the reasons already indicated, would not be purely 'theoretical' and neutral. They would lead toward practical and performative transformations and would not forbid the production of singular *oeuvres*. (2001, p. 50)

By *oeuvres*, Derrida means creative works of the humanities that inaugurate a new practice or a new institution, rather than merely describe the existing ones in the assertive mode.

Thus, contemporary thought marks a transition from the philosophy of analysis to the philosophy of synthesis by engaging in a riskier modality of "perhaps". Each act of analysis contains the possibility of a new synthesis.

# Possibilistic philosophy, informational society, and new technologies

I have already written about a new synthesis of philosophy and technology, and about *onto-technology*, which can bring forth new foundations of being in theoretical thought and then implement them through alternative forms of matter, life, and consciousness (see Chapter 9, "The Art of World-Making and the New Vocation for Metaphysics"). In the past, we had only one universe, one form of life, and one form of reason at our disposal. As a result, metaphysics was a speculative and unpractical discipline. But, as soon as we enter the era of proto-, the boundaries of this single world become transgressible, which allows us to create new forms of artificial, genetically, and technologically enhanced life and reason. Such "proteic" metaphysics becomes quite a practical and effective discipline of setting the foundational properties and universals for possible worlds as constructed by new technologies. In the past, the philosopher pronounced the last word about the existing world, consummated in reflection. Now the philosopher can pronounce the first word about something that has never existed or happened before. Philosophy as inquiry into first principles and universals does not speculate any more about what was in the beginning, but constructs beginnings and sets up metaphysical parameters for alternative physical and psychical worlds. As the *technology of the first day of creation*, philosophy turns to action. This way, the method of potentiation comes to full fruition in the new technological opportunities of metaphysics.

It became a truism that in the post-industrial era, information replaces capital as the resource of social wealth. However, some very non-trivial conclusions can be drawn from this fact, which are rarely pursued to their natural conclusion. The informational value of any text is defined by its unpredictability, which grows as the probability of its message becomes smaller. News of the first space flight contained more information than any report about the tenth or even the hundredth flight. The society of the future can be expected to increase the volume of information it possesses, since that is its main wealth.

But what is the growth of information if not an increase in the probabilistic character of social life? Information grows as the world becomes more and more unpredictable with less probable events. The cult of the new, when each person strives to be the first in something, is the main condition of the informational enrichment of society. In this sense, the expressions "the land of infinite possibilities" and "the information society" are synonymous. The more possibilities a given unit of reality possesses, the more informative it is. The volume of information in society grows through the increase of possible variants of each event. For example, in a totalitarian or traditional society it is usually possible to predict who the head of government will be or which party will be in power. In a "society of possibilities" the same event, a presidential election, carries much more information precisely because it is not predetermined. Thus, a society built on the basis of *information* resources due to the internal logic of its development, progressively becomes a society of *possibilities*.

In developed societies, the emphasis shifts from reality to possibility, because a life full of possibilities is richer and more eventful than a life reduced to the plane of actual existence. Human life is limited by the parameters that belong to *Homo Sapiens* as a generic creature. It is impossible to eat more than one is capable of eating, impossible to see more than one is capable of seeing, and these limits are close to being reached in the developed countries of the West, at least for a significant part of the population. But this depends more on the multiplication of its possibilities than on their fulfillment. If reality is a constant denominator, then possibility is a constantly growing numerator of civilization. This ratio is what defines the internal meaningfulness of life, its intenseness and significance. As civilization develops, *the number of possibilities for one unit of reality constantly grows*. Such is the transcendental side of progress, usually eclipsed by its practical side.

Thus, there are two major premises for the transition from the analytic philosophy of the actual to the creative philosophy of the possible. One is the transition from an industrial to an information society whose wealth is measured by the value of unpredictability. The other is a technological and biological revolution, which makes the formation of alternative realities, minds, and bodies increasingly possible.

The possibilistic philosophy reveals its uniqueness when compared with Hegel's absolute idealism, which was designed to reflect the results of the universal historical development. According to Hegel, philosophy consummates the process of self-development and self-awareness of the Absolute Idea, progressing through the worlds of nature, history, and reason:

> The present standpoint of philosophy is that the Idea is known in its necessity. ... The ultimate aim and business of philosophy is to reconcile thought or the Notion with reality. ... To this point the World-spirit has come, and each stage has its own form in the true system of Philosophy; nothing is lost, all principles are preserved, since Philosophy in its final aspect is the totality of forms. This concrete idea is the result of the strivings of spirit during almost twenty-five centuries of earnest work to become objective to itself, to know itself. (Hegel, 1995, pp. 512–3)

Now, in the early twenty-first century, it is possible to paraphrase Hegel as follows:

> The present standpoint of philosophy is that the Idea, having matured in the kingdoms of Nature and History, is known in its possibilities, which take it beyond the limits of Nature and History. The ultimate aim and business of philosophy at the stage of *potentiation* is to take concepts beyond the limits of reality. However, philosophy's goal is not to change or improve reality, which is the task for the concrete positive disciplines such as natural or social sciences, law and politics. The aim is, rather, to create new forms of being that have not yet taken historical or technological shape and are in need of metaphysical ideas and foundational principles so that, at a later date, they can be taken up by scientists, engineers, politicians and other practitioners of positive disciplines. The world's spirit has known itself through forms of cognitive and active

relationships with the actual being and now finds itself in the sphere of what is conceivable and possible. Philosophy turns into a starting point for experimental work aimed at designing and creating new worlds without any limits of space and time. This conceptive idea is the result of the striving of the spirit which characterizes twenty-five centuries of earnest work to become objective, to know itself as the origin of the existing world so that it can lay foundations for worlds yet to come.

From multiple interpretations of a single world, creative philosophy moves to multiple initiations of many different worlds. Philosophy stands at the beginning of new, ideational ways of being. It brings forth those thinkables that cannot fit into the realm of the actual and that display the excess of pure potentiality, which in its turn becomes the embryo of new existents. Just as the engineer is the maker of mechanisms, the artist is the maker of paintings, and the politician is the maker of social institutions and practices, the philosopher is the maker of thinkables and universals and their combinations in the form of conceivable worlds.

The philosopher's goal is to cognize the rational in reality, not in order to justify it the way it is (cf. Hegel's principle of the identity of reason and reality), but in order to find the extra-real and super-real in reason itself, in its capacity to transcend the real. What used to be perceived as "empty possibilities", ephemeral bubbles on the surface of reality, are, in fact, the hot growing seeds, *logoi spermaticus* of nascent worlds.

We belong to that historical stage where the methodology of the philosophical compression of the Universe comes to an end, and a new methodology of its conceptual expansion begins. While the main philosophical device for Hegel or, more precisely, the device of the World Spirit in Hegel's interpretation, is that of sublation, i.e. the final reconciliation of all previous contradictions of history, the logic of potentiation is that of *ex-lation*, i.e. extraction, abduction. The mind finds in reality blank spaces, flaws, unrealized meanings, and bubbles of possibility that might become entryways into other worlds. The factual universe is progressively dissolved in the universe of thinkables, signifiables, and beables. This way, reality passes into the subjunctive mode, which is a huge sphere of new spiritual experience, tolerance, hope, intellectual generosity, and creativity. *The best of all possible worlds is the world of possibilities*, to which this philosophy of the possible can serve only as an introduction[4].

---

[4]I give a much more detailed description of the change of modalities in philosophy and the rise of possibilist thinking in my book *Filosofiia vozmozhnogo (A Philosophy of the Possible)*. (Epstein, 2001).

# 20

# The mass of knowledge and the energy of thinking

Science is commonly viewed as the systematic knowledge of the world and its laws. The notion of knowledge is central to all contemporary definitions of science, which is further justified by the very origin of the Latin word *Scientia,* meaning "knowledge". The *Encyclopedia Britannica* defines science as "any system of knowledge that is concerned with the physical world and its phenomena and that entails unbiased observations and systematic experimentation. In general, a science involves a pursuit of knowledge covering general truths or the operations of fundamental laws."[1]

If science is identified with knowledge, the following questions, crucial for the self-definition of the human sciences, arise: "How is knowledge acquisition related to the activity of thinking?" and "Does thinking serve as a means for the enhancement of knowledge or, on the contrary, is knowledge simply an instrument of thinking?"

There is a significant semantic difference between *to know* and *to think. To know* means to possess information, to have established or fixed in the mind a true concept about a certain object. *To think* means to perform in the mind certain actions with concepts, to combine and separate them, moving from one level of generalization to another. Thinking is a dynamic operation, which works with concepts that are represented in the static form of knowledge.

Without a doubt, knowledge has its own dynamics expressed by the verb *to cognize.* Cognition is the process of knowledge acquisition that

---

[1]http://www.britannica.com/

eliminates false concepts while retaining and accumulating authentic ones. Cognition necessarily includes the activity of thinking; however, thinking cannot be reduced to knowledge because it can create concepts that do not correspond to anything in reality. On the contrary, reality can be gradually changed in order to correspond to such concepts. Thinking produces everything that humans add to the surrounding world, i.e. the entire trans-natural realm of history and culture. Thinking adds to knowledge a second reality, the handmade and the "headmade" world of ideas and values, art, and technology.

Thinking does not simply follow knowledge, but precedes it, creating a possibility of knowledge and its object. Even a commonly indisputable fact, for instance $2 \times 2 = 4$, is based on concepts such as number, unit, and equation. In the end, all concepts that lie in the foundation of knowledge turn out to have been constructed by thinking; these constructs, being so obvious and common, are perceived as the building blocks of facts. Thoughts that become part of "folklore", self-evident and known to all, appear as facts. For example, the units of time and space, such as a minute, an hour, a meter, or a kilometer, make up the very foundation of factual knowledge. Even such factual statements as "It is 5:30 p.m.", or "George Washington was born in 1732", or "There are 190 miles between New York and Boston" are based on the analytical work of thinking that divides the continuum of time and space into these particular units.

This priority of thinking is especially pertinent to such fields as history, culture, morals, and metaphysics. Most thoughts that have had a profound impact on humankind are not based on any facts whatsoever; rather, they contain collective experiences and cultural constructs, with different people often expressing polar views: "Love thy neighbor", "Man is wolf to man", "All people are born equal", "Man is a rational animal", "'Man is a fallen creature", "Society is a war of each against all", "The end justifies the means", "Life is a miracle", or "Life is meaningless". Theodore Roszak calls such thoughts, which do not need any logical proof or empirical verification to rule society, "master-ideas" (Roszak, 1994, pp. 92–4). He emphasizes that, although master-ideas are not based on any facts at all, they themselves have become the foundation for numerous facts of religious, social, and cultural history, studied by the human and social sciences. After all, if Shakespeare had not thought up his plays, or Napoleon had not thought up a new European order, literary critics and historians would be deprived of some of their most important subjects, the foundational facts of European culture and history.

Therefore, knowledge should be considered an aspect of thinking, and not the other way around. Even the natural sciences, while containing precise knowledge about nature, are constructed by humans and thus absent from nature itself. Physicists know something about time and space only because thinking has developed the very categories of time and space, which can now be correlated with the surrounding world through acts of cognition. Knowledge is not contained in the objects of knowledge, but is acquired through thinking about them.

Thinking employs knowledge as its adaptive mechanism. In order to transform the world effectively, we have to reflect it adequately. In the past, the concept of adaptation was heavily used in the Darwinian theory of evolution to describe organisms adjusting to their natural milieu. However, this view is now rejected by many biologists who opt for the position of constructionism: an organism not so much adapts to its milieu as constructs it, i.e. it adapts its milieu to itself. In the words of Richard Lewontin, a contemporary authority on evolutionary genetics:

> [O]ne can organize one's knowledge about organism and the world in a completely different [non-adaptational] way by using a metaphor of *construction*. To do so, one needs to abandon the alienated view of the organism and the environment, to say that it is not the case that environments have an autonomous set of laws, and organisms discover them, meet them, and have to cope with them but that, in fact, environments are a consequence of what Marx called "the sensuous activity of organisms ..... [O]rganisms have constructed the world in which we live. (1994, p. 506)

If constructionism is correct in describing the sensuous activity of organisms, then it should be even more applicable to the intellectual activity that is even more independent from the conditions of the material environment. Adaptation is only a means for construction. Knowledge is the mind's adaptive mechanism by which thinking coordinates itself with the environment, in order to transform it in accordance with its own needs. Everything that belongs to history and culture is the result of such an adaptation of reality to thinking. Any fragment of an artificial milieu, from a book to a car, from a sculpture to a skyscraper, can be viewed as a system of embodied concepts and thus bears the imprint of thinking. Thinking disrupts the established, cognized connections of facts and transforms them into pure concepts, intellectual visions and fictions, so that some of such fictions, through social practices, arts, and technologies, could become new facts.

The common field of thinking and knowledge can be designated by the compound term, "thinknowledge" (with one "k"), wherein "think" blends into "know". This epistemological category assumes that thinking and knowledge are two interrelated forms of intellectual activity. From an epistemological point of view, knowledge and thinking can be related as mass and energy are related in physics. We can apply Albert Einstein's famous formula as a heuristic device to describe the transformation of the mass of knowledge into the energy of thinking.

$E = mc^2$
*The energy of thought equals the mass of knowledge multiplied by the speed of conceptual dissociations and associations squared by reflexivity.*

By "dissociations and associations", I refer to the restructuring of those concepts and elements of propositions that comprise the mass of knowledge, i.e. the totality of established facts. "Reflexivity" means that, having fulfilled the restructuring of concepts on one level, we move to the meta-level of thinking that allows us to objectify and describe the previous one. Thinking moves by gradations of generalizations, ascending the ladder of "meta-", which is expressed by the sign of power ($^2$) that is the multiplication of a number by itself. Thus, according to this formula, the mass of knowledge is a positive factor that increases the potential of thinking. However, there are also other factors at play: the free-play of concepts, the intensity of their dissociations and associations, the speed of the restructuring and recoding activity, and, finally, the depth of reflection, i.e. the range of transitions between the levels of consciousness.

Let us take, as a simple example, a trivial proposition: *The city of Washington, DC is the capital of the United States of America.* This is an elementary unit of geographical knowledge concerning Washington, DC. Of course, we need to add the caveat that any proposition includes some implicit knowledge beyond what is explicitly stated. This particular example contains the implicit knowledge of what a city is, what a capital is, what a country is, and how these concepts are interrelated. We can generalize the above-cited proposition as follows: *The element "W" is the center of the system "U".*

Let us try to extract the energy of thinking from this short and plain fragment of knowledge, a well-known atomic fact: Washington, DC is the capital of the USA. The process of thinking can be compared to the bombardment of atomic nuclei by highly charged and accelerated particles. In our case, the role of such energizing particles is played by questions addressed to this seemingly static and self-sufficient statement. Thinking is the potentiation of knowledge, whose elements are disrupted and recombined, thereby producing new, more dynamic meanings as compared with their bound, fixed, and immobile existence within a certain fact.

Are all properties of the system "U" embraced by its central element "W", or does the specificity of the central element consist precisely in its being markedly different from all other elements in the system? In other words, is Washington, DC the most typical American city, or, precisely because it is the capital, the center of statehood, and the hub of foreign and international organizations, is it the least representative of the country it is called to represent? These questions reveal a contradiction in the very concept of a capital: on the one hand, it represents the most character-istic aspects of the entire country, as its symbol and quintessence; on the other hand, as a result of its special symbolism, it is sharply different from the rest of the nation. The most characteristic is simultaneously the least characteristic—this paradox refers us back to the dialectics of coincidence of the maximum and the minimum in the metaphysics of Nicholas of Cusa. Washington, DC is both maximally and minimally the "American city". To be the central element of a given structure means, to a certain degree, not to be an element of this structure at all, but rather to be located outside it. This is manifested by the unique administrative status of Washington as a "stateless" city, the District of Columbia.

This sequence of questions can be expanded to the next level of gener-alization: "Does the system need a central element at all?", "How can the meaning of a central government change with the increased dissemi-nation of knowledge and diffusion of communication systems, e.g. the internet?", "Does the state need a capital or, in the epoch of electronic communications, can it function without the concentration of power in one geographical point?", "Could it be ruled by the web community as a collective body, a syntellect, and synergy of citizens?", "How will various national states be transformed by the dispersion of their power centers and by the even distribution of their administrative functions around the entire territories?", "Can a political capital fulfill the functions of a cultural and industrial capital effectively?", "How desirable is the confluence of these functions of a capital in a democratic society?", "Does such a totalization of the central element strengthen or weaken the system as a whole?", "In which way is Washington, DC a non-capital or even the deep province of the United States?", "Which other US cities could claim the status of a capital and in which domains? For example, New York as the capital of architecture and ethnic diversity; Los Angeles—of arts and entertainment; Boston—of education; San Francisco—of electronic technologies and bohemian intellectuals". "How could various proposals about the status of Washington, DC, as a capital, be inscribed in the play of contemporary political forces?"

All these acts of thinking, in the form of questions, doubts, and proposals emerged from the nuclear fission of one trivial fact that combines two elements of knowledge: the city of Washington, DC and the country of the United States of America. We have found striking paradoxes within this seemingly obvious proposition: "Is Washington, DC really the capital of the US and in what sense?" or "How is it possible for an element to be simultaneously the most and the least representative of an entire system?" We have tried to separate these elements and to build some alternative visions of countries without capitals or with multiple capitals.

Thinking proceeds from facts and then ignites new meanings in the hearth of facticity that seemed to have burnt out. The elements of the initial proposition (a geographical cliché) are released from their rigid connections and recombined into new concepts, extrapolated into new thematic domains, and extended to new levels of meta-descriptions and generalizations.

As mentioned above, this process can be described by using Einstein's formula in its humanistic, cognitive application: the energy of thinking (E) mobilizes and accelerates (c) elements of knowledge (m) and squares them by reflexivity ($^2$). In other words, thinking (1) takes the mass of knowledge out of its inert state of known and self-evident facts; (2) splits its particles while accelerating them to their maximum speed ("the speed of light") by intensifying the processes of dissociation and association of logical qualities, similarities, and differences as they are being pulled together and pushed away from one another, and (3) multiplies the levels of the movements of these particles, turning them on themselves and thus squaring itself. The energy of thought is extracted from the body of knowledge by producing multiple, fast, light-like, fleshless, fictive, virtual combinations of its particles.

Such a humanistic rendition of a physical formula may be considered only a metaphor, or a very conditional analogy, emphasizing the similarity between energy-mass transformations in physical and mental spheres. However, one can also view such a transfer of these notions as a case of abduction or logical "stealing". Such "stealing" occurs when a conceptual term is taken from a discipline where it has already been accepted and is applied in another discipline where it is "estranged". Abduction is the extraction of a concept from that conceptual paradigm where it traditionally belonged, and its transference into different, multiple, diverging rows of concepts. The term *abduction* was introduced by Charles S. Peirce in order to differentiate this form of reasoning from induction and deduction, and mark it as a form of hypothetical thinking which occurs when a surprising fact receives a new interpretation. Pierce defines abduction as "a method of forming a general prediction without any positive assurance that it will succeed" (Peirce, 1932, p. 153).

I believe that the concept of abduction deserves further elaboration. It is obvious that, along with induction as reasoning from the particular to the general, and deduction as reasoning from the general to the particular, another form of logical reasoning exists when two notions, which are equal in scope, but come from different disciplines, each having its own subject, are interrelated. It is such a relationship that can be called "abduction". An abductor takes a concept from one field and applies it to another field thus enacting a sort of cross-fertilization or cross-pollination of various branches of knowledge. In this way Michel Foucault invented his "Archaeology of Knowledge", even though the concept of archaeology usually refers to the study of material cultures of the past. Karl Marx abducted a number of notions from Hegel's dialectics and philosophy of history, e.g. "unity of opposites" or "alienation", when he applied them to the field of economics and commodity production. Such transfers can hardly be called purely metaphorical when a term or a method belonging to a certain discipline is withdrawn from its traditional subject area and transferred into another. Semiotics, in part, "stole" its subject (signs and sign systems) from rhetoric, while the new discipline of memetics, as the evolutionary study of replicating ideas, signs, and units of information, abducted its subject from semiotics. Many disciplines are linked through abduction, which makes it possible to create new disciplines; for example, the notion of a quantum has been abducted from quantum physics and transferred into quantum metaphysics (see Chapter 13 *"Micronics: The Study of Small Things"*). Both abduction and metaphor transfer meaning by similarity. Abduction, however, is not a poetic technique, but rather a logical one, involving the enhancement of theoretical concepts as they migrate from one subject area to another.

Thought which moves "at the speed of light" is hardly a metaphor when seen from the perspective of the newest theories of the quantum nature of the brain operations (cf. Penrose, 1994). One might also recall the latest technologies of quantum computers that imitate the process of thinking by using the capacity of quanta to transmit information with a speed considered by some specialists to be even faster than the speed of light (the effect of quantum superposition). We can observe a structural isomorphism between the inert mass of matter and fixed knowledge of certain facts, on the one hand, and the explosive energy of nuclear and mental processes, on the other. Thus, as a heuristic formula, Einstein's equation is applicable to various domains of thinknowledge.

Knowledge is reified thinking, or thinking in its past tense, just like factories, machines, and other means of production represent reified labor. There is always a danger at universities and other academic institutions, which are engaged in the acquisition and dissemination of knowledge, that the mass of accumulated knowledge, in the form of data and other informational resources, will dominate and suppress the energy of living-thinking.

The main objective of academic activity is research, defined as "diligent and systematic inquiry or investigation into a subject in order to discover or revise facts, theories, applications, etc." (*Webster's New World College Dictionary*, 2000, p. 1141). Important as it is, academic work is not limited to research, but also involves intellectual creativity and imagination. Any component of knowledge is the result of a thinking process and a premise for further acts of thinking, which lead from the knowledge of what exists to the creation of what has never existed or happened before. Thinking de-objectifies knowledge, freeing its elements from their established connections and setting them into free-play, constructing a number of virtual, fictional objects. Some of them, through technology, industry, and social and political practices, become part of the surrounding reality, which thinking modifies in order to adapt it to itself. There is nothing in the artificial environment that would not already have been contained in brain cells, in the activity of neurons, in those concepts and images in which our mind operates.

An academic work should be evaluated not only on the basis of the scope of knowledge in its coverage of material, but also the extent of the transformation of knowledge into thought, or, to be more exact, on the basis of the relationship between these two measures. Is a scientific work supposed to contain references to all relevant sources? In general, it is better to have more references than fewer references. But, a conceptual coverage of more material is also better than that of less material. And, with more material covered, specific sections would contain fewer references. An individual life is short, while science's potential is limitless, so one has to make a careful study of details commensurate with the breadth of thought. Knowledge should not be confused with "*gnawledge*" obtained by "gnawing" facts rather than by conceptualizing and creatively interpreting them. When Bacon said "Knowledge is power", he hardly meant "gnawledge". Science is undertaken not by know-it-alls, but by people who are acutely aware of their ignorance. Those erudite in their own field rarely make a creative contribution to science, focusing primarily on editing, compiling, and commenting on the works of others, conducting research in archives, and composing bibliographies—all, unquestionably, worthwhile and useful pursuits. Firstly, since they know everything about their subject, they don't have anything to add to it. Secondly, one can know everything about some very limited subject, whereas real science brings together and integrates diverse subjects and fields of knowledge. One can, for instance, know everything about the life and works of Goethe, Hugo, or Pushkin. However, one cannot know everything about the style of Goethe, his way of seeing the world, his place in German and world literature; these fields call for constructive thinking. The problem of many scholars erudite in their fields is that they cannot problematize their knowledge by going beyond it; they are firmly grounded in their special area and do not see the abyss of the unknown which can be crossed only on bridges made from thought constructs. *Science begins at the point where knowledge ends and uncertainty starts.* This view of science goes back to Aristotle, who defined wonder as the starting point of the cognitive process: "For it is owing to their wonder that men both now begin and at first began to philosophize ... a man who is puzzled and wonders thinks himself ignorant" (1975, p. 258). Ideally, a scholar should acquire as much knowledge as possible while still being able to wonder, to be surprised. One can apply to the scholar what Faulkner said about Thomas Wolfe: upon being asked to name the best American writers of his day, Faulkner would say that Wolfe was the best because he was the greatest failure. Was it not a failure for Einstein to attempt to think up the general field theory for which he—or science itself for that matter—at the time did not have enough knowledge? Such a monumental defeat is surely worth many small victories.

In science, one can identify different layers and levels: (1) observation and collection of facts; (2) analysis, classification, and systematization; (3) interpretation of facts and observations; search for meanings, patterns, and conclusions; (4) generalization, i.e. creation of general concepts, comprehensive typologies, and overall characterizations of the subject area; (5) methodology, the study of various methods of analysis, interpretation, and generalization; (6) paradigmatic thinking, i.e. awareness of preconditions and biases that lie at the foundation of a particular discipline or its separate methods, and an attempt to change them, establishing a new way of seeing things.

It would be ideal for science to be progressing in a simultaneous and parallel fashion on all these levels, whereby finding new facts leads to their interpretation and creation of a new paradigm. However, scientific revolutions do not follow this "normal" path. Many established facts become ignored simply because they stand in the way of new and hitherto unnoticed facts, which can only be perceived thanks to a new paradigm. The new paradigm, in its turn, is already changing our perception of those established facts or even invalidating those facts. This way, to quote Thomas Kuhn,

> Chemists could not, therefore, simply accept Dalton's [atomic] theory on the evidence, for much of that was still negative. Instead, even after accepting the theory, they had still to beat nature into line, a process which, in the event, took almost another generation. When it was done, even the percentage composition of well-known compounds was different. The data themselves had changed. (1996, p. 135)

As the history of science shows, many ideas that revolutionized our scientific worldview appeared not as a result of accepting established facts, but rather in the process of a sharp collision with them. Paul Feyerabend, a philosopher of science, even formulated the rule of "counterinduction" that recommends "the invention and elaboration of hypotheses inconsistent with a point of view that is highly confirmed and generally accepted" (1975, p. 47).

This is even more apparent in the humanities where paradigms are much more fuzzy, and where professional communities are organized much less rigidly. Unfortunately, those in the humanities pay even less attention to this rule of "counterinduction" than those in the exact sciences, although the humanities are capable of more methodological breakthroughs and new insights due to the unstable nature of their methods and conventions. According to Feyerabend, an approach calling for the development of hypotheses that are not compatible with observations, facts, and experimental results, does not really need to be defended, since there is not a single interesting theory which is compatible with all known facts. Such a discrepancy between facts and conceptions acts as a catalyst for scientific thinking, allowing the discovery of new facts and the revision of old ones:

> Knowledge so conceived is not a series of self-consistent theories that converges towards an ideal view; it is not a gradual approach to the truth. It is rather an ever increasing ocean of *mutually incompatible (and perhaps even incommensurable) alternatives,* each single theory, each fairy tale, each myth that is part of the collection forcing the others into greater articulation and all of them contributing, via this process of competition, to the development of our consciousness. (Feyerabend, 1975, p. 30)

Thus, academic activity cannot be limited only to the realm of research consisting in the accumulation and multiplication of knowledge. It would be more accurate to define the task of scientific and academic institutions not as research, but as *thinknowledge, an intellectual activity in the forms of both knowledge and thinking.* This includes: (1) description and systematization of existing facts and principles; and (2) production of new concepts and ideas that may be effectively used in the development of our civilization. Knowledge is information about the present state and connections of facts, whereas thinking is the transformation of these connections in order to create new ideas and concepts that could be converted into objects or properties of a future world.

# In place of a conclusion: A new introduction to future thinking

## Scholarship or scholasticism?

The main problem with the humanities today is their self-enclosure in the past and their alienation from the contemporary society. Contrary to the meaning of their vocation, the humanities are not interested in humanity and humanness, i.e. in human beings as creators of history and civilization—heroes, conquerors, dreamers, martyrs, and discoverers. Instead, the humanities in today's academic world are interested mostly in texts and their critical interpretations, and in hypercritical interpretations of interpretations.

What can we do to restore the transformative potential of the humanities? I believe that the humanities need to grow a practical branch that would correspond to the role of technologies in relation to the natural sciences and politics in relation to the social sciences.

Imagine botany without agriculture, forestry, and gardening, i.e. without any cultivation and experimentation with plants. Or, imagine cosmology without cosmonautics and space technology, without rockets, satellites, shuttles, and astronauts, i.e. without any attempts at practical exploration of space. And yet, this is exactly the situation with the humanities today, where scholarship in not developing its own practical and experimental branches degenerates into scholasticism.

# Creative thinking in academia

Sometimes I encounter the objection that the practical branch of the humanities already exists in creative writing. However, it is not actually a branch of the humanities, but rather an object of their study, just as nature is the object of study in natural sciences. Literature, painting, music, theater, and cinema are all primary arts that are explored by humanistic disciplines, such as aesthetics, cultural studies, literary theory, art history, and musicology. What I suggest is an active application of these disciplines, a transition from theory to practice, which is qualitatively different from writing poems or novels, playing the piano, or acting in the theater. I call for a place in contemporary academia where humanistic inventors, such as Friedrich Schlegel, André Breton, or Walter Benjamin could teach students how to proclaim, shape, and direct new literary and intellectual movements. One might object that the literary manifesto is a creative genre that cannot be taught. However, the novel or poem (also creative genres) are taught by departments of creative writing. Why not build departments of *creative thinking,* where literary visionaries and intellectual engineers could find their proper place in academia?

Another objection that I hear: why is it not sufficient to practice this art of creative thinking outside academia? I agree: nobody should coerce creative minds into academia. But, if there are poets and fiction writers who choose an academic career in addition to their literary vocation, why deny creative thinkers the same opportunity? Napoleon may not deserve a Ph.D. for winning the Battle of Austerlitz, but we need to distinguish between heroes and authors. While Napoleon, as a hero and an object of historical studies, does not deserve a Ph.D. for his military campaigns, Nietzsche, as an author, does deserve one for his intellectual battles. Who could teach the ideas of the Superman better than the author who conceived them?

Of course, humanistic inventors can advance their ideas outside of academia; however, they will then be put at the disadvantage of having neither funds nor followers among students, and of being cut from the entire academic system designed for the dissemination of ideas. But the academic system that cuts itself from humanistic inventions loses even more, because the humanities, bewitched by the past, are doomed to stagnation.

# Disciplines

We need a place for the invention and propagation of new genres and disciplines, including those that cross the established borders between sciences and the humanities, between theories and practices, between art objects and art theories, and between novels and treatises. There should be a place in academia for new—at this point fictional or semi-fictional—disciplines emerging in response to the new intellectual and technological developments of the early twenty-first century. This new constellation would include such humanistic disciplines as the *techno-humanities*, focusing on the mutual transformations of humans and machines; *micronics,* investigating micro-phenomena across disciplines; *semiurgy*, aiming to synthesize new signs and rules of grammar; *horrology*, exploring self-destructive mechanisms of civilization; and *scriptorics*, centering on the psychology and anthropology of writing versus impersonal grammatology.

Where can we discuss projects for such new disciplines? How can we even attempt to inaugurate them as worthwhile intellectual practices? Currently, there are no specialists in the *transhumanities*, *semiurgy*, *micronics*, or *horrology*. There are no dedicated journals, no depart-ments, and no academic outlets for these prospective areas. Meanwhile, these "fictions" are meant to become disciplines in the precise academic sense of the word. I am not talking about interdisciplinarity as the interaction of existing disciplines (which is mostly formal and aimed at pleasing the university administration). I am talking about the birth of new disciplines, for which there is not yet any intellectual environment. It would be improper, if not simply ridiculous, to offer an introduction in *technosophia*, *micronics*, or *horrology* to philosophy departments since they specialize overwhelmingly in a restricted analytic tradition, or to offer courses in *semiurgy* or *scriptorics* to departments of linguistics. Ask a philosopher whether he is willing to collaborate with a designer of virtual realities and electronic games; or ask a linguist whether she would be interested in introducing new coinages into the language which she studies. The overwhelming majority of academics will be indifferent to, if not indignant at, such intellectual "provocations". It will take years before a new paradigm of the transhumanities can find its way into "monodisciplinary" departments.

Universities need a place for the conception and birth of new disciplines, new methods, and new genres of intellectual discourse. Francis Bacon believed that the most important kind of invention is precisely that of new arts and sciences:

> ... it cannot be found strange if sciences be no further discovered, if the art itself of invention and discovery hath been passed over. That this part of knowledge is wanting, to my judgment standeth plainly confessed. (1803, p. 132)

This branch of knowledge is still non-existent in today's academia. Bacon himself invented several disciplines that were fully established only centuries later, e.g. geopolitics, which came into its own only in the twentieth century. Should we wait for centuries to have a new discipline mature "spontaneously"? Or, should we create a space for the invention of new disciplines within the academy that will consistently and purposely transgress the boundaries of what is considered "academic"?

I am not for anarchy or the complete demise of the institution of genres and disciplines; but I am decidedly in favor of their infinite proliferation in all directions. I believe that it is necessary to establish clear boundaries in order to transgress them: this is the most efficient way to produce new meanings and values. Creative thinking programs will serve this purpose within academic institutions, in order to reinforce an intellectual ferment which is now lacking, especially in the humanities.

When a new discipline emerges, such as memetics, for instance, which purports to study "the genetics of culture", evolutionary models of cultural information transfer, how can humanists, philosophers, linguists, or literary theorists, learn promptly about it within the framework of their specialization? Academia needs units that could be fashioned after "rapid reaction forces", which are designed to intervene quickly in the most remote regions of the world (a rare case when a military metaphor is apposite). All existing, departmentalized and compartmentalized forms of knowledge either completely ignore emerging trends or react to them belatedly.

Thus, we need futuristic humanities. Why has the orientation to the future become the exclusive privilege of natural sciences and science-based technologies? Is nature more dynamic than civilization? Why does the study of civilization usually turn out to be so much more conservative than the study of nature? Why do philosophy and literary and art theories fail to project new futuristic forms of living, writing, or painting in the way that the sciences project and instigate the emergence of new technologies?

# Genres

If we look at today's academic journals in the humanities, we will find only two main genres of scholarly discourse: the article and the review. Where are all of the other genres that, over the course of centuries, have helped to exercise our human capacity for wonderment, imagination, and creative thinking? Where are the manifestoes, aphorisms, fragments, theses, programs, preambles, and essays? Can we imagine a collection of aphorisms or a manifesto on the pages of the kinds of journals circulated among members of professional organizations? When Friedrich Schlegel wanted to give proper generic shape to his ideas, he called them simply that: "ideas". And ideas they were, mostly 5–10 lines each, unlike many lengthy scholarly articles, from which it is often difficult to extract a single productive idea. Marx's *Theses on Feuerbach* gave rise to numerous scholarly books and directions of thought, but there would be no place  . today in a scholarly journal for publishing these 11 theses of two pages in length because the genre is not sufficiently "academic". The most creative, succinct, and energetic genres of intellectual discourse are banned from academic publications.

According to Nietzsche, "One shouldn't conceal and despoil the *facts* of how our thoughts have come to us. The most profound and inexhaustible books always have something of the aphoristic and sudden character of Pascal's *Pensées*" (1980, p. 35). It is noteworthy that Pascal's *Thoughts* were written only as drafts for a treatise on systematic theology and never completed according to the author's design. But the quality of being only drafts or pure ideas—seeds, rather than plants—of thinking endows them with that special energy peculiar to embryos. They have the potential of growing in the perception of readers rather than simply presenting them with full results of thought and thus diminishing the potential of co-thinking and co-creation. The way to expand academic discourse is by cultivating and institutionalizing micro-genres that are in tune with the accelerated modes of contemporary communication, e.g. short fiction or Twitter poetry. The humanities need their own genres of intellectual compression, promoting the art of concision, the capacity to pack the explosive energy of mind into but a few lines.

# The two tasks for the humanities

The humanities should reaffirm the human measure of things—not simply to effect a "re-enchantment" of the world, but to rehumanize the realities left out by the hard science. A soul, a spirit, beauty, or a human face is unobservable or even non-existent from the viewpoint of natural sciences. A face, when explored with a microscope, first reveals large pores, then the skin's outer layer formed from flattened, dead cells, then fatty tissues and bones, and eventually, its molecular structure. It is impossible to find such a "demystified" face beautiful or to fall in love with it. "The Face Delusion", "The Beauty Delusion", "The Soul Delusion"—many things, among them the most important for human self-awareness—will turn out to be delusions in the style of R. Dawkins' *The God Delusion* (2006) if our view of reality were reduced to scientific data obtained by instruments and based on calculations.

Thus, the first task of the humanities is to uphold the human measure of things by maintaining the immaterial values as they are revealed and perceived by humans: personality, soul, and spirit. It is particularly important to preserve the beauty of common, "irregular" language as distinct from the "precise" languages of sciences and computers. This is the task of *preservation*.

The second task is that of *transformation*, which calls for developing full human potential as it is increasingly explored and implemented by sciences and technologies. We need to understand that even the most dehumanized instruments and calculations are still the creations of a human mind, and that the essence of being human is not only to preserve, but also to surpass (and surprise) oneself, to transcend the limits of one's nature. What is common to both tasks is the necessity to *denaturalize* humans, i.e. to resist both the scientist fallacy of reducing humans to physical nature, and the retro-humanistic fallacy of reducing humans to unchanging human nature. To help people to *remain* human and to *become* human—these two sides of the mission of the humanities should complement each other rather than degenerate through their separation into technological scientism or philological conservatism.

# Vits: The units of transformation

In our discussion of the transformative humanities, it would be useful to elucidate the very category of *transformation*. How does it relate to information? What is the *basic unit of transformation* that could be compared with *bit* as the unit of information?

In my view, the processes of transformation and information, and their formative units, are correlative. As is known, the measure of information is the probability of the event that is presented in a given message. A *bit* (*binary digit*) is the basic unit of information in computing; it is the amount of information stored by a digital device or other physical system that exists in one of two possible states (0 or 1). The two states can also be viewed as logical values (*true/false*, *yes/no*), algebraic signs (+/−), activation states (*on/off*), or any other two-valued attributes. The information is gained when the value of such a variable, 0 or 1, becomes known.

Transformation is performed from the same binary values, with one distinct state *turned into* the other, for example, through the transition between *on* and *off*, *yes* and *no*, *false* and *true*, or + and −. A unit of transformation, both by analogy and by contrast with *bit*, can be called *vit*, from Latin "vita", meaning "life". Life is transformative and self–transformative, autopoietic. The property of all living entities is not just to transmit information, but also to transform it and to be transformed by it. Cells do not only exchange information in the process of living and do not only reproduce the information received from genes. Ultimately more similar to writers than to texts, cells, as contemporary biology shows, compose the organism, using genes as a toolkit.

Living organisms are engaged in processes of metabolism, development, evolution, reproduction, that incessantly cross borders between opposite states. The processes of metabolism, for example, are organized into pathways, in which one chemical is transformed into another chemical through a series of steps, by a sequence of enzymes as instruments. In enzymatic reactions, the molecules, which exist at the beginning of the process, called "substrates", are converted into different molecules, called "products". Life, in the broadest sense, can be defined as a transformational process, in which certain elements, such as particles, molecules, facts, concepts, words, and ideas are converted into other elements. Thus, "vit" is an appropriate name for a unit of transformation.

Information is produced through the choice of 0 or 1, whereas transformation is achieved through the change of 0 to 1 or 1 into 0. Transformation connects two poles, values, or states, by the process of their reversal. If we throw up a coin and call it heads or tails, it is one *bit* of information. If we change the sides of the coin, reversing up and down, this is a basic unit of transformation, one *vit*. The more *vits* that can be found in a certain event, the more *vital* (vibrant, dynamic) it is, and therefore, the closer it is to the processes of life in organic beings.

The more rare and improbable the event is, the higher its information value. In the same way, the force of transformation can be measured by the improbability of an action or an accomplishment (cf. Chapter 16, "What Is 'The Interesting'?"). Life is a highly intense transformational process, with millions of *vits* occurring per second within an organism. Ultimately, the resurrection of the dead may be viewed as the maximum possible magnitude of transformative power demanding a virtually infinite amount of *vits,* or transformative events.

Thinking is not antagonistic to life; on the contrary, it is one of the most intense forms of living that is relatively independent of material carriers, while still connected, rather mysteriously, with the activity of the brain. Thinking is the transformative work on concepts and various elements of information. Whereas information in the form of knowledge reflects the existing state of facts, thinking transforms them. It consistently crosses the borders between concepts, and overcomes or reverses their binary oppositions. To argue this, we do not need to look for a sophisticated example, such as the famous formula for the transformation of mass into energy: $E = mc^2$. Every routine and seemingly tautological act of thinking, such as the one expressed in the plain statement "Socrates is a man", is essentially transformative as it crosses the boundary between the individual ("Socrates") and the general ("man").

At the present point in history, when information becomes the main wealth (capital) of society, and when some scientists acknowledge that even the physical universe consists of nothing but information, it is time for us to take the next step by moving from the *informational universe* to the *transformational multiverse*. According to Michio Kaku, "We are making the historic transition from being passive observers of the dance of nature to becoming choreographers of the dance of nature, with the ability to manipulate life, matter and intelligence" (2006, p. 361). This brings forth the necessity for a transformative or "choreographic" approach to all areas of study, which can be creatively transformed by the living force of thinking. It is time to learn how to measure transformative practices to the same extent that we are now able to measure amounts of information. By using *vits* as units of living and thinking, and by collaborating with information/transformation technologies, the transhumanities can work toward this goal.

# Transformative thinking and education

To recognize the constructive potential of the humanities is only the first step in their methodological elaboration. Bakhtin's insights help us to specify the character of cognitive activity in the humanities as different from the sciences. The tendency in the "applied humanities", inasmuch as they have been called on to prove their practical value, has been to technologize or to politicize these disciplines, that is, to subject them to the practical modalities of the natural or social sciences. The humanities, however, have their own constructive potential that corresponds to their unique object. Bakhtin characterizes this object as "*expressive* and *speaking* being" (1996, p. 8). This being never coincides with itself and therefore is inexhaustible in its meaning and significance. He continues:

> [There are] various ways of *being active* in cognitive activity. The activity of the one who acknowledges a voiceless thing [as in natural sciences] and the activity of one who acknowledges another subject [as in human sciences], that is, the *dialogic* activity of the acknowledger. (1986a, p. 161)

Following Bakhtin's emphasis on the dialogical activity of cognition, we can single out a specific set of utterances, which I call *transformative*, that are crucial for the logic and ethics of humanistic discourse. *Transformative utterances* communicate something that changes the very process of communication and the roles of its participants. The simple sentence *I love you* is an example of a transformative utterance, as it refers to the relationship between communicators and radically changes this relationship in the moment of its declaration.

Humanistic discourse, like any discourse in the natural or social sciences, is addressed to human individuals. Only humanistic discourse, however, has human individuals as its subject matter. Not purely informative, humanistic discourse is potentially as transformative as a declaration of love (or of hatred); it addresses the same subject about which it speaks. Unlike technological or political activity, activity in the humanities is directed not to material objects or social masses, but to creative and responsive individuals, engaging them in events of creative communication. To technologize or to politicize the humanities is to ignore their specificity.

Education is one aspect of this creative potential of the humanities that the processes of technologization and corporatization of the university now challenge. Two questions are crucial with regard to the self-determination of the university in the twenty-first century: "Can computer-based educational technologies, such as distance learning, replace the University as the real Place, the community of collaborators and interlocutors?", and "What makes the University different from a shopping mall, a commercial center for buyers of diplomas and professions?" These two questions are interconnected and, in fact, call for a single answer. The university is neither an informational network nor an intellectual supermarket; the university is a humanistic institution. Its purpose is *to educate humans by humans for the sake of humanness*. The technologization or commercialization of education would fundamentally undermine the dialogical nature of the humanities as the thematic and methodological core of the university curriculum. Alexander Pushkin's poem *Conversation of a Bookseller with a Poet* (1824) includes one remarkable phrase: *Inspiration is not for sale, but you can sell a manuscript*. Teachers share with students not only their manuscripts, notes, books, and ideas, but also their inspiration. Education is, in Bakhtin's words, "the event-potential of dialogic cognition" (1986a, p. 161). Only the human sciences are fully commensurable with, and dialogically open to, their human subjects and addressees.

Education is one of the most mysterious and intimate moments in life—a truly existential experiment. Professional activity, even in the creative arts, is usually presented in premeditated forms and predetermined genres. Paintings, poems, and dances are all finished products from which their producers—artists, poets, and choreographers—have already distanced themselves. Even actors or singers demonstrate on the stage what they prepared in advance. In education, the mystery of human creativity is revealed most intimately and spontaneously as the self-creation of a personality here and now, through dialogue with others. Education is not only a social, but also an existential event, or, more precisely, a rare case of *existential sociality* where social and existential dimensions intersect.

Though "reproducibility" is considered a standard requirement for academic research, education involves *irreproducible* moments of human interaction, "becoming-through-knowledge", rather than a simple acquisition of knowledge. Sometimes I ask myself whether my instruction in the classroom could be computerized, transferred to a disk, and offered as a digital package. I sincerely hope the answer is, "No". Education is an improvisational activity that exercises the human capacity for wonder and unpredictability. Education is not just talking about what we already know; it initiates a social event of creative co-thinking, where what is unknown is revealed to us only in the presence of others.

Although commerce and technology are indispensable aspects of the university, they should never overrun its humanistic core. We should not diminish the value of the market economy that shaped the ethos of modernity, or the value of the information technology that shaped the ethos of postmodernity. I would suggest, however, that the next historical period may witness a new ethos of *eco-humanity*, an attempt to revive humanity as a disappearing species that requires preservation and cultivation. Let us adopt for a moment a pessimistic view on the future of our species: even then, the humanities will be necessary to advance its self-awareness and to warrant its survival. In the coming era of humanless production, robotic enterprises, self-managing plants, and electronic networks, the University can become a kind of refuge and preserve for *Humanitas*. Even if *arties*, i.e. the artificial creatures of the future, develop their own ecological awareness and treat *humies*, i.e. their human progenitors, benevolently, as we now try to treat wildlife, there will still exist a need for a haven to protect this threatened species. The university may then display the full redemptive potential of its humanistic heritage in an increasingly dehumanized world. Though this view of the fate of humanity as an endangered species is too pessimistic, it remains an optimistic view of the role of the University as the ultimate sanctuary for this species.

# The interrogativity of the humanities

My aim in this book was not to make any predictions about the future of the humanities, but to interrogate those possibilities that may or may not be realized. According to Bakhtin, "[I]f an answer does not give rise to a new question from itself, it falls out of the dialogue and enters systemic cognition, which is essentially impersonal" (1986a, p. 161). Questions have their own irreducible value as a source of existential anxiety and intellectual inspiration. To Bakhtin's famous thesis on the "answerability of art", we may want to add the idea of the "*interrogativity* of art theory" in relation to the humanities, as a whole.

There are good reasons to believe that interrogativity is becoming more important for humanistic discourse than ever before. The very quality of "being human" becomes more debatable in the age of artificial life and intelligence, when some intrinsic human properties, such as living and thinking, are transferred to technological and bio-technological devices. The humanities have to exercise the mode of self-interrogation in order to reflect upon the growing fragility and uncertainty of their human subject.

The natural and social sciences are at their best in answering human questions; the humanities, in questioning scientific answers. Any solution in the humanities ranks lower than the question it seeks to answer because a creative human individual, unlike objects of natural and social sciences, can never be objectified and determined from the outside. Great explorers and self-explorers of humanity, beginning with Socrates and including Bakhtin, bequeathed to us their modes of interrogation more than their systems of beliefs and convictions. Their answers are questionable, but their questions are irrefutable.

# A university center for the humanities innovation: A sample program

The Center for Humanities Innovation (or CHI, to invoke the "life-force" from Chinese culture) should serve as a focus for the activities of researchers both within and outside the university. Its goal is to develop highly creative new branches of the humanities that are capable of engaging with the rapidly changing intellectual climate of the twenty-first century, and in particular with the increasingly swift advances in science and technology. The Center would focus specifically on the transformative potential of the humanities and their capacity to change the objects of their study.

The central questions associated with this goal are as follows: "What does it mean to be human in an advanced technological age?", "Do the new bio- and info-technologies reaffirm and expand or rather undermine the potential of being human?", "How can the humanities elaborate their own visions and concepts of the humanity in response to and in distinction from sciences?", and, finally, "What would be the most efficient means of collaboration between the humanities and sciences and technologies for the future of the human kind?"

The Center will pursue the following objectives:

1   To focus specifically on the potential of the humanities to transform the objects of their study. Examples of the rich diversity of projects that the Center could pursue might include the impact of the discipline of linguistics on the development of languages, the influence of literary and aesthetic theory on the creative growth of

literature and art, and the role that philosophical inquiry might play in the creative design of virtual worlds.

2  To address problems of technical enhancement and biological transformation of humans, simulated reality and artificial intelligence from the humanistic perspective, in collaboration with researchers from the departments of Philosophy, Theology, Physics, Biology, and Information Technology.

3  To develop a "rapid reaction force" which has the capacity to respond swiftly to significant new trends or intellectual problems that transcend the boundaries of extant disciplines and call for establishing new fields of research.

4  To develop new disciplines in the humanities that respond to the socio-cultural challenges of the twenty-first century, such as micronics, biosophy, horrology, semiurgy, scriptorics, and humanology (the creation and exploration of technohumans through culture and technology). This presupposes a paradigmatic shift from analysis to synthesis across the humanistic disciplines.

5  To expand the genres of intellectual discourse, with particular emphasis on those creative and concise genres that have disappeared from scholarly writing: manifestos, theses, aphorisms, fragments, programs, ideas, and notes.

6  To examine how new informational technologies radically change, both in a defiant and enhancing manner, the profession of the humanist, the traditional concepts of text and knowledge, the methods of interpretation, and the ethos of the academic community.

7  To develop specific methods and criteria for the evaluation of the transformative power of thinking and intellectual creativity, imagination, inspiration, invention, and originality in the humanities, in the context of general theory of creativity as applied to arts, sciences, and the humanities.

8  An integral component of this vision would be the development of the "InteLnet" – an electronic portal for intellectual innovations that will accumulate and circulate new ideas in the humanities and transhumanities.

Overall, the Center would act as a point of mediation between existing disciplines, seeking to initiate interactions between traditional scholarship and transformative humanistic technologies in ways that will enhance intellectual creativity and foster academic cross-fertilisation.

# GLOSSARY

" " —a blank space. " " cannot be expressed in any phonetically motivated form, but can be presented in the form of air quotation marks or conveyed by quotation marks around a blank space. " " is what underlies every text and constitutes the very condition of its signification. " " is not simply the blankness of a sheet of paper or a computer screen; the blankness of " " is a sign, an object of reflection, and a means of communication. " " as the philosophical "primary word" is a sign of the absolute and pure being, revealed at the border of language and unexpressed. " " is a "blind spot" of consciousness, which generates new signs, but which itself can be cognized and named only as a meaningful blank space. Cf. **Ecophilology**.

**Abduction** (lit. "robbing", "taking away")—the extraction of a concept from that categorical paradigm where it traditionally belongs, and its transference into different disciplines and multiple rows of concepts.

**Ambiutopianism** (from Greek "amphi", meaning "around", "on both sides")—a combination of utopianism and anti-utopianism, an ambivalent attitude to the future (e.g. in Platonov's novel "Chevengur").

**Arties** (colloquial)—a positive name for *arti*ficial creatures (in distinction from the contemptuous —"mecho" used in Spielberg's film *Artificial Intelligence*).

**Chronocide** (from Greek "khronos", meaning "time" and Latin "cidum", from "caedere", meaning "to slay")—a murder of time, a violent interruption of historical succession and continuity.

**Conceptivism** (from Latin "conceptare", meaning "to form in the mind", "to imagine", "to conceive")—a philosophy of "conceptual initiation", a constructive activity of the mind in the area of concepts and universals. Conceptivism recognizes the conceptual "constructedness" of reality; however, conceptivism is aimed not only at criticizing and demystifying any constructed concepts, but also their creative generation. This way, conceptivism is aimed at unifying the theoretical and practical forms of reason.

**Contravocation** (from Latin "vocare", "to call")—an ethical category that refers to two moral voices that sound in a human soul with equal strength and can never be fully reconciled with each other. Due to contravocation conscience appears as if torn apart by equally justified duality of virtues, e.g. prudence and courage, generosity and thriftiness, self-giving and self-preservation.

**Cosmic art** (cosmo-art)—a total art characterized by the same sensory stimulations as reality itself, including smell and touch. By using new technologies, cosmic art makes it possible for artistic creations to appear practically indistinguishable from sensory objects of the real world.

**Critical universalism**—a worldview that emphasizes universal human values by critically distancing itself from racial, ethnic, class, gender, sexual, and any other self-contained cultural identities. Critical universalism is contrasted both with postmodern relativism and dogmatic universalism. Critical universalism's vision is one of the internal diversity of individuals in their dialogical openness to others.

**Culturonics**—a practical extension of study of culture; creation of new cultural movements, genres, institutions, etc. A discipline within transhumanies.

**Début de siècle** (Fr.)—a stable pattern of innovative orientation toward the future, as opposed to "fin de siècle"—a sensibility characterized by a sense of fatigue and exhaustion of creative impulses. Romanticism of the early nineteenth century, avant–garde of the early twentieth century, and proteism of the early twenty-first century are examples of début de siècle mentality.

**Diamond rule**—an ethical rule based on individual uniqueness as the main criterion of moral behavior: *Do that which others need and no one else can do in your place.* The diamond rule does not annul the universal character of the golden rule, which is based on the reciprocity of human wills, but

rather sets a diamond stone of the individual gift in its "golden frame": *Do that which anyone including yourself could wish and which no one else but you can do.*

**Differential ethics**—ethics based on the uniqueness of each personality that supplements a traditional ethics based on the idea of the universal self, cf. the golden rule. Differential ethics can be summarized as follows: *The best action is that through which the maximal capacity of one matches the maximal need of the other.*

**Ecognition**—see: Reconsciousness

**Eco-humanity**—humanity as a species endangered by the growth of the techno-sphere and artificial forms of intelligence; a bio-cultural form of intelligence that needs preservation and cultivation.

**Ecophilology** (ecology of text)—a discipline that studies the extratextual environment and the ways in which it can be inscribed within text, including blank spaces (cf. "          "). Ecophilology explores the role of any textual environment that represents the general condition of its signification—from ancient cave drawings and graffiti to contemporary electronic media.

**Futurologism**—a word preceding and anticipating that which it signifies. A futurologism does not simply describe something that is possible in the future, but also creates that very possibility by expanding the sphere of meanings enacted in language, cf. such futurologisms as "robot", invented by the Čapek brothers in the 1920s, or the word "cyberspace", invented by William Gibson in the 1980s.

**Futuroscopy**—a non-linear orientation toward the future as a multitide of co-possible thinkable projections and horizons; an orientation different from a linear, predictive futurology.

**Horrology** (from Latin "horrere", meaning "to bristle with fear")—a discipline that studies the self-destructive mechanisms of civilization, which make it susceptible to all forms of terrorism including its biological and technological forms.

**Humanology**—a discipline that studies the (self-)transformation of humans in an advanced technological society. Humanology studies humans as a part of the technosphere, focusing on their distinctive features compared to other intelligent beings, such as cyborgs, robots, and their gendered varieties, e.g. androids and genoids. Humanology is sometimes labeled "posthuman studies" or "trans-human studies". Humanology is both the *ecology of humans* and the *anthropology of machines*, i.e. a study of the mutual redistribution of their functions. Accordingly, humanology can be divided into *eco-humanology*, dealing with the specificity of humans irreducible to machines, and *techno-humanology*, dealing with human functions capable of being transferred to machines.

**Humies** (colloquial)—*hum*ans as possible partners of artificial intelligent beings; the term also invokes associations with natural beings "*humi*liated" in the developed technosociety of the future.

**Hyperauthorship** (from Greek "hyper", meaning "over", "above", "excessive")—the excess of functional or fictional authorship over factual authorship.

Kierkegaard and Nietzsche, Pushkin and Pessoa were hyperauthors who created or used the masks of their numerous hypoauthors (heteronyms) on behalf of which they wrote their literary or philosophical works that are not directly connected to any "real" or "biological" individuals. Hyperauthorship is popular in electronic networks where many fictional hypoauthors (avatars) come in increasingly oblique relationships to their biological parents. Another form of hyperauthorship is the excess of authors over texts whereby a number of different authorships ("signatures") can be ascribed to one and the same text (the case of the Japanese poet Araki Yasusada).

**Ichnosphere** (from Greek *ichnos*, "trace")—the totality of traces, material emanations (visual, audio, tactile etc.) that a living being spreads into the surrounding world.

**IntelNet** (intellectual network)—a communicational network connecting all thinking beings, both natural and artificial, in order to create and promote new ideas and intellectual movements through the Internet. IntelNet is a stage toward the integration of neuro- and electronic networks into a new form of communal co-thinking— *Syntellect*. This integral intellect will accumulate the potential of all thinking beings and operate on both biological and technical levels. We find ourselves now in the very first stage of electronic communal reason (co-reason, co-thinking). IntelNet was launched in 1995 as the first interactive network for discussing and sharing the humanistic ideas on the Internet.

**Interference**—fuzzy and "wavy"

intersections and overlapping
of different cultures (traditions,
mentalities) in the process of their
interaction (the term refers to
interferential patterns in physics;
this effect is found, for instance, in
the butterfly's colorful markings).
The interferential model in cultural
studies may succeed models based
on one-directional "influences" or
impenetrable "differences".

**Interlation**—a variation on the
same theme in two or several
languages. In contrast to
translation, in interlation the roles
of source and target languages
are interchangeable. Interlation
is a verbal art based on figurative
(metaphoric) relationship between
languages.

**Ipseism** (from Latin "'ipse",
meaning "self", "oneself")—a
view contrasting with physicalism
and assuming that the objective
foundations of one's experiences
are found inside one's subjectivity.
According to ipseism, the experience
of selfness lies at the basis of the
subject's cognitive acts aimed
at others and is common to all
living beings thus making possible
communication among them.

**Language synthesis** (synthetic
philosophy)—a theoretical
practice aiming to expand our
mental vocabulary by creating
new words, lexical fields, and
syntactical rules. This branch of
the transformative humanities
helps to increase the volume of
the speakable, conceivable and
thinkable, and, therefore, doable
and accomplishable. Synthetic
philosophy is a twenty-first
century response to the tradition
of language analysis dominant in
twentieth century Anglo—American
philosophy.

**Micronics** (from Greek "mikros",
meaning "small")—a discipline
studying the forms and functions
of micro phenomena in nature, art,
culture, economics, etc.

**Multiverse** (from Latin "multum",
meaning "much", and Latin
"universum" meaning universe, the
world) – the totality of worlds with
different physical laws, features,
and dimensions, as opposed to our
"universe", one and only.

**Multividual** (from Latin "multum",
meaning "much", and Latin
"individuum", meaning
"individual")—a technologically
or genetically enhanced individual
assuming various "bodies"
and material guises, while
simultaneously remaining conscious
of one's own unique vocation and
moral responsibility.

**Neurocosm**—a symbiosis of the brain
and physical reality, a fragment of
cosmos directly connected to, and
controlled by, the brain.

**Neurosociality** (neuromilieu)—a
symbiosis of the brain and
society, whereby the social
lives of human beings and the
physical structure of our brains
are co-determined. Neurosociality
is a cerebrally open society in
which brain signals are directly
transmitted through electronic
networks, affecting informational
and production processes. As a
result of the development of new
technologies, the future may see
cerebral (neural) and socio—
cultural lines of communication
merging.

**Noocracy** (from Greek "nous",
meaning "mind")—a form of
political government based on the
universal mind integrated through
communication networks (cf.
**Syntellect**).

**Ontotechnology** (from Greek "ontos", meaning "being")—advanced technologies with the power to change the foundations of human existence, to create a new spatio-temporal continuum, a new sensory environment and ways of its perception, along with new kinds of organisms and new forms of intelligence.

**Paleonoic** (paleonoic era; from Greek "palaios", meaning "ancient", and "nous", meaning "mind")—an era of technologically underdeveloped mind and primitive intellectual machines. (Similar to the *paleozoic* era, from Greek "zoe", meaning "life"). We now live in the paleonoic era when artificial intelligent forms are only beginning to emerge.

**Pertext** (from Greek "per", meaning "through")—a new textual configuration, the list of the Web pages on which a certain word or phrase is used. It functions as a table of contents for *supratext*. Pertexts contain the titles of the sites, the names of the authors, the relevant lines of their works, web addresses, and links to those pages where the entry word is used.

**Potentiation** (possibilization)—a historic and epistemological category denoting a transition of phenomena from actuality to potentiality, a growth of the degrees of the possible in reality itself. It is also thinking in the subjunctive mood, the transformation of theories into hypotheses and assertions into suppositions. Historically, possibilities grow faster than the ways of their realization. Unlike traditional (including revolutionary) ways in which an ideal can be realized, potentiation denotes a development from the real to the possible, not from the possible to the real. The goal of potentiation as a methodology in the humanities is to expand the scope of thinkable and "beable" meaningful realities.

**Predictionary**—a dictionary that does not register words already in use but introduces new words that may make their way into dictionaries of the future. Unlike traditional dictionaries (including those of neologisms), which are merely reactive, Predictionary is projective and is ahead of language, anticipating its possible future development. In Predictionary, a word's life only begins, and may continue in texts by various authors, thus becoming a part of language.

**Proteism** (from Greek "protos", meaning "first"; also a reference to the Greek god Proteus, famous for his power to assume any shape at will)—a methodology alternative to the "post-" (cf. postmodernism, poststructuralism, post-utopianism, and post-industrialism). It studies emerging, not yet-formed phenomena in the earliest fluid stages of their development, when they only promise, or tend to become. Proteism is a humble awareness of the fact that we live in the earliest stage of an unknown civilization; that we have tapped into some secret source of power and knowledge that can eventually destroy us; that all of our glorious achievements to date are only pale prototypes of what the coming bio- and info- technologies are pregnant with.

**Proto-** (from Greek "protos", meaning "first, original")—refers to a new sensibility that accentuates the beginnings of new things rather than the endings of old things, and also prospective rather than retrospective modes of theoretical thinking. While "post-" dominated the late twentieth century humanities, the mindset of the early twenty-first century can be best described in terms of "proto-"; for example, the present condition is "proto-global", "proto-virtual", "proto-quantum", and "proto-nootic".

**Protologism** (from Greek "protos", meaning "first, original" + Greek *logos*, word; cf. *prototype*, *protoplasm*)—a freshly coined word that for the first time is offered to public. A protologism is different from a neologism that is already used by the society though it is still perceived as a new word.

**Quantum metaphysics** (micrometaphysics)—a metaphysics focusing on a thing in its singularity, on the minimal units of meaning as the smallest elementary thinkables, including extra-conceptual and extra-linguistic, unnamable singularities.

**Realogy** (from Latin "res", meaning "thing")— a discipline that looks at that essence of the thing which cannot be reduced to the technical qualities of a *product*, the economic qualities of a *commodity*, or even the aesthetic aspects of a *work*. Things as representations of the personalities of their owners or users are the primary interest of realogy, and such ordinary things are collected in the *lyrical museum*. The task of realogy is to comprehend the sentimental and spiritual meaning of things independent of their commercial and utilitarian functions.

**Reconsciousness** (cf. *vossoznanie* in Russian; "ecognition")—a to-and-fro circular movement of consciousness that involves the ethical recognition and ecological reconstruction of the environment and preconditions of every cultural activity, for example, the restoration of blank surfaces and spaces as conditions of writing.

**Retextualization**—a performative method of reading through rewriting, supported by the textual economy of digital networks. Retextualization is a method alternative to the method of interpretation, which is based on the fixed, "paper" status of literary texts.

**Semiurgy** (from Greek "semeion", meaning "sign", and "ourgia", meaning "work")—an activity of generating new signs and their introduction into language.

**Sophian disciplines** (sophio-disciplines, from Greek "sophia", meaning "wisdom")—disciplines that view the object of their study as related to the holistic vision of the universe. In this sense, the *sophy-disciplines* can be distinguished from the *logy-disciplines*, which study their objects within more narrow methodological frameworks, cf. '-logy' in their names (from "logos", meaning "word", "reason"). One can identify a sophian counterpart of many *logy-sciences*, e.g. archesophy as a counterpart of archeology, psychosophy as a counterpart of psychology, geosophy as a counterpart of geology, biosophy as a counterpart of biology, and technosophy as a counterpart of technology.

**Sophiophilia** (the reversal of roots in the word "philosophy")—the search for wisdom conducted outside the limits of philosophy as an academic discipline, in the realm usually labelled metaphysics, spirituality, or higher knowledge. While philosophy has abandoned wisdom and turned into a rigid discipline of the systemic organization of notions and logical analysis of language, sophiophilia chooses new and non-academic venues such as the living wisdom of the ancient and other thinkers, e.g. Plato, Lao Tse, Pascal, and Goethe.

**Stereo-ethics**—an ethics based on the duality of life's purposes and virtues, such as courage and prudence, or self-sacrifice and self-preservation, neither of which presents the singular correct moral choice. Stereo-ethics combines different moral perspectives, just as sight combines two different projections of an object to allow a realistic perception of the world.

**Stereo-text**—a composition that uses a variety of languages to convey the multidimensional volume of thought and image as well as the multiplicity of their associative connections (cf. stereo music and stereo cinema).

**Supratext**—a textual unity of a higher, more general plane in relation to the given text. For example, "English romanticism" or the genre of "lyrical ballads" are supratexts for S. T. Coleridge's poem "The Rime of the Ancient Mariner." If *context* is the environment of a text on the same systematic level, then *supratext* is a unit of the higher level.

**Surreality** (surobject)—a fragment of online reality characterized by the same psycho-physical authenticity as offline reality, yet, as a technical device, subject to human control.

**Syntellect** (from Greek "syn", meaning "with", "together", and "intellect")—the unified mind

of civilization that integrates all individual natural and artificial minds through the mediation and accumulative effects of informational networks.

**Techno-angelism**—a tendency for humans to overcome, as a result of new technologies, limitations of their biological nature and take on angels-like characteristics.

**Techno-humanities**—technologies aimed to change human world on the basis of humanitistic studies.

**Techno-morality**—new moral possibilities and demands determined by the development of science, technology, and communication; for example, "threat reversibility" as interdependence of all political and moral subjects following the creation of nuclear weapon.

**Technosophy** (from Greek "techné", meaning "art", and "sophia", meaning "wisdom")—a sophian discipline that explores the spiritual, cultural, moral, and religious meanings of technology.

**Textoid**—a fluid, nomadic electronic text that wanders from site to site and is modified by users, much like an epic song was modified by a folkloric community.

**Thinknowledge**—an epistemological category assuming that thinking and knowledge are two interrelated forms of intellectual activity, in which the mass of knowledge (the totality of facts) is transformed into the energy of thinking which creates all of civilization, from the simplest material tools to the systems of ideas that shape the future of humanity.

**Transculture** (from Latin "trans", meaning "beyond")—a meta-cultural realm beyond any national, gender, or professional culture; a mode of being, located at the crossroads of cultures. Transculture is an emerging sphere in which humans position themselves free from the limitations of their primary, "inborn", naturalized cultures. The elements of transculture are freely chosen by people rather than dictated by rules and prescriptions within their given culture. Although transculture depends on the efforts of separate individuals to overcome their identification with specific cultures, on another level it is a process of interaction between cultures themselves in which more and more individuals today find themselves "outside" of any particular culture, "outside" of their national, racial, religious, social, ideological, and other "identities".

**Transhumanties** (Transformative Humanities)—an active transformation of culture as a result of its theoretical study. Transhumanities provide the disciplines studying culture with a practical extension, just as technology and politics are aimed at transforming what their disciplines study objectively— nature and society, respectively. Transhumanities constitute a discursive meta-level, different from the primary arts of literature, painting, or music, all of which comprise objects of inquiry in the humanities. For instance, one can view Andrei Belyi as acting in three roles—(a) a poet and novelist; (b) a scholar, a theorist of literature; and (c) a visionary, a transhumanist who inspired and transformed the Symbolist movement in early twentieth century Russia.

**Universics** (from Latin "unus", meaning "one", and "versus", from "vertere", meaning "to turn")—a discipline that would study the universal as a quality of individuals, in distinction from metaphysics, traditionally focused on generalities. Unlike metaphysics, which employs the most general terms and categories, such as "substance", "being", "unity", and "quality", universics focuses on the individual objects and their names, including proper names, because only singular objects and personalities possess universality.

**Virtomania**—a narcotic addiction to virtual worlds as they appear on a computer screen, including their 3D projections.

**Virtonautics** (cf. astronautics)— navigating virtual worlds. Virtonautics is currently still in embryo, but with the addition of the third and fourth dimensions to virtual reality, it may become more adventurous than aeronautics or even astronautics.

# BIBLIOGRAPHY

Adams, R. (1999). "Primitive thisness and primitive identity". In J. Kim and
    E. Sosa (eds.). Metaphysics. An anthology (pp. 172–83). Maiden, MA: Oxford:
    Blackwell Publishers.
Adorno, T. W. (1992). *Negative dialectics* (trans. E. B. Ashton). New York:
    Continuum.
Amato, J. (2000). *Dust: A history of the small and the invisible.* Berkeley, CA:
    University of California Press.
Aristotle (1916). *Politics* (trans. B. Jowett). Oxford: Clarendon Press.
—(1987). *Metaphysics,* Book 1, Ch. 2. In J. L. Ackrill (ed.). *A new Aristotle
    reader.* Princeton, NJ: Princeton University Press.
—(2001). R. McKeon (ed.). *The basic works of Aristotle.* New York: The Modern
    Library.
Bacon, F. (1803). *The works of Francis Bacon,* in 10 vols. London: H. Bryer.
—(1826). *The works of Francis Bacon.* London: Printed for C. and J. Rivington.
—(1978). *The works of Francis Bacon.* J. Spedding (ed.). Boston: Houghton,
    Mufflin and Co.
Badiou, A. (2002). *Ethics. An essay on the understanding of evil.* London, New
    York: Verso.
Bakhtin, M. (1979). *Problemy poetiki Dostoevskogo* (Problems of Dostoevsky's
    poetics). Moscow: Sovietskaya Rossiya.
—(1981). *The dialogic imagination: four essays.* M. Holquist (ed.; trans.
    C. Emerson and M. Holquist). Austin, TX: The University of Texas Press.
—(1984). *Problems of Dostoevsky's poetics.* C. Emerson (ed.; trans. C. Emerson)
    Minneapolis, MN: University of Minnesota Press.
—(1986a). *Speech genres and other late essays* (trans. V. W. McGee). Austin, TX:
    University of Texas Press.
—(1986b). "K filosofii postupka" (On the philosophy of an act). In I. T. Frolov
    (ed.). *Filosofiia i sotsiologiia nauki i tekhniki. Ezhegodnik 1984–1985*
    (Philosophy and sociology of science and technology). Moscow.
Barth, J. (1967). "The literature of exhaustion". *The Atlantic Monthly,* August,
    pp. 29–34.
Barthes, R. (1977). *Image, music, text.* New York: Hill and Wang.
Baudrillard, J. (1998). *The ecstasy of communication.* (trans. Bernard and
    Caroline Schutze). New York, NY: Semiotext(e).
Baugh, C. and T. Cable (2002). *A history of the English language.* London:
    Routledge.
Baynes, K., J. Bohman, and T. McCarthy (eds) (1986). *After philosophy: End or
    transformation?* Cambridge, MA: The MIT Press.

Belyi, A. (1994). "Magiya slov". In A. Belyi. *Simvolizm kak miroponimanie* (Symbolism as understanding the world). Moscow: Respublika.

Berdyaev, N. (1985). Smysl tvorchestva (The meaning of creativity). In N. Berdyaev. Sobranie sochinenii (*Collected works*), vol. 2. Paris: YMCA Press.

Bernshtein, N. A. (1966). *Ocherki po fiziologii dvizhenii i fiziologii aktivnosti* (Essays on the physiology of movement and physiology of activity). Moscow: Meditsina.

Berry, E. and M. Epstein (1999). *Transcultural experiments: Russian and American models of creative communication*. New York: St. Martin's Press.

Blackmore, S. (2000). *The meme machine*. Oxford: Oxford University Press.

Borges, J. L. (2000). *The library of Babel* (trans. A. Hurley). Boston, MA: David R. Godiner.

Bostrom, N. (2006). "Do we live in a computer simulation?" *New Scientist, 192 (2579),* 38–9.

Bruns, G. (1999). *Tragic thoughts at the end of philosophy: Language, literature, and ethical theory*. Evanston, IL: Northwestern University Press.

Buber, M. (1975). Tales of the Hasidim: The later masters. New York, NY: Schocken Books, Inc.

Burgess, G. (1914). *Burgess unabridged: A new dictionary of words you have always needed*. New York, NY: Frederick A. Stokes Company Publishers.

Cairns, D. (1984). Philosophy as a striving toward universal sophia in the integral sense. In L. Embree (ed.), *Essays in memory of Aron Gurwitsch* (pp. 27–43), Washington, DC: The Center for Advanced Research in Phenomenology, Inc. and University Press of America.

Čapek, M. (1961). *The philosophical impact of contemporary physics*. Princeton, NJ: D. Van Hostr and Company, Inc.

Caruth, C. (1996). *Unclaimed experience: Trauma, narrative, and history*. Baltimore, MD: Johns Hopkins University Press.

Chace, W. (2009). The decline of the English department. *The American Scholar*, Autumn. Retrieved from: http://theamericanscholar.org/the-decline-of-the-english-department/. Febr. 15, 2012.

Choi, C. (2005). Qubit twist bending: Nanotubes as mechanical quantum bits. Scientic American, April.

Cross, T. (2011). Homo ludens. Why video games will be an enduring success. *The Economist*, 10 December.

Crystal, D. (2007). *Words. Words. Words*. Oxford: Oxford University Press.

Damrosch, D. (2003). *What is world literature?* Princeton, NJ: Princeton University Press.

Darwin, C. (1871). *Descent of man, and selection in relation to sex*. London: John Murray.

Davis, R. C. et al. (eds) (1985). *Contemporary literary criticism. Modernism through poststructuralism*. New York and London: Longman.

Dawkins, R. (2006). *The God delusion*. Boston, New York: A Mariner Book.

Deleuze, G. and F. Guattari (1986). *Kafka: Toward a minor literature* (Theory and history of literature). Minneapolis and London: University of Minnesota Press.

—(1994). *What is philosophy?* (trans. H. Tomlison and G. Burchell). New York: Columbia University Press.

de Man, P. (1984). "Phenomenality and materiality in Kant". In G. Shapiro and

A. Sica (eds) *Hermeneutics: Questions and prospects*. Amherst, MA: University of Massachusetts Press.

Derrida, J. (1973). *Speech and phenomena* (trans. D. B. Allison). Evanston, IL: Northwestern University Press.

—(1997). *Of grammatology* (trans. G. Ch. Spivak). Baltimore, MD: John Hopkins University Press.

—(1982). *Margins of philosophy*. (trans. A. Bass). Chicago, IL: University of Chicago Press.

—(2001). "The future of the profession or the university without condition (thanks to the 'Humanities', what could take place tomorrow)". In T. Cohen (ed.), *Jacques Derrida and the humanities: A critical reader*. Cambridge: Cambridge University Press.

Donoghue, F. (2010). "Can the humanities survive the 21st century?" *The Chronicle of Higher Education*. 5 September.

Dugin, A. (1993). Zagadka sotsializma (The riddle of socialism). *Elements, 4*.

Dyson, F. (1988). *Infinite in all directions*. New York: Harper and Row.

Emerson, R. W. (1883). *Essays*. Boston and New York: Houghton Mifflin Company.

Epstein, M. (1995). "Thing and word: On the lyrical museum". In M. Epstein, *After the future: The paradoxes of postmodernism and contemporary Russian culture* (pp. 253–89). Amherst, MA: The University of Massachusetts Press.

—(2001). *Filosofiia vozmozhnogo* (The philosophy of the possible). St. Petersburg: Aleteia.

—(2008). "Hyperauthorship in Mikhail Bakhtin: The primary author and conceptual personae". *Russian Journal of Communication* 1 (3), 280–90.

—(2011). *PreDictionary: An exploration of blank spaces in language*. San Francisco: Atelos.

—(2012). "Hyper-Authorship: The case of Araki Yasusada". In B. Friend (ed.), *Scubadivers and chrysanthemums: Essays on the poetry of Araki Yasusada* (pp. 58–75). Bristol, UK: Shearsman Books.

Epstein, M. and G. Tulchinsky (2003). *Proektivnyi filosofskii slovar'. Novye terminy i poniatiia* (A Projective Philosophical Dictionary. New Terms and Concepts). St. Petersburg: Aleteia.

Faith, P. and H. Adam (2001). *Dictionary of the future. The words, terms and trends that define the way we'll live, work and talk*. New York: Hyperion.

Feyerabend, P. (1975). *Against method: Outline of an anarchistic theory of knowledge*. London: New Left Books.

Foucault, M. (1970). *The order of things: An archeology of the human sciences*. New York: Pantheon Books.

—(1996). "Truth and power". In L. Cahoone (ed.), *From modernism to postmodernism: An Anthology* (pp. 379–81). Cambridge, MA: Blackwell Publishers.

Frank, A. (1997). *The diary of a young girl*. The definitive edition. Otto M. Frank and M. Pressler (eds), New York: Random House.

Fukuyama, F. (2006). *America at the crossroads: Democracy, power, and the neoconservative legacy*. New Haven: Yale University Press.

Fuller, R. B. (1975). *Synergetics: Explorations in the geometry of thinking*. New York: Macmillan.

Galpin, R. (1998). "Erasure in art: Destruction, deconstruction, and palimpsest".
    Retrieved from http://www.richardgalpin.co.uk/archive/erasure.htm
Garreau, J. (2005). *Radical evolution: The promise and peril of enhancing our minds,
    our bodies—and what it means to be human.* New York: Broadway Books.
Genette, G. (1997). *Seuils.* Paris: Éditions du Seuil, 1987, translated as *Paratexts.
    Thresholds of interpretation,* Cambridge: Cambridge University Press.
Girard, R. (1987). *Things hidden since the foundation of the world.* Stanford:
    Stanford University Press.
Gleick, J. (1999). *Faster: The acceleration of just about everything.* New York:
    Pantheon.
Goethe, J. W. (1982). *Wilhelm Meister: The years of travel, or, the renunciants*
    (trans. H. M. Waidson). London: Jon Calder; New York: Riverrun Press.
Gogol', N. (1986). "Khristianin idet vpered" (The Christian goes forward). In
    *Vybrannye mesta iz perepiski s druz'yami.* Moscow: Khudozhestvennaya
    literatura.
Groys, B. (1993). *Utopiia i obmen* (Utopia and Exchange). Moscow: Znak.
Hartman, G. (1996). Talk delivered at Emory University.
Haverkamp, A. (1996). *Leaves of mourning: Hölderlin's late work.* New York:
    SUNY Press.
Hawking, S. (2001). *The Universe in a nutshell.* New York, etc.: Bantam Books.
Hayles, N. K. (1999). *How we became posthuman: Virtual bodies in cybernetics,
    literature, and informatics.* Chicago: University of Chicago Press.
Hegel, G. W. F. (1967). *Philosophy of right* (trans. T. M. Knox). Oxford: Oxford
    University Press.
—(1995). *Lectures on the history of philosophy* (trans. E. S. Haldane and F. H.
    Simson). Lincoln, NE: University of Nebraska Press.
Heidegger, M. (1968). *What is called thinking?* New York: Harper & Row.
—(2009). *Basic concepts of Aristotelian philosophy.* Bloomington, IN: Indiana
    University Press.
Hitt, J. (ed.) (1992). *In a word. A Harper's magazine dictionary of words that
    don't exist but ought to.* New York: Laurel.
Hodgin, R. (2009). *Virtual reality cocoon promises full sensory experience.*
    Retrieved from http://www.tgdaily.com/general-sciences-features/41622-virtual-
    reality-cocoon-promises-full-sensory-experience. May 3, 2012.
Hofstadter, D. (1999). *Gödel, Escher, Bach: An eternal golden braid.* New York:
    Basic Books.
Hofstadter, R. (1963). *Anti-intellectualism in American life.* New York: Vintage
    Books.
Horgan, J. (1997). *The end of science: Facing the limits of knowledge in the
    twilight of the scientific age.* New York: Broadway Books.
Horkheimer, M. and T. W. Adorno (2002). *Dialectic of Enlightenment:
    Philosophical fragments,* (trans. E. Jephcott; ed. G. Noerr), Stanford, CA:
    Stanford University Press.
Hoyrup, J. (2000). *Human sciences. Reappraising the humanities through history
    and philosophy.* New York: State University of New York Press.
Jakobson, R. (1985). "Lingvistika v ee otnohenii k drugim naukam" (Linguistics
    in its relationship to other sciences). In R. Jakobson. *Izbrannye raboty* (Selected
    works). Moscow: Progress.

Jameson, F. (1993). *Postmodernism, or the cultural logic of late capitalism.* Durham: Duke University Press.

Jaspers, K. (1977). *The origin and goal of history.* Westport, CT: Greenwood Press.

Jay, L. R. (1970). *Boundaries: Psychological man in revolution.* New York: Vintage.

Kabakov, I. (1998). *The palace of projects.* 1995–8. London: Artangel.

—(2000). *Der Text als Grundlage des Visuellen. The text as the basis of visual expression* (in English and German). Z. Felix (ed.). Koln: Oktagon.

Kafka, F. (1977). *Letters to friends, family, and editors.* New York: Schocken Books.

Kaku, M. (2006). *Parallel worlds: The science of alternative universes and our future in the cosmos.* London: Penguin Books.

Kamuf, P. (ed.) (1991). *A Derrida reader: Between the blinds.* New York: Columbia University Press.

Kant, I. (1949). *Critique of practical reason and other writings in moral philosophy* (ed. and trans. L. W. Beck). Chicago: University of Chicago Press.

—(1969). *Foundations of the metaphysics of morals,* (trans. L. W. Beck). Indianapolis, IN: Bobbs-Merrill.

Keats, J. (2011). *Virtual words: Language on the edge of science and technology.* New York, NY: Oxford University Press.

Kekes, J. (1983). "Wisdom". *American Philosophical Quarterly, 20(3),* 277–86.

Kenny, A. (ed.) (1994). *The Wittgenstein reader.* Oxford: Wiley-Blackwell.

Khlebnikov, V. (1928–33). *Sobranie proizvedenii* (Collected works). Yu. Tynyanov and N. Stepanov (eds). Leningrad: Izdatel'stvo pisatelei.

—(1986). "Nasha osnova" ("Our foundation"). In V. Khlebnikov. *Tvoreniya* (Creations). Moscow: Sovetskii pisatel'.

Kierkegaard, S. (1968). "Anguish and sin". In S. Kierkegaard. *The difficulty of being Christian.* Notre Dame, IN: Notre Dame University Press.

Klapp, O. (1986). *Overload and boredom: Essays on the quality of life in the information society.* New York: Greenwood.

Krippendorff, K. (1994). "A recursive theory of communication". In D. Crowley and D. Mitchell (eds). Communication theory today (pp. 78–103). Stanford, CA: Stanford University Press.

Kroker, A. and M. Kroker (eds) (1987). *Body invaders: Panic sex in America.* Montreal: New World Perspectives.

*Kto est kto v sovremennom iskusstve Moskvy* (Who is who in the modern art of Moscow). (1993) Moscow: Album.

Kuhn, T. (1962). *The structure of scientific revolutions.* Chicago: University of Chicago Press.

Kurzweil, R. (2005). The *singularity is near. When humans transcend biology.* New York: Viking.

Lakoff, G. and M. Johnson (1999). *Philosophy in the flesh: The embodied mind and its challenge to Western thought.* New York: Basic Books.

Landau, S. (1989). *Dictionaries: The art and craft of lexicography.* Cambridge: Cambridge University Press.

Large, P. (1984). *The micro revolution revisited.* Totowa, NJ: Rowman and Allanheld.

Leibniz, G. W. (1969). *Philosophical papers and letters* (trans. L. E. Loemker). 2nd edn. Dordrecht, Holland: D. Reidel Publishing Company.

—(1984). Ob universal'nom sinteze i analize. *Sochineniya* (On the universal synthesis and analysis. Works). Vol. 3, Moscow: Mysl'.

Lemkin, R. (1946). Genocide. *American Scholar 15(2)*, 227–30.

Lenin, V. I. (2008). *Lenin on literature and art*. Rockville, MA: Wildside Press.

Lentricchia, F. and J. McAuliffe (2003). *Crimes of art and terror*. Chicago: University of Chicago Press.

Levy, P. (1997). *Collective intelligence: Mankind's emerging world in cyberspace*. New York; London: Plenum Trade.

Lewis, D. (1979). "Possible worlds". In M. J. Loux (ed.), *The possible and the actual: Readings in the metaphysics of modality* (pp. 182–9). Ithaca and London: Cornell University Press.

Lewontin, R. (1994). "Facts and the factitious in natural sciences". In J. Chandler et. al (eds). *Questions of evidence. Proof, practice, and persuasion across the disciplines* (pp. 478–91). Chicago, London: The University of Chicago Press.

Lifton, R. (1970). *Boundaries: Psychological man in revolution*. New York: Vintage.

Lotman, Yu. (1977). *The structure of the artistic text* (trans. R. Vroon). Ann Arbor: The University of Michigan Press.

—(1988). *Struktura khudozhestvennogo teksta* (The structure of the artistic text). St. Petersburg: Iskusstvo.

—(1997). *O russkoi literature. Stat'i i issledovaniia: istoriia russkoi prozy, teoriia literatury* (On Russian literature. Essays and research: History of Russian prose, theory of literature). St. Petersburg: Iskusstvo.

—(2001). *Universe of the mind: A semiotic theory of culture* (trans. A. Shukman). Bloomington and Indianapolis: Indiana University Press.

Lotman, Yu. and B. Uspensky (1985). "Binary models in dynamics of Russian culture (to the end of the Enlightenment century)". In A. Nakhimovsky and A. Nakhimovsky (eds), *The Semiotics of Russian cultural history*. Ithaca, NY: Cornell University Press.

Lovelock, J. E. (1979). *Gaia: A new look at life on Earth*. Oxford, New York: Oxford University Press.

Lyotard, J.-F. (1984). The postmodern condition: a report on knowledge. (trans. G. Bennington and B. Massumi). Minneapolis: The University of Minnesota Press.

—(1988). *The differend: Phrases in dispute*. Minneapolis: University of Minnesota Press.

Malles, S., J. McQuain, and R. Blechman (1998). *Coined by Shakespeare: Words & meanings first penned by the Bard*. Springfield, MA: Merriam-Webster.

Mamardashvili, M. (1992). *Kak ya ponimaiu filosofiiu* (How I understand philosophy). Moscow: Progress, Izdatel´skaia gruppa 'Kul´tura.

Mann, T. (1990). *Meine Zeit, Gesammelte Werke in dreizehn Banden*. Franfurt a.M.: Fischer, XI: Reden und Aufsatze 3.

Marcel, G. (1973). *Tragic wisdom and beyond. Including conversations between Paul Ricoeur and Gabriel Marcel*. John Wild (ed.). (trans. Stephen Jolin and Peter McCormick). Evanston, IL: Northwestern University Press.

Martin, J. (2007). *The meaning of the 21st century: A vital blueprint for ensuring our future*. London: Transworld Publishers.

Marx, K. (1867). "Capital", vol. 1. Retrieved from http://www.marxists.org/archive/marx/works/1867-c1/ch10.htm. May 3, 2012.

McLuhan, E. and Frank Zingrone (eds) (1995). *Essential McLuhan*. London: Routledge.

McLuhan, M. and B. R. Powers (1992). *The global village. Transformations in world life and media in the 21st. century*. New York: Oxford University Press.

—(1967). "Theses on Feuerbach". In L. Easton and K. Guddat (eds), *Writings of the young Marx on philosophy and society*. Garden City, NY: Anchor Books.

Melville, H. (1938). *Herman Melville: Representative selections, with introduction, bibliography, and notes* (ed. W. Thorp) New York, etc.: American Book Company.

Menand, L. (2010). *The marketplace of ideas: Reform and resistance in the American university*. New York: W. W. Norton & Company.

*Milyi Angel* (1991). *Esoteric Review*. Moscow, Artogeia.

Montaigne, M. (1973). "Of cripples". In *The complete works of Montaigne*, vol. 3. (trans. D. M. Frame). Stanford, CA: Stanford University Press.

Moravec, H. (1988). *Mind children: The future of robot and human intelligence*. Cambridge, Mass.: Harvard University Press.

Nabokov, V. (1964). *Speak, Memory*. London: Weidenfield and Nicolson.

Nagel, T. (2000). "What is it like to be a bat?" In *The mind's I: Fantasies and reflections on self and soul*. Composed and arranged by D. Hofstadter and D. Dennet (pp. 391–402). New York: Basic Books.

Naisbitt, J. (1982). *Megatrends: Ten new directions transforming our lives*. New York: Warner.

Nicholas of Cusa (1997). *Selected spiritual writings*. (trans. H. L. Bond). New York, Mahwah: Paulist Press.

Nietzsche, F. (1968). *The will to power* (trans. W. Kaufman and R. J. Hollingdale). New York: Vintage.

—(1978). *Thus Spake Zarathustra: A book for none and all*. London: Penguin.

—(1980). *Sämtliche Werke. Kritische Studienausgabe*, 15 volumes. G. Colli and M. Montinari (eds). Munich: Deutscher Taschenbuch Verlag.

—(1997). *The twilight of the idols, Or how to philosophize with the hammer*. (trans. R. Polt). Indianapolis, IN: Hackett.

—(2006/1910). *Gay science*. Mineola, NY: Dover Publications.

Nussbaum, M. (2010). *Not for profit: Why democracy needs the humanities*. Princeton, NJ: Princeton University Press, 2010.

Orwell, G. (1968). "New words". In G. Orwell, *The collected essays, journalism and letters of George Orwell*. New York: Harcourt Trade Publishers.

*The Oxford Companion to Philosophy* (1995). T. Honderich, (ed.). Oxford, New York: Oxford University Press.

Paulson, W. (2001). *Literary culture in a world transformed: A future for the humanities*. Ithaca and London: Cornell University Press.

Peirce, C. S. (1932). Collected papers. Vol. II, Elements of Logic. Charles Hartshorne and Paul Weiss (eds), Cambridge, MA: Harvard University Press.

Penrose, R. (1994). *Shadows of the mind: A search for the missing science of consciousness*. Oxford, New York and Melbourne: Oxford University Press.

Plato (1956). "Phaerdrus". In I. Edman, (ed.), *The works of Plato* (pp. 263–332). New York: The Modern Library.

Platt, S. (ed.) (1992). *Respectfully quoted. A dictionary of citations from the Library of Congress*. Washington, DC: Congressional Quarterly Inc.

Plotinus (2009). *The Enneads*. (trans. S. Mackenna), B. S. Page. Retrieved from http://www.davemckay.co.uk/philosophy/plotinus/plotinus. php?name=enneads.52. May 3, 2012.

Polanyi, M. (1962). *Personal knowledge: Towards a post-critical philosophy*. London: Routledge & Kegan Paul.

Pseudo-Dionysius (1987). "The mystical theology". In Pseudo-Dionysius, *The complete works*, (trans. Luibheid). New York, Mahwah: Paulist Press.

Rescher, N. (1975). *A theory of possibility: A constructivistic and conceptualistic account of possible individuals and possible worlds*. Pittsburg: University of Pittsburgh Press.

Rilke, R.-M. (1935). "Letter to Witold von Hulewicz, November 15, 1925". In Rilke, R.-M. *Briefe aus Muzot* (pp. 335–6). Leipzig: Insel-verlag.

Roberts, A. (2005). *What might have been: Imaginary history from twelve leading historians*. London: Orion Publishing.

Roszak, T. (1994). *The cult of information. A neo-luddite treatise on high-tech, artificial intelligence, and the true art of thinking* (1986). Berkeley, CA: University of California Press.

*The Routledge encyclopedia of philosophy* (2008). Craig, E. (cd.), *10 vols*. London, New York: Routledge.

Russo, J. (2005). *The future without a past: The humanities in a technological society*. Columbia, MO: University of Missouri Press.

Sagan, K. (1994). *Pale blue dot: A vision of the human future in space*. New York: Random House.

Sartre, J.-P. (1964). The *words*. New York: George Braziller.

Schelling, F. W. J. (1856–61). *Sämmtliche Werke*, K. F. A. Schelling (ed.), I Abtheilung vols 1–10, Stuttgart: Cotta, 1856–61, 5, S. 125.

Schumacher, E. (1989). *Small is beautiful: Economics as if people mattered*. New York: Harper Collins.

Shapiro, M. (1985). "On some problems in the semiotics of visual art: Field and vehicle in image-signs" (1966). In R. Innis (ed.), *Semiotics. An introductory anthology* (pp. 206–25). Bloomington, IN.: Indiana University Press.

Shonagon, S. (1991). *The pillow book* (trans. I. Morris). New York: Columbia University Press.

Shvedova, N. (2005). "Paradoksy slovarnoi stat'i" ("The paradoxes of a dictionary entry"). In N. Shvedova, *Russkii iazyk. Izbrannye raboty* (Russian language: Selected works). Moscow: Iazyki slavianskoi kul'tury.

Skalkovsky, K. (1904). *Materaly dlya fiziologii russkogo obchestva: Malen'kaya khrestomatiya dlya vzroslykh. Mneniya russkikh o samikh sebe*. (Material on the physiology of Russian society: Russians' opinion of themselves). St. Peterburgh: A. S. Souvorin Publisher.

Smith, M. (1995). *Literary realism and the Ekphrastic tradition*. University Park, PA: Pennsylvania State University Press.

Solzhenitsyn, A. (1973). *The Gulag Archipelago: An experiment in literary investigation* (trans. T. Whitney). New York: Harper & Row, Publishers.

Spinoza, B. (1949). *Ethics* (ed. J. Gutman). New York: Hafner Publishing Company.

Taylor, M. (1986). "Erring. A postmodern A/theology". In L. Cahoone (ed.), *From modernism to postmodernism. An anthology* (pp. 435–46). Oxford: Blackwell Publishers.

Tindemans, J. P. A., Verrijn-Stuart, A. A., and Visser R. P. W. (eds) (2002). *The future of the sciences and humanities.* Amsterdam: Amsterdam University Press.

Tsvetaeva, M. (2002). *Zapisnye knizhki i dnevnikovaya proza* (Notebooks and diary prose). Moscow: Zakharov.

Turney, J. (2010). *The rough guide to the future.* London: Rough Guides.

Vernadsky, V. I. (1926). *Biosphera* (The Biosphere). Leningrad: Nauchnoe khimiko-technicheskoye izdatel'stvo.

Viereck, G. (1929). "What life means to Einstein". *The Saturday Evening Post,* 26 October, pp. 17, 110–17.

Vygotsky, L. (1993). *The collected works of L. S. Vygotsky: Problems of general psychology: including the volume Thinking and speech,* Volume 1. New York: Springer Publishing Company.

Wanner, A. (2003). *Russian minimalism: From the prose poem to the anti-story.* Evanston, IL: Northwestern University Press.

Weber, M. (1949). The logic of the cultural sciences. In *The methodology of the social sciences* (trans. E. A. Shils and H. A. Finch). New York: Free Press.

*Webster's new world college dictionary* (2000). 4th edn, M. Agnes (ed.). Foster City, CA.

Wells, H. G. (1937). *World brain: The idea of a permanent world encyclopedia. Contribution to the new Encyclopédie Française, August.* Retrieved from https://sherlock.ischool.berkeley.edu/wells/world_brain.html. May 3, 2012.

Whitehead, A. N. (1938). *Modes of thought.* New York: The Macmillan Co.

Wiener, N. (1954). *The human use of human beings: Cybernetics and society.* Garden City, NY: Doubleday.

Williams, R. (1985). *Keywords: A vocabulary of culture and society.* New York: Oxford University Press.

Wilson, A. (ed.) (1995). *World Scripture: A comparative anthology of sacred texts.* New York: Paragon House.

Wilson, E. (1999). *Consilience: The Unity of Knowledge.* New York: Vintage.

Windelband, W. (1919). "Über Friedrich Hölderlin und sein Geshick". In W. Windelband, *Präludien: Aufsätze und Reden zur Philosophie und ihrer Geschichte* (SS. 254–5). Tübingen: J. C. B. Mohr.

Wittgenstein, L. (1994). Filosofskie issledovaniya (Philosophical investigations). In L. Wittgenstein *Filosofskie raboty* (Philosophical works). Moscow: Gnozis.

—(2010). *Tractatus logico-philosophicus.* (contr. Bertrand Russell; trans. C.K. Ogden). Retrieved from http://www.gutenberg.org/files/5740/5740-pdf.pdf. May 3, 2012.

Wurman, R. S. (1989). *Information anxiety.* New York: Doubleday.

Wyse, P. (2009). *Wyse words: A dictionary for the bewildered.* Edinburgh: Chambers.

Yam, M. (2011). "Hackers could make a MacBook's battery explode". *Tom's Hardware: The Authority on Tech,* 26 July. Retrieved from http://www.tomshardware.com/news/hacker-macbook-battery-explode-overheat,13123.html

# INDEX OF NAMES

# INDEX OF SUBJECTS